Tools for Thinking

Modelling in Management Science

Third Edition

Michael Pidd

Department of Management Science,
Lancaster University Management School, UK

A John Wiley and Sons, Ltd., Publication

This edition first published 2009
© 2009 John Wiley & Sons, Ltd

Registered office
John Wiley & Sons, Ltd, The Atrium, Southern Gate, Chichester,
West Sussex PO19 8SQ, United Kingdom

For details of our global editorial offices, for customer services and for information about how to apply for permission to reuse the copyright material in this book, please see our website at www.wiley.com

The right of Michael Pidd to be identified as the author of this work has been asserted in accordance with the Copyright, Designs and Patents Act 1988.

Reprinted January 2011, June 2011, February 2012, November 2012

Wiley also publishes its books in a variety of electronic formats. Some content that appears in print may not be available in electronic books.

Designations used by companies to distinguish their products are often claimed as trademarks. All brand names and product names used in this book are trade names, service marks, trademarks or registered trademarks of their respective owners. The publisher is not associated with any product or vendor mentioned in this book. This publication is designed to provide accurate and authoritative information in regard to the subject matter covered. It is sold on the understanding that the publisher is not engaged in rendering professional services. If professional advice or other expert assistance is required, the services of a competent professional should be sought.

Library of Congress Cataloging-in-Publication Data
Pidd, Michael.
Tools for thinking : modelling in management science / Michael Pidd. – 3rd ed.
    p. cm.
Includes bibliographical references and index.
ISBN 978-0-470-72142-1 (pbk.)
1. Problem solving—Simulation methods. 2. Management science—Simulation methods. 3. Decision making—Simulation methods. I. Title.
HD30.29.P53 2010
658.4'0352—dc22

                                                                                    2009025976

A catalogue record for this book is available from the British Library.

Typeset in 10/12pt Baskerville MT by Aptara Inc., New Delhi, India.
Printed and bound by CPI Group (UK) Ltd, Croydon, CR0 4YY

Tools for Thinking

To my family, friends and colleagues

Contents

Preface

I wrote the first edition of this book because I had been teaching MBA students and found that, with the right approach, they could see the value of Management Science in tackling difficult problems. Initially, many were sceptical, arguing that the human side of management was all that mattered. I was also teaching specialist Management Science students who had difficulty in seeing that the human side mattered at all, although they loved the mathematical and computer algorithms that make up many textbooks.

This teaching experience has always pulled me in two directions.

To the Management Science students I want to say, 'Your maths and computer models are all very well, but what about the organizations in which you will work? Don't you think that the context of your work is worth some investigation?'. But many such students are too busy grappling with their computers to worry too much about these things. In popular parlance, these are the rocket scientists.

To the students and others who stress the human side of management, I want to say, 'Hold on a minute. Yes, of course management is through people, but isn't it important to think through the consequences of possible action before doing something? Perhaps you would be better managers if you were able to use the tools to do this?'. This group are often known as the poets.

This book is written for both rocket scientists and poets, whether they be students, academics or practitioners. It aims to give both sides a glimpse over the wall into the other playground. It argues the case for the rocket scientists to be much more thoughtful about organizational life. It stresses the need for the poets to see that methods do exist that will help them to think through possible consequences. For both camps, the idea is to stress that systematic thinking and analysis has a role to play in improving organizational life.

With this in mind, I had found no suitable text that discussed modelling in Management Science. There were plenty of books that explored the use of different techniques, such as linear programming or computer simulation. There were also books that covered the use of soft methods such as soft systems methodology and cognitive mapping. However, I could find none that brought these two areas together, showed how they related and placed them in the context of the building and use of models in Management Science.

As in previous editions, the book is divided into four parts.

Part I Modelling in Management Science

This provides the context for the rest of the book. It argues the case for rational analysis and tries to take account of some criticisms of rationality. It suggests a role for Management Science in contemporary organizations and proposes a few simple principles for modelling.

Part II Interpretive modelling – soft Management Science

Although Management Science is usually associated with mathematical and statistical approaches, the last decade has seen the development of powerful approaches that are essentially qualitative. They are intended to provide support for analysts to understand and interpret people's ideas and preferences. In this way, they are used to help think through the consequences of possible action.

Part III Mathematical and logical modelling

This part covers four techniques or approaches that are commonly associated with Management Science. There were many contenders for inclusion, and the reasons for my choice are given in the introduction to Part III. They are intended to illustrate modelling, as distinct from models or techniques.

Part IV Model assessment and validation

This single chapter discusses how models and modelling approaches can be validated so that participants may have some faith in their results.

Changes in the third edition

The main change in the third edition is the addition of a new chapter on decision analysis (Chapter 8) which approaches the subject as a bridge between the hard, more mathematical techniques of Management Science and the soft methods. As well as introducing decision trees, Chapter 8 provides an introduction to decision-making under uncertainty and shows how rational approaches can be applied when multiple decision criteria are needed. As with the other chapters, I have tried to present the material in an accessible way and with suitable examples.

When discussing decision analysis in Chapter 8 and static Monte Carlo methods in Chapter 10, I have used parts of the Decision Tools Suite (Palisade software: www.palisade.com) to show how suitable software can be a great help in developing and using Management Science models. Chapter 8 uses PrecisionTree an Excel add-in for decision trees, and Chapter 10 uses @Risk, another Excel add-in, for Monte Carlo sampling. There are other products on the market that can be used in similar ways. The coverage of discrete event simulation in Chapter 10 is based on Micro Saint Sharp, a simulation package that is well suited to non-manufacturing examples.

Where necessary I have also brought the other chapters up to date, although I have not changed aspects that already seemed to work well. John Wiley & Sons were kind enough to seek the opinions of several reviewers on what changes should be made to the third edition. As is often the case, many of their suggestions were contradictory, although several reviewers did ask for a chapter on decision analysis.

Acknowledgements

I am grateful to friends and colleagues from Lancaster and elsewhere who have given me food for thought during this book's various editions and its gestation period, which stretched over many years before I finally proposed it to John Wiley & Sons in the mid-1990s. In particular, I would like to acknowledge the help provided by comments from Vlado Ceric, Chris Chapman, Brian Dangerfield, Colin Eden, Richard Eglese, Robert Fildes, Allen Greenwood, Geoff Walsham, Stephen Watson, Mark Westcombe, Dave Worthington and Mike Wright. I am also indebted to a number of awkward thinkers who have stimulated my ideas over the years, especially John Crookes, Peter Checkland, the late Steve Cook and Ray Paul. Finally, I am grateful to my students and other readers who have suggested improvements and spotted mistakes in the previous editions. As ever, any mistakes that remain are mine.

Michael Pidd
Lancaster University
May 2009

PART I
MODELLING IN
MANAGEMENT SCIENCE

Introduction

Part I is a general introduction to the idea of modelling as a part of Management Science, stressing modelling as a part of Management Science, and stressing modelling as an activity rather than discussing types of model. The idea is to show how models are built and used, rather than exploring different types of model in any detail – there are plenty of books that do that very well. Thus, the approach taken is non-technical, but it does demand some stamina from readers who may not have come across the ideas before.

Part I begins with a discussion of the value of modelling, taking as the theme of Chapter 1 the idea that models are convenient worlds. They are artificial worlds that have been deliberately created to help with understanding the possible consequences of particular actions. It is important to realize that all models, as used in Management Science, are approximations, and that modellers must develop skills that enable them to decide what should and should not be represented in the model. Such models are almost never used without human intervention, but are designed to assist people making complex decisions – hence this book is called *Tools for Thinking*.

The modelling theme continues with Chapter 2, which looks at the role of modelling within organizations. Modelling approaches are often viewed as exemplars of highly rational schemes, and it is important to consider how they can be of use within organizational life, which may be far from rational in any classical or linear sense. Thus, Chapter 2 develops a definition of rationality from Simon's work, and then considers critics of this view, most notably Mintzberg and his colleagues, who argue for a more intuitive approach to the crafting of strategy. Putting these two together suggests that a role for modelling is to attempt to make sense of strategic vision: the vision stemming from processes that are, at least in part, intuitive.

Chapter 3 faces up to the common view that the main role of Management Science is in problem-solving. But this carries with it the idea that, once solved, problems stay that way. Organizational life is rarely so kind, and it is important to recognize that modelling is used as a way of coping with change and turbulence. Chapter 3 discusses various ideas about the nature of problems and suggests the role for modelling within them. It concludes with an extensive discussion of the nature of problem-structuring, taking the view that this 'naming and framing' (Schön, 1982) is fundamental to successful modelling.

Chapter 4 ends Part I on a thoroughly practical note with a discussion of six principles of modelling that I (and others) have found useful. As part of this discussion, it also reviews the different ways in which models are put to use in Management Science, because this affects the amount of simplification possible within a model. There is no sense in which this is a complete list of useful ideas about modelling, but it will at least serve as a starting point from which readers may develop their own ideas.

Reference

Schön D.A. (1982) *The Reflective Practitioner. How Professionals Think in Action.* Basic Books, New York, NY.

1 Models as convenient worlds

Managing complexity and risk

Our lives are increasingly complex, whether we consider only our individual lives, sharing with our families or working in some kind of organization. Those of us in the Western world depend on artificial aids for our survival: we travel long distances by car, boat or plane; we cook food on devices fuelled by gas or electricity; and we take for granted that computers enable us to communicate instantly across the globe. We are very much part of an interconnected world in which our decisions and those of others can have major consequences for us and for other people. This became very clear in the second half of 2008, when overliberal availability of credit, reckless lending, little-understood and complex financial instruments and an out-of-control bonus culture led to the effective insolvency of large banks and finance houses. These symptoms, which first appeared in the USA and the UK, quickly affected all nations in our global economy and blighted the lives of millions, possibly billions. We live in a complex, fast-moving and highly interconnected world in which we must make better use of resources or face a very uncertain future.

When our decisions turn out well, we expect that we and others will benefit from what happens. But we are also aware that, when things go wrong, the consequences can be dire indeed. The same is true of businesses. For example, the costs to a manufacturer that decides to build a new factory on a green-field site, or to re-equip an existing factory, can be huge. Clearly, managers will make such an investment only if they expect the business to gain some return from doing so. But how can they be sure that their decisions will turn out as they intended? How can they be sure that there will be sufficient demand for the products the factory will produce? How can they be sure that the technologies used within the factory will work as intended? The consequences of failures can be very expensive and may even be dangerous. One way to help improve such planning is to find ways to learn from the failures that sometimes occur (Fortune and Peters, 1995). This learning implies that the investigators have something – a model – against which the performance of the system can be compared.

On a different theme, the high population of our planet serves to increase the awful effect that natural and man-made disasters can have. For example, modern societies rely on large-scale chemical plants for the production of materials to be turned into foodstuffs, drugs and components for goods. But these plants can be dangerous to operate, a fact that the people of Bhopal in India are unlikely ever to forget. There, in 1984, poisonous gas drifted over the town after escaping from a nearby chemical plant, killing about 3000 people and injuring another 250 000 (Fortune and Peters, 1995). We rely on electricity to power our factories and our household devices, and many of the generating plants are based on nuclear reactors. As we know from the events of Chernobyl in 1986, an explosion and a major release of radiation may have terrible consequences. How can managers of these plants try to ensure that they have minimized, or reduced to zero, the risks of dangerous accidents? How can those with the task of evacuating an area and cleaning up afterwards be sure that they are working as effectively as possible?

The effects of natural disasters such as earthquakes and floods also threaten our lives. These disasters affect both highly developed countries – for example, the earthquakes in Kobe in Japan in 1995 and in San Francisco in the USA in 1989 – and poorer countries such as Bangladesh, whose land is very vulnerable to annual floods, lying largely within the Ganges and Brahmaputra deltas. Such natural disasters not only threaten lives but also disrupt normal life and make it impossible for people to live as they would choose. How can natural disaster experts assess the risk of such hazards? How can they ensure that they are able to warn people when a disaster threatens? How can they ensure that they evacuate people quickly and safely from danger zones?

It is, of course, impossible to be sure what will happen when we make changes in complex systems, for we can be sure of what will happen only when we have complete control over events. However, there are ways of minimizing risk and of managing complexity. The complexity of modern life is here to stay, and we must therefore adopt approaches to cope with this. The risks, too, are evident, as are the rewards for being able to manage those risks. The main argument of this book is that the development and use of rational and logical analysis can be a great aid in managing that complexity and in recognizing and managing the inevitable risks.

Thinking about consequences

Whenever we make a decision and take some action, there will be consequences. The consequences may be within our control, or there may be considerable risk or uncertainty. When we have full control of the consequences of our decisions and actions, we have only ourselves to blame when things go wrong and we can take the credit when they turn out well. In these cases, it clearly makes sense to think through the consequences of our actions and our decisions. For simple decisions, this process is itself simple. All we have to do is list the possible outcomes and choose the most desirable, ensuring that we know which course of action will lead to this outcome. Thus, if we wish to invest some cash in one of a small number of investments, all of whose returns are known and are certain over some defined period, simple arithmetic will help us to choose the best investment. In terms that will be defined later, in doing so we have used a simple decision model. We have applied logical analysis to our circumstances.

Often, however, life is not so simple and we are at the mercy of other people's actions or of the intervention of events we cannot control. Decisions about farming and food supplies are, for example, at the mercy of the weather. When our decisions are affected by other people's, this may be because we are in competition with them, and we must try to consider carefully how other people might respond to the actions that we take. As a classic example, consider the game of chess, which has been much studied by students of Artificial Intelligence. Chess has no chance element, everything is determined, and the winner is the player who follows the best strategies. There is considerable evidence (Simon, 1976) that the better players are able systematically to analyse current and possible future positions very quickly by procedures that can be modelled by computer programs. Other competitive situations are much more complex than chess. For example, a manufacturer of fast-moving consumer goods must develop marketing policies, but competitor companies will do the same and customers' responses are not wholly predictable. This situation is, therefore, more complex than that of a game such as chess.

Does this mean that logical analysis is a waste of time? Not really. Consider the example of the captain of a commercial airliner about to make a long-haul light. Before take-off, the captain must file a flight plan specifying the intended route, timings and other aspects. However, few long-haul flights follow their precise flight plans because there may be changes in the weather, turbulence, military flights or emergencies affecting other aircraft during the flight. Nevertheless, the plan has its value for it serves two purposes. First, it serves as a standard against which progress on the flight can be monitored, which is much better than setting off in the vague hope of landing in Australia! Second, it allows the organization (the airline) to build a body of knowledge about flights and how they can be affected by studying why the flight plan could not be followed. That is, it allows an after-the-event audit to occur.

One major argument of this book is that rational and logical analysis is crucial in our complex and complicated world. However, it might be instructive to think about what other ways there might be to take such decisions, and these include the following.

- *Seat of the pants.* This term usually implies rapid decision-making based on intuition, with no real attempt to think through the consequences. Sometimes this approach can be quite effective, but it can also be rather dangerous. Few of us would wish to be flown on a commercial airline flight by a crew who made no attempt whatsoever to plan their route; flying by the seat of our pants can be exciting, but some kinds of excitement are grossly overrated.
- *Superstition.* This term is used here to indicate a mystical belief that examining some other system will shed light on whatever decision we are facing, even when there is clearly no link whatsoever between our decision and the system that we are using as a reference. This is very similar to the attitude people adopt when they read horoscopes in newspapers with a view to planning their day. A related notion is the idea that use of a lucky charm or method of doing something will guarantee a desirable outcome. For example, a soccer player might always put his left boot on before his right in the belief that doing it the other way round will cause him to play badly. It may not be stretching the analogy too far to suggest that some organizations seem to operate in a similar manner.
- *Faith and trust.* This term is used to denote an approach that is close to superstition, but with the one important difference that there is some proper link postulated between the parallel system and the decision to be faced. Thus, there is the idea that proper observance of the one will guarantee a favourable outcome in the other. Some people would argue that certain politico-economic theories could be classified in this way.
- *Do nothing.* This is the classical 'head in the sand' approach, closing our eyes and hoping that the problem will go away or that it will be sorted out in some other way. There are times when it may be best to do nothing, but, paradoxically, we can only know this when we have thought through the consequences of doing nothing. An example of this might be sitting tight during an earthquake.

Probably most people use one or more of these approaches in making personal decisions that have no major consequences. But most of us would be unhappy with the thought that they were being used by others to make major decisions that might have a significant impact on us.

It should, of course, be noted that even logical approaches can fail – especially if they are blinkered. There is a wonderful example of this in the Andalusian hills of southern Spain. There, set among beautiful scenery, close to Montejaque, about 30 kilometres from Ronda, is a dam built by the Seville Electricity Company in the 1920s. They had found a valley into which an existing water source flowed. The valley was wide and deep and had a narrow exit – perfect for a dam. Even better, the valley was high in the hills and water flow could be used to generate hydroelectric power as well as providing water supplies. So, with Swiss engineers as the main contractors, work started and continued for several years. Walls were demolished, roads rerouted and the main dam wall, the first U-shaped dam in southern Europe, rose above the valley floor to an impressive height. Eventually, all was completed and the river was diverted back into the valley. A lake began to form behind the dam, and slowly it filled with water. Over weeks, the water level rose and the Seville Electricity Company congratulated itself on its wise planning and its use of the Swiss engineers. Meanwhile, the locals were watching with keen interest, for they knew something that no outsider had thought to consider.

When the reservoir was nearly full, the water level suddenly fell and did so very quickly, leaving just a small pool behind the dam. What the locals knew, and what every visitor can see to this day, is that the hills are mainly composed of limestone. Limestone itself is impervious to water but contains many fissures through which water may pass – which is why there are many caves in this type of rock. Presumably the huge downward pressure of the water opened up small fissures, and, like water in the bath, away it went. So, after all that effort, the water just drained away and the huge expenditure on the dam was wasted. Visitors can still walk across the dam and admire its fine engineering as they smile and look down at the small pool of water several hundred feet below them. The design was wholly logical, its dam was at the forefront of technology, its designers were good and conscientious people – but they forgot to ask the basic questions. Analysis without basic thought and rigour is a waste of time.

Simple physical models

The Lake District is one of the most popular tourist areas of Britain, with rugged mountains and beautiful lakes. Its fells were the site of much early industrial activity that led to the growth of the small villages that are scattered across the landscape. Tracks that connected these villages are now the paths along which walkers explore the area. The Lake District is wet as well as beautiful, and its attractive streams cascade down the fell-sides into the lakes. Many bridges have been built where the tracks cross the streams. The most appealing of these are made from a single self-supporting arch of stones (a good example is to be found behind the Wasdale Head Hotel). Figure 1.1 shows the basic design of these bridges.

A common method of building the bridges was to erect a wooden framework across the stream. This framework would be an arch on which the stones of the bridge would be placed.

Figure 1.1 A simple stone arch bridge.

The builders would securely locate the sides of the bridge in the solid ground on the stream banks and would carefully place selected stones on the wooden arch, starting from the banks. Eventually, the builders would reach the stage where only the keystone remained unplaced. The keystone sits at the top of the arch in the centre and would be forced into place to ensure a tight fit. If all the stones were properly fitted tightly together, then the arch would be self-supporting once the keystone was in place.

When the builders were happy that the stone arch was finished, they would set fire to the wooden arch that had supported it while being built. The question in their minds was whether the stone arch would collapse. Would it hold up its own weight, and would it support the weight of the traffic (people and animals) that walked over it? Someone would have to be the first to walk over the bridge and test it. On most occasions, the arch would hold and the bridge would be safe. But there were probably occasions when it collapsed along with the plans and reputations of the builders.

If a newly built bridge did collapse, it was unlikely to be a major catastrophe – apart from the effect on the builder's future prospects. Building such a bridge was not expensive and did not take a long time. The builders could try again until they produced a safe bridge. In the old adage of engineers, they could 'suck it and see'. This 'suck it and see' approach does not imply that the builders did not carefully plan the bridge. Certainly they were careful to select a site and careful in their choice of stones, in preparing these stones and in placing them. They were probably working from a mental image of the bridge. They could probably envisage what it would look like and what size of loads it would bear. Hence, they were able to make the bridge on site and adapt it and rebuild it until it worked as intended.

Small bridges over streams have probably been constructed in this way for centuries, but it would clearly be inappropriate to attempt work on a large-scale civil engineering project such as a motorway bridge in the same way. We take it for granted that the bridge will be planned by qualified engineers and architects who understand how to go about this job. Indeed, in many countries, bridges must be designed and their construction supervised only by fully qualified people. The work of the designers might begin with implicit mental models, their first ideas about the bridge, but we would expect them to move quickly on to formal and explicit models, which would lead to a bridge that would both meet its specification and be safe to use.

There are various types of model the bridge design team might employ. The simplest to envisage are two-dimensional drawings that show, at different levels of detail, how the bridge will look and how its different components will be fastened together. These drawings may exist on paper or might be held in some form of computer-aided design (CAD) system that allows drawings to be displayed on screen and manipulated in different ways. It might also be important to test out the bridge's performance under extreme conditions, such as high winds. For this, the designers may build scale models and test rigs, using wind tunnels and scaled tests to see how their design will perform.

The designers will also be working within cost limits. They will try to ensure not only that the bridge is strong enough to meet its specification but also that it is not overengineered. They will need to consider very carefully the size of the beams and supports that make up the bridge. To do this, they will use well-established mathematical models and equations to describe how the components will perform. They will use these different types of model as ways of managing the sheer complexity of the physical design and to minimize the risk that the bridge will not perform as intended. There is, of course, still no guarantee that the bridge will be safe under all conditions. For example, there is the well-known case of the Tacoma Narrows Bridge which collapsed in 1940 under moderate wind stress after starting to sway. However, in such cases, a model of the bridge may be used to try to discover what went wrong so as to ensure that a similar tragedy does not happen again.

Beyond the physical models

The designers need to go well beyond these models of the physical design for such large-scale projects. If, say, the bridge is part of a larger traffic scheme, they will wish to know what effect their design will have on the overall traffic flow. One way to do this would be to simulate on a computer the likely operation of the bridge. Such a simulation model (see Chapter 10) would allow the designers to develop control strategies for traffic on the basis of the capacities of the bridge and of the rest of the road network.

They will also need to assess how long it will take to build the bridge, and will organize themselves to control the project properly and ensure that it runs according to plan. To do this, they are highly likely to use a model of the different activities that are needed to complete the project, and thus they may resort to network planning tools such as the critical path method (CPM) and the programme evaluation and review technique (PERT) to plan the project and to control its operation. These tools allow the builders to see the effect of possible delays or accelerations in the building works. For example, what happens if the concrete cladding arrives a week late owing to shipping delays? Will that delay the whole project, or are there ways of rearranging the work to catch up the lost time? These are simple questions on small projects but immensely complicated questions in large-scale activities.

The purpose of this book is to demonstrate how different types of model can be useful in helping to manage complexity in order to reduce the risk of wrong decisions. The book also aims to show how different approaches to developing and using models can affect their value in practice. It is perhaps obvious how models and modelling can play a useful part in large-scale civil engineering projects, but it may be less clear how they can be used in other areas of life. After all, complex models must be expensive to build and cannot possibly include the full complexity of a situation, so does this not imply that modelling is a good idea but one that always falls down in practice?

Carefully built models can be of great use in areas of life very different from the design of physical structures. An idea central to this book is that one distinguishing characteristic of management scientists (meaning operational research professionals, business analysts and others who use rational and logical methods) is their use of explicit models. In spite of the analogy of the bridge-builders, the work done by management scientists cannot be regarded as a type of straightforward engineering. As will become clear, it is important for management scientists to be very careful in the assumptions that they make about organizations and in their treatment of other human beings.

What is a model?

There are many definitions of 'model' in general, and also many definitions of the term as used within Management Science. One of the earliest definitions simply says that *a model is a representation of reality* (Ackoff and Sasieni, 1968). This definition is appealing in its simplicity, but it ignores the question of why the model is being built. This aspect is crucial, for a model is always a simplification, and such simplification must be done with an eye on the intended use of the model. If this issue is ignored, a modeller could go on modelling forever in the safe and sure knowledge that parts of reality have been left out. This simple definition must therefore be expanded to consider the purpose for which the model is being built. Thus, a suitable definition for the present discussion is that *a model is a representation of reality* **intended for some definite purpose**.

This definition is still very wide-ranging and needs a more precise statement of purpose for the model and for modelling as an activity within Management Science. Management scientists aim to help managers to make better decisions and to exercise better control over the things for which they are responsible. It is therefore important that the definition of a model (and consequently of modelling) includes this idea so as to restrict the area of discussion. That is, in Management Science, models are often built to enable a manager to exercise better control or to help people to understand a complicated situation. Thus, a third stage definition is that *a model is a representation of reality intended* **to be of use to someone charged with managing or understanding that reality**.

This definition, in turn, could be criticized because it suggests that models in Management Science are only of value to those at the apex of a power structure, as in a business organization. Work in the UK in the 1980s and 1990s demonstrated that Management Science could also be of value to people who are not in positions of such power (Ritchie, Taket and Bryant, 1994). It would therefore be sensible to extend the definition yet further so as to include these possibilities. Thus, the definition becomes *a model is a representation of reality intended to be of use to someone* **in understanding, changing, managing and controlling that reality**.

Any reader who is a trained management scientist may be irritated by this definition and its development. Why does it not mention the term 'system'? Why not say that 'a model is a representation of some system'? This is because, to me at least, the term 'system' simply has too many connotations, some of which will be explored later in this book. But what, then, about the term 'reality' which is included in the definition. Does this assume that everyone will agree about what constitutes reality? Suppose they are wrong? This is an important point and explains why 'system' is not used in the definition. However, it also means that the term 'reality' must itself be qualified.

It is important to recognize that, in terms used by Checkland (1981), people may have legitimately different 'Weltanschauungen'. This German word, popular among philosophers, translates into English as 'world-view', but it is intended to convey the bundle of 'taken for granted' meanings and assumptions most of us employ in our daily lives. Some of us, for example, may take for granted that a car is a means to get from A to B with the minimum hassle. Others may regard it primarily as a status symbol, or as a hobby, or as a necessary evil that drinks away money and pollutes our world. Needless to say, anyone who attempts to consider how road space should be used in our crowded world must think through these different Weltanschauungen. Our world-views affect what we see and how we describe our experiences. They also affect our choices. To cope with this realization that different world-views may lead to different descriptions of reality, we need to adopt an approach to modelling that is, using Zeigler's (1984) term, multifaceted. That is, we may need to accept that multiple models are possible for a single apparent reality.

We also need to accept, although it is already implicit in the definition, that no model can ever be complete. This is for two reasons. First, were a model to be a complete one-on-one mapping of something, it would be just as complex as the real thing, and we would then have two of those somethings. This may be satisfying for an art-forger, but rather negates what we shall see later to be some of the advantages in modelling. The second reason is that, unless we include the entire universe in our model, there is always the risk that something will be missing.

There may be some relationship between our area of interest and another part of reality that is missing from the model. This may not matter now, but it may matter later.

Our definition now becomes *a model is a representation of* **part of reality as seen by the people who wish to use it to understand, to change, to manage and to control that part of reality**. A further criticism might be that this definition has no mention of improvement. Surely people engage in modelling because they wish to improve something? The only sensible answer to that question is to recall that multiple Weltanschauungen are possible, and that one person's improvement may be regarded as a disaster for someone else. Hence, our definition deliberately excludes any statement about improvement.

We have one more refinement to make. This involves the realization that most of us operate our lives with a set of assumptions that form our mindset. This causes us to carry around informal, mental models of our world. These models are modified by experience, sometimes because they fail to deliver and sometimes because they are challenged by other people. But internal and implicit mental models are not the main concern of this book – here we are concerned with models that are explicit and external. Hence, our definition becomes *a model is* **an external and explicit representation of part of reality as seen by the people who wish to use that model** *to understand, to change, to manage and to control that part of reality.*

Why bother with a model?

Our definition of a model, as it is to be used in Management Science, includes the idea of the user, for such models are generally built with some use in mind. But what are these uses? Much of the rest of this book will explore those uses and will show how they affect the ways in which models may be built, but it would be as well to discuss here the general reasons for building and using a model. Perhaps the clearest way to do this is to think of the alternatives. What approaches might be followed if a modelling approach is not adopted?

This discussion assumes that some critical issue is being faced that requires a decision to be taken or some control to be exercised. It does not assume that the decision will be taken immediately, nor that rational analysis is the only consideration. Similarly, it does not rule out the notion of 'decision fermentation', said to characterize some successful Japanese companies, nor the gradual process of dealing with issues (see Langley *et al.*, 1995). In such gradual processes, an issue is discussed over considerable time by many people in the organization, at different levels and with different viewpoints. Through this lengthy process, a consensus emerges that develops into a commitment to act. Thus, decisions are often not taken at a definite point in time; they emerge as different considerations and are accounted for by those participating in the process. Nevertheless, when a decision is to be taken, whether immediately or by some emergent process, there are approaches that could be followed that differ from the use of explicit models as advocated here. These options will always include the status quo; that is, we could leave things just as they are.

Do nothing!

This possibility – the favoured option of the lazy and often the only option open to the powerless – has at least the attraction that the analyst will not be blamed for what happens as a result. This is not always an option to be sneezed at, for inaction can sometimes be the best initial response when faced with uncertainty. Sometimes, an overhasty response is much worse than doing nothing. However, if we do have the discretion to act, then we need to ask how we know that inaction is an appropriate response, and the answer, surely, is that we can only know this if some analysis has been conducted. This implies that we have either internal and implicit models or external and explicit models.

Experiment with reality

Considering this option takes us right back to the building of single-arch bridges from stone. The same arguments apply here as they do for bridge-builders. Trying out possible options for real is all very well, and can be very exciting, but it can also be disastrous for the following reasons:

- *Cost.* In most situations in which we need to respond or to exercise some control, we have a range of options open to us. The range may be quite small (do we place the new factory in Wales, or should it be in France?) or it may be almost infinite (what control algorithm should be developed to ensure aircraft safety in crowded airspace?). Trying out any option in practice always incurs cost. The cost per option may be quite small, and, if the range of options is limited, this may be a very sensible way to operate. But if the cost per option is high or the range of options is almost infinite, experimentation with reality can be very expensive.
- *Time.* There is often not enough time to try out all the options in practice, even when the range is small. To be sure where to locate our factory, we may need to see how the option works out over a 10-year period if we are to get a realistic return on the investment. This would clearly be impossible. On a smaller scale, if we need to decide how best to route service vehicles around an urban area, there may be too many options to make it worthwhile even attempting to experiment in practice. Thus, the times taken to conduct the experiments mean that experimentation on reality is likely to lead to very restricted experiments.
- *Replication.* Linked to these two is the need, on occasions, for replication. Sometimes a case has to be argued for a change or for some control to be exercised. This can mean arguing the case at different levels within an organization and with different groups of people. They may wish to see the effects of the policy, and they may wish, entirely legitimately, to try out the same experiments themselves. Another reason for replication is statistical variation. For example, the demand for most products is variable and unpredictable, except in statistical terms. Any policy to be investigated may need to be examined under a wide range of demand patterns to check its sensitivity. Thus, replication may be needed, and this is both time-consuming and costly on the real system.
- *Danger.* When things go wrong, catastrophe may result. The analogy here with bridges is obvious: no one would wish a bridge to collapse, injuring hundreds of people and costing huge sums. The same is true in the realm of Management Science. The result of trying to cram more aircraft into a restricted airspace may be to increase the risk of collision to an unacceptable level. Most of us would rather that this were established by experiments on models of the airspace and the control policies rather than by the use of real aircraft. Especially when we are on those aircraft!
- *Legality.* There are times when we may need to see what effect a change in the law might have. One possibility is to break the law and then see what happens. This may be all very well if you are employed by the Mafia, but is unlikely to endear you to the rest of society. Hence, it is much better to develop a model of how things would be were the law to be different. This can be used to see the effects of various changes and allows us to see whether it might be worth pressing for a change in those laws.

Models as appropriate simplifications

The value of simplification

It is important to understand the limitations of model-building and of model-use, for a model will always be a simplification and an approximate representation of some aspect of reality. This is clearly true even of architects' and engineers' drawings of bridges: for example, they are not usually concerned to show the exact colour of the steel and concrete to be used to build the bridge. They are much more concerned with the general appearance and detailed functioning of the structure. Hence, their models are approximations, and none the worse for that.

Models do not have to be exact to be of use. As an example, consider the problem of navigating the subway systems, which are part of mass transit in many large cities around the world. The operators of these systems usually display their various routes by the use of maps displayed on the subway stations. The interesting thing about these maps is that they allow the reader to understand the possible routings by deliberately distorting reality. This is done in two ways. First, the physical layout of the subway lines is distorted on the map so as to emphasize their general directions and their interchanges. Thus, routes that may share the same tunnels in the physical world are shown as separate on the logical map. Second, careful use of colour allows the reader to identify the various lines from a key. As yet, in spite of adding coloured markers on the station walls, no subway operator has attempted to colour the steel rail track to match their maps!

Therefore, it is not a valid criticism that models are simplifications, for it is precisely such approximation that makes them useful. Hence, the important question to ask is what degree of simplification is sensible and can this be known in advance? As part of an answer to this question, consider Table 1.1, which identifies some of the important differences between a model and reality, using the term 'reality' to represent the part of the real world being modelled.

Complex reality and simple models: Occam's razor

There can be no clear answer to the question of how complicated a model needs to be – it depends, as was discussed earlier, on its intended purpose. One helpful idea is to consider Occam's razor. According to Doyle (1992), 'William of Occam, or Ockham, b. Ockham, England, c. 1285, d. c. 1349, ranks among the most important philosopher–theologians of the Middle Ages'. He is remembered especially for the principle of analysis known as Occam's razor, which he used to dissect the philosophical speculations of others. Two of the many statements of Occam's razor are as follows:

- do not multiply entities unnecessarily;
- a plurality (of reasons) should not be posited without necessity.

A contemporary interpretation of this would be that, if two explanations seem equally plausible, then it is better to use the simpler of the two. In one sense, a model will be used in an attempt

Table 1.1 Reality versus model.

Reality	Model
Complex	Simple
Subtle	Concrete
Ill-defined	Well-defined

to provide an explicit explanation of something or other, and Occam's razor supports the view that simplification is not merely acceptable, it is desirable. Consider, for example, a model that includes the arrival of customers at a service point. If observation data are available, they might show that the arrival rate can adequately be modelled by a Poisson distribution (a simple way to represent random arrivals). This simple Poisson process may be perfectly adequate for deciding what resources are needed at a service point. To people trained in queuing theory and stochastic processes, the use of such a probability distribution is commonplace. However, in real life, the customers may have their own individual reasons for arriving when they do. Some may be earlier than they intended (less traffic than expected?), others may be later (the bus was late?) and others may have called on the off-chance. Thus, a complete model of the real-life system would need to account for each of these and other factors for each customer. But this detail may be quite unnecessary unless the aim of the model is to study the effect, say, of changing road traffic patterns on the operation of a service centre.

Thus, in modelling terms, the application of Occam's razor should lead us to develop models that are as simple as possible and yet are valid and useful for their intended purpose. That is, whether an element of a model is necessary (in terms of Occam's razor) will depend on its intended purpose. This, too, can be difficult, for only with perfect hindsight can we be sure that a model adequately addresses the reality being modelled. Nevertheless, it is important that management scientists do attempt to assess the degree to which their models are valid. Chapter 12 will deal with this issue in more detail.

An analogy about complexity

Another reason for simplicity in modelling comes from a common joke about complexity. To a mathematician, a complex number is the square root of a negative number; it has two parts, known as the real and imaginary parts. Complex systems also have real and imaginary parts. The problem is to differentiate between the two, which is difficult because one person's reality may be another's imagination. Models, on the other hand, are simple in the sense that they are entirely explicit and can be tested by other people. Models are imagination made explicit.

Subtle reality and concrete models

Although this book takes for granted that reality does exist in a form external to the observer, the modelling of reality is still not straightforward for the reasons identified in the analogy about complex numbers. Even if we accept (as I do) that reality is 'out there', we still have the problem that we must rely on our own perceptions in attempting to understand and to experience that reality. The adversarial principle of justice that is dominant in the UK and USA stems, at least in part, from the view that witnesses to events can produce totally or partially different accounts of events without lying. Two people might enter a street at the same time to see a youth standing over an elderly person lying on the side of the road. One witness might be sure the youth is helping up a frail person who has fallen, the other absolutely certain he is stealing the old person's handbag. In reality, the youth had knocked the woman down, but only because he dashed across the road to push her out of the way of an oncoming car.

The point of a model is to make explicit or concrete whatever aspect of reality is being investigated. In some cases, the model is being developed in order to gain some understanding about how the real world operates. In this sense, the model becomes a theory that tries to explain what has been observed to occur. One test of such a model's validity would be a Turing test of the type devised by the mathematician Alan Turing. He argued that a good test of an artificial

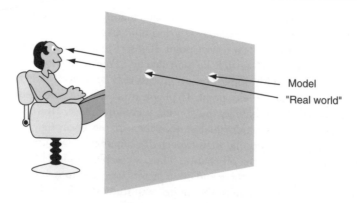

Figure 1.2 A Turing test.

system (model in our case) is to see whether a judge, knowledgeable about the aspect of the real world being modelled, can distinguish between a stream of data coming from the real world and one coming from the model. The basic idea is shown in Figure 1.2.

The problem with this kind of argument is that it assumes that the observer is both omniscient (all-knowing) and unbiased. The observer might simply be wrong in declaring the model to be acceptable or not. This may be because, when most of us talk about reality, what we actually mean is our own impressions about reality. Reality itself lies under those impressions, and the best way to understand it may be to consider carefully many such impressions. On the other hand, the model is concrete and entirely explicit. People may also, of course, misunderstand the model or its output, but its parts can be written down and may be unambiguously addressed. This is one distinct advantage that a model, albeit a simplification, has over the real world.

Ill-defined reality and well-defined model

In one familiar passage in the New Testament, the apostle Paul wrote about perfect love and ended by writing that 'Now we see but a poor reflection in a mirror, then we shall see face to face' (I Corinthians 13:12). Our impressions of the world are always partial, both in the sense that we do not experience everything and also in the sense that we may well be biased. Thus, our concept of what is going on in the real world will consist of ill-defined views and arguments unless they are properly codified and documented within a formal and well-defined model. In Figure 1.3, reality is shown inside an ill-defined cloud, and the model is shown as a fully defined box.

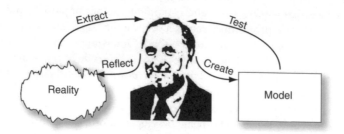

Figure 1.3 Models and reality.

The task of the modeller is to take these ill-defined and implicit views of reality and cast them in some form well enough defined to be at least understood and argued over by other people. In the case of Management Science, this model may need to be represented in some computable form to allow for rapid experiments on the model so as to make inferences about the real world. This can only be done if the model is fully specified, although the specification may only emerge while trying to translate it into a computable form. Thus, one major development in the 1980s was the idea of visual interactive modelling, in which a computer is used as a device to build a model in a stepwise manner. Thus, the analyst develops a simple model by, perhaps, developing some form of representation on a computer screen. This model is then 'run' – that is, used in some way or other – and it will, most likely, be found wanting. Its faults are considered, and these are then remedied until the model is held to be adequate, or valid, for its intended purpose. Thus, the full specification may only emerge from the modelling process.

Models for decision and control

Much of what has been said so far in this chapter could apply to any kind of model, but the main focus of this book is on models and modelling in Management Science. That is, the attempt to use explicit models to improve decision-making and control in organizations, whether they are businesses, charities, social agencies, community groups, churches or whatever. For this purpose, the book takes the view that two important aspects of management are decision-making and control. This does not mean that these are the only important aspects of management; for example, Mintzberg's early work on the realities of managerial life (Mintzberg, 1973) demonstrated that one characteristic of managerial life is a constant stream of meetings and interruptions. Time to think or to take an Olympian perspective is rare, whereas interacting with people is frequent.

Nevertheless, most organizations are made up of people working towards goals of various kinds. Those people sometimes do take decisions and also spend much of their time with other people in trying to achieve those goals. To this end, they establish policies and devise rules, which they then attempt to enforce and implement. It would be extremely foolish to argue that management is wholly about decision-making and control, but some of it is, and it is to these two aspects that a modelling approach can make a very useful contribution.

Decisions

A decision needs to be made when an individual, a group or whatever faces a choice in which there is more than a single option. The range of possible options might be small, or it might be near-infinite. An example of the former might be the decision about whether a confectionery product is priced at 40p or 50p. An example of the latter might be the exact target weight of the pack (assuming that this is not specified in weights and measures legislation). Decisions are further complicated when they turn out to be a sequence of decisions, each of which affects subsequent options. The armoury of Management Science has many weapons to use in fighting this particular modelling battle. Parts II and III of this book are devoted to descriptions of some of these weapons. Some of them are based on mathematical and logical models, others are ways of helping people to think through the consequences of situations as they interpret them. As will be made clearer in Part II, there is no need to assume that a narrow view of rationality dominates organizational decision-making; the point of a model is to explore what might happen if a particular decision were to be taken. Similarly, it is not necessary to assume that decisions happen in an instant after massive and purposeful deliberation; they can occur as streams of issues are dealt with over time (Langley *et al.*, 1995).

Control

Control is related to decision-making. Often, making the decision is the easy bit! What is much harder and takes much more time and energy is getting a decision fully implemented and then managing the continued operation of the new system. In most organizations, whatever their type, this involves a process of persuasion, consultation and argument, which can be very time-consuming. It also involves battling with the changes in the rest of the world as they occur during implementation, and ensuring that the decisions taken are still sensible in the light of those changes.

For example, analysis via a model may make it clear to a group of senior managers of a supermarket chain that it would be best to concentrate their delivery system around a small number of large depots. The problem is that they currently operate with a larger number of small depots, and the transition will take time. In addition, the staff in some of the smaller depots are likely to lose their jobs and so are unlikely to be cooperative in implementing the changes. The implementation of that decision, therefore, is likely to be a fraught process involving many meetings, some formal and some informal, some arranged ahead of time, others on the spot. People will need to be persuaded and to be enthused, and may need to be rewarded in some way for their cooperation. All of this takes time, and all is part of the day-to-day life of management.

As an analogy, consider again the task of the pilot of a long-haul aircraft. The flight may be about 14 hours non-stop, but the pilot (with computer assistance) must file a flight plan specifying the intended route and expected timings, all in advance. This is done with the aid of computer-based models of aircraft performance, computerized navigation systems and computer-based weather forecasts. This supporting technology is designed to make a difficult decision as straightforward as possible. Yet the pilot knows very well that it will be an extremely unusual flight if changes are not made to the plan en route. Winds may be unexpectedly strong, there may be air-traffic-control problems or the plane may be rerouted to avoid turbulence. This does not mean that the original plan is a waste of time; rather, it means that the plan serves as a basis for control, against which progress can be measured.

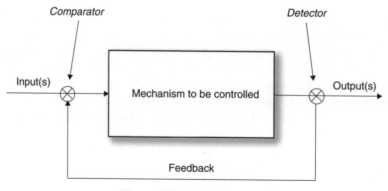

Figure 1.4 A feedback system.

Control systems are usually based on the idea of feedback, as shown in Figure 1.4. This diagram shows a mechanism controlled by the detection of its performance, which is then fed back and compared with some target level of performance. This concept, although mechanistic in appearance, may also be used at a conceptual level to think about control within organizations. Most often the feedback is negative, that is, differences between the target value and the actual value are used to guide the system towards its target. Thus, if the airline pilot realizes that the plane is ahead of schedule, then the air speed can be reduced to bring the flight back on to schedule.

Control systems depend on the availability of information about system performance which is fed back to a manager, who is able to compare it with what is wanted and change the system's performance as necessary. In doing this, organizational managers are using models (often implicit) about what is likely to happen if they take certain action. For example, they may believe that increasing the shelf space devoted to soft drinks in a supermarket may increase sales of those drinks. If increasing sales of those drinks is one of their aims, then making such a change may seem a reasonable thing to do. But a formal and explicit model of the link between sales and shelf space would be so much more useful than a set of hunches for exercising this control.

Soft and hard modelling

Few people would disagree with the notion that some kind of formal model is involved in most Management Science, but many books on Operational Research or Management Science imply that only mathematical models are of interest. One of the aims of this book is to demonstrate that successful Management Science involves the use of other types of formal model, as well as those that are mathematical in form. Mathematics and mathematical models are very useful, and Part III will explore some aspects of their construction and use. But it is important to realize that the value of models and modelling approaches extends way beyond the realm of mathematical models for decision and control. This issue will be discussed in much greater detail in Part II, but some mention needs to be made here of two other types of model that are of great value in Management Science.

Business process models

The 1990s saw an increasing interest in business processes, especially in business process re-engineering (BPR) (Hammer and Champy, 1993). To some extent, such BPR was just another fashionable term for taking a fundamental look at the way a business operates so as to exploit appropriate technologies – not a new idea. Yet there were some new emphases in BPR that are to be much welcomed. The first is the view that managers need to focus on business process as well as business structure. A process is a sequence of dynamic activities needed to get something done that will add value in the business. Thus, the concern is not so much with questions such as 'What departments and managers do we need to serve our customers?', but with ones such as 'What tasks must we do in order to serve them?'. The stress is on verbs rather than on nouns, on actions rather than on static systems, on processes rather than on structure.

These ideas are in vogue because changes in technology have made it possible to imagine ways of carrying out tasks that are radically different from the ways in which they were done in the past. For example, a national post office operates regional sorting centres in which mail is sorted for subsequent distribution. In most countries, addresses have associated postcodes or zip codes to aid this sorting and distribution. One remaining problem, however, is that many envelopes are handwritten or poorly typed, and high-speed character recognition systems cannot be used to sort these automatically. People are employed to mark these envelopes with machine-readable codes to enable automatic sorting. The traditional approach to this task is to employ a number of these coders in each sorting office, but modern technology means that, by using video cameras and remote keyboards, these coders could be located almost anywhere in the world. Hence, shifting workloads might draw on variable pools of labour. The shifted process still involves people reading handwritten codes and marking them with machine-readable ones. This process is needed at the moment. But the changes in technology allow the process to be shifted in space (to another location) or in time (to another time zone).

Before such a process is re-engineered in this way, it makes great sense to model it in order to discover the essential and sensitive components where improvement will make a difference. As another example, insurance companies in the UK must meet certain deadlines in responding to requests and in allowing leeway on contracts for different types of insurance. When launching new products, which these companies do surprisingly often, they need to plan staffing levels and computerized support to meet these legal requirements. In order to be able to operate quickly in the marketplace, the companies need rapid ways to assess the likely support levels needed to service a product. To this end, they sometimes use computer-based simulation models as an aid to this business process engineering (not re-engineering this time) (for an example of this, see Davies, 1994).

Soft modelling in Management Science

Whereas the affinity between business process modelling and the models used in engineering may be fairly clear – indeed the term 're-engineering' in BPR gives much of the clue – other types of much less concrete modelling are also carried out under the Management Science banner. A detailed treatment of these appears in Part II, but some discussion is important here so as to set things in context. These approaches are usually known as 'soft OR/MS' [Operational (or Operations) Research/Management Science], and they have a number of features distinguishing them from decision modelling, control modelling and business process modelling. Most of them are intended to aid in strategic management and planning, a field that has a number of distinctive features.

A strategic decision is one that will have a large effect on the continued survival of the organization. Indeed, it could be argued that the development of a strategy is an attempt to take control of the future by managing or creating that future. Strategic decision-making is rightly considered to be complex, and this complexity has a number of different dimensions:

- A huge quantity of both quantitative and qualitative data and information that could be considered. This does not mean that such data are immediately to hand, but that it is easy to conceive of huge amounts of data that one or more participants might consider to be important. Usually, the available data are incomplete and may be ambiguous in their interpretation.
- Considerable confusion and lack of clarity about problem definition except at the basic level (we want to continue to exist). This stems from disagreement and uncertainty about what should constitute legitimate issues for inclusion in decision-making.
- The different participants who make up the strategic team may have conflicting objectives and may be in direct opposition to one another. Within this conflict, power relationships are important and need to be considered if any kind of negotiated consensus is to be reached.

The aim of soft OR/MS is to explore the disagreements and uncertainties that exist so that an agreed consensus and commitment to action can be reached among the senior management team. In such approaches, the modeller must act in a facilitative role and cannot take for granted that the participants share the same view about reality, and must, instead, work with the perceptions of those who are involved. The resultant models are used to show the consequences of these different perceptions and the relationships between them. This allows for exploration of areas in which consensus and commitment to action may be possible. A good introduction to these methods is given in Rosenhead and Mingers (2001).

Part II of this book is devoted to some of these 'soft' methods, which will be summarized as interpretive approaches. This is because they are attempts to enable people to understand how other people interpret their experience and what is happening. It is common for different people at the same event to interpret it in quite different ways. Take, for example, the case of a scandal within the Church of England over a radical church in the North of England whose vicar was accused of the sexual abuse of women from the congregation. There were calls for an inquiry to uncover how this could have happened and to suggest what might be done to prevent this happening again. Interviewed on TV, the bishop in whose diocese the church was located said, in all sincerity, that there would be no point in such an inquiry as everything was known already. This did not satisfy those who were calling for the inquiry. Why should this be? One possibility is that those calling for the inquiry did not believe that the bishop and his colleagues knew all there was to know about what happened. But it is more likely that the bishop and those calling for the inquiry interpreted its purpose in quite different ways. The bishop may well have been logically correct to say that the inquiry would uncover nothing new; on the other hand, setting up the inquiry would have shown that the issue was being taken seriously. The two parties interpreted their reality very differently, even without accusing one another of lying or of distortion.

In contentious areas of life and in strategic management, such differences of interpretation are not unusual. Part II shows that these interpretations can be modelled and can be used to help people find enough agreement and consensus to agree to take action. Of course, in one sense, any model can represent only a perspective on what is happening, and, as mentioned earlier, different perspectives will lead to different models. The interpretive approaches are distinctive because they are deliberately designed to work with multiple interpretations and aim to make use of these differences. By contrast, although quantitative models do embody different perspectives, they are usually not, of themselves, multifaceted. Multiple quantitative models can be used, but this is rarely a deliberate strategy. It is an essential part of interpretive approaches.

Summary: models as tools for thinking

In an increasingly complex and interconnected world, it seems vital that we find ways to explore the possible consequences of decisions and plans before taking any action. One way of doing this is to use an approach that is based on external and explicit models that capture the essence of some situation. The models are simplifications, abstractions of features deemed to be important, and there can be no guarantee that they will be valid. However, used sensibly, models and modelling approaches provide one way of managing risk and uncertainty. In this sense, models are 'tools for thinking'. Just as hand and power tools add to the physical power and aptitude of humans, so these tools for thinking may be used to add leverage to human thought and analysis. But there are some obvious dangers.

The first danger is summarized in the anonymous comment that 'if the only tool you have is a hammer, then you tend to treat everything as if it were a nail'. In Birmingham, in the West Midlands of the UK (known as Brummagem to the locals, or Brummies), a common joke is that a hammer is a 'Brummagem screwdriver', the idea being that screws can always be hammered into place if you can't be bothered to do the job properly. The result is that the assembly looks OK at first, but the problems come later. In a similar way, models may be grossly misused in the name of OR/MS, and there are no substitutes for intelligence, humanity and intellectual rigour in developing appropriate models and in using them properly.

The second danger is that of 'nothing-but-ism'. As has been repeated many times in this chapter, models are simplifications, and that is part of their power and attraction. There are therefore always things missing from a model, and the analyst and those using the models need to be well aware of this. Even if the model is substantially valid for the task in hand, there may be things missing from it that mean that analysis based on it can be safely and sensibly ignored. As used in OR/MS, models show the rational and logical consequences that are known or expected to follow from certain actions. Given that reality is multifaceted, a model and its results should be as open to question as any other product of the human mind. In spite of these dangers, models within OR/MS have much to contribute to improving the worlds in which we live. The rest of this book aims to give sensible advice about how they can be built and how they might be used.

References

Ackoff R.L. and Sasieni M.W. (1968) *Fundamentals of Operations Research*. John Wiley & Sons, Inc., New York, NY.

Checkland P.B. (1981) *Systems Thinking, Systems Practice*. John Wiley & Sons, Ltd, Chichester, UK.

Davies M.N. (1994) Back-office process management in the financial services – a simulation approach using a model generator. *Journal of the Operational Research Society*, **45**(12), 1363–1373.

Doyle J.P. (1992) William of Occam, in *Software Toolworks Multimedia Encyclopedia*. Software Toolworks, Novata, CA.

Fortune J. and Peters G. (1995) *Learning from Failure: the Systems Approach*. John Wiley & Sons, Ltd, Chichester, UK.

Hammer M. and Champy J. (1993) *Re-engineering the Corporation*. Nicholas Brealey, London, UK.

Langley A., Mintzberg H., Pitcher P., Posada E. and Saint-Macary J. (1995) Opening up decision making: the view from the black stool. *Organizational Science*, **6**(3), 260–279.

Mintzberg H. (1973) *The Nature of Managerial Work*. HarperCollins, New York, NY.

Ritchie C., Taket A. and Bryant J. (eds) (1994) *Community Works*. APVIC Publications, Sheffield, UK.

Rosenhead J.V. and Mingers J. (eds) (2001) *Rational Analysis for a Problematic World Revisited*. John Wiley & Sons, Ltd, Chichester, UK.

Simon H.A. (1976) From substantive to procedural rationality, in *Method and Appraisal in Economics*, ed. by Latsis S.J. Cambridge University Press, Cambridge, UK.

Zeigler B.P. (1984) *Multifaceted Modelling and Discrete Event Simulation*. Academic Press, New York, NY.

2 Management Science – making sense of strategic vision

Background

Chapter 1 discussed why management scientists build external and explicit models. The main reason is to support decision-making and control within organizations by helping people to see the possible consequences of their actions. The models may employ mathematics and statistics, and they are an attempt to bring reason to bear on complex issues. But what do we mean by 'reason' in this context? A popular book on soft operational research (OR) is entitled *Rational Analysis for a Problematic World Revisited* (Rosenhead and Mingers, 2001). This implies that these methods are based on a rational approach in a world that may not be wholly straightforward. This chapter will explore what might be meant by 'reason' and 'rationality' in an attempt to point out some of the pros and cons of using models within Management Science. It will do so by using ideas developed by Simon in his work in Economics, Psychology and Artificial Intelligence, and by laying these alongside the work of others, such as Mintzberg, who argue that factors other than reason need to be considered.

Rational choice

Some people see Management Science as a form of decision modelling based on an extension of managerial economics in which optimal choices need to be made between competing alternatives. That is, they argue that Management Science is an attempt to support rational choice. A concise description of this view of rational choice is given by Simon (1954) as follows:

> *The most advanced theories, both verbal and mathematical, of rational behaviour are those that employ as their central concepts the notions of:*
>
> *1. A set of alternative courses of action presented to the individual's choice.*
> *2. Knowledge and information that permit the individual to predict the consequences of choosing any alternative.*
> *3. A criterion for determining which set of consequences he prefers.*
>
> *In these theories, rationality consists in selecting that course of action which leads to the set of consequences most preferred.*

The value of the various outcomes needs to be measured consistently, and the term 'utility' is commonly used in the Economics and Psychology literature for that purpose. Utility is some measure of welfare or value. For the time being we will leave aside the question of how this is to

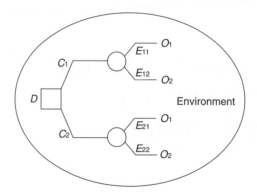

Figure 2.1 The basic idea of classical rational choice.

be computed, although, as we shall see later, this is an issue of some importance. The decision criterion (item 3 in Simon's list) usually has two parts:

- a statement of the utility measure that will be employed;
- a statement of the selection mechanism, such as choosing the most profitable or the cheapest.

Another view of the same approach is given in Figure 2.1. The ellipse depicts the environment within which the decision-making process occurs. In the simplest case, as depicted, there are at least two possible courses of action (C_1 and C_2) open to the decision-maker D. In the simplest case, each of the courses of action could lead to an outcome that is desirable (O_1) or undesirable (O_2). The modelling task is to establish the relationships (E_{ij}) that exist between the courses of action (C_i) and the outcomes (O_j). In effect, these E_{ij} values reflect the efficiency of each choice in leading to each outcome. Some choices are more likely to get to a particular outcome than others, and therefore their E_{ij} values will be higher. For present purposes, we can ignore the question of how these E_{ij} relationships can be obtained or approximated in some way or other, but this is another question that must be faced at some stage. There is no need for D to be a single decision-maker, provided there is agreement among participants about the various C_i, E_{ij} and O_j values and variables. Obviously, there can be many more than two courses of action (that is, $i > 2$), and the outcome set may be rather more sophisticated than just a simple division into those that are acceptable and those that are not.

Without too much imagination, it is possible to see Figure 2.1 as a form of road map or maze in which the aim is to get from one end to the other. Indeed, this notion of decision-making as navigation across known terrain is, as will become clear, very pervasive. Some people refer to this view of decision-making as sequential search.

A simple investment decision

A simple example that fits this set of assumptions would be a straightforward choice between two alternative investments that allow you to place some cash on deposit for a known period of time. Suppose that you could place £1000 with the Reliable Bank or with the Trusty Building Society, and that both institutions are guaranteed by the government should they get into difficulties. Suppose, too, that Reliable offers a compound interest rate of 7.5% p.a. and Trusty offers 7.0% p.a., both rates guaranteed for 2 years, and that no other investment is available.

A straightforward application of the theory of rational choice would lead you to invest your £1000 in the Reliable Bank. This fits the notions listed by Simon as follows:

1. There is a known set of choices – three in fact:
   - do nothing;
   - invest in Reliable Bank;
   - invest in Trusty Building Society.
2. We have complete knowledge and can predict the consequences of each option:
   - do nothing – producing £1000 after 2 years;
   - invest in Reliable Bank – producing $£1000 \times (1.075)^2 = £1155.6$ after 2 years;
   - invest in Trusty Building Society – producing $£1000 \times (1.07)^2 = £1149.0$ after 2 years.
3. The criterion of choice is clear: select the investment that produces the best return after 2 years – the Reliable Bank.

Hence, in simple cases of this type, there is little doubt that classical rational choice is a useful approach to adopt.

At the risk of labouring the point, it is important to see how the assumptions and the example are well suited to one another. First, the set of options is relatively small and is fully known – not only now, but over the full 2-year period of the intended investment. Second, the consequences of each option are known and are subject to no variation whatsoever – the return is fully guaranteed and will not change. Third, the decision criterion is entirely unambiguous and can be directly applied by computing the promised returns over the known time period. Clearly, such an approach could be entirely automated in a computer program, and this would be wholly satisfactory if its assumptions held.

Relaxing the assumptions

Each of these assumptions could be relaxed without entirely invalidating the classical rational approach. Considering each in turn:

1. The set of choices need not be small – computers are capable of analysing millions of choices if this is necessary. The set could even be infinite over a known range, such as when there is a need to decide how much to invest. The range might be from zero up to many millions, with every possible value in between. Such cases can be modelled by a continuous variable over that known range. This is the basis of mathematical programming models (see Chapter 9) and other optimization approaches.
2. The information and insight needed to predict the consequences of each of the options need not be immediately known or available. Within Management Science, much modelling effort goes into attempts to make these predictions by developing models that link options to consequences by establishing the *E*s (efficiencies of choice) of Figure 2.1. This may involve the use of statistical forecasting techniques, of scenario analysis, of computer simulations or of other techniques from the standard toolkit of Management Science.
3. The decision criterion applied need not be a simple single dimension variable; a multi-criteria choice could be made. That is, attempts could be made to find the option that does best against a whole range of criteria, and, sometimes, this turns out to be possible (see Chapter 7). For example, it may be important to the investor that the investment produces a high return and is made with an ethical institution. Sometimes, both criteria can be satisfied by the same

choice. A further refinement, which links this notion and the second one, occurs when the consequences of an option are uncertain and the choice must then be made on the basis of expected utility. In these cases, probability theory may be brought to bear on the problem, and the choice is then made on the basis of what is expected to produce the best outcome, although there is no guarantee that this expectation will be met. This is known as risky choice (Slovic, 1990) and implies that objective probabilities are known. This idea can further be refined when there are only subjective views of likely outcomes, and in such a case the concern is to maximize the subjective expected utility. As we move from utility to expected utility to subjective expected utility, the computations grow more complicated, but the basic idea remains the same.

Thus, the simple classical and rational approach most certainly has its place within Management Science. Its application has been advocated since the early days of the subject. As an example, see Ackoff and Sasieni (1968) who, like many others at that time, suggested that modelling of this type requires the analyst to establish and to link the following:

- the set of alternative courses of action (often known as the controllable variables);
- the set of other variables relevant to the issues under consideration (often known as the uncontrollable variables);
- some form of decision criterion that is consistent and that permits the model to be used so as to select the most appropriate course of action.

Modelling proceeds as the analyst attempts to link these sets of variables together to show their effects in terms of the decision criterion. Their suggestion fits rather well with the notions of rational choice shown in Figure 2.1. To illustrate this point, consider the following short case study, which will be used at various points in the book. As the chapters unfold, the case will be used in different ways to develop the later ideas of the book.

Case study: TICTOC – a hose by any other name

The InCorporated Transitanian Oil Company (TICTOC) was formed around 1980 when the Transitanian government completed its 10-year programme of nationalizing the oil companies engaged in extracting its oil. The oil comes from wells on the mainland and is piped directly to the supertanker port at Ventry. Here, it is either refined or shipped to the consumer countries as crude oil. The Ventry port installations are controlled by TICTOC.

Your role

You are part of a Management Science project team and are employed by TICTOC. You have just attended a meeting that may lead to a Management Science study. The meeting will be reconvened tomorrow so that you may sketch out your proposals for work that you believe to be worthwhile.

Background

Today's meeting was with the Director of Port Services (DPS) at Ventry, the Controller of Pumping Operations (CPO) and the Maintenance Manager (MM). You discussed the pumping of crude oil from the Ventry storage tanks into waiting tankers. The technology used is fairly standard and involves sections of flexible hose about one metre in diameter that connect the Ventry tanks, via pumping stations, to the tankers in the harbour. Because of tidal rise and fall, the hoses are subject to shearing and twisting forces of some magnitude, and this sometimes causes the hoses to fail in service. When this happens there is a large spillage of crude oil until the pumps are switched to auxiliary hose lines.

Until recently, the hoses have been bought from a UK supplier who claims to sell the best available hoses. This supplier, UKHose PLC, was the originator of these flexible hoses and has been selling its current range of hoses for about 10 years. The original Ventry pumping installation was bought from UKHose, and, until now, the same company has provided replacements as necessary.

Over the last 2 years, two new suppliers of large flexible hose have appeared. YankHose is from the USA and JapHose is from Japan. Both companies claim that their hoses are at least as good as the UKHose product – although their production technology is somewhat different and allows them to undercut UKHose prices by up to 40%. New ancillary equipment may be needed to adapt pumping operations away from the UKHose product.

The DPS is very keen to reduce his costs and has insisted that one of the pumping stations be switched to JapHose for a trial period. There have been problems during this trial, and the CPO is unhappy about what he feels is a much higher rate of failure in service than was the case with UKHose products. At one stage in the meeting, the conversation went something like this:

DPS: . . . Yes, 1 know that the hoses seem to fail a bit more often, but look at the price. We save 40% on the prices charged by UKHose. I'm not bothered about shorter service lives with that reduction.

CPO: Even if the life is only 50% of UKHose?

DPS: Come on! It's much higher than that.

MM: Well, I'm not too sure about that. But I don't really know what the failure rates are. I'm sure that we could improve things by better maintenance.

CPO: But if we stop the pumping just for preventive maintenance then it costs money. There's all the demurrage to pay to the tanker owners for a start.

MM: It's still cheaper than having a hose blow oil all over the harbour when it fails. Then we still have to stop pumping, but we also have to replace the hose section. Then we have to clean up the harbour. We also have the Greens on our backs about pollution. I'm sure that better maintenance is the answer.

DPS: But it all costs money. There must be some way to work out what to do. What about you whiz-kids in the MS Division, do you have any ideas?

Applying classical, rational analyses to TICTOC

Following the usual advice, the first task is to identify the variables relevant to the issues being faced. The primary issue of choice is the selection of flexible hoses to be used at the Ventry installation of TICTOC. An attempt to divide the various factors and variables into those that are controllable by TICTOC and those that are not reveals another issue. We need to decide which person's or group's perspective will determine whether a variable or factor is controllable or not. In this case it seems straightforward enough: you are the management scientist and the problem has been posed by the DPS at Ventry whose perspective should therefore be taken. That is, to use common terminology, we will treat the DPS as the client for this study.

Options or controllable variables

There appear to be two sets of options:

1. The type of hose selected – UKHose, JapHose or YankHose.
2. The maintenance policies applied to the hoses once they are in use.

That is, the decision problem is to select a hose type and to decide what maintenance it should have when in service.

Uncontrollable variables

The most important of these would seem to be the following, bearing in mind that their identification here does not guarantee that we will be able to evaluate them:

- the expected life of the different types of hose – this may be expressed as a probability distribution;
- the likely purchase price of the hoses;
- the likely costs of spillages, should they occur – this may also be expressed as a probability distribution;
- the costs of the different maintenance policies.

Decision criterion

Taking the perspective of the DPS at Ventry, it seems as if the main idea is to control costs while still providing an adequate service to the tanker-operators. Hence, the problem resolves to one of cost minimization. That is, some solution must be found to the following:

$$\text{Minimize [Expected(total cost)]}$$

where

$$\text{Expected(totalcost)} = \text{Expected(total purchase price)}$$
$$+ \text{Expected(maintenance expenditure)}$$
$$+ \text{Expected(spillage costs)}$$

Thus, we need to compute the Expected(total cost) for each of the three types of hose, and for each one we need to do this under a range of feasible maintenance policies.

Data requirements

In the account of the problem given above, no data are provided – just as in real life. A basic principle (see Chapter 4) has to be that the model drives the data collection and not the other way round. It is therefore important to consider the data requirements for this simple cost model, which will help to illustrate yet more pitfalls that are open to the unwary modeller, even in simple situations:

1. *Hose prices.* To simplify matters, assume that the only point at issue here is the actual prices of the hoses, that the same ancillary equipment will fit all three types, and also that all three types give identical pumping performance. Even then the issue may be far from straightforward, as there may be no 'price list' for such expensive items and, instead, the prices may be negotiated between TICTOC and the hose supplier. Thus, even the prices may be uncertain, and it may be better to think of Expected(prices).
2. *Expected maintenance expenditure.* A number of factors will determine how easy it will be to get these data. First, are there any proper records of the cost of existing maintenance policies? If so, they may be used to estimate the likely cost of applying similar policies. The complications then begin. Is it reasonable to assume that similar policies will be needed for any type of hose? Probably not if we take seriously the views of the MM: 'I'm sure that we could improve things by better maintenance'. This means that the apparently simple decision model based on cost minimization may depend on at least one other model that attempts to show the costs of different maintenance policies.
3. *Expected spillage costs.* This will have at least two components. First, some estimate of the likely costs of a spillage – this may be available if such an event has occurred in the past on the Ventry site or elsewhere in the world. The second component is rather more difficult, and it concerns the number of spillages likely to occur. That is, some estimate of the life/failure distribution is needed for each of the three hose types. A further complication is that it seems reasonable to assume that the service lives will depend on the maintenance policies, otherwise there is no point whatsoever in having a maintenance policy. Thus, some model showing the link between maintenance and hose life will be needed.

Another, hidden, complication is that the hoses in question have expected service lives of several years, making it necessary to estimate long-term costs. This means that price and cost inflation need to be taken into account, and that the timing of various payments needs to be considered as well. Thus, some method of comparing costs incurred at different times will be needed, for which one approach would be to use a costing model based on net present values.

Net present value

Net present value (NPV) methods involve a little algebra but are straightforward in their basic principles. They assume that money can be invested to bring a return, which can be expressed in terms of a proportion or percentage of the capital invested. This represents an interest rate, often known as the discount rate, and, the higher the discount rate, the greater is the return from the investment. Suppose that we invest an amount P now, at an annual compound rate of interest i. We can compute the value of the investment in 1 year, 2 years, 3 years or n years ahead, as shown in the second column of Table 2.1.

NPV calculations simply reverse these investment valuations so as to compute the value now of some sum in the future, assuming that any sum available now could be invested at that rate i. Hence, suppose that a sum worth, say, T would be available in n years' time; then, if T is its value at that time point, its present value (assuming a discount rate of i) is as shown in the third column of Table 2.1.

Table 2.1 Compound interest and present values.

Year end	Value of an investment P made at the start of year 1	Present value of a sum T to be received at the end of year n
1	$P(1+i)$	$T/(1+i)^n$
2	$P(1+i)^2$	$T/(1+i)^{n-1}$
3	$P(1+i)^3$	$T/(1+i)^{n-2}$
$\vdots$	$\vdots$	$\vdots$
n	$P(1+i)^n$	T

The present values become net present values when there are payments in and out to consider, the present value calculation being applied to the net flow of cash at the particular time point. Hence, in the case of TICTOC, it may be possible to compute the net cost at each year over, say, the next 10-year period. To allow for the time value of money, we then compute the NPV for each of the annual cash values, to bring the whole computation back to today's monetary values. In this way, we allow for the fact that cash may be invested elsewhere if not in the hose systems. This computation would, of course, be completely inappropriate if the TICTOC were in an economic system that did not permit or encourage the payment of interest on investments.

Thus, an apparently simple situation that seems to involve a choice among only three known alternatives can turn out to be more complicated than it would seem at first sight. Nevertheless, with careful analysis along the lines suggested above, it should be possible to analyse the three hose options and their related maintenance policies so as to suggest which type of hose should be purchased. Whether the analysis will be completed in time to be of use is another question.

Some points emerging from the TICTOC case

Later chapters will return to the TICTOC case to show how other aspects of the decision can be considered by using some of the methods discussed in them. It is clear that the problem as discussed so far is very simplistic. For example, we have assumed that the viewpoint of the DPS should be given preference over any others, and we have also assumed, with very little discussion, that cost minimization is the agreed aim of the three participants in the discussion.

Linked models may be needed

At first sight, the issue of hose choice could be resolved by the use of a cost model that could make use of existing, or easy to obtain, cost data. The resulting computations would also be straightforward and could be based on a simple spreadsheet. However, there are complications lurking beneath because many of the data are unlikely to be available and many of the data are not just single-point estimates but are probabilistic as well. We cannot be sure how long a hose will last in service, even if we have data available to estimate this. It is extremely unlikely that all hoses of the same type will last for the same length of time. All we can say is that there is a probability function that seems to govern the life of a hose of a particular type, and there are likely to be different probability distributions for each of the three hoses. Further, the effect of maintenance on these life distributions needs to be analysed. Thus, we find that the simple cost model is like an iceberg in which most of the mass and volume are below the surface – and this is where the danger lies.

Suitable data may not be available

The use and abuse of data are discussed in more detail in Chapter 4. For present purposes we should note that we are rarely presented with perfect data. Normally, they must be sought, collected, analysed and carefully considered. Data collected for one purpose may not be suitable for another.

As one example of this hazard in the TICTOC case, consider the issue of the prices of the hoses. It may seem obvious that the prices of UKHose, at least, are known. But this simply may not be true. As mentioned earlier, prices are often negotiated and may shift over time. It seems unlikely that UKHose would insist on charging the same price to TICTOC if they start to believe that a small price reduction might win them the order. Most negotiations are based around such beliefs, whether they turn out to be true or false.

As another example, consider the question of the costs of maintenance. Although these may be logged in TICTOC's accounting systems, they may be collected for the purpose of assigning costs to particular pumping contracts or for a payroll system. In either case, assumptions will have been made about what to include and what to leave out in stating the costs. There may be no guarantee that the cost elements included are the ones needed for the purpose of modelling any variations from current practice. For example, the costing system would sensibly include the labour costs in its monitoring of the maintenance system. Some of these costs will be related to the scale of the operation (such as skilled manpower employed directly on the job), but others will be fixed (some office costs, for example). Thus, when modifying current costs to allow for new, possibly higher, levels of maintenance, care must be taken to scale up only the direct variable costs. Other costs, such as that for office space, may be left unchanged unless that cost will change.

Old hands at modelling often make statements such as: 'If you want data, then collect it yourself'. This view does not stem just from world-weariness or cynicism, but from sensible reflection on experience. Attempting to collect data oneself at least has the advantage that the collector is aware of the accuracy or otherwise of the data and of the ways in which missing data may be synthesized. The increased dependence of most organizations on computer-based information and decision support systems means that the collect-it-yourself approach is becoming increasingly difficult. This is a pitfall of which analysts need to be aware.

Changes over time are important

Most decisions have only a finite life, and it may be more important to select an option that appears to be robust and, contrarily, more adaptive than one that is immediately attractive. Robustness (Rosenhead, Elton and Gupta, 1972) is the ability of a solution to withstand major changes in circumstances. Adaptiveness is the ability of a solution to be modified, or to self-modify, as circumstances change. Perversely, both attributes are valuable and may be preferable to apparently optimal solutions that are attractive in the here-and-now but turn out to be dangerous if circumstances change.

Constrained choice

The discussion so far has assumed that the decision criterion being employed is something simple, such as: maximize expected return over 2 years. One obvious extension to this is to consider constrained choice; that is, circumstances in which, although there exists a straightforward and agreed decision criterion, there are other aspects to consider as well. This is usually managed by

Table 2.2 Six investments.

Investment	Guaranteed annual return (%)	Ethical status
1 Reliable Bank	7.50	OK
2 Trusty Building Society	7.00	OK
3 Nice Investment Trust	6.75	Unknown
4 Triad Friendly Society	10.00	Awful
5 Mafioso Bank	10.50	Even worse
6 Ecological Business Trust	7.25	OK

treating the other aspects as constraints that will be applied before the decision criterion. Thus, the basic idea is that all options are assessed first against the constraints. Only from within this set of acceptable alternatives, usually called the feasible set, can the best option be selected by the use of the decision criterion. This is the basic idea of constrained choice.

A simple investment decision revisited

As a very simple example, consider the investment decision mentioned earlier in this chapter and suppose that it was a little more complicated. Suppose that there are now six possible investments, as shown in Table 2.2, but that you are only willing to place your cash with financial institutions you regard as ethically sound.

If you were to ignore the ethical stance of the investments, the most attractive is to place your cash with the Mafioso Bank. However, this is clearly unsatisfactory, and your feasible set consists of {Reliable Bank, Trusty Building Society, Ecological Business Trust}. Your ethical preferences have been used to reduce the set of options down to a feasible set from which you would select the Reliable Bank if you were to apply your decision criterion of the maximum return over 2 years. Sometimes, of course, there is no conflict between such concerns – as would be the case if the Reliable Bank were able to offer a rate of 10.5% or more.

It is important to realize that, in any form of constrained choice, the choice is made subject to the constraints. That is, the constraints restrict the choice. This means that the use of the decision criterion (maximum return in the above example) is subordinate to the constraints (ethical acceptability in the above example). Only those options or courses of action that satisfy the constraints will be allowed into the feasible set. There are a number of modelling techniques associated with Management Science that are used to support this form of constrained choice. Two of the most commonly applied ideas are discussed later in Chapters 9 and 11. Mathematical programming methods, discussed in Chapter 9, allow the analysts to express some constrained choice problems in an algebraic form that, with the use of computer packages, can be used to find the best choice. Heuristic methods, discussed in Chapter 11, offer no guarantee that an optimal choice will be made, but they are used to search for acceptable options among the feasible set.

Risk and uncertainty

This chapter began by recounting Simon's summary of classical rational choice. This was shown to have some application in its immediate form and also in a slightly relaxed form in which choices are constrained or may be multidimensional. A further relaxation of the assumptions is needed in cases of risk or uncertainty. These conditions occur when no one can be sure that a particular choice will lead to a particular outcome. For example, there may be no guarantee that any of the investment options considered earlier in this chapter are certain. There could even be the possibility that one of the banks might fail.

Extending classical rationality to cope with such circumstances involves the realization that the world is not deterministic. A deterministic world would be one in which precise prediction was possible because things ran like clockwork. This may be true of some mechanical systems, but it is unlikely to be true in complex human systems. To consider non-deterministic outcomes, we must resort to ideas of probability. That is, we need to estimate how likely it is that a particular event, or set of events, will occur.

Some writers make a clear distinction between decisions taken under uncertainty and decisions taken under risk, although both cases assume that outcomes are non-deterministic. A risky decision is one in which it is possible to know the probabilities of the different events. An uncertain decision is one in which these probabilities cannot be known at all. This section follows de Neufville and Stafford (1971) and regards this as a purely artificial distinction.

Uncertain decision-making and decision criteria

We are faced with making a decision under uncertainty when we are clear what options are open to us but unsure what the consequences will be of taking any or all of those courses of action. In such cases, we can construct a pay-off matrix to show the consequences of each option–outcome combination. For example, suppose a sales manager thinks there may be increased demand for the products made by his company and, after discussions with colleagues, concludes that the company could prepare for this in three ways:

1. Invest in new, faster manufacturing equipment.
2. Pay production workers to work overtime shifts.
3. Do nothing.

If all goes well, he reckons that sales of the company's products will increase by 15%. However, competitor businesses are also aware of the possibilities, and another possible outcome is that the company's sales could actually fall by 5%. What should he recommend?

A payoff matrix shows the outcome of each option, expressed in some consistent measure. In this case the measure is cash, and Table 2.3 shows revenue and costs that are expected to follow for each option–outcome combination. These data can be used to construct the payoff matrix of Table 2.4, which shows the net return from each option–outcome combination. What should the sales manager recommend? The standard advice is that this depends on his attitude

Table 2.3 Revenues and costs (£000s) for payoff matrix.

	Demand up 15%		Demand down 5%	
	Revenue	Costs	Revenue	Costs
New equipment	650	440	560	420
Overtime	650	450	560	450
Do nothing	600	410	560	410

Table 2.4 Payoff matrix.

	Payoffs (£000s)	
	Demand up 15%	Demand down 5%
New equipment	210	140
Overtime	200	110
Do nothing	190	150

to risk, and that this should be reflected in the decision criterion that he uses to compare the options. If he is relaxed about downside risk and is keen to gain the highest possible return, then this should be reflected by his choice of the option–outcome combination that maximizes the company's possible return. This is known as the *maximax* criterion and should lead him to recommend that the company buy new equipment to meet the anticipated demand increase, leading to a maximum possible net return of £210 000. However, the payoff table shows that, if they do buy the new equipment and demand falls, the company will only gain a net return of £140 000, which is less than they would gain under the same outcome if he had recommended they do nothing.

He may, on the other hand, be much more cautious and decide to recommend the option that, if demand falls by 50%, will lead to the highest return. This is known as the *maximin* criterion, as it attempts to maximize the minimum return received. The minimum returns all occur when demand falls by 5%, and in such cases the least worst (maximin) return of £150 000 is achieved by recommending that the company do nothing.

There is a third way of looking at this decision, which is from the viewpoint of possible regret. The value of a regret is the difference between the net return from an option–outcome combination and the maximum net return from that outcome. Table 2.5 shows the regret matrix for the current decision. If demand increases by 15%, the maximum net return is £210 000, which occurs if the company decides to buy new equipment. Thus, the regret from deciding to work overtime if demand rises by 15% is £10 000 (£210 000 minus £200 000), and so on. The final column of Table 2.5 shows the maximum regrets, and the minimax regret of £10 000 occurs if the company buys new equipment and sales fall by 5%.

Finally, we might suppose that the sales manager is in his job because he is rather good at peering into the future and also discovers some way to find out what competitors are likely to do. Hence, using his expertise and inside knowledge, he may decide that there is a 60% chance that sales will increase, and therefore a 40% chance that sales will decrease, because of action by competitors. These probability estimates can be used as the basis of a fourth decision criterion: expected value. The expected value of an option is simply a weighted average of the net returns from each outcome, using the probabilities as the weights. Hence, the expected value of buying

Table 2.5 Regret matrix.

	Regrets (£000s)		
	Demand up 15%	Demand down 5%	Maximum
New equipment	0	10	10
Overtime	10	40	40
Do nothing	20	0	20

new equipment is:

$$(0.6 \times £210\,000) + (0.4 \times £140\,000) = £182\,000$$

The equivalent values for working overtime and doing nothing are £164 000 and £174 000 respectively. Hence, to maximize the expected return, the sales manager should recommend that the company prepare for increased sales by buying new equipment.

Of the four criteria that we have examined for the sales manager, three point to the same option, buy new equipment, as being preferable. The maximax return of £210 000 comes from this option, as does the minimax regret of £10 000 and the maximum expected return of £182 000. When we consider the maximin return criterion, this favours the do nothing option, although the buy new equipment option is only £10 000 behind it. Hence, it looks as if selection of the buy new equipment option is fairly robust across different decision criteria. However, note that even this conclusion depends on how accurately the sales manager and his colleagues can estimate the costs and revenues from the three options, and, if the expected return is used as the criterion, on how well he can estimate the probabilities of the two outcomes. With a spreadsheet it is easy to experiment with the sensitivity of the decision to different probabilities; doing so shows that, when the probability of increased sales drops below about 33%, the scales tip in favour of the do nothing option.

Some difficulties

Note that the use of expected values relies on the estimation of probabilities for future events. This may be straightforward, say, for a grand slam tennis match between two top professionals who play one another regularly on their international tours. Current form may show that player A almost always beats player B, whatever type of court they play on, so a gambler may be fairly confident about placing a bet on the result. Whether she will place the bet will also, though, depend on the odds offered by a bookmaker, who is also aware of the form. The punter makes a profit if she is better at estimating the probabilities than the bookmaker. The tennis games between the pros are sufficiently similar to regard each game as a repeat of the same event; however, there are many situations in which this is not the case.

Because the events are non-repeatable, there is no empirical way of checking the values assigned to the probabilities. Instead, recourse must be had to subjective probability estimates. These should not, of course, be divorced from past experience, but they are still subjective. This is not necessarily a bad thing if the approach is used to help people think about their views on the likelihood of different events. In the sense in which the term will be used in Part II of this book, the approach can be employed to help people to 'interpret' what is happening or what might happen. A refinement is to use a Bayesian approach (for more details, see Raiffa, 1968), which provides a more rigorous framework for the use of subjective probabilities. This is a subject covered in Chapter 8, which discusses decision analysis.

The computations required in this type of decision analysis are simple enough, but the underlying assumptions deserve a brief mention here, for they are crucial. They also assume that it is possible to measure the value, or utility, of any outcome. The example above carefully avoided mentioning this issue, but it is very important. If monetary values are being used, this removes one difficulty – although it may simply be untrue that, for a particular individual, £1 000 000 is worth 10 times £100 000. For some business decisions, however, monetary value will suffice.

When other values are being considered, things are far from simple. There are well-established techniques for attempting to build a non-monetary utility function for an individual (for details, see Watson and Buede, 1987). These methods are fine for simple situations whose complication is that people may not have a monetary utility function – as mentioned above, a return of £1 000 000 may, for an individual, have a value that differs from 10 times the value of a return of £100 000. However, in many complex decisions, it is important to recognize that different people and groups will have different value systems. For example, in principle, the approach could be used to investigate the value of a sequence of medical investigations. But who will determine the value of each outcome and on what basis? This illustrates that this type of decision analysis needs to be used with some care. Used sensitively, it can help participants see the effects of different utility functions, which then provides a way of exploring their preferences. Chapter 8 discusses the use of value functions to establish utility functions in the SMART approach to multi-criteria decision analysis.

A great degree of care is needed in using and interpreting these apparently simple methods. As was stated before, their main value may be in helping people and groups to explore their beliefs and preference systems. That is, their best use may be descriptive and interpretive, rather than normative.

Bounded rationality

So far, this chapter has introduced the classical idea of rationality and has shown how some of its assumptions may be relaxed so as to make the notions more usable. However, there have been many critiques of classical rationality, and the rest of the chapter will consider two of them.

Dissatisfaction with approaches based on this classical view of rationality led Simon (1972) to propose the notion of bounded rationality. Awarded the Nobel Prize for Economics, one of Simon's main concerns was to make economics more relevant and useful to the real world. One of his justifications of bounded rationality was that: 'We prefer the postulate that men are reasonable to the postulate that they are supremely rational'. In essence, bounded rationality is based on behavioural notions and upon observations of the ways in which decisions are actually taken in practice. It assumes that human rationality has its limits, especially when operating in conditions of considerable uncertainty.

Substantive rationality and procedural rationality

In developing his case for bounded rationality, Simon (1976) discusses two alternative views of rationality, which he terms substantive rationality and procedural (or behavioural) rationality. In Simon's terms, substantive rationality is dominant in classical economics, and it corresponds to the basic tenets of classical, rational decision-making as discussed so far. Behaviour is considered, in these terms, to be substantively rational when it is goal-oriented within limits imposed by some given conditions and constraints. Thus, a substantively rational choice is one that is the best way to achieve a given goal. In terms of classical economics and decision analysis, this implies the maximization of utility, which, as shown earlier, may be extended to allow for risk and uncertainty.

By contrast, procedural rationality is concerned not so much with the outcome of a deliberation than with the nature of the deliberation process. Behaviour is said to be procedurally rational when it results from some appropriate deliberation. Thus, the focus is the process of decision-making; on how it is done or on how it should be done. In these terms, irrational behaviour is impulsive behaviour that occurs without adequate consideration and thought. Procedural rationality is thus closer to the common-sense view of reason than might be the case with substantive rationality. In these terms, the focus is on developing procedures that may enable people to make better decisions. Thus, Simon argues that, to be of use in the real world, discussions of rationality ought to focus on procedural rationality as well as on the substantive rationality that dominates classical decision theory. That is, the stress should be on the process of rational choice-making. Soft systems methodology, cognitive mapping and system dynamics, the methods covered in Part II, can be regarded as approaches that are intended to be procedurally rational.

Limits to rationality

Simon (1976) proposed the notion of bounded rationality, which takes as its starting point a number of assumptions about situations in which decisions may have to be made:

1. In many complex situations there is considerable uncertainty and risk about the consequences of choices that might be made. There are several reasons for this. The first is that information about these consequences may simply be unavailable and may have to be forecast or modelled in some way or other. This is obviously an important issue in situations that include considerable novelty. The second reason is that the actions of other players may influence the consequences of any action. For example, although an action to select a price for a product may seem sensible and may appear to lead to maximum profits, a competitor's promotional activity may negate this pricing policy.
2. In many situations it is ludicrous to assume that the decision-maker has complete information about all feasible options. This is clearly nonsense for most personal decisions such as marriage or even buying a car. To take another example, buying an air ticket at the cheapest price available to you does not guarantee that you have paid less than the person in the next seat. He or she may simply have had more information than you did, or may have found some way to modify the real world so as to create more options.
3. The complexity of many decision problems means that the actor or decision-maker is unable to compute the best course of action, even if all possible options are known. This is due to the limited computational capacity of the human brain. Clearly, the use of computer-based analysis allows this limitation to be pushed somewhat further away than was the case when Simon first proposed bounded rationality.

Because of these limitations and problems, Simon proposed that practical rationality is procedural and is thus bounded. Simon argued that rational choice embodies two aspects: search and satisficing.

Search

In this bounded rationality, one essential component of rational decision-making is a systematic search for options that are, it is hoped, feasible. This contrasts with the classical approach, which seems to assume that a full set of feasible options is known at the outset. One implication of the inclusion of search in this view of rational choice is that account can be taken of the costs incurred in making such a search. If the search is sequential – one option after another – there may come a point at which the marginal cost of the search becomes too high. Thus, none of us conducts an exhaustive search for a life-partner, for life is simply too short. We may, none the less, be very happy in our choice!

A second implication of option search is that there may be no need to accept only the set of options that is available and presented at the start of decision-making. When faced with options that we don't much like, many of us will engage in all sorts of behaviour to find ways to improve the set that seem to be available. In the terms of constrained choice, we look for ways to break the constraints that define the feasible set. Thus, people move house or emigrate to find jobs in the hope of a better life when they are unable to find suitable work where they currently live. We may also stall and prevaricate when making hard decisions, trying to make time in the hope that better options may emerge. It is important to note that these behaviours are highly rational in a procedural sense and, indeed, are part of good decision-making. Making a snap decision is often very unwise.

A third implication is that decision-making and problem-solving can be regarded as a creative process, rather than one that is purely routine and mechanistic. This is because one aspect of decision-making becomes the process of generating suitable options worthy of consideration. This can be viewed at two levels. It legitimates the use of creativity techniques such as brain-storming (Evans, 1991) and the methods introduced in Part II, which are ways of encouraging people to generate useful ideas and proposals. It also makes sense of the ways in which managers and other people operate. Few successful managers spend their lives isolated from other people, thinking grand and highly rational thoughts about the world. Instead, they are in constant interaction with other people (Mintzberg, 1973, 1989). This is not just because they are social animals; in many cases they are in the process of searching for ways to get things done and are trying to negotiate agreement about what will constitute an acceptable, and satisficing, solution.

Satisficing

The other, better-known feature of bounded rationality is the idea of satisficing, perhaps the term most closely associated with Simon in his contribution to Management Science. The classical approach assumes, in its most sophisticated form, that a decision-maker will attempt to maximize subjective expected utility. Instead, a procedural or bounded rationality assumes that people will search for options that appear to be good enough. That is, they have in mind a level of aspiration that defines solutions and options that are not only feasible but are acceptable as well.

At this point it might be argued by some that the above account of satisficing is equivalent to optimizing within a set of options, the only difference being that the set of options is not believed to be complete. However, this would be to misunderstand Simon's position, for satisficing is related to search. That is, a satisficer will cease to search as soon as the first option to satisfy the level of aspiration is found. In a further refinement, the levels of aspiration may change over time. You may begin your search for a life-partner with very unrealistic ideals and may need to temper them over time. In a different context, your unhappy (and squashed) experience in a small car may be acceptable when childless but lead you to look for a larger and more comfortable car when children arrive on the scene. This view of procedural rationality is close to the ways in which a designer may gradually refine a design over time, searching all the while for ways to achieve whatever is required of the design. As mentioned above when discussing search, the notion of changing levels of aspiration makes sense of the ways in which most of us tend to operate, whether as managers or in other aspects of our lives. As we experience events, meet other people, observe what is happening and interact with the world, our views tend to change and so do our needs. In this way, our aspirations may well change, affecting the search process referred to above and also affecting our definition of what may constitute acceptable, and satisficing, solutions. Bounded rationality sees choice as a form of sequential search, which may be informal, and from which choices are made by satisficing rather than optimizing.

Planning, intuition and rationality

So far we have discussed the classical notion of rational choice, seen how its apparently restrictive assumptions can be relaxed, examined two techniques that stem from these assumptions and looked at the idea of bounded rationality as proposed by Simon. In this way, we have placed the use of rational and analytical models in the wider context of rationality. However, it would hardly be reasonable to claim that anybody acts entirely rationally, whether in a bounded sense or in the classical sense, for the whole of their lives. Fans of the old TV series 'Star Trek' will recall that only Mr Spock was able to do this. Acting non-rationally does not necessarily mean that we will make wrong decisions, nor that we are being fools. There is a place in life, and in decision-making, for intuition and emotion. One advocate of the place of intuition in organizational life is Henry Mintzberg, and it is worth exploring his argument in this section.

The nature of managerial work

Henry Mintzberg was originally employed in the Operational Research Branch of Canadian National Railways. He made his academic reputation with a study of the actual working lives of senior managers, which is described in *The Nature of Managerial Work* (Mintzberg, 1973). The main findings of this early empirical research are rather in contrast to the view that senior managers are strategists who spend much of their time engaged in deep rational analysis. It is sometimes suggested that this is what they do when developing and managing strategies that will enable their organizations to prosper. By contrast, some of the findings of Mintzberg's early work in a range of organizations, public and private, in the late 1960s and early 1970s were as follows:

1. Many senior managers worked long hours at an unrelenting pace. In discussing this, Mintzberg (1973) writes:

   > One major reason is the inherently open-ended nature of the job. The manager is responsible for the success of his organization and there are really no tangible mileposts where he can stop and say, 'Now my job is finished'. . . . No matter what kind of managerial job he has, he always carries the nagging suspicion that he might be able to contribute just a little bit more.

   This could seem a never-ending task.
2. Their activity was characterized by brevity, variety and fragmentation. A typical day was composed of many small, short-lived interactions with a few scheduled meetings that occupied much of the day. Although the longer meetings were often scheduled to last more than one hour, the senior manager may have chosen not to stay for the whole meeting. There was also variety in the tasks performed, which ranged from short phone calls, through unscheduled meetings and conversations, to ceremonial tasks such as making long-service presentations, negotiations and action requests. Many of these activities and tasks were fragmented and were sometimes interrupted by other pre-empting tasks. The manager was constantly switching between tasks.

3. The managers in the sample seemed to prefer the more active elements of their workload and disliked tasks such as reading mail and reports, even though they might have contained 'hard' data. They much preferred to spend time searching out current information, which may have been 'soft' – that is, based on opinion. Recently received 'hot' communications would cause scheduled meetings to be rearranged at short notice. This is rather in contrast to the view that such managers are contemplative planners who spend much of their time in the type of rational analysis discussed in the first part of this chapter.
4. Linked to the point about activity, most of the managers seemed to prefer verbal media when communicating with people. Face to face was especially preferred, with phone conversations coming second. (This was before the days of email.) Many of these conversations were informal, with formal meetings being reserved for ceremony (e.g. long-service awards), strategy-making and negotiation, which needed prior arrangement as they often involved many people. The verbal communications were almost all about gaining and giving information, often soft information.

The picture is of continuous activity, of rapid decisions and consultations with individuals, together with longer, scheduled meetings that involve many people. Throughout this activity, the manager is continually receiving and sifting information, seeking out what is relevant now or what might be useful in the future. It is not an image of a life of detached, contemplative reason. Mintzberg's observations, albeit based on a limited sample, shed considerable doubt on the view that management is an inherently rational activity, whether procedural or substantial. Perhaps even bounded rationality may be too idealistic.

The 'crafting' of strategy

Later work by Mintzberg and his associates explored the process of strategy formation as it occurs within a range of organization types and sizes. A useful summary of this work is given in *Mintzberg on Management* (Mintzberg, 1989). He argues that many earlier accounts of strategy formation attempt to place it within a strongly rational framework in which options are sought out and compared, and then strategy is agreed upon. Such views stress the role of analysis and decomposition in their reliance on formal planning cycles and the development of operational plans from the strategies. They fit well with Simon's notions about search in bounded rationality. Indeed, the search for possible strategies and their subsequent evaluation is a major part of many accounts of what was once known as corporate planning (see, for example, Argenti, 1968).

By contrast, Mintzberg argues that many successful strategies are 'crafted' rather than planned. What he means by this is that humans are very adaptive and can be very good at learning from what happens. Thus, strategy formation does not usually take place in some isolated ivory tower where abstract ideas are contemplated. Instead, it takes place in the current context of the organization, which may include a host of smaller activities, some of which may develop into strategies for the whole organization. Thus, the senior managers of an organization, as they attempt to think and debate about their strategy, may realize that they have developed some strength and expertise in certain areas of work. That is, small-scale actions from one part of an organization may start to converge into patterns, which may then become deliberate strategy. The same could apply to external opportunities – they begin as one or more small clouds 'no bigger than a man's hand', but the visionary is able to see patterns in their development and may thus develop appropriate strategies.

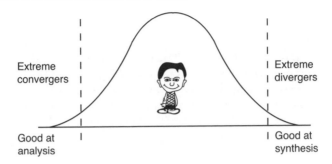

Figure 2.2 Convergers and divergers.

The term 'crafted' is used as a metaphor because it reflects the ways in which, say, a sculptor begins with an idea of what he or she wishes to produce. But the variations in the material and shifts in mood lead to the development of something rather different from the original intention. The final object may be altogether more pleasing than the original idea could have been, because it fits well with the materials and with the developing expertise of the artist. In short, the vision changes because of experience.

This view has a number of interesting implications. The first is that organizations must do their best to preserve and, preferably, to develop individuals with creative vision. That is, organizations need people who are able to recognize patterns: both in what the organization already does well and in what seems to be happening elsewhere. In *Contrary Imaginations*, a fascinating book written in the 1960s, Liam Hudson (1967) describes some of his early research into creativity. This led him to suggest that the spectrum of Figure 2.2 could be proposed. This shows two extreme groups of people, with the majority (perhaps 70%) in the unclassified middle. The extreme points are the convergers and the divergers. Convergers are extremely good at analysis and at following established procedures. Divergers are more likely to be good at synthesis, at producing new ideas and seeing new patterns in things. In a prospective study, Hudson found that schoolboys who were convergers tended to study maths and science at university, whereas the divergers tended to follow creative arts and humanities degrees. Management Science analysts tend to be drawn from the pool of convergers, and this suggests that many will not find it easy to fit roles that require the type of creativity implied by the 'crafting' of strategy.

The second implication of crafting is that successful senior managers need deep knowledge, both of their business's internal operations and of the external environment. Useful patterns cannot be imagined if there is no understanding and appreciation of what is happening. Thus, the notion that a senior (or any other kind of) manager is likely to be successful without some deep knowledge seems very dangerous. This re-emphasizes the need for strategy formation to be an integral part of managerial work at all levels and not some adjunct operation performed by planning professionals. The crafting of strategy is about detecting small changes that may lead to big things; that is, helping emergent patterns take a desirable shape. This does not mean that planning cycles have no place within successful organizations, far from it. But it stresses that classically rational analysis, which tends to dominate formal planning cycles, may not play a major role in strategy formation. Much of the analysis takes place later, when the implications of possible strategies have to be explored, turning hunches into policies and plans. Thus, one role for modelling might be in making sense of the strategic vision that emerges as strategy is crafted. Other chapters of this book, especially those on 'soft' Management Science (in Part II), will have something to say about this.

Intuition and insight

The third relevant theme in Mintzberg's work stems from an article he wrote for the *Harvard Business Review*, 'Planning on the left side and managing on the right' (Mintzberg, 1976). This argued that, based on then current views of brain physiology, human brains employ two quite separate approaches to processing information. In shorthand terms, these are usually referred to as left and right brain processing. More recent research on brain function (Damasio, 1995) shows this shorthand to be misleading, as brain function appears much more complicated than this, but the ideas are at least interesting as metaphors:

- *Left.* This is the type of processing that fits well with the notions of rationality and logic as discussed so far. It refers to linear sequential processing, in which information is processed one bit after another in an ordered way. This occurs in much the same way as linear speech, with words in a definite sequence.
- *Right.* By contrast, this is simultaneous processing, which seems to be much more relational and holistic. It refers to the 'feeling' side of our natures, in which we sense things and experience emotion. In Mintzberg's terms, it refers to gestures rather than to speech; most of us can gesture simultaneously with our hands and our faces.

Thus, in the sense in which the terms were used above, convergers tend to operate on the left and divergers on the right. To quote Mintzberg (1989), 'a politician may not be able to learn mathematics, while a management scientist may be constantly manipulated in political situations'. There are, of course, many exceptions to this type of generalization, but there is some truth in it too. Awareness of emotion and intuition, alongside rational analysis, can contribute to better decision-making.

Referring back to the section on managerial work, it is clear that many of the actual and preferred modes of operation of the senior managers observed in the studies could be classified as right brain rather than left. So, in the same way, can the talents required to see patterns and to 'craft' strategy. On the other hand, the abilities needed to spell out the implications of different strategies may be regarded as left brain rather than right. Perhaps only the rare polymath will be good at both, and this suggests a good reason for teamwork in senior management.

Linking reason and intuition

It seems clear that successful management and wise decision-making require the dual support of creative intuition and rational analysis. The vexing question is, how can this be achieved? The answer seems to be that neither of the two factors should be abused or downgraded. Someone, probably Russell Ackoff, once wrote that 'a difference between managers and analysts is that analysts recognize every value of probability except zero and one; on the other hand, managers recognize only zero and one'. This may be an exaggeration, but it does emphasize the importance of partnership in finding ways to help organizations operate more effectively.

An overreliance on formal reason, as against intuition, can be dangerous, and so can the opposite. Sometimes common sense is helpful, sometimes not. As an example, one summer weekend I planned to go hiking in the English Lake District. The previous evening, I phoned the Lake District weather service to listen to their recorded forecast for the following day. It was bad. First thing next morning I phoned again and listened to the update – bad again: rain promised, low cloud and chilly for the time of year. Looking out of our house windows it was a beautiful morning, so I cycled a short distance to a point where I could see the Lake District mountains in the distance. It looked beautiful, the sky was blue, the clouds were sparse and high and the sea sparkled in the sun. I felt good and I suspected that the weather forecast might be wrong. But I'm a rational man and I know that the weather forecast is based on all sorts of clever mathematical models, and I don't trust my feelings. So I stayed home – apparently it was a lovely day in the Lake District! I did make some progress with this book, however.

Damasio (1995) is a fascinating book that reviews evidence about brain function, based on the author's own medical work and that of others with people whose brains have been damaged in accidents or by illness. He argues that the concept of mind cannot really be separated from the body, and that to think in these terms is to fall into a false dualism. He argues that both reason and emotion/intuition are distributed across several areas in the brain and that together they constitute mind. In particular, he quotes a number of sad case histories of people who, after brain damage, not only had their emotions blunted but were also unable to plan, although their day-to-day functioning seemed normal enough. Damasio argues that, in a healthy mind, emotion and reason are strongly linked through the physical body and brain. Effective and thoughtful analysis may then depend on mind, which is also steeped in the juices of emotion.

In the end, the role of analysis can only be to explore the possible consequences of different courses of action. Rational, analytical approaches do not, by themselves, provide direction or identify alternatives. We can rarely predict, with complete certainty, that events will happen. If we could be sure of the future, then there would be no problem – reason and intuition would be happy bedfellows. Perhaps the role of reason is to test out intuition and perhaps the role of intuition is to prevent paralysis by analysis. Intuitive crafting helps to provide direction and vision. Analysis helps to make sense of this vision. Each one places the other in context.

Summary – making sense of strategic vision

Chapter 1 made a case for taking seriously the idea that modelling approaches, as found in Management Science, can help people to explore the consequences of their actions and decisions. It is sometimes assumed that such models must be built and used within a highly restricted view of human action – classical rationality, in which ends are clearly related to means, and in which everything is known. This chapter has pointed out that this classical rationality needs further elaboration before it can be of use. Simon's development of bounded rationality, with its emphasis on the limitations of human action and thought, was one attempt to do this. Another was the extension of classical rationality into risky and uncertain decision-making. However, these various extensions all seem to treat humans as information-processing machines whose capacity may be limited in some way or other.

Alternative perspectives on these same issues are provided by writers such as Mintzberg who emphasize the apparently non-rational side of organizational life. It is clear from his work, and that of others, that people do not operate according to these highly rational models. It might, of course, be argued that people should operate rationally, and that those who do will always win out over those who do not. This is not an argument that will be presented in this book, for to do so would be to miss the most important point, which is that models should be regarded as tools for thinking. They provide ways in which people may reflect on what is proposed and decide whether or not certain things should be done and certain risks should be taken.

A model will always be a simplification of certain aspects of the real world. The next chapter examines how people frame the part of the real world in which they are interested; that is, how people decide what simplification and approximation might be appropriate. Chapter 4 then provides a few principles for modelling, the first of which is 'model simple, think complicated'. This stresses that the model and its users form a system that can help people to examine the possible consequences of their proposals. In this sense, models should be part of the process of making sense of the strategic vision; they form a link between the intuitive and the rational.

References

Ackoff R.L. and Sasieni M.W. (1968) *Fundamentals of Operations Research.* John Wiley & Sons, Inc., New York, NY.

Argenti J. (1968) *Corporate Planning. A Practical Guide.* George Allen & Unwin, London, UK.

Damasio A.R. (1995) *Descartes' Error: Emotion, Reason and the Human Brain.* Picador, London, UK.

de Neufville R. and Stafford J.H. (1971) *Systems Analysis for Managers and Engineers.* McGraw-Hill, Maidenhead, UK.

Evans J.R. (1991) *Creative Problem Solving in the Decision and Management Sciences.* South Western Publishing, Cincinnati, OH.

Hudson L. (1967) *Contrary Imaginations. A Study of the English Schoolboy.* Penguin, London, UK.

Mintzberg H. (1973) *The Nature of Managerial Work.* HarperCollins, New York, NY.

Mintzberg H. (1976) Planning on the left side and managing on the right. *Harvard Business Review,* July–August, 49–58.

Mintzberg H. (1989) *Mintzberg on Management.* The Free Press, New York, NY.

Raiffa H. (1968) *Decision Analysis.* Addison-Wesley, Reading, MA.

Rosenhead J.V. and Mingers J. (eds) (2001) *Rational Analysis for a Problematic World Revisited,* 2nd edition. John Wiley & Sons, Ltd, Chichester, UK.

Rosenhead J.V., Elton M. and Gupta S.K. (1972) Robustness and optimality as criteria for strategic decisions. *Operational Research Quarterly,* **23**, 413–431.

Simon H.A. (1954) Some strategic considerations in the construction of social science models, in Simon H.A. (1982) *Models of Bounded Rationality: Behavioural Economics and Business Organization.* MIT Press, Cambridge, MA.

Simon H.A. (1972) Theories of bounded rationality, in Simon H.A. (1982) *Models of Bounded Rationality: Behavioural Economics and Business Organization.* MIT Press, Cambridge, MA.

Simon H.A. (1976) From substantive to procedural rationality, in Simon H.A. (1982) *Models of Bounded Rationality: Behavioural Economics and Business Organization.* MIT Press, Cambridge, MA.

Slovic P. (1990) Choice, in Thinking: an Invitation to Cognitive Science, Vol. 3, ed. by Osherson D.N. and Smith E.E. MIT Press, Cambridge, MA.

Watson S.R. and Buede D.M. (1987) *Decision Synthesis: the Principles and Practice of Decision Analysis.* Cambridge University Press, Cambridge, UK.

3 Problems, problems . . .

Management Science as problem-solving?

The opening chapter of this book was a general introduction to modelling which argued that, carefully used, even simple models can be of great value in helping people to manage in today's complex world. Models, as used in Management Science, are ways of applying rational analysis to complex issues, and hence Chapter 2 focused on the meaning of rationality and tried to locate the role of reason in decision-making. Against this background, it is now time to think about problems and problem-solving. This is because, to many people, Management Science is a rational attempt at problem-solving. Hence, it is important to understand what we mean when we use the word 'problem'. As will become clear in this chapter, people use this term in different ways, and this can cause some confusion.

At one extreme, this is seen in the view that the main role of Management Science analysts and groups is to 'solve managerial problems', whatever form these might take. On another dimension, it is common to hear management scientists speak of 'an interesting distribution problem' when referring to work on the physical movement of goods. Another example would be when people speak of 'a linear programming problem'. The word 'problem' is being used in three different ways here, and there are many others ways in which it could be used. What these different usages have in common, however, is the idea that problems exist and that they can be solved. The idea of solution also carries with it the notion that, once solved, a problem stays solved. As will become clear later, this particular notion of permanent solution can be very dangerous and should be avoided. The purpose of this chapter is to consider these ideas and to develop them into something that is more useful and intellectually defensible.

Problems, puzzles and messes

The starting point will be to explore, in a little detail, what might be meant by the idea of a problem, especially as this is used in Management Science. This discussion is based on the views of Ackoff (1974, 1979), who distinguishes clearly between problems and messes. As shown in Figure 3.1, this idea can be extended to three points on a spectrum: puzzles, problems and messes, each being intended to depict a different way in which people use the word 'problem'. These, however, are not the only ways – they serve as archetypes on the spectrum of possible uses. Each of the three have in common the notion, made explicit in Chapter 2, that the concern is with situations in which one or more choices must be made, often in conditions of uncertainty and risk.

Puzzles

In these terms, a 'puzzle' is a set of circumstances in which there is no ambiguity whatsoever once some thought has been given to what is happening or needs to be done. The issues that

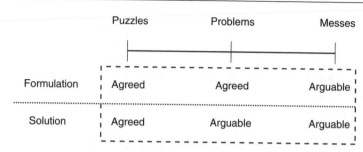

Figure 3.1 Puzzles, problems and messes.

need to be faced are entirely clear, the range of options is completely known and there exists a single correct solution to the puzzle. Thus, in the terms to be used later, the puzzle is fully structured, and it is possible to be sure that a solution to the puzzle is correct once it has been found. The term 'puzzle' is used here because common parlance refers to crossword puzzles and jigsaw puzzles. These are exercises with well-understood structures and, usually, a single correct solution. Puzzles are very different from open-ended tasks in which many different approaches are possible. There may be various ways to attack a crossword puzzle, but the definition of the puzzle is complete and there should only be a single correct solution (although the British newspaper *The Guardian*, often known as The Grauniad because of its occasional typos, has been known to print crossword puzzles that contain mistakes!). The same is true of a jigsaw puzzle; some people start with the edges, some start in the centre and others start with the corners – but there is only a single correct solution. With this in mind, people who have studied mathematics will recognize that when they were told to 'complete all the problems on page 42' or to 'have a go at this problem sheet', they were being asked to engage in a puzzle-solving activity. In most cases, the problem sheet contains a set of similar puzzles, usually getting harder as the student works down the page. The idea is to give practice in the use of particular methods and to help students to generalize their use.

If their maths is less than perfect, such students may find themselves turning to the back pages of the textbook in the hope of finding the answers. They are likely to be upset (and confused!) if those model solutions turn out to be wrong, as sometimes they do. Why should they be upset? There seem to be two reasons for this. The first reason is their inevitable disappointment after putting in a lot of hard work. The second reason is that we expect puzzles to have a single correct solution, and, if the 'solution' offered turns out to be wrong, then this can cause great frustration. Most of us can often learn quite a lot by trying to work back from the given answer, if it is correct, to the question. Indeed, this is one of the strategies suggested by Polya (1957) in his book on problem-solving in mathematics and also by Wickelgren (1974).

Although the nature of puzzles is simple, they are not always simple to solve. Sometimes they are, but setters of exam papers are quick to learn how to devise puzzles that will stretch their students, whether these are first-graders or postgraduates. So puzzles are not necessarily easy, but they are solvable and the correctness of the solution can be demonstrated. There may even be several different ways to get from the puzzle, as presented, to the correct solution. I well recall, at the age of 12, taking a geometry exam in school and being faced with the need to prove a small theorem and being totally unable to recall how to do it. In a panic I invoked a theorem that I could prove, and tried (unsuccessfully) to get to the result that I needed. Needless to say, my exam performance that day was not good. However, the maths teacher took me on one side and asked how I'd thought of tackling the puzzle the way that I had. At the age of 12 all I could do was blush, mumble and apologize. Later I realized that he was intrigued by my enforced creativity rather than angry and that he wished to encourage me.

Problems

The middle point of the spectrum in Figure 3.1 is designated as 'problems'. A problem is more complicated than a puzzle, but less complicated than a mess. This complication stems from the fact that a problem has no single answer that is definitely known to be correct. At the heart of a problem is an issue that must be tackled. In real-world Management Science, an analyst is more likely to face a problem than a puzzle. An example might be, 'How many depots do we need in order to provide daily replenishment of stocks at all our supermarkets?'. As a question, this seems straightforward enough and is relatively unambiguous; however, this is just the tip of the iceberg. Such a question, based on an important issue, rarely has a single correct solution, for it depends on how you, or someone else, decide to construe it. Thus, for problems, in the way the term is used here, there may be agreement about the core issue to be tackled but there might turn out to be several, equally valid, solutions.

Consider again the issue of the number of depots needed to service a set of supermarkets. One way of construing this issue might be to reformulate it as something like the following: 'Assuming that the depots stay at their current size and the supermarkets do the same, how many depots would we need to meet current demand and to guarantee delivery to each of the stores within an agreed 30 minute time window each day?'. Once formulated in this much tighter way, there may indeed be only a single correct solution. But to achieve this, a problem, with its core issue, has been transformed (some would say reduced) to the form of a puzzle. To illustrate this point yet further, an alternative formulation of the problem might be something like: 'Assuming that the supermarkets and depots stay at their current sizes and are grouped into regions as now, how many depots would be needed to meet current demand in each region and to guarantee delivery to each of the stores within an agreed 30 minute time window?'. Not only is this formulation longer than the first one, it is also a little different. It now includes an extra feature, which could turn out to complicate things or might be a simplification – the depots and supermarkets must have a regional organization. This presumably implies that a depot in Region A will not normally deliver to a supermarket in Region B. Needless to say, the second formulation may produce a solution different to that of the first one.

There is a further reason why problems, as defined here, may lead to a range of solutions that are all acceptable, and this is to do with the approaches taken in working towards a solution. As an example, consider the type of case exercises, often known as Harvard-type cases, with which most business administration students are familiar. When used for teaching, the normal mode of use is to distribute copies of a case to the class in advance of a discussion session. The case papers, often 20 or more pages long, give background on a company or market, provide extensive data and pose some issues. Later, possibly the following day, the class will assemble and, under the guidance of an instructor, students will propose approaches and solutions. Clearly, given a range of suggested approaches, some of them will be wrong, but more than one may be plausible. There are likely to be several possible approaches, each of which may be used in sensible attempts to tackle the core issues of the case. Even when people are agreed about how to construe the basic issues, they may employ different approaches in an attempt to solve the problem. This may be due to their backgrounds, to their expertise or whatever. But there may be no real way of declaring one solution to be superior to all others, even after the removal of those that are obviously wrong. This is why the case method is a good way of encouraging discussion in a class of bright students. It is also the reason why the case method of teaching business administration is preferred by some teachers who do not regard management as a generalizable science.

Messes

The other extreme point on the spectrum of Figure 3.1 is the 'mess', as Ackoff defined it. A mess is a set of circumstances in which there is extreme ambiguity and in which there may well be disagreement. In a puzzle there is complete agreement about the nature of the puzzle (a single correct definition) and also a single correct solution. In a mess there is a whole range of possible definitions and descriptions of what is going on, and there may be no way of knowing whether a solution, as such, exists at all. Some writers (see, for example, Rittel and Webber, 1973) reserve the term 'wicked problem' for this idea of a mess. In a mess, there are many issues to be faced, they are interrelated and the interrelationships are often as important as the issues themselves. A mess is a system of problems with multiple stakeholders who may hold quite different views of what is feasible and desirable.

In most organizations, strategic decision-making and management is closer to the idea of a mess than to the idea of a puzzle or a problem, as these terms are used here. Strategic decision-making is often characterized by ambiguity about objectives (other than survival), uncertainty about outcomes (they may be several years ahead) and great risk if things turn out badly. A strategic decision may be one that puts all, or a significant part, of an organization at risk. Thus, what constitutes a strategic decision for a small company ('Do we move our manufacturing base to this new site?') would be considered tactical to a multinational business such as Ford. This does not mean that the decision is unimportant, simply that its scale and impact do not affect much of the company in the latter case.

It would, however, be a mistake to assume that the notion of 'mess' is only of relevance in strategic decision-making or analysis. Even in smaller-scale work the notion can apply. Consider again the question of supermarket deliveries. It would be reasonable to ask whether interrelated issues have to be faced. For example, is it likely that the support technologies used in the system will be constant over a reasonable time period? The 1990s saw all large supermarket chains invest heavily in electronic point-of-sale (EPOS) computer systems, which provide rapid and accurate information about sales, stocks and receipts. This investment, in turn, affects the timing of the reorder cycle and may be expected to alter delivery requirements. As a second example, is it reasonable to assume that the type of goods stocked will be constant over the time period? Again, probably not, because the large supermarket chains stress their fresh goods rather more than in the past. Presumably the margins are higher, which is why most also offer clothing nowadays, and the fresh goods create a pleasant ambience in the stores. Shifts in the type of goods mean different storage and transport requirements. We could also question whether road transport systems will remain constant. Will vehicle sizes change? Will speed limits be reduced? Will maximum driver hours be changed? Finally, are there any new technologies that may shift the whole business? Some supermarkets allow customers to order via the Internet – what impact might this and other developments have? The list is almost endless.

Note, too, that the various issues over which the basic depot question grows more complicated might depend on one another. This is typical of messes, even in non-contentious areas. Thus, to work with messes requires the analyst to be able to see the links as well as the separate issues. That is, the links may be as important as the separate parts of the mess, and these may need just as much attention. One of the greatest mistakes that can be made when dealing with a mess is to carve off part of the mess, treat it as a problem and then solve it as a puzzle, ignoring its links with other aspects of the mess. It is crucial that the various issues are dealt with while keeping a watchful eye on the links to other aspects of the mess.

Issue streams – the dynamics of decision-making and action

Further light is shed on the question of messes by Langley *et al.* (1995), arguing that much academic research on organizational decision-making has tended to focus on the extremes, stressing either that it is highly rational or highly opportunistic. By contrast, they argue, it should be recognized that meetings, discussions and debates within organizations revolve around 'linked issue streams'. These issues constantly recur over time and are rarely transformed into fully solved problems. Examples might include the following:

- A manufacturing company faces the constant need to keep its costs low and its quality high and consistent. Through time this has been managed in a variety of ways, initially by installing flow-line production and using mathematical stock control models, later by swapping to just-in-time (JIT) systems and so on. Around this quest swarm a number of issues such as stock control, raw material quality, process quality and management, supplies to customers and so on. These issue streams periodically throw up a series of problems such as: 'Should we integrate with our customers' computer systems, and, if so, how?' or 'How can we run on minimum stocks while product variety is increasing?'. Although these issues are resolved for some time, they are rarely solved in any permanent sense.

- A supermarket chain must constantly have a full product offering on its shelves, must provide good customer service, must attract customers, must maintain low stocks and must make a profit. As people strive to achieve these aims, this throws up a continuing stream of issues through time. Examples might be the extent to which EPOS systems should be installed and used, or the question of how to get stocks from the manufacturer into the stores. At one time or another, different approaches will be adopted after careful scrutiny, argument and analysis. Sooner or later, these policies will be revised and others will be substituted.

- A health care system faces the need to provide emergency units to deal with walk-in patients and people brought in by ambulance. Some of the patients may need intensive care, requiring highly skilled staff and expensive equipment. Others may only need dressings or even just reassurance. How should this emergency care be provided? Should it be concentrated into a small number of large units, which forces patients to travel but which guarantees access to high-quality care? Or should there be a network of casualty units, each of which can send on patients to more remote large units when needed? There is no single, perfect answer to these questions, which must be debated and faced through time. The changes in the external environment such as technology, transport and patients' expectations will all affect what is felt to be acceptable practice. But this view will probably change as the issues re-emerge from the issue stream.

It should be obvious why this happens. The world that provides the environment for the organization is constantly changing: new technologies appear, competitors find other ways to operate, consumer preferences alter and so on. Thus, the same basic issues tend to occur, alongside new ones, within any organization. One of the tasks of managers is therefore to manage these issues and their relationships. In doing so, decisions and actions tend to be mingled and may not be easy to separate.

Hence, Langley *et al.* (1995) argue that organizational decision-making may usefully be regarded as a dynamic process that emerges from attempts to manage this issue stream. The issue stream itself is a complex network of issues, linked in a whole host of ways, and those linkages may result in issues that are tightly or loosely coupled. This view, which stems from Organization Theory rather than from Management Science, fits well with Ackoff's notion of a mess as a system of problems. Whether we choose to refer to issue streams or to messes, it is important to realize that any solved problem remains solved for only a period of time. The process is highly dynamic.

Problems as social constructs

What should be becoming clear from the discussion so far is that it may be best, in Management Science, to regard problems, puzzles and messes as social constructs. That is, like beauty, there is a sense in which they are defined in the eye of the beholder. This does not mean that every aspect of the issues to be faced is within the mind of the analyst or the participants. That a business is heading for bankruptcy or that an ambulance service is failing to provide adequate response times may be beyond dispute. But the interpretation of those 'facts' is less certain, and different people may interpret the same 'facts' in different ways. In other words, there may be several valid views of what is happening and of what might be done about it. Some of these interpretations may turn out to be wrong, in the sense that they cannot be defended. However, it is very common to find more than one plausible explanation.

Writing many years ago, John Dewey (quoted in Lubart, 1994) produced the maxim: 'A problem well put is half-solved'. It seems as if he had in mind that a poorly posed problem will be very hard, if not impossible, to solve. If this maxim is combined with the realization that problems, in organizations at least, are social constructs, then the importance of problem-structuring becomes obvious.

Case study: TICTOC

Different points of view

Chapter 2 introduced the TICTOC case study, which revolved around the selection of replacement flexible hoses to be used to connect ocean-bound bulk tankers to crude oil storage tanks on the mainland. In Chapter 2 we treated this case as an application of the ideas of classical decision modelling. We identified the Director of Port Services (DPS) as the client or decision-maker and, from that perspective, developed a cost model. The idea was to select the hose system that produces the lowest total expected cost over some time period. The preceding discussion in Chapter 3 should suggest that far more than this could be read into the text of the case. There are, for example, stakeholders other than the DPS, and these can be divided into internal and external stakeholders. This is important, because 'the selection process must also consider the distribution of the benefits and costs among the interest groups affected by the project' (de Neufville and Stafford, 1971).

Internal stakeholders

Three people, plus you as analyst, are mentioned in the text, and each one will have a view about what could or should be done. It may seem obvious that the DPS is the boss, but that does not mean that everyone else's view should be ignored. We might consider why this should be, using the Maintenance Manager (MM) and Controller of Pumping Operations (CPO) as examples. It seems that the main job of the CPO is to guarantee a continuous flow of oil from the tanks to the ships whenever this is needed. Further, this should be done in a safe way. Thus, from the point of view of the CPO, a hose type that causes minimum hassle may be most desirable. Cost may not be the highest priority from this perspective, although this does not mean that cost is irrelevant. Wearing the MM hat, things may look a little different. Here may be a chance to show just how good the maintenance operation can be, and there may also be the chance to boost the department's budget.

Clearly, given the brief account provided in the text of the case, the above comments are speculative, but they are not ridiculous. How, then, should they be dealt with? The basic principle has to be: do not ignore these perspectives. There are two reasons for this, and they are linked. The first is that these people may know much more about some of the detailed issues of hose use than the DPS, and thus much of the information needs to come from them. The same point relates to a comment made in Chapter 2 about the need for deep knowledge; such knowledge may lie with the MM and CPO rather than with the DPS.

The second reason has to do with the implementation of the work if it is successful. Mintzberg (1989, p. 69) comments that management scientists are wont to complain when their recommendations are not implemented: 'They have claimed that managers don't understand analysis, . . . that the politicized climates of organizations impeded the use of analysis'. If analysis proceeds without taking account of significant stakeholders, then it is hardly surprising that people do not cooperate; nor should it be a shock that they use political means to achieve their ends. Thus, it is crucial that major internal stakeholders – in this case, the CPO and MM – are involved and consulted.

External stakeholders

A fundamental, and often ignored, issue in any analysis is the way in which boundaries or limits are drawn around the mess. Later, we will look at systems approaches, particularly soft systems methodology (Checkland, 1981) to see what contribution they can make to this. In the TICTOC case, it is quite clear that there are external stakeholders who may have some involvement in the decision. Some possible examples are as follows:

- *The tanker operators.* They may have experience of collecting and delivering oil from installations elsewhere in the world at which these different hose types are used. It may be important to check on their experience and preferences.
- *Transitanian politicians.* TICTOC is a nationalized company, and there may be political pressures to buy hose systems from one country rather than another. This does not imply that TICTOC gives in to these pressures, but they should certainly not be ignored. If a careful analysis shows that a politically undesirable choice is preferable from a business perspective, then a further analysis may be needed to show what would be the financial effect of making the political choice.
- *The 'Greens'.* Assuming that this label applies to local environmental activists, it may be important to gauge their reaction to the different proposals. This would be important, whether or not the DPS, CPO and MM regard themselves as having 'green' credentials.
- *Local residents in and around Ventry.* Far-fetched though it may seem to some, these people might also be regarded as external stakeholders whose views must be accounted for. Some of them will work on the terminal site, and any moves to replace substantial pieces of equipment will not pass without comment.
- *The hose vendors.* Bearing in mind the fact that prices for the equipment will be negotiated rather than taken from a published list, the likely behaviour of the suppliers can hardly be ignored.

These groups are not clients or decision-makers, but they cannot be ignored if a choice is to be made that boosts TICTOC's effectiveness.

Possible reformulations of the TICTOC 'problem'

As cast in Chapter 2, this is described as a problem of hose choice, but we know little or nothing about the history of the issue. We do not know why this group, led by the DPS, has decided to search for a possible new supplier of these expensive hoses. It could be pressure from one of the external stakeholders; it might be dissatisfaction with the existing UKHose; it might be that other pressures within the larger TICTOC organization make it important that something is seen to be done at Ventry. There are myriad such possibilities, and the wary analyst does not ignore them, but nor should they necessarily be accepted. They all form part of the 'mess' with which we have been asked to work. Later, we will make use of some of the 'soft' Management Science techniques in an attempt to explore this a little further.

The use of the TICTOC case here in this chapter is intended to shed some light on what is meant by the idea of problems being organizational constructs. The idea is that 'problems' do not exist in a vacuum but exist in people's minds and relate to their experience of the world and to their expectations. Hence, structuring these messes into problems is very important.

Problem-structuring

As most of the important issues in organizational life emerge as parts of systems of problems, or messes, how should we attempt to develop definitions of problems to which a useful contribution can be made? This process is often known as problem-structuring, and it carries with it the idea that problems are malleable and can be moulded into a variety of shapes and forms. Rather than do this in an informal way, we need methods (Smith, 1988, 1989) to increase our success rate. Problems are not things that appear as if from above and on which the analysts must struggle until some suitable solution is found. Problems are constructs that emerge from ongoing issue streams and to which attention is paid. To understand how this occurs, it might be helpful to consider the views of Schön (1982) and Goffman (1974), who explain why one person might identify as a problem something other people might ignore.

In this chapter, problem-structuring is developed as a way to understand the context of a problem before any detailed analysis. In Part II, the same term is used of methods that are an end in themselves; that is, with some wicked problems, problem solution is impossible, but problems can be structured so as to shed enough light on them for action to be taken.

Framing and naming

Monty Python is a well-known British TV comedy series from the late 1960s that poked fun at a number of targets. One such target was the long-running BBC Children's TV programme *Blue Peter*, which always had serious educational aims. One *Monty Python* sketch had one of the cast playing a *Blue Peter* presenter teaching children how to play the flute. 'Right', he said, 'You pick it up, blow in this end and waggle your fingers around. Got it? Good. Next week we'll show you how to become a brain surgeon'. Some things are so simple if you know how!

The same sketch could have been applied to photography, especially with today's cameras that automate almost everything except taking the shot. Thus, photography is easy: 'You pick

Frame 1

Frame 2

Full scene

Figure 3.2 Framing.

it up, look through this hole and waggle your fingers over this button. Got it? Good'. However, a few minutes spent looking at someone's holidays snaps (or, even worse, their holiday video) makes it clear that things are not so simple. In photography, there is quite an art in framing the shot. If we look around us, there are many possible subjects within our field of view. A good photographer knows how to include only what he or she wants to see on the final picture, and Figure 3.2 shows an example of this effect. To do this, the viewfinder is used as a frame deliberately to include some things and exclude others. Photographers frame their shots very carefully to capture their selective view of the world. Poor photographers do not do this – hence the familiar shots of distant black dots against the snow: 'That's Dave skiing, doesn't he look good?'. Thankfully, although they have disadvantages in bright light, the viewing screens on the backs of digital cameras seem to reduce framing errors in photography.

Framing is a term introduced by Goffman (1974) as a way of explaining how we make sense of events by employing a scheme of interpretation (a framework). When we come upon some new experience, we tend to interpret it in the light of our existing frameworks even if we are unable to articulate what these frameworks may be. Goffman was concerned to understand how individuals make sense of events that might, to a detached observer, seem puzzling, nonsensical or even immoral. One example he quotes is the view, in most societies, that men do not handle the bodies of women with whom they have no relationship. Medics are, however, freed from this taboo in many countries and may even handle the most intimate parts of a woman's body. This does not appal most of us, and we do not regard it as immoral because we have a frame of reference within which we make sense of what is happening.

Goffman argued that people develop frames of reference that are layered, with primary frames as the basic layer that makes sense of the rest. Returning to the analogy of framing in photography, a frame or framework enables us to see some things and to miss or ignore others. It is rather more than a perspective or viewpoint, being something that we have built up and that enables us to make sense of what we see and do. When people do not share common frames, they literally see things differently. This can be the case within organizations, and is often the case when people from different backgrounds come together in a team or to negotiate.

Schön (1982) discusses the ways in which professionals operate when they are attempting to work with and, possibly, serve their clients. One part of this process is the way in which the professional, whether consciously or not, frames the role that he or she will fill and also frames the situation being faced. Schön calls this process 'problem-setting': 'a process in which, interactively, we name the things to which we will attend and frame the context in which we will attend to them' (p. 40). Problem-setting is thus a deliberate and conscious process in which we choose what to study but which is guided by frames that may be unconsciously or subconsciously applied.

Taking this discussion further, Schön argues that successful practitioners strive to do two things. First, they try to relate new experiences to their existing repertoire of past experiences. This may be done consciously: 'Now, I recall that we saw something like this a couple of years ago', or it may be unconscious, in that we find ourselves asking certain questions and anticipating certain responses. If we do either of these things as practitioners, we are using a frame in order to make sense of a new situation. Second, the practitioner tries to maintain the uniqueness of the current situation. This may well be interpreted in terms of prior experience and knowledge. However, the good professional does not just apply a standard response but tries to keep in mind what is different and special about the current circumstances. In this way, we need not be a prisoner of our own experiences and history; instead, these may be used as part of the context that enables us to set the problem.

Thus, in the terms being used here, problem-structuring is a process of naming and of framing. In this sense, it is closer to an art than to a science, which should hardly be surprising given the struggle to maintain the unique nature of current circumstances. Problem-structuring is a bit like setting ourselves an exam, but this is to be done with the client also involved in the process. That is, effective problem-structuring is part of effective Management Science and depends on active cooperation between the analyst and the client. At the very least this is because the two parties bring different insights. The analyst is familiar with the modelling approaches and may be able to think about the situation in abstract terms. The client and user know the detail and context of the situation and wish to ensure that the modelling work is of value. This suggests that their problem-structuring should be a joint process of framing and naming.

In so doing, it is clear that there are two obvious pitfalls to be avoided: the dangers of oversimplification and overelaboration.

The danger of oversimplification

Given that problems need to be defined from messes, one obvious pitfall is the risk of oversimplification. This can occur in a number of ways. The first occurs if we attempt to tackle one aspect of a messy situation in complete isolation from other aspects that may be equally or more important. In this context we have already considered the case of a supermarket chain needing to reorganize its distribution to stores around the country. Within this system of problems there are many aspects that could be tackled, and most of them are interrelated. At some stage, those people responsible for developing the new systems will need to carve off pieces of work that are manageable within a reasonable time period. Thus, decomposition is inevitable, but it should only be done in the light of the expected links between the different issues. Ignoring the linkages may have undesirable effects on other aspects of the mess.

The danger of premature or overenthusiastic decomposition is that resolution of one issue may worsen another aspect. These knock-on effects may be immediate or may only be apparent after some time. As an example of an immediate but unforeseen effect, consider the case of a chain of short-order restaurants that wished to improve efficiency. A Management Science consultant advised them, and his analysis concentrated on better and tighter control of foodstuffs in the restaurants. The idea was to move towards an automated system in which EPOS equipment recorded item usage, which would permit replenishment requests to be placed with suppliers on some agreed basis. Attractive though this idea may seem, there is a downside to it. It implies a shift in the role of the restaurant manager and also in the relationship with the suppliers. Unless these other aspects are carefully thought through, there is a risk that increased efficiency of stock control may reduce the effectiveness of the service offered in the restaurant.

As an example of longer-term consequences, consider the case of a tea packing and blending company that wishes to automate its blending process. Most of the packaged tea on sale in grocery stores is actually blended from up to 40 teas from around the world. The blending is overseen by blenders who, like wine tasters, taste small samples of different teas and develop a pilot blend so as to achieve consistent tastes and appearance. The pilot blend is then scaled up for a large-scale batch production process, each batch coming from a separate pilot blend. Could this batch process not be reorganized on continuous lines so as to produce a consistent blend by the use of consistent teas? The answer is, yes it can. Analysis of the blends devised by the tea blenders over several months showed very consistent patterns in their blends, and this should lend itself to automated, continuous blending. But there is an important snag, which might only become clear after some time. The individual teas are bought on the world commodity markets where both prices and qualities vary as bids and offers are made. Thus, the teas needed for a constant blend may not be available in the right qualities or quantities. Also, a competitor company might realize that the tea company only ever bought certain teas, and could force them into an uncompetitive position in the commodity market. Thus, the long-term consequences of a short-term improvement could be dire.

The second way in which oversimplification may occur is through our natural tendency to see what we prefer to see, for it is very easy to be bound by frames of which we may not be aware. When we approach new situations, we bring with us our past experience and our successes and failures. Many of us are apt to apply our own favourite remedies, which fit well with our own expertise, but in doing this we may ignore other aspects. Much of my own technical expertise is in discrete computer simulation, for example, and, whenever I am asked about aspects of certain dynamic systems, I envisage the system in terms that make it easy to simulate. Needless to say, this applies a set of blinkers that enables me, like a racehorse, to make rapid progress, but I do so at the risk of running in the wrong direction or even in the wrong race. This risk is almost inevitable if it is true that the notion of what constitutes a problem is socially and psychologically defined.

The danger of overelaboration

As is so often the case, there is a chasm on the other side of the narrow road walked by the analyst: the risk of overelaboration or overcomplication. A commonly expressed truism about systems is that they are interconnected internally and externally. Or, as the advocates of chaotic notions in complex systems would have it, the flap of a butterfly's wings in Beijing may trigger a hurricane in Florida (Kelly, 1994). Where do we draw the boundaries around what we are attempting? Must a study of inventory control in motor spares take in a full examination of the prospects for all kinds of transport over the next 20 years?

There is clearly no general answer to this question, but there are some principles to bear in mind when the question is asked. Probably the two most important principles are that it depends on the systems being studied and on the questions that need to be answered. Later on we shall see that these two principles are highly interrelated, but they can be considered separately at this stage. Although it may be true that all systems are interconnected in some way, there is no doubt that some connections are stronger and more important than others. This is why organizations are often organized into hierarchies. Waddington (1977, p. 49) points out that it is appropriate to view a system in hierarchical terms when, 'having analysed the complex into a number of elementary units, we look at the relationships of those units and find that the interrelations fall into separate classes with few intermediaries'. If the analysis is intended to have only short-term impact, then operating at a specific point in the hierarchy may be acceptable.

As an example, consider the job of planning an extension to the New York subway system, for which it would seem perfectly reasonable to exclude the fact that the Moon orbits the Earth. As far as we know, the gravitational pull of the Moon is insufficient to make trains run faster or slower, and we are not dependent on moonlight for the illumination of the platforms. Surely, therefore, the Moon need not be considered as a component of the New York subway system.

However, things may not be so simple. Ridiculous though it may seem, knowledge about the Moon and its effects may be important for the operation of the New York subway system! Consider two possible reasons for this. First, the phases of the Moon will affect the number of people who travel at certain times of year. Easter (a Christian festival) and Passover (a Jewish festival) are classic moveable feasts, because their calendar dates depend on the phases of the Moon. Needless to say, the number of people travelling and their trip distribution may be very different from normal at those times of year. Second, all subway systems suffer from water seepage, and, in the case of New York, much of the subway is close to the sea. The sea is pulled by the Moon's gravitational field, which shows itself as tides of different levels. The sea defences have to be designed to withstand high tides and to pump water back at the correct times.

Hence, absurd though it may seem, the Moon may need to be included in some analyses of the New York subway system. It is clearly not within the control of anyone who manages or uses the subway system, but it does have an influence. It may perhaps be best to regard it as part of the environment of the system, but for some purposes it cannot be ignored. Thus, one way of answering the question, 'how do we decide what is inside a system', is to consider its function. This is a question we shall return to in Chapter 5, which discusses soft systems methodology.

Problem-structuring as exploration

The notion of problem-structuring in Management Science is simple enough, although it is rather harder to put into practice. The idea is to develop some definition of the problem that is to be tackled without losing sight of the relationship between this problem and other things. There is no need for it to carry the idea that problems are solved in any permanent sense. Because problems are constructs of the human mind and of people working together, they need to be defined. In one very important sense, they do not exist 'out there' but exist within ourselves. Thus, the idea of problem-structuring is to come up with some problem definitions that are manageable and that seem likely to help manage the issue stream or mess.

In a way, problem-structuring goes on throughout the life of a Management Science project. It is sometimes only when the project is over that we can see clearly what we were doing. This is a bit like climbing a sand dune in the dark. We struggle and slip, we may even curse, and we're not too sure if we're doing things the best way. But the direction of the slope tells us that we're headed in the right direction. Once at the top, after the dawn breaks, we can see our footsteps in the sand. We see where we've been and how we got there, and we might even learn from the experience. So, throughout a Management Science project there tends to be a continuing questioning about the work being done. Nevertheless, the start of such a project is when most such activity takes place; this at least ensures that we are setting off in the right direction.

Many years ago a colleague and I carried out a small empirical study of how Management Science groups in part of the UK attempted to structure the problems that they tackled (Pidd and Woolley, 1980). We concluded that the best metaphor to describe our observations was that the practitioners whom we met and observed could be seen as 'explorers'. They were attempting to map out new territory in a way that would make for its later exploitation. We concluded that, as well as employing a few techniques, this exploration approach could be characterized as follows:

- The approach was inclusive. What we meant by this was that the practitioners were concerned with much more than the technical and 'official' issues that were apparent at the start of a project. As well as exploring the problem as it had been specified to them, they also wanted to understand the people involved and their concerns. The exploration covered the people as well as the problem. This did not imply that they had a well-formulated set of notions about how their organization functioned or about the politics of the circumstances. Far from it. Indeed, many of them found these considerations rather frustrating. Yet they recognized the importance of including them in their initial work on a project.
- The approach was continuous. That is, they engaged in a cycle of enquiry, as shown in Figure 3.3. Looking back on this work, we made this observation in complete ignorance of the literature on organizational and other learning (see Argyris, 1983; Kolb, 1983), with which it fits rather well as a form of single-loop learning. In fact, the cycle would be better expressed

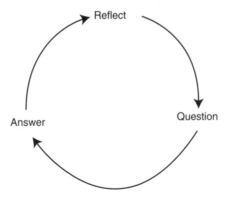

Figure 3.3 Problem-structuring as continuous exploration.

as a helix through which the analyst makes gradual progress, all of the time reflecting on what has been learned and adapting his or her views at the same time.

- The work of Management Science groups was, in some senses, hierarchical, which relates to the point above about continuity. What seemed to happen was that work on one 'problem' would often spawn further work as other issues of importance emerged. Sometimes these secondary issues turned out to be more important than the work that uncovered their existence, and they would come to dominate the analyst's time. On other occasions, these secondary issues could just be noted and left to some later date.
- What we observed was generally informal, by which we meant that there was little evidence of use of formal creativity techniques such as brainstorming or synectics. Instead there was the general chatter and banter of people working together who bounced ideas off one another, expecting to give and to gain from the exchanges. We were a little surprised by this lack of formal technique.

Since we carried out that research, a few techniques such as soft systems methodology (see Chapter 5) and cognitive mapping (see Chapter 6) have emerged into the limelight and are used by some people in their problem-structuring. It might, therefore, be the case that contemporary efforts in problem-structuring are rather more formal than we observed in the late 1970s. But this may well depend on the Operational Research/Management Science (OR/MS) group involved.

The practicalities of problem-structuring

In a way, much of this book is about problem-structuring, and this is because experience suggests that, once usefully structured, a problem may already be half-solved. This section will concentrate on some of the very practical ways in which problem-structuring may be made more effective. Bear in mind that these assume a backdrop formed by the features of the exploration approach as described above.

The idiot questions: critical examination – Kipling's wise men

One feature of method study that can be safely adopted in Management Science practice is the idea of critical examination. This is the routine use of a standard set of questions that are well captured in Rudyard Kipling's famous verse from the *Just So Stories* ('The elephant's child'):

> I keep six honest working men
> (They taught me all I knew);
> Their names are What and Why and When
> And How and Where and Who.

This gives us six lines of enquiry to be pursued at the start of a project that will help us in our structuring or framing of the problems to be tackled. They stem from the realization that problem-structuring needs to be an inclusive process that stretches far beyond the technical issues of the work. They are what I call 'the idiot questions', and I call them this because they can only be asked openly at the start of the project. If asked then, they tend to make the project client, assuming one exists, think the analyst is smart for asking such perceptive questions. However, if they are asked later in the project, the client will tend to think the analyst is an idiot who should know that by now. It is also important to realize that these are not intended as direct questions.

Starting a project is like any other form of social interaction in which there are many ways of finding things out other than asking a direct question. Considering each of these six in turn:

- *What* is going on and what do people want? These are two very basic questions to face, and they are concerned with digging into the content of the issues that led to the request for Management Science support. This is the most basic enquiry line, and one that most analysts are likely to follow without thinking much about it. In effect, the analyst is operating almost as a detective or anthropologist. As with all these lines of enquiry, it is important to ask the same questions of a number of people. A navigator fixes position by locating several reference points, and a sensible analyst will do the same.
- *Why* have we become involved in this project and why does the client wish for help? This is also a fundamental question but may be less likely to be asked by a naive analyst. It requires digging beyond the surface and reflecting on the contributions Management Science might make to resolving the issues. As is known by experienced practitioners, their help may be sought for all sorts of reason – some positive, but others rather negative. It may be due to their expertise; it may be due to the failure of others; it might be a result of desperation; and it might be because their involvement will postpone things for a while. Whatever the reason, it seems crucial that the analyst gives some thought to this question, otherwise there is a great risk of later misunderstanding. The analyst is, of course, free to attempt to renegotiate the implicit or explicit terms of his or her involvement, and this may be an essential part of problem-structuring or setting. But this is impossible unless this basic question has been addressed.
- *When* did all this start to happen, and what is the history of it all? Most interventions in organizations have a history to them, and trying to understand it can shed great light on what might be done. For example, this may be a long-standing issue to which the managers of the organization return from time to time and to which they expect to return in the future. Thus, they are not expecting a once-and-for-all-time fix, but are looking for some way to operate more effectively. The question also relates to the urgency of the work: is it to be done to a very tight timetable or can things be done at a slightly more leisurely pace? Once again, this is all part of getting things in context.
- *How* did all of this start to emerge? Clearly this and the other five 'honest working men' are close relatives or friends, and in this form it relates closely to the Who and When questions. But it also relates to the What question in facing up to how things are done at the moment or how people might envisage things operating in the future. This depends both on the analyst's reflection and deliberation and on the opinions of the people who are interviewed at this stage of the work.
- *Where* is all this happening, and does it have to happen here? This is another fundamental question for the analyst to face. Location can be very important even in these days of instantaneous electronic communication around the world. Physical distance can cause enormous problems, and may create misunderstandings that can be ironed out only by people spending time physically together. Tasks that once had to be located in one particular place may now be located elsewhere in the world – for example, some large software companies locate their entire European telephone help-desks in the Netherlands because of the linguistic prowess of the Dutch. If callers are talking to helpers in their own language (and the call is free), it makes no difference in which country the help-desk is located.
- *Who* are the people involved (the stakeholders), and what do we know about them? Put in these terms, this question can seem rather aggressive and intrusive, but it is very important to face up to it. Organizations are made up of people who behave in all sorts of ways, and analysts who ignore this do so at their own risk. To quote an extreme example, some large companies are still family-owned, and to treat a request from the owner in the same way as

one from a junior manager may lead to an interesting situation. As with the other questions, the analyst needs to use the answer to this question as valuable information that will inform the approach that should be taken.

In a sense, these six questions are the framework for a story or narrative in which people explain what happened and why. Bruner (1990) argues that people employ narrative; that is, they tell stories to account for experiences and events that seem odd in some way or another. The storyline explains why things are as they appear to be. He argues that we do this in an attempt to relate the incongruity to aspects of our frameworks of understanding. Telling a convincing story is part of the sense-making that we do as humans, which suggests that problem-structuring is an attempt at sense-making.

Spray diagrams

A second approach to problem-structuring, used by some people, is the graphical approach known as spray diagrams, suggested by Fortune and Peters (1995) as part of their methodology of learning from failure. This methodology has a preanalysis phase that corresponds, roughly at least, to the way in which problem-structuring is being described here. The diagrams are intended as working tools that display relationships. They should be revised and enhanced as thought, analysis, interviews and deliberation proceed. An example of a spray diagram for TICTOC is given in Figure 3.4.

The diagram has a clear focus around the main issue of hose choice, with an indication that the prime issue here is whether or not to stay with UKHose. The major preoccupations of the players are also noted on the diagram, although the central character of the DPS is only there by implication. It certainly illustrates the range of pressures that he faces.

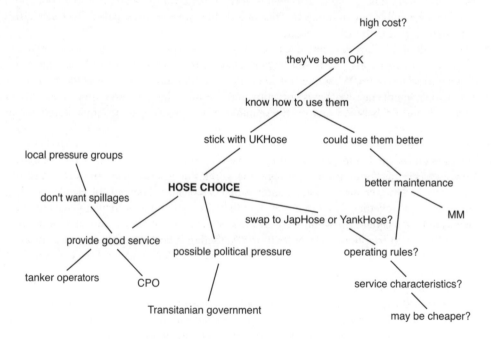

Figure 3.4 Spray diagram for TICTOC.

Rich pictures

Checkland suggests the use of rich pictures as part of soft systems methodology (see Chapter 5), but they also can stand alone in their own right. They form part of the attempt to capture the problem situation that characterizes problem-structuring. As with the 'idiot questions', rich pictures are intended to be inclusive, and, as with the 'idiot questions', they are primarily for the benefit of the analyst. They are an attempt to sketch out the main participants in the work and to show their interests and interactions. The idea is to include information that could be regarded as 'soft' (such things as people's attitudes, roles and assumptions) as well as 'hard' or technical data (such as numerical data and details of computer systems). In the sense that will be discussed in Chapter 5, they are intended to be holistic devices.

A moment's reflection on the notion of 'framing' introduced earlier in this chapter should indicate how close a rich picture is to this idea. An artist, when drawing a picture, even a portrait, is attempting to capture what he or she 'sees' as the essence of the subject and to convey that to the viewer. One room of the Picasso Museum in Barcelona is devoted to a number of studies made by the artist in his reworking of a famous painting by Velázquez, Las Meninas. This series includes many studies of the small girl from Velázquez's canvas, in which her shape grows steadily more and more abstract until only the essence of her form is left on the canvas. It takes skill, insight and practice to capture the essence of anything in a picture, and part of this is the framing of the subject. Rich pictures are intended to help the analyst to do the same by providing an abstract representation of the problem situation.

Figure 3.5 shows an example of a rich picture that was drawn while thinking about the TICTOC example introduced in Chapter 2 and developed further in this chapter. It is clear that, unlike Picasso's paintings, this is no work of art – but nor was it intended to be. Rich pictures are devices for thinking about the problem. They differ from lists in two important ways. The first is that they make it clear that there is, as yet, no definite sequence in which the issues will be

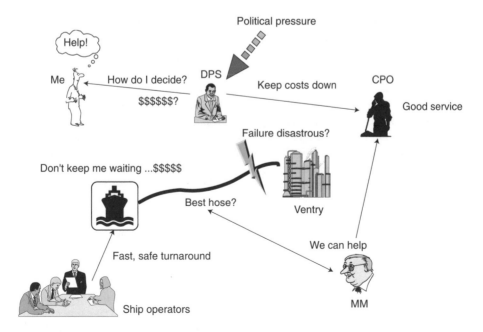

Figure 3.5 Rich picture for TICTOC.

handled. The second is that they focus on relationships between issues, people and systems in a way that lists do not. There is no particular reason why an analyst should not use this device as a way of capturing the perceptions of the different people (the Who of the 'idiot questions'). There may thus be a number of rich pictures from a range of viewpoints. Note one important feature: the analyst figures on the picture, too. This may not be obvious to the analyst, but it will be very obvious to the other people involved as stakeholders in the study. It is crucial that the analyst develops this self-awareness, for organizational systems are not inanimate objects, they are made up of people, including the analyst, who react, who respond and whose views change.

Brainstorming

A third practical and well-known approach is brainstorming, a term that probably originated with Osborn (1953). Brainstorming is one of several techniques that are intended to increase people's creativity, a subject that Saaty (1998) feels is perhaps underrated in Management Science. According to Gilhooly (1988), brainstorming has two main principles:

1. The evaluation of ideas is to be postponed until a definite time point at which idea production has ceased. This is to avoid inhibiting the person or people who are producing the ideas. Ideas that may not be useful in themselves may be a stepping stone to others that are useful.
2. Quantity breeds quality. The idea behind this is that, the greater the number of ideas produced, the greater the chance that there will be some useful ones.

These are to be implemented via four rules, which are often expressed as follows:

1. Criticism is ruled out.
2. Freewheeling is welcomed.
3. Quantity is wanted.
4. Combination and improvement are sought.

These rules are intended to encourage participants freely to associate positively with ideas that have been produced, to produce ideas themselves, however odd they may seem, and to look for ways to combine and improve suggestions that have already been generated.

The basic idea of brainstorming is simple: participants propose ideas and insights that are displayed as they are proposed. The first stage is to gather the ideas, and during this stage no criticism is allowed. Instead, people are encouraged to build on ideas suggested by others. Once the gathering stage is complete, the group may proceed to cluster the ideas and then start to evaluate them. It seems that a facilitator is needed to make the best use of brainstorming, otherwise there is a tendency for evaluation to occur too early.

Gilhooly (1988) provides evidence that brainstorming is effective, both for individuals and for groups. In this context, effectiveness means that the ideas produced are unique and valuable, and that the quantity of ideas is large. Other studies quoted by Gilhooly appear to show that the best way to employ brainstorming is to use nominal groups. This variation starts with the individual group members, alone and in private, suggesting the ideas. This avoids group pressure and too early evaluation of other people's ideas. The resulting ideas are then pooled (so as to increase the quantity of ideas), and there is no particular reason why the pooled ideas cannot be fed back to the participants to give them the chance to build on the ideas produced. A variation on these nominal groups is used in the first stage of what Chapter 6 calls the SODA II (Strategic Options Development and Analysis) approach of Eden and colleagues.

Brainstorming also illustrates one of the important principles of successful problem-solving if oversimplification and overelaboration are to be avoided. This is the realization that a group, or individual, must sometimes think expansively, must broaden their thinking, in a search for ideas and insights. Equally, it is important to realize that there are times when evaluation, that is, a narrowing of the options and ideas, is needed. As in Figure 3.3, which shows problem-structuring as exploration, there may be a need to return several times to expansive thinking and to evaluation in successful problem-solving. Expansive thinking without evaluation is fun, but likely to be unproductive. Evaluation without proper expansive thinking will be sterile and uncreative.

Summary

This chapter serves as a bridge between the theoretical concerns of Chapter 2, which looked at rationality and how it is regarded within Management Science, and the various approaches advocated to help in model-building, which will be the focus of later chapters. It discussed the notion of problem-solving, as often used by management scientists, and warned of some dangers in an oversimplified view of this. In particular, it looked at the ways in which 'problems' are socially defined and emerge from messes (to use Ackoff's term) or issue streams (to use Langley's term). What emerges from this discussion is the need to be aware that 'problems' are socially defined; they are constructed or construed by individuals and groups. It is thus important for management scientists to be very careful and deliberate in their problem-structuring.

To help with this framing and naming, a few simple techniques that have been found useful in practice were introduced. They relate to the notion that problem-structuring is a form of exploration in which the analyst develops a map of what is happening and of what might be done about it. Finally, the need for both expansive thinking and evaluation was discussed.

References

Ackoff R.L. (1974) *Redesigning the Future: A Systems Approach to Societal Planning*. John Wiley & Sons, Inc., New York, NY.

Ackoff R.L. (1979) The future of operational research is past. *Journal of the Operational Research Society*, **30**(2), 93–104.

Argyris C. (1983) Productive and counter-productive reasoning processes, in *The Executive Mind*, ed. by Srivasta S. Jossey-Bass, San Francisco, CA.

Bruner J.S. (1990) *Acts of Meaning*. Harvard University Press, Cambridge, MA.

Checkland P.B. (1981) *Systems Thinking, Systems Practice*. John Wiley & Sons, Ltd, Chichester, UK.

de Neufville R. and Stafford J.H. (1971) *Systems Analysis for Managers and Engineers*. McGraw-Hill, Maidenhead, UK.

Fortune J. and Peters C. (1995) *Learning from Failure. The Systems Approach*. John Wiley & Sons, Ltd, Chichester, UK.

Gilhooly K.J. (1988) *Thinking: Directed, Undirected and Creative*, 2nd edition. Academic Press, London, UK.

Goffman E. (1974) *Frame Analysis*. Penguin Books, Harmondsworth, UK.

Kelly K. (1994) *Out of Control: The New Biology of Machines*. Fourth Estate, London, UK.

Kolb D.A. (1983) Problem management: learning from experience, in *The Executive Mind*, ed. by Srivasta S. Jossey-Bass, San Francisco, CA.

Langley A., Mintzberg H., Pitcher P., Posada E. and Saint-Macary J. (1995) Opening up decision making: the view from the black stool. *Organizational Science*, **6**(3), 260–279.

Lubart T.I. (1994) *Creativity, in Thinking and Problem Solving*, 2nd edition, ed. by Steinberg R.J. Academic Press, London, UK.

Mintzberg H. (1989) *Mintzberg on Management*. The Free Press, New York, NY.

Osborn A.F. (1953) *Applied Imagination*. Scribners, New York, NY.

Pidd M. and Woolley R.N. (1980) A pilot study of problem structuring. *Journal of the Operational Research Society*, **31**, 1063–1069.

Polya G. (1957) *How to Solve It. A New Aspect of Mathematical Method*, 2nd edition. Doubleday, New York, NY.

Rittel H.W.J. and Webber M.M. (1973) Dilemmas in a general theory of planning. *Policy Sciences*, **4**, 155–169.

Saaty T.L. (1998) Reflections and projections on creativity in operations research and management science: a pressing need for a shifting paradigm. *Operations Research*, **46**(1), 9–16.

Schön D.A. (1982) *The Reflective Practitioner. How Professionals Think in Action*. Basic Books, New York, NY.

Smith G.F. (1988) Towards a heuristic theory of problem structuring. *Management Science*, **34**(12), 1489–1506.

Smith G.F. (1989) Defining managerial problems: a framework for prescriptive theorizing. *Management Science*, **35**(8), 963–981.

Waddington C.H. (1977) *Tools for Thought*. Paladin, St Albans, UK.

Wickelgren W. (1974) *How to Solve Problems. Elements of a Theory of Problems and Problem Solving*. W.H. Freeman, Reading, UK.

4 Some principles of modelling

The purpose of this chapter

This book discusses some hard and soft modelling approaches that have been found useful in Management Science. This is the final chapter of Part I, which is concerned with some of the general issues faced in Management Science. Chapter 1 developed a definition of 'model' as the term is used in Management Science, and argued that models are useful because they are tools for thinking that enable us to investigate what might happen if we (or someone else) did something. Chapter 2 was an introduction to rational decision-making and argued that practical rationality is, in Simon's terms, procedural. Empirical studies of how managers actually manage show that other factors as well as reason are at work in decision-making and control. These need to be accounted for in any ideas about modelling. Chapter 3 explored what we mean by the idea of a problem as the term is used in Management Science practice. It also looked at some methods of problem structuring, so as to avoid tackling the wrong problem. This requires the analyst to take account of the circumstances that lead people to believe that there is a problem for which modelling might be of some help.

This chapter covers some general principles that can be applied when developing a model that will be useful in Management Science. Other people, notably Powell (1995) and Morris (1967) have proposed principles that they and others have found useful. The focus here is avowedly practical, the idea being to provide some issues to consider and some principles that may be useful. It is important, though, to bear in mind that some of these principles are almost matters of style. Such matters need to be internalized and personalized. An example I often use with students is to recall the medical training of my wife, a doctor. As a student she was taught the importance of physical examination, and, as a novice, was given a strictly defined sequence of instructions to follow when examining a patient. She and her fellow students followed this to the letter until it was second nature to them. By that stage, however, each student had personalized it to some extent. One student might be rather better at hearing strange sounds, another at feeling changes in skin texture and so on. Each slightly adapted the formula but internalized its structure and aims. The same should occur with these principles of modelling.

Finally, a caveat. This set of principles will be neither complete nor eternal. One of the hazards of writing a book is that the author's past comes back like a ghost to haunt him. Things I wrote 20 years ago are sometimes quoted back at me – and I find that my own views have shifted and that I don't agree with what I wrote then! These principles, therefore, are not to be treated as if they were carved into tablets of stone. They are ideas that I hope will prove useful and to which I hope others will add. Principle 5, 'do not fall in love with data', is itself subdivided into a number of principles, but it seems best to keep the overall number small, within the 'seven, plus or minus two' rule (Miller, 1956).

Principle 1: model simple, think complicated

Complexity and complicated models

Chapter 1 argued a case for modelling from a view that our world is complex and that the consequences of decisions and plans can be large-scale and wide ranging. Given this, must models be complicated to be of any use? Do complex situations always require complicated models? It is important to consider this, because a common mistake is to try to build a model that is as complete and accurate as possible. Paradoxically, this is almost always a mistake.

A tenet of cybernetics, the science of control, is the principle of requisite variety (Ashby, 1956), which might seem to support the view that complex systems require complicated models. The principle of requisite variety can be stated in many ways, one of which is that 'variety must match variety'. Its origin lies in the design of control systems that are intended to operate in complex environments. In its simplest form it suggests that, to be effective, a control system must be able to match the system it is controlling. For example, if a furnace can get too cool as well as too hot, the control system should include some way of detecting and responding to low temperatures as well as to high ones. Stated in this form, the principle of requisite variety is almost a truism. Ashby took it rather further than this commonsensical notion and developed a mathematical theory of its use.

What of its applicability to models and modelling within Management Science? Must a model be as complicated as the reality being modelled? Thankfully, the answer is no – for a reason that may not immediately be obvious, but which is illustrated in Figure 4.1. Models are not just built, they are also used – a rather obvious but vitally important point. It is crucial that the combined variety of the model and the user(s) can match that of the system being modelled. This does not mean that either one of the two components (model and user) must separately be able to do so. Chapter 5 discusses systems approaches and points out that a system comes to our notice because it displays behaviour not apparent in its components. This is known as emergent behaviour. In the context of modelling it is important to realize that the model and the user form a system. Requisite variety is an emergent property of that human–model system and not of its components.

Model simple, think complicated

The implication of this idea is captured in the aphorism 'model simple, think complicated'. That is, a simple model should be supplemented by highly critical thinking and rigorous argument and analysis. This view could, of course, be taken to a ludicrous extreme. For example, a verbal

Figure 4.1 Model and user as a system.

model might be: 'The world is hideously complicated and dangerous when things go wrong'. No amount of critical thinking or analysis could take such a verbal model much further forward. At the opposite extreme, if a model itself does have requisite variety, then there might be no need for much critical thinking. In such cases the model could be built into a computer system that is used for day-to-day operation and control with no human intervention. Indeed, as Ashby pointed out in the principle of requisite variety, such complexity is essential if the model is to provide full and automatic control. Between these two extremes lies the realm within which most Management Science is conducted. The models are neither trivial nor fully requisite. Instead, they simplify and aggregate.

One advantage of simple models is that they are easier to understand than complicated ones. Writing about the desirable features of decision models, John Little (1970) argued that one essential property was that they should be simple. This is because transparency is easier to achieve with simple models. Therefore, these stand a greater chance of being used than very complicated ones. Within Management Science, models are built in order to help people and organizations to become more effective in what they do. This means that their results need to be used, and this requires trust on the part of the user. Trust is easier to achieve when the user is at least able to appreciate the overall workings of the model. It is important not to misread this as suggesting that a Management Science model must always be limited by the technical prowess of the people sponsoring the work – this, too, would be ludicrous.

Instead, the idea of simplicity needs to be linked with another suggestion of Little (1970): that the model should be easy to manipulate. As an analogy, there is a world of difference between the car driver and the skilled motor engineer. Most of us can drive cars, although we may have only the vaguest notion of how the car works. We can drive because we have been trained to so, but also because the car itself gives us rapid feedback about our driving. For instance, we go off the road or hit other vehicles if we steer wrongly. After some training, a car is easy to manipulate and meets our preference for personal mobility. In a similar way, a model that is easy to manipulate (e.g. its user interface might be made to resemble a spreadsheet) and that produces results that seem relevant will be used. Thus, simplicity has a second aspect, ease of use.

There are, of course, occasions when this metaphor collapses. In the world of travel, if we need to traverse the Pacific, driving across is not a viable option. Instead, we climb aboard a jet aircraft and surrender control to the aircraft crew with their own expertise. Similarly, there are some models that require the user to place their trust in the skills of the analysis team, because only they fully understand its workings. But users should only do so if the model produces results and insights that are relevant and appropriate to their situations. It is the joint responsibility of the analyst and the users to ensure that this is the case. Complicated models have no divine right of acceptance.

This idea that we might 'model simple, think complicated' brings us right back to the idea that models are 'tools for thinking'. It would be wrong to interpret that phrase as being 'tools to replace thinking'. Instead, they are tools to support and extend the power of thinking. Thus, a complicated model that is poorly employed may be worse than a simple model used as a tool for careful thought.

Chapter 10 introduces computer simulation as a way of modelling complex dynamic systems. As almost anything can be simulated given enough time and money, it is tempting to assume that a highly detailed model is always needed. This is a great mistake. A model should help people to think things through and cannot replace that thinking.

This principle means that a relatively simple model can support complicated analysis. A model intended as a tool for thinking needs to be adequate for the task, and it must be skilfully used if the task is to be done well. At a conference I attended, a plenary speaker, a distinguished and senior manufacturing manager of one of the world's most successful companies, told the audience that he wanted a model to simulate all his company's worldwide factories at almost any level of detail. As he was our distinguished guest, it would have been rude to disagree. The appropriate response, though, is that given by Evelyn Waugh's character Boot to his boss, Lord Copper, in the novel *Scoop*. Whenever Lord Copper expressed some outrageous view, Boot's polite response was, 'To a point, Lord Copper, to a point!'. No model can or should do everything.

How are models used?

It would be impossible to list all the different ways in which models are used, but understanding types of model use can be helpful in considering how simple a model can be – that is, how closely it must resemble what it is intended to represent. Figure 4.2 shows a simple spectrum of model use, with four archetypes of model use, each defined by the amount of human interaction needed (the strength or weakness of the arrows in Figure 4.1) and by the extent to which models are intended for frequent or one-off use. Clearly there are more than four ways in which a Management Science model is used, but the four shown in Figure 4.2 usefully highlight the different types of use.

The extreme left of the spectrum of model use is labelled *decision automation*, which refers to models that completely replace human decision-making. These are likely to be used very frequently, possibly many times each day. They might include models used for the monitoring and replenishment of low-value stocks and parts for an organization that keeps thousands of different items. It is relatively straightforward to develop computer software to implement algorithms that will determine which items need to be reordered and in what quantities these are needed. Using e-commerce links, orders can be placed automatically with suppliers. In their routine use, models intended for decision automation do not require human involvement and can be further developed to monitor their own performance so as to make appropriate adjustments to parameter values. Any human intervention is limited to high-level monitoring.

Models intended for decision automation usually rely on accurate and up-to-date data for their parameterization, are intended to be accurate representations and are usually subject to severe tests of validity. This is important, because the models will replace humans in making decisions, which requires people to be confident that the models are appropriate to the task in hand. Thus, if Figure 4.1 were redrawn to show the relative importance of models and humans, the humans would virtually disappear.

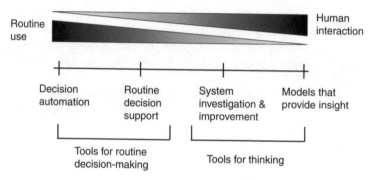

Figure 4.2 A spectrum of model use.

Moving from the left-hand end of Figure 4.2, the next point on the spectrum of model use is labelled *routine decision support*. This refers to models that are regularly used, but much less frequently than those intended for decision automation. Also, they do not replace human decision-making, but support it. Examples might include models used to support rostering decisions, for example to determine how an airline might allocate cabin crew to its flights. This rostering requires consideration of the flight departure and destination points, the type of aircraft, the cabin crew available and the hours they have worked and are allowed to work. It is possible, although difficult (Day and Ryan, 1997), to develop and implement models that will propose a set of rosters to fit an airline schedule so as to minimize the cost of staffing the flights. However, these models cannot be used fully to automate decisions, because they can never take account of the daily occurrence of staff absences through illness, changes to the schedule owing to weather and other unforeseen circumstances. They can, though, provide a schedule that humans, who are aware of these problems, can adapt to fit unanticipated circumstances. In this way, the model may be able to produce a roster that is 90 or 95% satisfactory, freeing the people involved to deal with what are often ambiguous situations that cannot be satisfactorily modelled in advance.

These models for routine decision support must, like those intended for decision automation, be based on accurate data, but there is no pretence that the model will cover all circumstances. There is an explicit trade-off between the cost of the model and the degree to which it fits all conceivable circumstances, and a recognition that the model is intended to support and not to replace human decision-makers.

The third point on the spectrum of model use in Figure 4.2 is labelled *system investigation and improvement*. This refers to models that are typically developed as part of a project that has been set up to understand why a system is behaving as it seems to be or to consider options for its improvement. In such situations, models and their human users would have almost equal weight in Figure 4.1 if it were redrawn to show their relative importance. Discrete computer simulation models, discussed in Chapter 10, are often used in this way. The model typically represents the structure of the system of interest, and users then suggest options for change that can be simulated to show their likely effects. Sometimes, the model will need to be modified to allow the investigation of particular options, revealing a very close relationship with users.

These models intended for system investigation and improvement are usually mush less precise than those for routine decision support. They will typically focus on only some aspects of the system being modelled and treat the rest in a very approximate way. The data used are often approximate and aggregated, rather than very detailed. Validation becomes a delicate dance between the user, the purpose for which the user requested the model and the model itself. Validation is often problematic because the models may be used to hypothesize how a future state may affect performance, and there is thus no 'real system' with which to compare the model.

Finally, the right-hand end of the model use spectrum in Figure 4.2 is labelled *models that provide insight*. These are rather like a compass of the type used by hikers to navigate their way across difficult terrain. This type of compass requires considerable skill for proper use, which relies on the hiker being able to determine her current location; by contrast, a GPS will tell the hiker where she is. Essentially, the compass provides a sense of direction that the user must combine with a map so as to navigate safely. Models intended for providing insight are very strongly reliant on the user in Figure 4.1 and have little value without an intelligent user. The modelling approaches discussed in Part II of this book are often used to provide insight. There is no pretence that they are wholly accurate, and, as discussed in Chapter 12, their validation is highly problematic. Likewise, any data used are often highly aggregated and may be very approximate. The models themselves may have been developed very quickly and are likely to be discarded after use.

Principle 2: be parsimonious, start small and add

Unfortunately we have no metric for simplicity, no way of knowing whether our models are optimally simple (to coin a strange term). Presumably, we can put a crude lower bound on this optimal simplicity. For example, the mental models in use before Management Science modelling could serve as a lower bound, as we would otherwise have no reason to develop the formal model. After that we must act like an army approaching a well-defended city at night, using a little stealth and cunning.

We do this by employing the principle of parsimony, which I have long found useful in computer simulation modelling (Pidd, 1998). In its more memorable form, this principle is sometimes known as KISS, an acronym for Keep It Simple, Stupid. The idea is that models should, ideally, be developed gradually, starting with simple assumptions and only adding complications as they become necessary. Instead of attempting, from the outset, a wonderful model that embodies every aspect of the situation in a realistic form, we begin with something manageable, which may have unrealistic assumptions. The intention is to learn what we can from this simple model and then to refine it gradually, wherever this is necessary.

There are two variations on this theme. The first, as discussed above, is to add successive refinements to a model until it is good enough for the purpose in hand. The second is to employ what Powell (1995) calls 'prototyping', in which successive models may be abandoned and replaced with more complex ones until a good enough model has been developed. Both variations carry the idea that it is best quickly to develop a working model, even if it is imperfect. It can be refined, or even abandoned, later.

A simple example: ping-pong balls

To use this principle, the model-building should begin with the well-understood and more obvious elements that are thought to be most relevant to the intended purpose of the model. Once these are properly modelled and validated, the more complicated and less well-understood elements can be added as required. The temptation to dive straight into the complicated aspects should be resisted, in spite of its siren sounds. In a fascinating book on quantitative modelling in general, not particularly aimed at a Management Science audience, Starfield, Smith and Bleloch (1990) develop this idea in some detail through a series of examples that increase in complexity. One of their earliest examples is the following: 'Look around the room you are sitting in. How many ping-pong balls could you fit in this room?'. They take the reader through a series of attempts to answer this question by a modelling approach.

Their first suggestion is that the reader should produce an answer to this in just 60 seconds. Faced with the problem put in this way, most people make a vague estimate of two volumes, that of a typical ping-pong ball and that of the room in which they are sitting. Those reading this on a palm-fringed beach should use their imagination or should go for a swim! Hence, the first simple model that many people employ to tackle this is

$$\text{Number} = \text{room volume/ball volume}$$

They use this idea to make a guess at the number, having also guessed the rough dimensions of the room. Of course, this makes a lot of assumptions. Most people assume their room to be rectangular, that there will be no furniture in the room, that ping-pong balls will not compress under pressure and so on. Nevertheless, such a model is better than throwing our hands in the air and crying, 'Oh I don't know, hundreds, thousands maybe!'.

Their second suggestion is that the reader spends a further five minutes addressing the question, preferably working with a partner. What many people do at this stage is to refine this earlier model. Thus, they make a better estimate of the dimensions of the room and use this to compute its approximate volume rather than making a guess. This gives the following simple equation:

$$\text{Room volume} = L \times W \times H$$

where L is length, W is width and H is height.

Similarly, people tend to estimate the volume of a ping-pong ball and usually treat such a ball as if it were a cube. They may do this to avoid computations with π, or because they imagine that this is the correct formula for the volume of a sphere, or even to allow for the fact that there will be gaps between the balls as they are packed. Thus

$$\text{Ball volume} = D^3$$

where D is diameter.

Hence, after the five minutes (six in total), the overall model becomes

$$\text{Number} = \frac{L \times W \times H}{D^3}$$

This has now transformed the simple guess into a symbolic model with parameters L, W, H and D. Each of these could be estimated, or even measured given more time, to provide an estimate for the number of ping-pong balls. The implicit model has been made explicit.

As a next stage, Starfield, Smith and Bleloch suggest that the modeller might spend a little more time developing the model into one with upper and lower bounds. This is simpler than it might seem, because the cubic model developed after six minutes is one easy way of producing a lower bound on the solution. It assumes that the balls will not compress and treats them as if they were cubes, which tessellate in three dimensions. If the balls actually compress, or just settle into one another, then more could be packed in than the cubic model would suggest. An upper bound, in this case, could be produced by a different simplification. This treats the balls as perfect spheres that do not compress and that, by some magic, can be packed in with no air gaps at all – clearly impossible, but that doesn't matter. In this case the volume of a single ball is

$$\text{Ball volume} = \frac{4\pi}{3} \left(\frac{D}{2} \right)^3$$

Hence, the overall upper bound model is

$$\text{Volume} = \frac{L \times W \times H}{\frac{4\pi}{3} \left(\frac{D}{2} \right)^3}$$

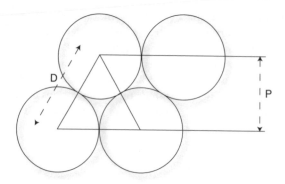

Figure 4.3 Trapezium model for the ping-pong ball problem.

Dividing the upper bound model by the lower bound model gives an upper:lower ratio of $6/\pi$, which is just lower than 2.

Further refinements can be made by examining the assumptions made when developing these simple solutions. For example, we made assumptions about how the balls are packed, about the room being a simple rectangle, about there being no furniture in the room, about air pressure having no effect and so on. Each of these assumptions is, strictly speaking, wrong. Nevertheless, our models tell us much more than a simple guess. They are more likely to be closer to the truth, and they are general symbolic statements about general rooms and general spheres. One way forward would be to develop a more realistic treatment of the way in which the balls rest on one another. A two-dimensional example of this is shown in Figure 4.3, with the balls resting on one another within a trapezium. Simple trigonometry then allows us to proceed as follows.

Imagine, as shown in Figure 4.3, a triangle with each apex at the centre of a ping-pong ball. If the balls settle into one another without compression, then this will be an equilateral triangle if all the balls are the same size, and this enables us to estimate the packing distance P as follows:

$$\sin(60) = \frac{P}{D}$$
$$\therefore P = D\sin(60)$$
$$\therefore P = 0.866D$$

The height of the trapezium containing four balls is $P + D$, whereas the cubic model assumed that a square with sides $2D$ was needed. Hence, the volume needed for four balls is rather less than might be expected using the cubic model. Working in two dimensions, as in Figure 4.3, this suggests that 13–14% less space would be needed. Or, putting it another way, we could pack in something like 13–14% more balls than the cubic model might suggest. In similar ways, the model can be gradually refined until its accuracy is suitable for the intended purpose.

A second example: cloud cover

A rather more realistic exercise is described in Miser and Quade (1990a), which discusses a model for estimating how much of a runway would be visible to pilots through partial cloud cover. This might be an important consideration for an aircraft coming in to land in cloudy conditions. There are various types of cloud, but at a height relevant to a plane seeking visual contact with an airport runway, only some need be considered. The first question is, how could these be represented in a model? As before, the principle of parsimony suggests that starting simple might be the best approach, and thus some simple geometric shape has much to commend it. One possibility is to treat discrete clouds as if they were discs. As Miser and Quade point out, using discs in this way is reasonable, as the relevant types of cloud do tend to be compact. It is also a helpful simplification, as the geometry of discs is well understood.

Cloud cover is often measured as a percentage of the sky that is visible from points on the ground, and its pattern may be specific to the location of the airport. For example, nearby hills or ocean may cause certain patterns to predominate. These patterns could then be modelled at different heights by the use of simplified circles to represent the clouds, and in this way it should be possible to estimate the visibility of the runway from different points in the sky. Whether this model is close enough to the likely 'real' distribution of cloud cover is the crucial question. This could be at least partially assessed by having an aircraft fly past different points under known cloud conditions and then attempting to compare the actual visibility with that predicted by the model. If the model is found to be too simple, it can be further refined by, for example, using shapes closer to the actual shape of clouds. For instance, each cloud could be modelled as a set of overlapping circles (producing shapes that resemble Mickey Mouse's face in one form). Again, this refinement might be chosen because the geometry of circles is simple, and thus the model is tractable. In this way, the model may be gradually refined until it is adequate for its intended purpose. As with the ping-pong ball example, with this example and with real modelling in Management Science, the principle of parsimony has much to commend it.

Principle 3: divide and conquer, avoid mega-models

This is common advice given to anyone trying to understand how a complex system operates. Powell (1995) calls this decomposition, as well as divide and conquer. Howard Raiffa (1982, quoted in Miser and Quade, 1990b) has the following to say:

> Beware of general-purpose, grandiose models that try to incorporate practically everything. Such models are difficult to validate, to interpret, to calibrate statistically and, most importantly, to explain. You may be better off not with one big model but with a set of simpler models.

Raiffa's point is partially related to the first two principles above, but also relates to the need to build a model from components, each of which should be developed parsimoniously. In a way, this principle was implicit in our treatment of the ping-pong ball problem earlier in this chapter. We developed separate, extremely simple models of the room and of the balls themselves. Each could easily be understood and their relationship could be controlled.

As an example, consider a manufacturer of packaging items that wishes to provide a better service to its geographically scattered customers. One measure of this service is the proportion of orders that are met on time and in full. One way to tackle this is to build three separate models and to link them in order to help understand how to improve customer service:

1. A model of the demand for the main classes of product, showing the variation from day to day and by season and the growth trends. In essence, this is a standard time-series model.
2. A model of the production capacities for the range of products, allowing for different product mixes of the materials (e.g. bubble wrap) that form the items the manufacturer sells.

3. A model of the process by which stock may be allocated to customers, which depends on the priorities placed on particular orders and on the likely sizes of trailers available for distribution.

Case study: Lancaster Bus Company Dial-a-Bus

Consider the need to provide modelling support for the Lancaster Bus Company (LBC), which is planning a new Dial-a-Bus service to a number of satellite villages that cluster around a large town. The idea is that, instead of following a fixed route, the buses will respond to phone calls from potential passengers and will pick up and drop off as required – although within some overall timetable. LBC need to know how many buses to provide and what fare levels to charge so as to cover their costs (if they are a public utility) or to make a profit (if they are a private company). The temptation is to assume that some type of all-inclusive model, possibly a large simulation, is the way to approach this. But it might be better to develop a series of small models that link into one another.

To simplify matters here, suppose that other towns have attempted similar systems and that they are willing to talk to LBC about their experience. However, even though the managers of LBC have some detailed data from these towns, suppose that these were heavily subsidized pilot projects. This means that, although the LBC proposal has some similarities with services elsewhere, there are some important differences. To cope with this, suppose that LBC have conducted a survey among residents to see how likely individuals would be to use the service at different fare levels.

There are major differences between the LBC project and the earlier pilot projects, not least because the pilot projects were heavily subsidized in a way that LBC cannot do. However, it may be possible to model the actual demand recorded in the pilot projects in a way that has some relevance to the situation of LBC. One approach might be to collect socio-economic data from each of the pilot project towns. Examples might be car ownership, number of elderly people, total populations and so on. Analysis of these data, say in a linear regression model, might reveal that ridership (the proportion of people using the service) is related to one or more of these variables in the pilot projects. Hence, we have model 1: *ridership in pilot projects is a function of several variables*. For example:

$$\text{Ridership} = f(\text{car ownership, proportion of elderly})$$

If the same data were available for the villages in the study, then model 1 could be used to estimate the likely ridership of the LBC service if it were heavily subsidized. The resulting estimate could then be modified by model 2, the results of the price sensitivity survey. This is likely to show that, the higher the fares, the lower the actual ridership is likely to be. The model-1 estimate could be treated as if it were equivalent to the demand at a fare level at which all interested people would use the LBC service. Hence, we have model 2: *actual proportion of potential users at different fare levels*. For example:

$$\text{Proportion} = f(\text{fare levels})$$

This can now lead us to model 3, which might be related to the frequency of the service to be provided. The two extremes here would be the option of running just one circuit each day to each village and the opposite option of running entirely on demand. The greater the frequency, the greater will be the proportion of model-2 numbers willing and able to use the service. Thus, model 3 might be a financial spreadsheet that shows the sensitivity of the revenues and costs to service frequency, given different fare levels. Hence, we have model 3: *financial out-turn at different fare levels and frequencies*. For example:

$$\text{Net returns} = f \text{ (service frequency, ridership, proportion of users)}$$

Of course, these three simple models could be combined into a single model, but this would be a mistake for several reasons. First, there would be a significant loss of transparency. Each of the simple models is easy to understand and has implications that can easily be grasped by people. This is so important when it comes to persuading people that the results of a model are worth taking seriously. Another reason is that each model can be used for a sensitivity analysis. Different relationships could be tried, for example between potential ridership and socio-economic variables, and their effects should be clear.

Principle 4: use metaphors, analogies and similarities

Rather than being restricted to a direct consideration of the problem at hand, it can be helpful to try to get another perspective on things. This use of other perspectives should be distinguished from the use of a model to understand different viewpoints and interpretations. Here, the idea is that devices such as metaphors, analogies and related problems can be of great help in themselves. Morris (1967) recommended that modellers seek an analogy with some other system or an association with some earlier work. In seeking such an association, the modeller relies on her previous experience or stands on the shoulders of those who have gone before. In either case, the idea is to search for previous well-developed logical structures similar to the problem in hand.

Metaphors, analogies and similarities

In their early book on operations research, Ackoff and Sasieni (1968) devoted a chapter to the subject of modelling, which included a discussion of the use of analogue models within operations research. In such an analogue model, one property of the system is replaced with another property that is easier to represent or to manipulate. Thus, in an everyday example, hikers use maps that represent the physical property of altitude by the use of lines, or contours, on the map. Locations at the same altitude above sea level are linked by the contours, and an experienced map-reader may use them to gain a good impression of the physical terrain. Contours are used because they are more convenient than the obvious device of scaling the actual terrain on to the map in a relief form. Such a relief map would hardly be convenient on a hike, as its solid form would make it unwieldy.

Analogues of this type are sometimes employed in Management Science, although perhaps not as often as some introductory books might suggest. Cognitive mapping (see Chapter 6) is one example in which related concepts are drawn as a map in two dimensions. This makes their relationships visible, although it might be argued that such maps might be better represented in three or more dimensions as far as their relationships are concerned. This would, however, lose the convenience that comes from a two-dimensional map.

Analogies are also useful in modelling as an activity. A common, but misconceived, view of creativity is that it is the ability to conjure new ideas, apparently from nowhere. In practice, much creativity comes from realizing that ideas and notions developed gradually in one field can be usefully applied in another; that is, from seeing links that others have ignored or could not see. Saaty (1998) described this as deductive creativity. Saaty, however, was pleading for a new paradigm in which analysts employ what he termed inductive creativity, a deliberate attempt to look at experience and to induce a larger and more general system view of what is happening. We should thus strive to see a particular problem as merely an instance of a general case.

Another use for metaphors and analogies is to try to gain some insight into how a system may operate. In an example outside the world of Management Science, Gerrig and Banaji (1990) discuss this and mention some interesting experiments by Gentner and Gentner (1983). They took a group of people who were 'fairly naive about physical science' and tried to help them to understand some concepts of electricity. They did this by the use of two metaphors. The first was of water flows through pumps, valves and reservoirs. The second was of a moving crowd passing through locations at different rates. The water flow analogy helped the class to use their prior knowledge of pumps and reservoirs to understand about batteries, but it did not help them to understand resistors. The moving crowd analogy helped them to understand about resistors as if they were gates restricting the movement of people between two points, but it did not help with their understanding of batteries. They found that the proper use of analogy or metaphor aided the learning process, but that a badly chosen metaphor could slow things down. We may infer, therefore, that metaphors can be useful in developing learning if they are chosen properly.

Creativity, analogies and different viewpoints

One view of creativity is that it comes from the ability to associate apparently unrelated ideas. In his book on creativity in management science, Evans (1991) suggests several uses for metaphors and analogies. He quotes the early paper of Morris (1967) who also advocated the use of appropriate analogies in modelling. One approach that stresses analogies is synectics, in which analogies are used to examine an issue from different perspectives. For example, participants in synectics sessions are encouraged to use four types of analogy:

1. *Personal*. Participants are asked to imagine themselves within the problem being discussed: 'Now, if I were one of these widgets, I'd have been sitting on that shelf for hours while nothing much happened'. I sometimes encourage my students to devise better algorithms by getting them to imagine themselves as a bored computer that knows there must be a better way of doing things.
2. *Direct*. This is closer to the normal idea of analogies, as in Ackoff and Sasieni (1968), and asks participants to think of parallel situations from real life: 'Well, in some ways, the demands on emergency services are just a form of queuing system'. In this way, lessons from one system may be transferred to the analysis of another. This transfer may not be complete, but it may still spark off useful ideas and insights.
3. *Fantasy*. The idea is to be totally idealist and ask for the impossible. Just suppose ... What if ...: 'Just suppose goods could be delivered to customers instantaneously'. 'Just suppose whole-body scanning could be done with a portable device'. This approach encourages the modeller to find ways of getting from the current position towards some idealized state.
4. *Symbolic*. This is the use of a compressed description of the problem or of its possible solution. Gilhooly (1988) quotes Stein (1974, p. 189) about a group who used the idea of the Indian rope trick in developing a new jacking mechanism.

The idea of these analogies is to get people to take new views of things that might be too familiar or, at the opposite extreme, are not understood. In terms of Management Science modelling, this means trying to gain new insights that might lead to useful models.

Principle 5: do not fall in love with data

The model should drive the data, not vice versa

The availability of friendly computer packages has produced a generation hooked on data: data-junkies. I am not arguing that data and their analysis are unimportant and can be ignored. Rather, I observe that many students seem to imagine that modelling is impossible without data, preferably lots of them. They treat data as a form of Linus's blanket. They assume that, because a model is a representation of some system, examination of data from that system will reveal all that they need to construct the model. Such an assumption may be a mistake, even though exploratory data analysis is very useful, and I would not wish to return to the days before modern computer software appeared for this purpose. The slapdash use of exploratory data analysis can never replace careful thought and analysis.

Modelling should drive any data collection, and not the other way around. The modeller should think about the type of model that might be needed before attempting large-scale data collection. Conway *et al.* (1995) comment on the use of data in the discrete simulation of manufacturing systems, including the following assertion:

> *... you should resist the temptation, or the instructions, to collect real data with all the ingenuity you can muster. The collection process is much less valuable than you might think.*

Although this is an extreme view, it is a useful counter to the familiar greeting of the naive modeller to his client, 'Take me to your data'. Only after thinking about the model can the analyst know what type of data to collect.

Attitudes to data mark a key difference between mathematicians and management scientists. For example, it may be possible to develop a complex mathematical model of the production schedule in a factory. However, this will be of no value if it is impossible or horrendously expensive to collect the data needed to parameterize the model. Some compromise will be needed. Thus, Management Science modelling proceeds pragmatically; the modeller bears in mind what is possible as well as what is desirable.

In like mind, the ping-pong ball exercise did not begin by suggesting a data collection exercise. A common failing of students when learning about modelling is to insist that progress cannot be made unless there are some (or more) data available. Their assumption is that examination of the data will provide some clues to extend their understanding. This may well be a mistake, even though exploratory data analysis is a very valuable technique. Modern statistical software and spreadsheets enable the rapid plotting and summary of large amounts of data from which patterns may quickly be gleaned. Sometimes these patterns exist, but at other times they are, like beauty, in the eye of the beholder. Exploratory data analysis has much to commend it as an approach, but it is no substitute for careful thought and analysis.

Some of the dangers and pitfalls that await the unwary in their treatment of data are discussed below, but there is a fundamental point that should not be missed. This is that the model should drive the data, and not vice versa. This means that the analyst should try to develop some ideas of the model and its parameters and from this should think about the type of data that might be needed. One of the problems with some case-style teaching of business administration is that the cases are often intended to be self-contained. That is, the students know that all the data they may need are available in the papers issued with the case. This is quite unlike real life, in which data must be requested, justified and collected before they can be analysed. Data are not free, their collection has a cost, as does their interpretation and analysis.

How, then, should the use of data be linked into the parsimonious, gradual approach advocated earlier in this chapter? If circumstances permit, the best approach would be to develop a simple model and then to collect data to parameterize and test it. It may then be clear that the simple model is fine for the intended purpose, or it may be that the model needs to be refined – which may need more data or different data. These new data will have a cost that should enable some rough cost:benefit calculation to check whether their collection and analysis will be worthwhile. And so on, until some point is reached at which the costs outweigh the benefits.

Of course, these ideal circumstances may not pertain, and it may be necessary, especially when acting as a fee-charging external consultant, to set up a complete data collection exercise at the start of the work. If this can be resisted, then it would be a good idea to do so.

Data mining and data grubbing

'Data mining' entered the language of statisticians in the 1990s and refers to attempts to develop statistical models from available data using powerful computer packages that search for patterns. A debasement of this is data grubbing, which some use as a term of abuse for approaches in which many different data series are unthinkingly collected and then read by one of today's powerful statistical packages. These packages allow complicated analyses to be conducted on the data in a very short space of time. Regressions can be tried, linear and non-linear. Other types of multivariate plastic surgery can be applied to the data, such as transforming the original data series by taking logarithms and the like. Most worryingly, this can all be done very quickly by someone who knows very little about the statistical tools being used in the computer software. This is rather like an attempt to bake a cake by collecting ingredients that look interesting. These might then be mixed together until boredom sets in. The resulting melange is then popped into the oven, and we wait until the smoke appears. Cakes cooked in this way should only be given to people with whom scores need to be settled.

The original intention of statistical techniques such as regression was to investigate relationships that were thought to be plausible. Old-timers can recall having to compute regressions on mechanical calculators – which was hard work (this may be why so many older statisticians were of a slim build) and very slow. Hence, data grubbing was not a practical proposition – life was too short and the calculators were too unreliable. To stay sane, modellers of the earlier epochs would do a lot of hard thinking about possible relationships before embarking on multivariate analysis.

This criticism of data grubbing should not be interpreted as a call for a ban on friendly, powerful statistical packages. They are much too useful for that, and they take the drudgery out of statistical modelling. However, they should not be a substitute for thought. Also, just because data are available, it should not be assumed that they are useful.

Data are useful in model-building

This criticism of data grubbing and of a reliance on available data might be interpreted, wrongly, to imply that modelling is best carried out in an abstract way. It is certainly not the intention that data should be ignored in this way. It might therefore be helpful to divide data and information into three groups. First, there are preliminary or contextual data and information. Chapter 3, which discussed the nature of problems in Management Science, suggested that the What, Why, When, Where, How and Who questions of Kipling's 'honest working men' were a useful guide in preliminary investigation. Clearly, the results of these questions may be qualitative or quantitative. In the latter case it may be necessary to conduct significant analyses of the data thus produced. But these data are collected with a view to understanding more about the context of the problem, rather than the development of a detailed model. It is not unusual for this preliminary analysis to reveal enough insights for there to be no real need to take a project any further.

The second type of data are those that might need to be collected and analysed in order to develop the model in some detail. This is model parameterization, or model realization (Willemain, 1995). However, as will be repeatedly stated under the general heading of this fifth principle, the model structure should drive the data collection and analysis, not the other way around. The third type of data are discussed below under the heading 'Avoid using the same data to build and to test a model'.

Beware of data provided on a plate

An old adage among management information system professionals is that information is data plus interpretation. One feature of modern organizations is that computer systems collect almost every conceivable type of data about what is happening – except the data that you really need for a particular model. When taking data straight from a corporate information system (IS), one risks misinterpreting them. In this way, MIS information becomes misinformation. In today's global organizations, many people work in virtual teams, and this issue becomes particularly important. Just like liquids to be pumped, data put into an MIS are usually filtered and cleaned up. This filtering and cleaning may have such an effect that the data are of little use in analysis and modelling.

For modelling purposes, data are best ordered à la carte rather than table d'hôte. For example, in attempting to develop models for production control, it may be necessary to produce submodels of customer demands for the products being made. Most companies monitor their sales using data produced by the sales order processing systems that are used to take orders and issue invoices. The obvious way to get hold of demand data might be to take it from the customer order files, but there are at least three reasons why this might be a mistake. The first is that such systems often only record the actual despatches to customers, and this may be as much a reflection of the available finished stock as it is of the actual demand from customers. They may request one thing, but, if the company is unable to supply it, the customers may either go elsewhere or accept a substitute. The second reason is that, if the customers suspect that a required item is out of stock (in the light of past experience), they may not even request the item. Finally, the whole idea of implementing a new production system might be to make the company more attractive to customers who normally order from other suppliers. Hence, for all these reasons, the data from a sales order processing system might be treated with some caution.

As a second example, suppose a hospital wished to reduce its waiting lists and was proposing to model some aspects of its operation in order to decide whether to do so. Again, it might be thought that the best way to obtain data about patient referrals to the hospital would be to examine the referral database that contains information about actual referrals. As in the previous examples, these data might be very misleading for a number of reasons. The first is that other doctors who refer patients to the hospital may have a choice of hospitals to which they could refer and may make it their business to know how long the waiting lists are. Thus, they may choose to refer people to hospitals with shorter lists. Slightly more subtly, they may choose to refer to hospitals that they believe have shorter lists. A further point is that the waiting lists are a symptom of a problem, but are not the problem themselves. As doctors know, symptomatic or palliative treatment is given only when there are no other options; it is usually better to treat the underlying causes. Thus, it may be better to treat the waiting lists as outputs from a model rather than as inputs.

In these and other cases there may be no substitute for proper and well-organized data collection if a useful model is to be constructed. It may also be possible to take existing data and massage them in such a way as to account for some of their shortcomings. Thus, a small-scale data collection exercise might be used to reveal the discrepancies in the full, system-produced data, which may then be modified to take account of this. However, it must be borne in mind that such data massage implies that a model of the data themselves is being used as part of the modification process.

Data are just a sample

It is also important to remember that, in the vast majority of cases, data are just a sample of what could be used or might be available. This is true in a number of dimensions. First, the time dimension, this being the simplest to understand. When data are being used to build or to test a model, then those data will have been collected at a particular time and over a certain period. If we say that the data are believed to be representative, we are implying that they are representative of a larger population that displays some regularity through time. We are not expecting someone to come along later and surprise us with data that differ drastically from those that we have already obtained. Nevertheless, this may happen and is always a risk, which is clearest when we realize that the results of a model may be used to extrapolate into the future. The future may simply differ from the past; that is, the population from which the data sample comes may behave differently in the future.

Data are also a set of observations. This is the second aspect to note in the realization that data are a sample of what might be obtained given enough time and other resources. Any observation process is subject to errors of different types. Examples might include the following:

- Recording errors – for instance, a product code may be wrongly entered into a computer system. The risk of this can be reduced by careful checking, by proper training and also by the use of automatic devices such as bar codes, which may be read as the item passes a scanner.
- Transcription and analysis errors – for instance, when data are transferred from one system to another or are aggregated in some way. Sales data compressed into monthly slots may mislead if the sales actually show in-week variation.

Hence it is reasonable to be very sceptical about data, especially if they are readily available.

Avoid using the same data to build and to test a model

Most models used in Management Science make use of data in one form or another. The model, as illustrated in the ping-pong example, has parameters that must be given values. This process of parameterization is usually based on data, whether specially collected or generally available. The trap to avoid, if possible, is the use of the same data to parameterize the model and then to

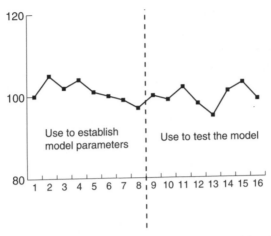

Figure 4.4 Data for model parameterization and model testing.

test it. As an example, suppose that a company wishes to understand the sales pattern for one of its products. Careful data collection proceeds, and they eventually have a time series of their weekly sales over the last 2 years. A management scientist then develops a forecasting model that is intended to suggest how sales might behave, given certain assumptions, over the next few months. The idea is that the model might be used, say, monthly, each time with an updated data series, to suggest likely future sales.

There are several types of forecasting model that could be employed, most based on the analysis of historical data. Under skilful hands, computer programs are used to estimate the parameters of equations that lead to a model that is a good fit to the recent historical data. The goodness of fit can be expressed in standard statistical terms and is always an evaluation of the degree to which the model fits the historical data. It is also important, where possible, to test how well the model predicts what might happen in the future. A tempting short-cut is to quote the goodness-of-fit statistic from the parameterization exercise, but this might be a mistake. A better approach, as shown in Figure 4.4, is to divide the available data into two sets. The earlier data are used to parameterize the model, and then the second set is used to test the model. This test set has not been used in the parameterization and is being used as a surrogate future. Goodness-of-fit measures can be used to assess how well the model predicts this surrogate future.

Principle 6: model-building may feel like muddling through

Most Management Science models are would-be representations of the real works that are built so that action may be taken or understanding may be increased. As these are rational artefacts, it might be thought that model-building is a linear and highly rational process. There have been few attempts to investigate this issue as it relates to Management Science, but the evidence suggests that model-building is not a linear process, nor is it classically rational (see Chapter 2). Instead, people seem to 'muddle through', making use of insights, perhaps taking time away from the modelling, trying to look at things from different perspectives and so on. This does not, of course, imply that modelling must be done this way, but it may well indicate how successful analysts actually operate.

How expert modellers work

A fascinating attempt to investigate this issue is reported by Willemain (1994, 1995). He gained the cooperation of a group of 12 experienced modellers, a mixture of practitioners and academics. All had completed graduate study in Management Science, and they averaged 15 years of experience since finishing graduate school. They were not, in any sense, novices. The first paper (Willemain, 1994) summarizes what the modellers said when given the chance to describe themselves, to express their views on their own approaches to modelling, to say what experience they had in modelling and to capture something important in a short, personal modelling story. Their self-descriptions and experience showed them to work mainly in areas in which they 'pursue specific objectives towards fundamental changes in complex, existing systems'. They claimed to 'develop a unique model for each problem, though all their models involve extensive computation'. From this we can conclude that their work could in no way be described as 'airy-fairy', for their concerns seem down to earth.

Of their approach to actually building and developing models, Willemain (1994) summarizes their responses thus: they 'develop their models, not in one burst, but over an extended period of time marked by heavy client contact'. Also, they are 'guided by analogies, drawing and doodling, they develop more than one alternative model, in each case starting small and adding'. Thus, many of their claimed approaches are a good fit with the other principles of modelling discussed in this chapter. They are very different from the idea that a modeller just sits down in a quiet place and writes some equations until the model is complete. It seems as if models are developed in fits and starts, and that client interaction is part of this.

In a second paper, Willemain (1995) reports an experiment with the same 12 people who were given modelling tasks and were asked to think aloud as they spent 60 minutes figuring out how best to develop suitable models. This is clearly an artificial task for two reasons. First, it compresses their activity into just 60 minutes, when their expressed preference was to work 'over an extended period of time'. Second, the request to think aloud as they worked might distort their normal patterns of work. There can be no certainty that their talking accurately reflected their thinking; however, in spite of these reservations, analysis of taped transcriptions reveals some interesting things.

To analyse the transcriptions, Willemain (1995) classifies their concerns under the following headings:

- *The problem context*, which he relates to problem structuring as defined by Pidd and Woolley (1980). That is, the process of gaining a sufficient understanding of the problem to proceed to some form of formal modelling.
- *The model structure*, which he takes to be the process of deciding what category of model to use and of analysing data prior to actually building it.
- *The model realization*, which is the process of parameter estimation for the model and/or the calculation of results.
- *Model assessment*, which is deciding whether the model will be valid, usable and acceptable to a client.
- *Model implementation*, which is working with the client so as to gain some value from the model.

The tapes show that about 60% of the modellers' time was devoted to considering model structure, which many would regard as the core of model-building. About 30% of the time was divided equally between concerns about problem context and model assessment, with similar time spent on each issue. Only 10% was devoted to model realization, and almost none to questions of implementation.

As the study gave the modellers just 60 minutes to work on a problem, it should be no surprise that so little time was devoted to model realization or implementation. But what is significant is that so much time was spent on thinking about problem context and model assessment. What is also very important is the fact that the time spent on these three major concerns was scattered through the modelling session. The modeller kept picking up a concern for a while, dropping it and then returning to it. Presumably this would be even more marked were it possible to follow how they operated over a much longer time period in their 'real' work.

Links with the other principles

Perhaps it is an exaggeration to say that modellers muddle through. However, it is equally an exaggeration to assert that modelling proceeds as a linear step-by-step process. It did not in Willemain's study, and it probably does not in most of our experience. The other principles presented here should be used to provide some order to the muddling through. It is quite normal for a modeller to think in parallel while working on a model. Discussing ill-defined problem-solving in general, Holyoak (1990) discusses how people tend to operate in parallel lines of thought and how they are continuously restructuring their ideas. A concern to understand the problem context goes hand in hand with a desire to produce a model that will be useful, as well as technically correct.

Summary

This chapter serves as a bridge between the general, fundamental ideas of Chapters 1 to 3, which underpin rational modelling. It discusses different ways in which models are used and introduces a few simple principles for modelling, as follows:

1. *Model simple, think complicated.* There is no need for the model to be as complicated as the system being modelled, for the model will have been built with some intended use in mind. It is, however, very important that the model is critically evaluated and subject to rigorous thought.
2. *Be parsimonious, start small and add.* Rather than attempting to build a complete model from scratch, it is much better to proceed gradually, preferably from some outline model towards one that becomes realistic enough and valid enough for the purpose in hand.
3. *Divide and conquer, avoid mega-models.* In some ways this is an extension of the principle of parsimony. The idea is that it can be much better to build small, relatively self-contained, models that can easily be understood than to aim for an all-inclusive model that has little hope of being used.
4. *Use metaphors, analogies and similarities.* Try to think about new things using whatever insights that previous experience may bring. One very useful way of doing this is to imagine yourself as part of the system being modelled.
5. *Do not fall in love with data.* This principle covers many possible sins of omission and commission. The basic idea is that the conceptual model should drive the data collection and analysis, and not the other way around. Data are no substitutes for careful and critical thought.
6. *Model building may feel like muddling through.* Nobody should imagine that modelling as an activity is one in which smooth progress is made and in which everything fits neatly together. Instead, most experienced modellers jump from topic to topic while modelling and need to keep refining their ideas. But they enjoy it and produce something useful!

References

Ackoff R.L. and Sasieni M.W. (1968) *Fundamentals of Operations Research.* John Wiley & Sons, Inc., New York, NY.

Ashby R. (1956) *An Introduction to Cybernetics.* Chapman and Hall, London, UK.

Conway R, Maxwell W.L., McClain J.O. and Worona S.L. (1995) *User's Guide to XCELL Plus: Factory Modeling System, Release 4.0.* Scientific Press, Palo Alto, CA.

Day P.R. and Ryan D.M. (1997) Flight attendant rostering for short-haul airline operations. *Operations Research*, **45**(5), 649–661.

Evans J.R. (1991) *Creative Problem Solving in the Decision and Management Sciences.* South Western Publishing, Cincinnati, OH.

Gentner D. and Gentner D.R. (1983) Flowing waters or teeming crowds: mental models of electricity, in *Mental Models*, ed. by Gentner D. and Stevens A.L. Lawrence Erlbaum, Hillsdale, NJ.

Gerrig R.J. and Banaji M.R. (1990) Language and thought, in *Thinking and Problem Solving*, ed. by Sternberg R.J. Academic Press, San Diego, CA.

Gilhooly K.J. (1988) *Thinking: Directed, Undirected and Creative*, 2nd edition. Academic Press, London, UK.

Holyoak K.J. (1990) Problem solving, in *An Invitation to Cognitive Science.* Vol. 3. *Thinking*, ed. by Osherson D.N. and Smith E.S. MIT Press, Cambridge, MA.

Little J.D.C. (1970) Managers and models: the concept of a decision calculus. *Management Science*, **16**, B466–B485.

Miller G. (1956) The magical number seven, plus or minus two: some limits on our capacity for processing information. *The Psychological Review*, **63**, 81–97.

Miser H.J. and Quade E.S. (1990a) Validation, in *Handbook of Systems Analysis: Craft Issues and Procedural Choices*, ed. by Miser H.J. and Quade E.S. John Wiley & Sons, Ltd, Chichester, UK.

Miser H.J. and Quade E.S. (1990b) Analytic strategies and their components, in *Handbook of Systems Analysis: Craft Issues and Procedural Choices*, ed. by Miser H.J. and Quade E.S. John Wiley & Sons, Ltd, Chichester, UK.

Morris W.T. (1967) On the art of modelling. *Management Science*, **13**(12), B707–B717.

Pidd M. (1998) *Computer Simulation in Management Science*, 4th edition. John Wiley & Sons, Ltd, Chichester, UK.

Pidd M. and Woolley R.N. (1980) A pilot study of problem structuring. *Journal of the Operational Research Society*, **31**, 1063–1069.

Powell S.G. (1995) The teacher's forum: six key modeling heuristics. *Interfaces*, **25**(4), 114–125.

Raiffa H. (1982) *Policy Analysis: A Checklist of Concerns*, PP-82-2. International Institute for Applied Systems Analysis, Laxenburg, Austria.

Saaty T.L. (1998) Reflections and projections on creativity in operations research and management science: a pressing need for a shifting paradigm. *Operations Research*, **46**(1), 9–16.

Starfield A.M., Smith K.A. and Bleloch A.L. (1990) *How to Model It: Problem Solving for the Computer Age.* McGraw-Hill, New York, NY.

Stein M. (1974) *Stimulating Creativity, Vol. 1.* Academic Press, London, UK.

Willemain T.R. (1994) Insights on modelling from a dozen experts. *Operations Research*, **42**(2), 213–222.

Willemain T.R. (1995) Model formulation: what experts think about and when. *Operations Research*, **43**(6), 916–932.

PART II
INTERPRETIVE MODELLING – SOFT MANAGEMENT SCIENCE

Introduction

Management Science (MS), or Operational Research (OR), first appeared in World War II (Waddington, 1973; Morse, 1986) as a way of harnessing rigorous scientific method in pursuit of victory in wartime. Its first practitioners were mainly physical scientists, engineers and mathematicians whose training in observation, experimentation and analysis enabled them to develop better strategies and tactics, rather than just better weapons. At the end of the war, many of its practitioners returned to their earlier academic work, but some were recruited to develop OR and MS in business and government. A few found their way into universities to develop academic programmes in OR/MS.

During the 1960s, the first OR/MS textbooks were written to meet the demand for training in the subject, and these established a pattern in which OR/MS was taught as quantitative analysis in support of decision-making. Thus, in many people's minds, OR/MS is a set of mathematical and statistical techniques of the type introduced in Part III of this book. These methods grew popular for two reasons. First, they were found useful, and there are many cases describing their application in journals such as *Interfaces*, a publication of the US-based Institute for OR and Management Science (INFORMS). Second, although understanding and using the techniques may require some mathematical and statistical sophistication, they are easy to package in a book or course, at least at an introductory level.

There are, though, many different views of OR/MS, and some of them are discussed in Pidd (1995), which presents six different views found in the literature:

1. *OR/MS as decision mathematics.* In this view the job of the analyst is to develop one or more decision models based on the type of rationality captured in Figure 2.1. The resulting models and techniques rely on a view that organizations can be viewed as machines, as discussed by Morgan (1986).
2. *OR/MS as optimization.* This is an extension of the first image above, with a belief that OR/MS is characterized by optimization methods of the type introduced in Chapter 9.
3. *OR/MS as problem-solving.* This is an appealing idea, but, as discussed in Chapter 3, it rests on a view of problems and problem-solving that may not be defendable. Properly defined, though, the idea of problem-solving is certainly useful.
4. *OR/MS as Management Science.* This is a term much used in this book, but many would argue that it is an oxymoron – like deafening silence, a contradictory combination of two words that would be meaningful on their own. However, in a more restricted sense, it can be a helpful idea if used to indicate a scientific outlook.

5. *OR/MS as a systems perspective*. Chapter 5 discusses this idea in much more detail. In essence it rests on a view that the world is, or can be viewed as, a set of interacting systems. In this view, analysis must begin by an attempt to understand those interactions.
6. *OR/MS as intervention and change*. This view is exemplified in the SODA (Strategic Options Development and Analysis) approaches of Eden and colleagues in Chapter 6. It is based on a view that OR/MS is about helping organizations and individuals to reflect on what they do, and to make appropriate changes.

Which of these views is correct? In some sense, all are correct and all are wrong, for each one presents part of the rich picture that OR/MS has come to be. Once we move beyond a view that OR/MS is about optimization and on to views 3 and 6, it becomes clear that we need methods that offer more than mathematics.

Soft methods

This book takes a view of rationality rather wider than simple (or even complicated) mathematics, and Part II assumes that different people may share the same experience and yet may interpret it in quite different ways. Thus, just as quantitative models may be used to demonstrate the effect of different policies, so other types of model may be used to explore the consequences of different ways of seeing the world. This is particularly important when operating at levels above the merely operational, where the issue is not so much about how to do something as about what should be done. That is, there is more of a concern with ends than with means, for in strategic analysis it is quite normal for people to argue and debate from different presuppositions. As this part of the book tries to make clear, modelling approaches can help people to understand one another's viewpoints and can help a disparate group develop a commitment to sensible action. This is important in tackling what Rittel called 'wicked problems' (Rittel and Webber, 1973) that have to be tamed before they can be solved.

Therefore, this part is concerned with describing two approaches that are often regarded as exemplars of 'soft operational research'. These two approaches, soft systems methodology (Checkland, 1981) and SODA/cognitive mapping (Eden and Ackermann, 2001; Eden, Jones and Sims, 1983) were developed in the belief that exploring the consequences of people's perceptions is crucial, especially in circumstances where there may be disagreement about objectives. Some writers – notably Rosenhead (1989) and Rosenhead and Mingers (2001a) – regard these approaches, especially soft systems methodology and SODA/cognitive mapping, as formal approaches to problem-structuring. As is made clear in Chapter 3, the term 'problem-structuring' is often used in two different ways. The first use envisages problem-structuring as a prelude to more formal, usually mathematical modelling. Thus, the idea is to understand the context before attempting detailed modelling. The second use regards problem-structuring as an end in itself, the idea being to help participants find their own way through the mess they are tackling.

Unlike the mathematical methods introduced in Part III, there is an essential link between the content of soft methods and the way, or process, in which they are used. Their use requires the analyst to operate in a mode rather different from that of the technological expert. The idea of the methods is that they should be used to help individuals and groups to think through the consequences of their beliefs and preferences. They are thus ways in which the analyst may facilitate this, by recording what people say or claim and playing this back to them inside a formal structure. The formal structures of the 'soft' methods provide a language to talk about these things, and may also take some of the heat out of a conflict-ridden situation by forcing the debate to operate at a different level of abstraction. In essence, they may separate a viewpoint from its advocate. The soft models are partial interpretations of how an individual or group believes things to be. This does not mean that the analyst must collude with someone whose views of the world may be clearly ludicrous. Rather, the idea is to open people's interpretations to a more public scrutiny. Needless to say, this must be done with tact and care.

Soft versus hard

Several places in this book have used the term 'soft' in contrast to the word 'hard', and it is important to unpack this a little. Checkland (1981) devotes considerable space to this question, as do Rosenhead and Mingers (2001b), and, rather than duplicate that effort, a slightly different approach will be taken here. The following discussion covers some of the main differences between 'hard' and 'soft' approaches, although it must be borne in mind that the discussion is intended to isolate the distinctions between two stereotypes and that there are many shades in between.

Problem definition

First, soft approaches begin with the assumption that problem definition is not straightforward but is itself problematic. As discussed in Chapter 2, problems are social or psychological constructs that are the result of framing and naming (Schön, 1982). This contrasts with the view, common in engineering, that work begins once a need is established. Thus, as mentioned before, in soft analysis, the work focuses on ends as well as means to those ends. Soft approaches are based on an assumption that people's perceptions of the world will vary and that their preferences may also differ. Thus, it is important to try to understand the different ways in which the different stakeholders may frame the issues being addressed in the study.

As an example, in the TICTOC case introduced in Chapter 2, we saw, in Chapter 3, that there are internal and external stakeholders, and these may each frame the issues somewhat differently. Soft approaches see problem definition as multifaceted – much as a jewel has facets that sparkle in the light and that create different appearances from different angles. Thus, soft approaches are pluralistic in their assumptions about problem-structuring. Linked to this, they must therefore assume that problem definition is not straightforward in many cases but will only emerge through debate and discussion. Chapter 2 discussed Simon's idea of procedural rationality, which stresses the incomplete search for options and data. Soft approaches are attempts to provide procedurally rational support as people consider how best to structure and frame the issues they face.

The nature of organizational life

Second, soft approaches do not take the nature of organizations for granted. In particular, they do not assume that organizations are just 'human machines' in which people are organized according to their functions, all of which are geared to some unitary objective. Instead, they assume that people may, rightly or wrongly, fight their own corner rather than be subsumed into some overarching objective. Thus, these approaches make different assumptions about the nature of organizations.

The soft systems methodology (SSM) of Checkland is based on the assumption that human activity systems are a useful way of thinking about organizations. Thus, SSM takes a systems view of organizations. On the other hand, the SODA I approach developed by Eden and his colleagues is individualistic, as it focuses on how individual people see their world. In doing so, it takes account of the fact that people behave politically within organizations. Neither assumes that an organization is a machine that grinds on regardless of the people who compose it. Instead, both focus on helping the humans who work in organizations to find the improvements and policies they seek.

Models as representations

Third, hard and soft approaches differ in the view they take of models themselves. In a hard approach, it is typically assumed that a model is a would-be representation of part of the real world. It is accepted that the model will be a simplification and an abstraction of the real world, and hence it is important to consider whether it is a valid representation. In this view it is vital that the model is properly representational, and its operation must therefore be validated against the part of the real world being modelled. If the model is found not to be a suitably accurate representation, it is regarded as poor and in need of improvement.

By contrast, in soft approaches, the idea is that models are developed so as to allow people to think through their own positions and to engage in debate with others about possible action. Thus, the main concern is that the models should be useful in doing this and in supporting the cyclic nature of their supporting methodologies. This does, of course, raise the question of whether any old model will do in soft OR/MS. The methods introduced in Part II certainly do require the analyst to take great care in seeking models that participants find helpful in mapping out the world as they see it and in coming to terms with inconsistencies and misinterpretations. It is, though, true that the question of validation is problematic for soft models. In what sense can confidence be placed in the model if the main criterion is its immediate utility?

Outcome as product or as learning

The final feature of these soft approaches is that they stress the importance of organizational and individual learning. They do not guarantee that a set of recommendations, or a definite product (such as computer software), will emerge for a project. They stress that, when people face problematic situations, this is a chance for them to learn how to cope with such circumstances in such a way that their performance is improved. This does not mean that there will be no tangible product or recommendation from such a project, but this may only emerge gradually as a consequence of the learning that occurs. Hence, exponents of soft methods tend to present the approaches as, in some sense, cyclic and as part of an ongoing stream of organizational life. They are closer to the view, expounded by Langley *et al.* (1995), that this stream of issues may, at times, deposit decisions and new systems on the banks as it flows past. The aim is to find ways of operating with this rather dynamic and loosely structured view of organizational life.

Complementarity

What about mixing methods and methodologies (Gill and Mingers, 1997)? Can hard and soft approaches be mixed? The immediate answer must be yes, because people do every day. However, like mixing alcoholic drinks, this should be done with care if the after-effects are not to be worse than anticipated. If soft methods are kept under control as problem-structuring approaches, then it is clear that they are likely to be used in conjunction with hard approaches when that is appropriate. For example, if a problem-structuring exercise using SODA or SSM reveals that physical distribution depots need to be resited and delivery vehicles should be rerouted, then some of the heuristic methods discussed in Chapter 11 will come into play. However, there are times when it may be impossible to combine soft and hard approaches. This is, perhaps, most likely when both consultant and client are expecting some hard OR/MS to take place but neither has a world-view that allows the use of soft approaches as well. The opposite may also be true, for an overemphasis on the human side of decision-making may make it impossible to convince people that hard methods are of value.

However, it is important to realize that even the hard modelling approaches of Part III can be used in a non-normative way. For instance, the decision trees introduced in Chapter 2 need not be regarded as models of how the world is. Instead, they can be used as tools to investigate how people see the world so as gradually to build confidence about a course of action. The same is true of optimization and heuristic approaches, although their complexity can make this rather difficult. The emergence of visual interactive modelling systems in computer simulation has enabled much small-scale simulation modelling to be done in this way. That is, the model is built to enable people to explore possible decisions in a highly interactive way.

Thus, the question of whether hard and soft methods should be combined is one that can only be answered in the context of a particular intervention by particular people. But it should certainly be encouraged (Pidd, 2004). With this in mind, Part II has two further chapters introducing methods that are often regarded as useful links between hard and soft approaches: system dynamics (Chapter 7) and decision analysis (Chapter 8). Both approaches have an underpinning set of assumptions that are rooted in the world of hard Management Science, but their success in practice depends upon skills and insights from the world of soft Management Science.

References

Checkland P.B. (1981) *Systems Thinking, Systems Practice*. John Wiley & Sons, Ltd, Chichester, UK.
Eden C.L. and Ackermann F. (2001) SODA – the principles, in *Rational Analysis for a Problematic World Revisited*, ed. by Rosenhead J.V. and Mingers J. John Wiley & Sons, Ltd, Chichester, UK.
Eden C.L., Jones S. and Sims D. (1983) *Messing about in Problems*. Pergamon Press, Oxford, UK.
Gill A. and Mingers J. (eds) (1997) *Multimethodology*. John Wiley & Sons, Ltd, Chichester, UK.
Langley A., Mintzberg H., Pitcher P., Posada E. and Saint-Macary J. (1995) Opening up decision making: the view from the black stool. *Organizational Science*, **6**(3), 260–279.
Morgan G. (1986) *Images of Organisation*. Sage, London, UK.
Morse P.M. (1986) The beginning of operations research in the United States. *Operations Research*, **34**(1), 10–17.
Pidd M. (1995) Pictures from an exhibition: images of operational research. *European Journal of Operational Research*, **81**, 479–488.

Pidd M. (ed) (2004) *Systems Modelling: Theory and Practice.* John Wiley & Sons, Ltd, Chichester, UK.

Rittel H.W.J. and Webber M.M. (1973) Dilemmas in a general theory of planning. *Policy Science*, **4**, 155–169.

Rosenhead J.V. (ed.) (1989) *Rational Analysis for a Problematic World.* John Wiley & Sons, Ltd, Chichester, UK.

Rosenhead J.V. and Mingers J. (eds) (2001a) *Rational Analysis for a Problematic World Revisited.* John Wiley & Sons, Ltd, Chichester, UK.

Rosenhead J.V. and Mingers J. (eds) (2001b) A new paradigm of analysis, in *Rational Analysis for a Problematic World Revisited*, ed. by Rosenhead J.V. and Mingers J. John Wiley & Sons, Ltd, Chichester, UK.

Schön D.A. (1982) *The Reflective Practitioner. How Professionals Think in Action.* Basic Books, New York, NY.

Waddington C.H. (1973) *O.R. in World War 2: Operational Research against the U-boat.* Elek, London, UK.

5 Soft systems methodology

Background

The term 'system' is in common use, and few people think about its meaning when, for example, speaking of their digestive system or nervous system. Similarly, we speak of transport systems, economic systems, systems of government, the Solar System, mechanical systems and computer systems. In some ways, the word 'system' has become so commonplace that it has almost lost its meaning. We generally use the term to describe something in which we are taking an interest and whose behaviour we wish to study. This chapter will develop a much tighter definition in its coverage of Checkland's soft systems methodology (SSM). It seems that the ideas that are usually included under the banner of 'systems approaches' originated in the study of biological and mechanical systems. Later, they were applied to Management Science, but this required some significant modification.

Checkland (1981) discusses the development of SSM and describes its development from a realization that 'hard' systems analysis was of limited use. Having worked for about 20 years, latterly as a senior manager, Checkland could see few points at which 'hard' systems analysis had been, or could have been, of value to him. This worry was increased by the term 'Management Science', for he could see little in Management Science that justified the use of the word 'science'. When he moved to academic life at Lancaster University, he set out to see if it would be possible to develop other systems approaches that could be of demonstrable value to managers. SSM evolved through a process of action research in which analysts tackled real-world problems and reflected on their success or failure in doing so. SSM was developed by trying things out, generalizing from these experiences and communicating the results to other people. It was not devised by people sitting in a detached place, observing what other people did and then suggesting how they might do better.

The main text on SSM is Checkland's own (Checkland, 1981, 1999). In addition, readers may also wish to look at Checkland and Scholes (1990), which addresses some of the criticisms levelled at Checkland's 1981 account of the approach. Checkland and Poulter (2006) deals less with the theory of SSM and more with its practical application. Other books of possible interest are Wilson (1984, 2001), mainly concerned with the application of SSM rather than with its justification, and Checkland and Holwell (1997), which uses SSM to think through aspects of information system development.

A slightly different perspective on similar issues is to be found in Vickers (1983), who was concerned with more than the development of a methodology. Vickers discusses how the development of ideas that first emerged in biology can be used, after modification, in the world of human systems. Indeed, both he and Checkland show how the careful use of systems ideas can be of great value in helping people to manage and govern themselves better. Equally, both of them are insistent that the inappropriate use of some systems ideas can do great harm. Rather like the old joke – 'How do porcupines make love?'. Answer: 'Carefully' – so must the user of systems ideas take great care. A useful, gentle critique of systems views is given by Morgan (1986), who places systems ideas alongside other ways of understanding the workings of organizations and the people within them.

Systems, wholes and holons

As discussed earlier, the term 'system' is often used casually, and this can create problems when trying to think carefully about systems methodologies. There are many books and papers that devote considerable space to defining what is meant by system, examples being Ackoff (1971), von Bertalanffy (1971) and Boulding (1956).

General characteristics of systems

For present purposes, any system is taken to have four characteristics:

1. *Boundaries*. Some things are inside the system, others – constituting the environment of the system – are not. Note, though, that the boundary may not be obvious. Where, for example, is the boundary of the system that we call a human being? Is it the skin? Does it include clothes? What about body odours?
2. *Components*. More than a single element is contained within the boundary. A boundary that contains nothing is not a system, and nor is a boundary that contains a single element.
3. *Internal organization*. The elements are organized in some way or other and are not just chaotic aggregations.
4. *Behaviour*. The system is recognized as such because it has properties that belong to it as a system and that do not come just from its individual components.

Thus, a human nervous system has a boundary – the extent of the body; it has components that can be studied, damaged and, sometimes, repaired; it has an internal organization, which causes enormous problems if damaged; and its behaviour can be observed. As a second, inanimate example, the CPU of a computer has a boundary defined by its physical extent; it contains components, including millions of transistors etched into silicon; it is organized – the transistors are not randomly etched into the silicon; and it behaves, it receives requests and instructions and it performs the required operations.

One part of the study of a system is to consider the component parts of that system and their organization, what Vickers (1983) terms 'the internal relations of the whole'. These internal components interact with one another and may themselves be considered as systems. Thus, a production control system may include computer programs, computer hardware, shop-floor data capture instruments, the people who operate the system and the set of rules that define its operation. To study a system, we need to investigate its components and their organization and relationships.

Human activity systems

SSM developed as a way to use systems ideas within human organizations to help human beings make changes and understand their effects. Thus, SSM is concerned with human activity systems, which have a number of further characteristics:

1. *They are open systems*. The system boundary is permeable in both directions, and there is communication and interaction across the boundary. The cross-boundary exchanges constitute the external relations of the system.

2. *They include human activity.* What people do and how they do it are prime concerns of SSM. It follows from this that human activity systems are dynamic as a result of human action.
3. *They include human intent.* People are not just machines that do things. What they do has meaning and significance for the individuals and groups concerned. Why people do things is often at least as important as what they do and how they do it.
4. *They have a limited life.* They are not eternal, and their life may be quite short.
5. *They are self-regulating.* A process of regulation, control or governance, which maintains it through time, is a characteristic of an open system. Such systems may be in equilibrium, but this stability is not the same as stasis.

These five further characteristics are very important, for they point to why simple-minded attempts to apply systems ideas in human organizations often come to grief.

A production control system will, sensibly, be regarded as a human activity system because it has the latter five characteristics. It exchanges information with other systems, both within and outside the organization – for example, those for buying raw materials and those for stocking finished goods. It includes human activity; indeed, it exists to support humans in deciding how much of a product to make and when to make it. It includes human intent, for it is typically based on assumptions about lean production or the need to satisfy customer needs. Further, a properly designed production control system has a limited life and must be scrapped or improved if it is no longer fit for purpose. Finally, it will include its own performance monitoring so that its operational success can be evaluated. Like all human activity systems, such a production control system will have been designed with a purpose in mind, against which its performance can be monitored.

Human activity systems are soft systems

Checkland's approach carries the title 'soft systems methodology' for two reasons. The first is that human activity systems are 'soft' in some of the senses in which the term is used in the introduction to Part II.

The question of what lies within and outside a system boundary is rarely straightforward in human activity systems and must be negotiated, discussed and agreed. This is all part of the idea of problem-framing introduced in Chapter 3 when discussing the dangers of oversimplification and overelaboration. When we frame a set of issues for consideration, we focus on some in considerable detail, but we simplify or even omit others. Human activity systems are not fully defined entities on whose precise characteristics everyone will agree. Instead, the components to be included in an analysis of a human activity system are the subjects of debate. As will become clear later, the assumptions from which the system derives should be a major determinant of what should be included.

The behaviour of a human activity system is also soft because it, too, may be construed by different people in quite different ways. Consider, for example, the financial control systems in many universities. In the UK at least, most universities have very little or no free cash and must run a tight financial ship. To the university's finance director, the financial control system is a way of ensuring that there is enough money throughout the funding year and that it is legitimately spent. The behaviour of the university that the finance director observes through the financial control system is one that measures income and expenditure. However, the behaviour of the university that students see and experience consists of their day-to-day contact with staff and other students and their use of facilities. A university may be seen as successful in financial terms but as unsuccessful in terms of the learning that students experience. Both are legitimate ways of describing the behaviour of a university. As a further example, what is the function of a prison? Is it to punish, to reform, or what? The anarchist Kropotkin (1927) wrote: 'Have not prisons – which kill all will and force of character in man, which enclose within their walls more vices than are met with on any other spot of the globe – always been universities of crime?'. Surely, not the original intention for prisons?

In a similar vein, it is especially true that human intent forces us to regard systems as soft. It is not always possible to infer people's intentions by observing their behaviour. This is partly because people may deliberately disguise their intentions, but also because the same activity may be carried out for quite different reasons, and the observer may simply misunderstand what is happening. This is a perennial problem in anthropology, particularly in ethnology, in which the behaviour of individuals and groups is observed with a view to understanding what is happening. This understanding will always be incomplete unless the observer has access to the set of assumptions and goals within which activity is conducted.

As mentioned earlier, human activity systems differ from biological systems because they have been created and designed by humans. Their behaviour and stability is a consequence of that design. By contrast, biological and ecological systems come into being as a result of happy accident (for atheists) or divine intervention (for believers). Their stability is a pleasing result of their interaction with the world around them. Therefore, in human activity systems, the question of system design is a central issue, as neither accident nor divine intervention is invoked. Sadly, human activity systems are not always well designed. There are, for example, many examples of production control systems that turned out to be useless, in spite of massive expenditure. This is often because the design has concentrated on computer hardware, software and control algorithms, sometimes at the expense of any real thought about how the system would be used and about its consequences for the rest of the organization. The same is true of many computer-based management information systems.

Thus, in human activity systems, design is a key feature. The criteria that will guide the design will often be a subject of great debate and even of some controversy. For example, is this to be a system that will 'guarantee ex-stock delivery on the next working day'? Or is it to be one that 'meets customer requirements, where these include guaranteed ex-stock delivery on the next working day'? A key feature of SSM is that it aims to provide a way for those involved in a human system to address its design and the criteria that will guide it.

Do human activity systems exist?

This may seem a strange question, but it is a very important one to face. Is the world actually composed of interacting sets of entities that combine to create systems? Or is the notion of a system simply a convenient way of describing the world? In the final analysis, we simply do not know. We do know that people, ourselves included, experience a world separate from themselves – of that we can be sure. However, we have no really effective way of ensuring that our own perception of the external world is the accurate one and that others are wrong. In a sense, objectivity can be regarded as a consequence of different people agreeing that their perceptions are similar. They could, of course, all be wrong (see Janis, 1972, on groupthink), but our confidence tends to increase as others agree with us.

In this chapter, we start from the viewpoint that the real world can be usefully regarded as being composed of systems of interacting entities. This allows us to accept that the question of system definition is at least partially arbitrary. That is, we define a system because we are looking for something, and the notion of a system provides some way of explaining what we have observed. For instance, were we to arrive at a subway station as aliens from another planet, we would probably try to understand what was going on by noting the different entities (passengers, trains, station, tracks and so on), how they interact and why they do so. But our description of this system would be somewhat different from that given by the person responsible for the subway network as a whole. In the sense in which this notion was introduced in Chapter 3, we employ our existing schemata to make sense of what we experience. Thus, our own position as observer cannot be ignored when considering the whole question of system definition.

Therefore, to understand SSM, we must add to our notion of human activity systems the idea that systems are artefacts. They are useful creations of the human mind. There is no need to argue that the world is systemic, we need only argue that it is useful to envisage it as a set of interconnected systems. Furthermore, different people may define a system in quite different ways, and each may be, in some sense, correct. Consider, for example, a student bar. Is this: a pleasant place for students to socialize, a money machine for the brewery, a way of the university making money from its students, a useful service to summer conference visitors, a den of iniquity or something else? Each of these stereotypes is a way of describing a student bar, and each may, in some sense, be regarded as a valid point of view. It is important that any notion of system can cope with the fact that different people may, quite legitimately, have different points of view.

An outline of SSM

Methodology and its underpinnings

SSM is both a methodology and an approach. Chambers Concise Dictionary gives several definitions for 'methodology', including 'a system of methods and rules applicable to research or work in a given science or art'.

Within Management Science, the term has come to have two quite distinct meanings. The first, common in the USA, uses the term 'methodology' to refer to what people in the UK would describe as 'techniques' – academics from the USA sometimes refer to the methodologies of linear programming (see Chapter 9) or of forecasting. That is not the usage intended within SSM.

In SSM, the word 'methodology' is used in two ways. First, it provides a set of rules that guide the conduct of a study using soft systems ideas. Figure 5.3, which will be discussed in some detail in this chapter, provides a common way of describing some of the main features of the approach. It depicts a sequence of activities in which an SSM study might be conducted. For example, it suggests that, before a system can be modelled in some way, its essence should be captured via a set of root definitions. In this sense, SSM includes a method of enquiry, although it should not be assumed that the method has to be followed in a rigorous, step-by-step manner.

The second sense in which SSM provides a methodology is that it embodies a set of guiding principles and beliefs that, although not rules for action, embody the basic ideas of soft systems. For example, an important, guiding principle is that the methodology itself is systemic, it being a cyclic learning system. Figure 5.1 shows a problem situation and a would-be problem-solver to illustrate the basic idea. The would-be problem-solver, the analyst, is not wholly separate from the problem situation but is connected to it and may be a part of it. This is quite unlike the world of laboratory science in which the scientist can carve off part of the world for experimentation and takes great steps to ensure that she is a separate observer of that experiment. SSM, however,

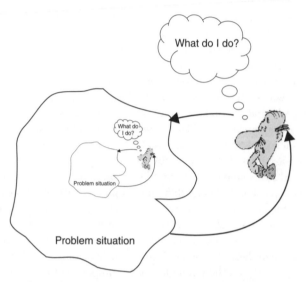

Figure 5.1 SSM as an involved, personal learning cycle.

takes for granted that humans have the ability to imagine themselves as separate from the problem situation being investigated. Indeed, they are able to imagine themselves standing outside that problem situation, observing themselves within it.

Not just how, but also why?

The SSM enquiry process, discussed below, is the second reason why SSM is regarded as 'soft'. This use of the term 'soft' is in contrast to approaches commonly used in many engineering projects in which the objectives of the study are agreed upon and taken as unambiguous. Thus, an engineer, working with an architect, might have a brief to design a bridge to meet stated weight and traffic requirements in a given location. When such objectives are specified, the job of the engineer is to find some way to meet the defined requirements. That is, the focus is on how to meet the given objectives and not, except in extreme cases, to question why the bridge is needed at all, or whether the weight and traffic requirements are correct. The same comment would apply to a Management Science study in which objectives are taken as given and incorporated in a decision model that is then used to explore the consequences of possible actions taken to achieve the objective.

By contrast, 'soft' approaches such as SSM are concerned with the why question before moving on to consider the how. It is clear that both questions are fundamental in most human activity systems, for these are designed and inhabited by people. Of course, there are cases where the objectives are agreed upon and unambiguous to all concerned – it will not take long to establish this using the methods of SSM. However, in most cases, SSM is specifically intended to help participants to discuss and move towards agreement about the objectives of a study or system. It does this through the cyclic approach shown in Figure 5.2 (based on Rosenhead and Mingers, 2001, p. 72). This shows a cycle of activities in which a process of representation through models supports a debate between participants. As in Figure 5.1, this assumes the ability both to be within an enquiry process and to reflect on it as it proceeds.

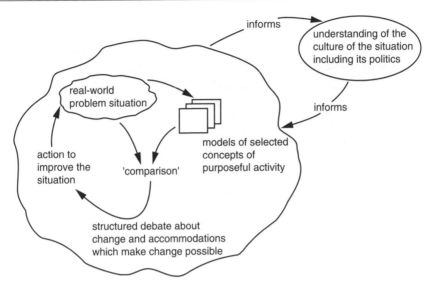

Figure 5.2 The basic idea of SSM.

Foundations of SSM

To use SSM successfully, the analyst must inhabit two worlds, often at the same time. The first is the 'real world' of human activity in which day-to-day business and interaction are conducted. This is a highly personal world of experience, memory, emotion and intent. The second is the world of systems thinking in which the analyst works on abstractions derived from the real world that may later be used for intervening in that real world. As a learning system, SSM is cyclic or multipass, and there is no assumption that work is necessarily complete in a single cycle. During each cycle, learning occurs, which then feeds into the study. It is important to realize that the shape in Figure 5.1 representing the problem situation will contain people other than the would-be problem-solver. The diagram illustrates SSM as a process of learning that depends on self-awareness.

An SSM approach

This section briefly describes the approach of SSM, and more detail is given in later sections. Figure 5.3 shows a commonly used diagram that summarizes the approach based on Checkland (1981, 1999). In later accounts of SSM, Checkland prefers a less detailed picture of SSM of the type shown in Figure 5.2, which has no explicit stage numbering and seems, therefore, less like a recipe. Hence, it is very important to realize that Figure 5.3 is intended as a framework to guide action, and is not intended to be a step-by-step recipe for success.

Several things are apparent in Figure 5.3. The first is that this is not a systematically linear approach that starts at one point (activity 1) and ends at another definite point (activity 7). Instead, as discussed earlier, it is a cyclic approach rather like the learning cycle of Kolb (1983). This should be no surprise given that soft approaches tend to stress the learning that will emerge from their use. Checkland (1981, p. 162) claims that the approach can be started, in principle

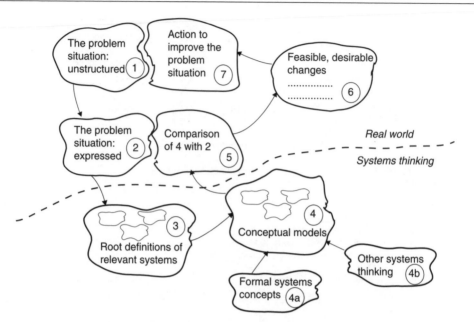

Figure 5.3 Soft systems methodology (Checkland, 1981).

at least, at any of the points in the cycle. He also stresses, sensibly, that real-life use will involve backtracking (going back to do the same thing again, even though it had been hoped to have finished that activity) and iterations around the loop as well.

The second thing to notice is the line that runs more or less diagonally and separates activities 1, 2, 5, 6 and 7 from activities 3, 4, 4a and 4b. This line indicates that the analyst using SSM must wear two hats: one for the real world and the other for the realm of systems thinking. The term 'real world' is meant to indicate the everyday world in which people live and to which they relate. To use SSM, we must investigate this world by working with at least some of these people, hoping to be of use to them and hoping to understand how they interpret the world. This requires what Checkland (1981, 1999) calls 'cultural analysis'. This work in the real world must not ignore the meanings that people attach to what they and others do, because these meanings are fundamental to the cultural analysis.

By contrast, the realm of 'systems thinking' represents a deliberate withdrawal from the real world while the analyst uses systems concepts to try to understand what is happening there. This requires what Checkland (1981, 1999) calls 'logical analysis'. In doing so, however, it is important to maintain a defensible view of the real world. Checkland's (1981) account of SSM was criticized for taking a view of organizational culture that was naive; the methodology is stated in somewhat different terms in Checkland and Scholes (1990) to counter some of those criticisms. In particular, this affects the across-the-line links between the real-world activities of SSM and the realm of systems thinking. Nevertheless, the analyst must, at some stage, think about the system in terms that may differ from those used by the people who are part of the system itself.

SSM steps 1 and 2: exploration and finding out

The first two activities in Figure 5.3 are labelled as 'The problem situation: unstructured' and 'The problem situation: expressed'. Note that the concern is with the circumstances, the situation in which someone feels there is a problem to be tackled. These activities aim to uncover different perceptions of why the intervention is needed and what it is that appears to be going on. The idea is to find some way of understanding and exploring the present context on the basis of the assumption that the world can be usefully regarded as systemic, rather than assuming that the world is composed of systems. In a way, this corresponds to problem-structuring as exploration, as discussed in Chapter 3. This exploration is rather like a first attempt to drill for oil: the ground must be surveyed and trial bores will be drilled, but there is no real intent to build a production rig at this stage. Instead, enough information will be gained to allow proper and detailed work to proceed. Continuing with this analogy, circumstances may change (e.g. oil prices), which may mean that this stage of the work has to be scrapped or reworked. Hence, the need, sometimes, to revisit this exploration stage.

The practical approach most commonly associated with the finding-out stages of SSM is the use of rich pictures, as discussed in Chapter 3. These are simple, graphical representations of what people feel are the important features of the situation being investigated. Unlike textual descriptions, they are non-linear and can display complex relationships. If constructed by a group working together, they form a public display on which each person can comment and which can be used as the basis for discussion. Trivial though it may sound, the opportunity for each person in a group to see what other people regard as the important factors and their relationships is very important.

It is clear that other approaches that allow a shared representation may also be useful in this stage of the work. One possibility might be a brainstorming session in which participants write on Post-it® notes the various factors they think are important. These may be stuck on a display board and moved around into groups and/or joined by lines drawn between them. The idea is the same as rich pictures, but uses words to cater for the artistically challenged!

Whatever methods are used, Checkland argues that it is crucial to consider a number of aspects of the situation being studied. The first is the structure of the situation, which refers to the relatively static aspects, such as physical layout, official and unofficial power hierarchies and communications systems (whether formal or informal). To use an analogy, until the creation of the Premier League, the shirt numbers of UK soccer players more or less indicated their playing position. Lower-numbered shirts were worn by defenders and higher numbers by attackers. In addition, the captain often wore an armband to indicate his status. Useful though such information is, it does not tell us much about the dynamics of what might happen on the pitch. It does not describe the tactics employed, nor their shifts during the different stages of the game. Nowadays, the numbers usually have no such significance, but they do have their value – they allow us to identify the players by linking the number to that in the match magazine. In the same way, structural ideas do not tell the whole story, but they can be useful.

In addition to the structure, we need to understand how things are done and what people are trying to do – these are the process aspects of the situation. In our analogy of a football game, this corresponds to the ways in which the game is actually played and the roles that people actually occupy. In a newspaper report of a soccer match, this is much more interesting than the team sheet or a list of the rules of the game. It probably makes sense to investigate the structure and process aspects simultaneously, as they are unlikely to be independent. However, it is important to be clear about which is which.

Finally, it is important to understand the climate of the situation: the attitudes of the people involved and the culture of the organization. How does the situation feel? How do people value what they do? What meanings do people ascribe to their actions? In our football analogy, a match may be wonderful or awful, depending on which team we support? In Checkland's terms, climate is the relationship between process and structure. Thus, the three aspects, like a three-legged stool, are a stable way of thinking about the problem situation.

To do this, Checkland and Scholes (1990) suggest three analyses that should be performed during the finding-out stages of SSM:

- *Analysis 1.* Identifying the people who occupy the various roles in an intervention, as follows. First, the 'would-be problem-solver': the person who has decided, been told or has requested to investigate the situation. Second, the 'client': the person for whom the investigation is being conducted. Finally, the 'problem-owners': the various stakeholders with a range of interests. Note that any or all of these roles may overlap – for example, someone may be using SSM to help support their own work.
- *Analysis 2.* Analysing the situation as a social system, building on knowledge of the significant roles that people have, to investigate the norms and values that are expressed. Roles are taken to be the social positions people occupy, which might be institutional (teacher) or behavioural (clown). Norms are the expected, or normal, behaviour in this context. Values are the local standards used to judge people's norms. The idea of this analysis is that the analyst should try to understand how people play out their roles.
- *Analysis 3.* Looking at the situation as a political system, in an attempt to understand how different interests reach some accommodation. This is an explicit recognition that powerplay occurs in organizations and needs to be accounted for. Needless to say, this analysis needs to be undertaken carefully and, maybe, covertly. There is little point asking people what their powerplays are!

SSM step 3: root definitions of relevant systems

SSM is action oriented and is used to understand something better and, possibly, to improve things. This is achieved by taking our structured exploration and expressing some aspects of it in systems terms. The idea is to think about the systems that might be put in place to achieve what people want and need, which requires the development of hypotheses about how things might be – that is, hypotheses about possible systems. At this stage, these root definitions need not be in any immediately implementable form, but are idealizations that capture the functionality of the systems of interest. Note that SSM's soft credentials are very clear at this point, for we are invited to develop root definitions of relevant systems (both plural), which accommodates different people and different groups that may see things in different ways. Root definitions are idealized interpretations of the systems of interest as seen from a range of viewpoints. They capture the essence of a system that has the functionality to achieve the aims, objectives and viewpoints of stakeholders. Note that, in Figure 5.3, we are still above the line in the abstract world of systems thinking, and, as they are idealizations, there is no need for root definitions to map on to existing organizational systems. A root definition is the first stage of an idealization of what might be. This is quite different from the question of what is or what should be.

Prior to developing root definitions, it can be helpful to address three related questions, which are often abbreviated as 'do P, by Q, to achieve R'. The R relates to the 'why' question discussed earlier and to the essential purpose of the system of interest. The Q relates to the means by which this will be achieved, and the P refers to the activity of the system. For example, Brown, Cooper and Pidd (2006) describe the use of SSM in a study of the UK personal tax system and include an example of a PQR used to establish a root definition of a proposal to provide a single interface linking the various computer systems used in collecting personal tax in the UK, as follows:

- **P**: What activity will be done? A system to give staff access to a single, coherent, summary record of taxpayers' affairs.

- **Q**: How will it be done? By providing a single IT interface that accesses all tax records for an individual, presenting that information in a single view and allowing single edit revisions to those records.
- **R**: Why will it be done? To enhance customer service, provide proactive advice to taxpayers, improve efficiency and, over time, lead to more reliable, up-to-date records.

A root definition, as a verbal account, is usually reckoned to have six components summarized in the mnemonic CATWOE, which stems from the initial letters of the following six terms:

1. *Customers.* These are the immediate beneficiaries or victims of what the system does. It can be an individual, several people, a group or groups. This is very close to the total quality management (TQM) notion that the customer is the next person to receive the work in progress. It indicates what happens to the output from the system and forms part of the external relations of the system.
2. *Actors.* In any human activity system there are people who carry out one or more of the activities in the system; these are the actors. They form part of the internal relations of the system. There may be several actors or several groups, and their relationships also form part of the internal relations of the system.
3. *Transformation process.* This is the core of the human activity system in which some definite input is converted into some output and then passed on to the customers. The actors take part in this transformation process. The process is an activity, and its description therefore requires the use of verbs. Ideally, a root definition should focus on a single transformation.
4. *Weltanschauung.* This is the often taken-for-granted outlook or world-view that makes sense of the root definition being developed. It is important to specify this because any system definitions can only make sense with some defined context. Thus, a root definition needs only a single Weltanschauung.
5. *Ownership.* This is the individual or group responsible for the proposed system in the sense that they have the power to modify it or even to close it down. This can overlap with the actors of the system.
6. *Environmental constraints.* All human activity systems operate within some constraints imposed by their external environment. These might be, for example, legal, physical or ethical. They form part of the external relations of the system and need to be distinguished from its ownership.

One way of understanding CATWOE and the idea of Weltanschauung is captured in Figure 5.4. This shows a simple input–output process, a black box. The process involves a transformation, carried out by the actors, and the results of the transformation pass through to the customers. External control is maintained by the owners, and the whole system sits inside an environment. The Weltanschauung, shown as the beam of a flashlight, illuminates the picture and enables things to be seen in context.

Root definitions of relevant systems in TICTOC

The best way to understand the creation of root definitions and the use of CATWOE is to consider an example. Consider the TICTOC case study introduced in Chapter 2, in which the initial dialogue introduces four people: the Director of Port Services (DPS), the Controller of Pumping Operations (CPO), the Maintenance Manager (MM) and you – the would-be

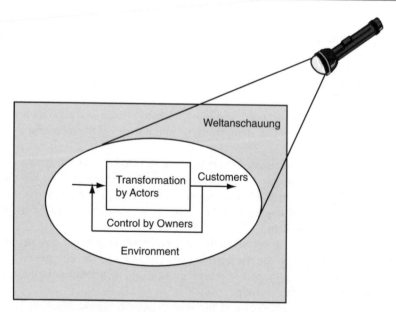

Figure 5.4 CATWOE as an input–output system.

problem-solver. In a real situation we could interview the other three people, but here we will need to infer things from the dialogue. For simplicity's sake, we will assume that each person's viewpoint can be expressed in its own, single root definition. Clearly, there will be cases where one person may construct several root definitions. Bear in mind that the following root definitions are what I infer from the dialogue. You may read things somewhat differently.

The DPS is responsible for the entire operation of TICTOC at Ventry; we have discussed in earlier chapters that he wishes to keep down his overall costs. We might thus develop a CATWOE for him as follows, taking the hose system as the relevant one. The easiest place to start is with the transformation, which is probably that the hose takes crude oil from storage tanks to tankers at minimum overall cost. The customer for this transformation may be, in the DPS's view, TICTOC itself. The actors are TICTOC workers, plus workers on the tankers. The system is owned by the government of Transitania and operates under constraints set by pumping rates, sea conditions and environmental concerns. Finally, what is the Weltanschauung of the DPS that makes sense of all this? This is presumably a belief that there is a need to supply world markets with Transitanian oil. Thus, our PQR statement might be: 'Transfer oil from Ventry tanks into bulk carriers using large flexible hose to supply world markets with Transitanian oil at minimum cost'. Hence, the CATWOE of the DPS might be as follows (note the obvious point that there is no need to develop a CATWOE in the sequence of its letters):

- *Customers*: TICTOC.
- *Actors*: TICTOC workers and tanker operatives.
- *Transformation*: transfer oil from Ventry tanks into bulk carriers.
- *Weltanschauung*: need to supply the world markets with Transitanian oil at minimum cost.
- *Ownership*: Transitanian government.
- *Environmental constraints*: pumping rates, sea conditions and environmental concerns.

Alternatively, we might capture this in the following sentences:

A system owned by the Transitanian government and operated by TICTOC staff, with the cooperation of tanker operators, to transfer oil from the Ventry tanks to waiting bulk carriers at minimum cost. It must operate within physical constraints such as pumping rates and sea conditions, plus environmental constraints. The system is needed so that Transitanian oil can be supplied to world markets at minimum cost.

What about the other two principal internal stakeholders, the CPO and MM? Considering the CPO next, then, it would appear that he sees the hose system as follows. A CATWOE for the CPO's view is:

- *Customers*: tanker operators.
- *Actors*: TICTOC workers and tanker operatives.
- *Transformation*: hose takes crude oil from storage tanks to tankers.
- *Weltanschauung*: my job is to provide a reliable service to tanker operators.
- *Ownership*: TICTOC.
- *Environmental constraints*: pumping rates, sea conditions and environmental concerns, need to keep costs down.

Note that there are some differences between the CPO and DPS root definitions. The CPO sees the tanker operators as the customers, and he treats cost as a constraint imposed from outside. His view of 'outside' differs from that of the DPS, for he sees the ownership as vested in TICTOC itself – whatever that may mean. Thus, the CATWOE can be expressed in something like the following form:

A TICTOC-owned system to transfer oil from the Ventry tanks to waiting bulk carriers as reliably as possible, operating within physical constraints such as pumping rates and sea conditions, plus environmental constraints and within cost limits. The system is operated by TICTOC workers and tanker operators, and is needed because my job is to provide a service to tanker operators.

Once again, your interpretation of the CPO's position as you look back to Chapter 2 may be slightly different. Checkland stresses the need to be aware that the analyst is one of the players in the drama of SSM. This is why it is much better to involve the participants in developing the root definitions, so as to reduce the chance of these being your misinterpretation of their interpretation!

Finally in this example, we need to consider the MM as the third internal stakeholder. His CATWOE might be:

- *Customers*: TICTOC.
- *Actors*: TICTOC workers and tanker operatives.
- *Transformation*: hoses that would have failed early now last longer.
- *Weltanschauung*: better maintenance helps provide a better service and saves money.
- *Ownership*: TICTOC.
- *Environmental constraints*: pumping rates, sea conditions and environmental concerns, need to keep costs down.

This third CATWOE includes yet more differences. The MM's Weltanschauung stresses his belief that better maintenance helps to provide a better service and should also save cash.

The transformation is therefore the process of improving the service life of the hoses. He sees TICTOC and the tanker operators as customers for this transformation. Thus, this CATWOE can be expressed as follows:

A TICTOC-owned system of maintenance to improve the service life of hoses used to transfer oil from the Ventry tanks to waiting bulk carriers at low cost. It must operate within physical constraints such as pumping rates and sea conditions, plus environmental constraints and within cost limits. The system is operated by TICTOC workers and tanker operators for the benefit of TICTOC.

Looking at the three root definitions, it is clear that any attempt to resolve this will need to take account of these three different perspectives. The DPS is interested in low-cost operation; the CPO wants to provide a better service with minimum hassle; and the MM thinks that better maintenance could help all this. Of course, things get even more complicated if we attempt to develop root definitions for the external stakeholders that were identified in Chapter 3. It may also be the case that other root definitions could be developed for the DPS, CPO and MM. As an exercise, you may like to do this now.

SSM step 4: conceptual modelling

Fascinating though the production of root definitions may turn out to be, it is not intended as an end in itself. Root definitions are a means to an end, and that end is the development of conceptual models intended to embody, in outline terms, what a system must include in order to deliver the functionality implied in the root definitions. Conceptual models are intended as minimal descriptions of the subsystems or components that would be necessary in any embodiment of the root definition. They are intended to take the verbs included in the root definitions and to show how they might relate to one another. Step 4 is still below the line in the realm of systems thinking, and so, as with root definitions, conceptual models are not intended to refer to any particular implementation within any particular organization. A detailed treatment of the place of conceptual models in SSM can be found in Wilson (2001).

In terms of SSM, a conceptual model is a diagrammatic representation of the interconnections of the activities that must be present for the root definition to make sense. It thus focuses on the verbs from the root definition and links them logically in quite conventional ways. Checkland and Scholes (1990) suggest that a conceptual model should contain between five and nine activities; any more than that and some aggregation would be needed, any less and the model would be too simple to be of use. Note, however, that the examples in Checkland (1981) do not meet this criterion. The activities must include processes for monitoring and control, as this is a fundamental part of the notion of an open system. Figure 5.5 shows a first attempt at a conceptual model for the root definition ascribed to the DPS in the case study. Clearly, conceptual models for the other two people would be a little different from this.

The next stage in conceptual modelling is to consider each of the activities in the broad-brush conceptual model by looking 'inside' them. For example, the activity of monitoring environmental constraints might be separated into those that are legally imposed and those that seem sensible for other reasons. Once again, it is important to note that this part of SSM assumes that the analyst is currently within the realm of systems thinking – there is no need to consider whether such systems really do exist (although this is a hard temptation to fight).

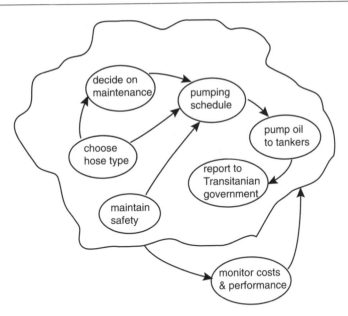

Figure 5.5 DPS conceptual model for the hose system.

Looking back to Figure 5.3, there are two subsidiary activities linked to activity 4: the use of the formal system concept and the use of other systems thinking. A conceptual model within SSM is to be judged against the formal definition of open systems and of human activity systems in particular. Clearly, this means that there must be ways for the system to communicate across its boundaries with the outside world. That is, there must be established relationships between the activities and subsystems, and there must be control systems that guarantee that the system will continue to operate for some time. In addition, the model can be checked against other systems ideas such as the notion of a viable system model (Espejo and Harnden, 1989). If it can be made to fit none of them, then its validity, in systems terms, must be in doubt.

Chapter 12 discusses the validation of models as used in management science. It asks how we can be sure that a model is correctly built and can be safely used to provide insight or to make decisions. As will be clear in that chapter, this seems a simple enough question at first – surely we just compare the model with the real world? However, it should be clear by now that different people may experience different real worlds, which somewhat complicates matters. Also, the model may be used to investigate options for change, in which case there is no real world against which to make a proper comparison. In what sense, then, can SSM conceptual models be validated? A valid conceptual model is one with activities that capture the root definition and are faithful to the principles of human activity systems. Thus, validating an SSM is not a comparison with the real world, but an examination of its adequacy against root definitions and systems concepts.

The discussion of a later version of SSM presented in Checkland and Scholes (1990) suggests that there may in fact be no need to use formal system concepts in developing the conceptual models. Instead, they argue that it is sufficient that the pairing of the root definition and model be defensible. That is, each activity in the model should be traceable back to words or concepts within the root definition. That is, the model is validated only against the root definition.

The three Es: criteria for evaluating conceptual models

Checkland (1981) suggests a set of three criteria, the three Es, against which alternative conceptual models can be assessed:

1. *Efficacy.* Will it do what is required; that is, will it work as intended?
2. *Efficiency.* If it works, what resources are required and can these be minimized?
3. *Effectiveness.* Does it meet the higher-level goals within which the system must operate?

To answer critics who regard these three Es as rather mundane and utilitarian, Checkland and Scholes (1990) expand them to five Es by adding:

4. *Ethicality.* Is it moral, does it meet required ethical standards? This is important if analysts are not to be mere technicians who do whatever those in power require.
5. *Elegance.* Is it beautiful and aesthetically pleasing, or rather clumsy and utilitarian?

Each of these Es must be consistent with the Weltanschauung of the root definition if it is to be of use, and their importance will vary between different projects. Each E may also serve as the basis for a measure of performance for the system, should some way be found to implement it in the real world.

SSM step 5: comparison – conceptual models versus what is there already

Conceptual models are developed to ensure that people's perceptions are captured in terms that fit the notions of an open system in the belief that this is an effective way to design human activity systems in the real world. When the aim is to bring about improvement, it is important to compare the current, as-is, situation with the conceptual models, so as to think through what action and changes may be needed. Checkland (1981) suggests four ways of doing this:

1. Using the conceptual models to support ordered questioning. The models are used as a source for a set of questions to be asked of people involved in the actual, as-is, or proposed situation. In effect, the analyst should keep the conceptual models under wraps and should use them to open up debate about change, to get people to think whether it is needed and, if so, in what form. This is an attractive way to proceed, for it permits the analyst to work with the people in developing possible changes, and it avoids the accusation that he or she knows a lot about systems but little about 'what goes on here'. If necessary, only the analyst need be aware of the conceptual models.
2. By walking through the conceptual models with sequences of events that have actually occurred in the past. The idea here is to investigate how they would have been handled, had the systems of the conceptual model existed, compared with what did happen in practice. It is obviously important to realize that people's memories of events can be very selective when doing this. Needless to say, this approach needs to be used with some care so as to avoid antagonizing those who might have been involved in whatever led to the request for a soft systems study.
3. By conducting a general discussion about the high-level features of the conceptual model in relation to the present situation. This requires the analyst to spend time with the major actors, explaining the models to them and discussing with them the differences and similarities.

Unlike mode 1 above, the major actors must be made aware of the conceptual model. As ever, this may require some tact.

4. By model overlays, which means attempting to compare the detail of the conceptual model with the detail of what is. It must be noted that this really means a comparison of the conceptual model with another model of what currently exists and operates; hence the term 'model overlay'.

Of course, if the study is focused on a novel system that does not exist, none of these methods can be used. In such cases, the conceptual models serve to focus people's attention on what might be done to implement their vision.

It cannot be stressed too highly that, in crossing the boundary from systems thinking to the real world, we are re-entering a world in which considerations other than just the cerebral and logical apply. Hence, Checkland and Scholes (1990) emphasize the crucial importance of maintaining two streams of enquiry, and this becomes especially important at this stage in the work. The first stream they term the 'logic-driven stream', by which they refer, primarily, to the analysis carried out below the line in the realm of systems thinking. Here, rigour and logic are needed to develop conceptual models that are valid in systemic terms. In addition, though, a second stream, the 'cultural enquiry stream', is also vital, and this features most strongly in the first two stages of SSM (exploration and finding out) and these latter phases (comparison and implementation). Implementation, in particular, is not just a cerebral act. Deciding to do something in such a way that the outcome will be as desired demands commitment and agreement. This takes time and is an emotional and psychological response at least as much as a logical one. Thus, the three enquiry streams mentioned earlier must be maintained with special vigilance at this stage and the following ones.

SSM steps 6 and 7: implementing feasible and desirable changes

This stage in SSM encompasses activities 6 and 7 in Figure 5.3. This is the stage at which the client for the study may be expecting a payoff, which may not be entirely straightforward with soft methods. In most cases there are also changes recommended as a result of such a study, and further work may be needed, possibly involving 'hard' management science, to demonstrate their value. The changes might be large scale, such as the implementation of a planning and control system where no such effective system existed prior to the study. On the other hand, they might be smaller in scale and may require adjustments to existing ways of doing things. A further outcome – the learning that accrues as a result of people participating in the study – is also to be expected.

During the exploration stages of SSM, investigations of the structure, process and climate of the situation were three important aspects. It should be no surprise, given the cyclic nature of SSM, that these should loom large at implementation time. Indeed, there are many similarities between the exploration and implementation stages of a methodological approach (Pidd, 1988). Thus, we might expect possible changes in the ways in which people are formally organized and controlled (the structure, which changes slowly); in the ways in which work is done and the people interact to do the work (the process, which is always in flux); and in people's attitudes about their work, the customers and one another (the climate).

The definition of these changes should emerge from activity of the SSM approach, the comparison of the conceptual models with the real-world problem situation as it was expressed. Whether the production of a set of feasible and desirable changes and the implementation

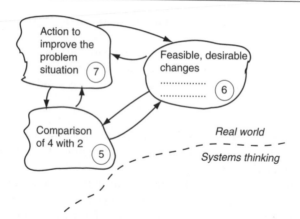

Figure 5.6 Cyclic activity in the 'real world'.

process can be fully separated from that comparison seems dubious. It may be better to regard this part of the approach as explicitly cyclic, as in Figure 5.6. That is, there is likely to be explicit movement between these three activities in an effort to ensure that the client gains from the study.

In deciding whether a change should be made, Checkland (1981) and Checkland and Scholes (1990) argue that any change must be systemically desirable and culturally feasible. This statement is unfortunately open to misinterpretation. What it seems to mean is that, taking the notion of a human activity system as an ideal type, any changes should be ones that can be defended in terms of that ideal type. If the change cannot be defended in systemic terms, it should not be recommended. Alongside this, the idea that changes should be culturally feasible is a swipe at impractical ideas of optimization and rationality. They are arguing that, no matter how attractive an idea may seem in the realm of systems thinking, unless it is acceptable, given the culture of the organization at that time, there is little chance of it being implemented. This, of course, could be taken as an argument for a form of short-term, fudge-and-mudge approach. However, major changes often do take years to put into place, and having an acceptable, or feasible, plan for their implementation is crucial.

Summary – some reflections on SSM

In his book *Images of Organization*, Morgan (1986) compares different metaphors in common use for the idea of organization. Of these eight metaphors, three are in everyday use:

- the organization as a bureaucratic machine;
- the organization as an organism or system;
- the organization as the expression of a culture.

The first metaphor, that an organization is a machine deliberately designed to perform certain functions, is extremely pervasive. It stresses the structural aspects of organizations, the formal roles people take and the explicit rules they may follow in carrying out their work. In manufacturing it is most strongly expressed in the approach of 'scientific management', often known as Taylorism, which stresses the need to organize work so that interchangeable people can carry out well-defined and highly structured tasks managed by explicit coordination. In these terms, the aim of management is to design the machine so that it works, to maintain it so it remains in good condition and to coordinate the different tasks on which people are engaged. This mechanistic approach fits well with highly bureaucratic organizations that are governed by rule books and in which task and role divisions are clearly defined.

The second metaphor, the idea that the organization is a form of organism, is virtually the same as regarding it as a system. The idea is that the organism does not need to be preprogrammed to respond to different, rather limited, circumstances. Instead, it expresses its organic nature by interacting with its environment in an adaptive way. Hence, the role of management is to develop appropriate systems that will support that adaptation and that will have some form of internal control. These are the same assumptions, in fact, that underlie many systems approaches. Morgan writes that the organismic view is really that of a machine in soft focus. What he means by this is that both metaphors, when used, pay scant regard to the nature of the social world. Both tend to take it for granted and assume that it can be dealt with in intellectual and logical terms. This was one of the criticisms made, fairly or not, of Checkland's (1981) account of SSM.

By contrast, his third metaphor, also in common use, is that an organization is an expression of a culture that is shared by its members. This culture might be cooperative, action oriented, research based or whatever. As an example, a British Home Secretary sacked the Director General of the British Prison Service. Commenting on this, a spokesman for the association that represents prison governors described the Prison Service as a 'command culture'. This was not intended as a criticism, merely a recognition that the service is organized on a military model in which orders are not to be questioned, they are to be obeyed. This could, presumably, be contrasted with the notion of a cooperative culture in which people are highly self-motivated. Use of the idea of organizational culture implies that changes will only be made if they can be accommodated within the culture – apart from deliberate efforts to change the culture.

How does this relate to SSM? Perhaps it is best to regard SSM as a way of taking a systems or organismic approach and adapting it to fit with the idea of organizational culture. Hence, the stress in Checkland (1981), which is magnified in Checkland and Scholes (1990), on the need to engage with the culture of the organization. Mingers and Taylor (1992) report on a postal survey of people who knew of SSM and who might have been expected to use it in some way. The proportion of users was quite high, and, of these, the majority claimed to use SSM with a view to easing a problem situation or to develop understanding. They also claimed that a main benefit of SSM was that it provided a strong structure within which they could achieve these aims. These findings seem to support the view that SSM provides a formalized approach to gaining understanding within an organization, paying due regard to cultural issues.

The next chapter explores another 'soft' approach, cognitive mapping and SODA, developed by Colin Eden and his colleagues. It takes a rather different view of the same issues, although outwardly it appears to be similar in some ways.

References

Ackoff R.L. (1971) Towards a system of systems concepts. *Management Science*, **17**, 661–671.
Boulding K.E. (1956) General systems theory – the skeleton of science. *Management Science*, **2**, 3.
Brown J., Cooper C. and Pidd M (2006) A taxing problem: the complementary use of hard and soft OR in the public sector. *European Journal of Operational Research*, **172**, 666–679.

Checkland P.B. (1981) *Systems Thinking, Systems Practice.* John Wiley & Sons, Ltd, Chichester, UK.

Checkland P.B. (1999) *Systems Thinking, Systems Practice: Includes a 30-year Retrospective.* John Wiley & Sons, Ltd, Chichester, UK.

Checkland P.B. and Holwell S. (1997) *Information, Systems and Information System: Making Sense of the Field.* John Wiley & Sons, Ltd, Chichester, UK.

Checkland P.B. and Poulter J. (2006) *Learning for Action: a Short Definitive Account of Soft Systems Methodology and its Use for Practitioners, Teachers and Students.* John Wiley & Sons, Ltd, Chichester, UK.

Checkland P.B. and Scholes J. (1990) *Soft Systems Methodology in Action.* John Wiley & Sons, Ltd, Chichester, UK.

Espejo R. and Harnden R. (1989) *The Viable Systems Model: Interpretations and Applications of Stafford Beer's Viable Systems Model.* John Wiley & Sons, Ltd, Chichester, UK.

Janis I.L. (1972) *Victims of Groupthink.* Houghton Mifflin, New York, NY.

Kolb D.A. (1983) Problem management: learning from experience, in *The Executive Mind*, ed. by Srivasta S. Jossey-Bass, San Francisco, CA.

Kropotkin P. (1927) Anarchism: its philosophy and ideal, in *Kropotkin's Revolutionary Pamphlets*, ed. by Baldwin R.N. Vanguard Press, New York, NY.

Mingers J. and Taylor S. (1992) The use of soft systems methodology in practice. *Journal of the Operational Research Society*, **43**(4), 321–332.

Morgan G. (1986) *Images of Organization.* Sage, London, UK.

Pidd M. (1988) From problem structuring to implementation. *Journal of the Operational Research Society*, **29**(2), 1–7.

Rosenhead J.V. and Mingers J. (eds) (2001) *Rational Analysis for a Problematic World Revisited.* John Wiley & Sons, Ltd, Chichester, UK.

Vickers G. (1983) *Human Systems are Different.* Harper & Row, London, UK.

von Bertalanffy L. (1971) *General Systems Theory: Foundations, Development, Applications.* Allen Lane, London, UK.

Wilson B. (1984) *Systems: Concepts, Methodologies, and Applications.* John Wiley & Sons, Ltd, Chichester, UK.

Wilson B. (2001) *Soft Systems Methodology: Conceptual Model Building and its Contributions.* John Wiley & Sons, Ltd, Chichester, UK.

6 Cognitive mapping, SODA and journey-making

Introduction

The introduction to Part II stresses that 'soft' methods are pluralistic and aim to be interpretive. That is, they do not assume that there will be agreement about objectives when working within an organization. Instead, they assume that there may be different perspectives on the same situation for many reasons. The last chapter described the soft systems methodology (SSM) developed by Checkland and colleagues. A key part of SSM is the use of root definitions of alternative, relevant systems, as SSM accepts that there will be alternative viewpoints and tries to express these in systems terms. A criticism of SSM is that it provides little guidance about how such conflict or disagreement might be handled. By contrast, the approaches to cognitive mapping suggested by Eden and colleagues, described here, give very specific advice about this.

A technique and two methodologies

As with SSM, the approach summarized here as cognitive mapping is more than just a technique. It consists of a technique, cognitive mapping, used in a rigorous way within one of two linked methodologies. The original methodology was known as SODA (Strategic Options Development and Analysis), and its clearest exposition is in Eden (1989). This original approach will be called SODA I in this chapter and is based around an approach in which individual cognitive maps are merged to help groups think through complex problems.

Its later version, here called SODA II, dispenses with individual cognitive maps and makes use of group decision support technology to build cause maps directly with a team. Both SODA I and SODA II have been used by Eden and colleagues in strategic thinking and planning and are part of journey-making (JOintly Understanding, Reflecting and Negotiating stratEgY) as described in Eden and Ackermann (1998). Both methodologies rely on a skilled facilitator to help construct the maps and to guide the group towards joint understanding and agreement.

The roots of the cognitive mapping employed in both versions of SODA lie in cognitive psychology, the discipline that tries to understand how humans think and make sense of their experiences. Similar methods have been developed to support the design of computer systems (Buckingham Shum, 1996) and for the analysis of conflict in political science (Axelrod, 1976). The technique itself is simple to understand, although it takes some practice to feel confident in its use. Computer software is available to support the construction and analysis of large maps, but its use is not essential, and some people may feel that it gets in the way of human interactions. This problem can be avoided if the map is built manually and then entered into a PC. Bryson *et al.* (2004) is a good introduction to the ways in which maps can be built for specific problems.

Process and content

In both versions of SODA, cognitive maps are used to capture people's thinking about a set of issues so as to develop an explicit model of them. The idea is that the analyst should interview people or work with a group in a semi-directed way and try to sketch out a map of their thinking that represents the concepts that they use and how they are linked together. It assumes that individual people work together, sometimes cooperatively, sometimes not, and that, to be effective, team members need to appreciate one another's thinking enough to develop a joint commitment. When working with groups, the idea to is develop shared understanding and appreciation. In doing so, it is important to note Eden's (1989) point that the outcome of any attempt to work with people results both from the content of the help and from the process through which it is delivered and experienced. This is captured in the notional equation

$$Outcome = process \times content$$

Thus, if the analyst concentrates only on the content of the help that is given, which might mean the techniques used or the responses gained from people, the outcome of the intervention is unlikely to be of much use. Similarly, any attempt to offer help that focuses only on a process of some kind is likely to be vacuous and is unlikely to produce anything of much value. The analyst, therefore, needs to master technique, but also must be consciously managing the process of what is happening. Although Checkland places rather less stress on this in SSM, it is clear that the same argument must hold if SSM is to be of much use. This is one reason why the introduction to Part II refers to these two approaches as interpretive.

Varieties of cognitive maps

Different disciplines use the term cognitive mapping to mean different things. In the wider literature of psychology (Tolman, 1948), the term usually denotes attempts to depict a person's mental image of physical space. For example, most people have a very distorted (i.e. non-physical) map of their surroundings; that is, our spatial memory is not just evoked by conjuring up an image of a scene in our minds but also depends on how important objects within that space seem to us. Thus, many factors are at work when we collect, organize, store, recall and manipulate information about our spatial environment. In fact, we tend to distort things in different ways according to our interests. For a brief discussion of this issue, see McNamara (1994), and, for more substantial coverage, see Downs and Stea (1977).

This chapter will focus on the term 'cognitive mapping' as suggested and used by Eden *et al.* in Management Science. The idea is to develop a simple two-dimensional representation of the concepts that an individual or people express, and to show their links – as expressed by the person or group involved. It would be hopelessly overoptimistic to describe the maps as models of thinking or as maps of thought. Instead, they are 'tools for reflective thinking and problem-solving' (Eden, Ackermann and Cropper, 1992). They are to be developed by a mapper who tries to capture the ideas of the interviewee or group, using the words used by the participants. Hence, they represent the mapper's honest interpretation of what is said in the interview or group session. The maps are preferable to verbal accounts because they enable the links between the concepts used by a person to be shown on the map in an unambiguous way. Verbal accounts of many linked concepts tend to be ambiguous.

A number of mapping approaches have been devised for use within organizations, especially for helping senior managers with their strategic thinking. A short overview of these is given in Fiol and Huff (1992), and a longer discussion is to be found in Huff (1990). The different approaches are based on a range of assumptions, which, for Eden and his colleagues (Eden, 1989; Eden, Jones and Sims, 1979, 1983), stem from personal construct theory (Kelly, 1955) in cognitive psychology. Personal construct psychology is 'an attempt to understand the way in which each of us experiences the world, to understand our "behaviour" in terms of what it is designed to signify and to explore how we negotiate reality with one another' (Bannister and Fransella, 1986). Associated with this theory are techniques such as repertory grids, which are attempts to develop ways of isolating and representing people's personal constructs. The techniques can become ends in themselves for some people and may obscure the insights to be gained from the rest of the theory (Rowe, 1983). Here we are concerned with the ways in which the theory can be used to help people understand and interpret other people's views of reality. Eden developed the cognitive mapping technique with this in mind, intending its use to be simple, transparent and flexible. It should be noted, however, that recent accounts of cognitive mapping make little or no explicit reference to construct theory, and there is some doubt whether this theory provides a justification for the cause maps of SODA II.

Assumptions of cognitive mapping and SODA

Eden has provided a number of accounts of cognitive mapping and SODA, the most straightforward of which are Eden (1989) and Eden and Ackermann (2001). The latter is a short account conveniently placed alongside Checkland (2001), which is Checkland's own abbreviated description of soft systems methodology. At first glance there are many similarities between the two approaches, which is interesting because they are based on different assumptions. There are also some major differences in the two approaches. The specific assumptions underlying cognitive mapping and the SODA approaches are discussed in this section.

Action orientation

Fascinating though it can be to explore people's perceptions via cognitive maps, this is not an end in itself. Instead, there is an orientation in which the aim is to help people decide what to do and how to do it. Indeed, there is a specific assumption that people are working towards a commitment to action and not just taking part to understand themselves. This is not intended to belittle the need for analysis and understanding – indeed, finding ways to help other people understand one another's perceptions is at the heart of the approach. However, the aim is to move people towards some commitment to act.

Individualistic focus

Whereas SSM assumes that it can be useful to regard organizations and their parts as if they were human activity systems, SODA and cognitive mapping make no such assumption. Instead, the initial stance of SODA I is thoroughly individualistic, although this mellows somewhat in SODA II. In general, though, SODA assumes that organizations are composed of individual people who may or may not choose to operate together in a system. Each of these individuals is assumed to hold views on what is happening to them and about what they would like to see happen. The idea of cognitive mapping is to model these perceptions and desires. The aim of SODA is to find ways for groups to develop a commitment to joint action in spite of those differing perceptions and desires. Given its roots within construct theory, this view of individualistic perception should come as no surprise.

The idea is to work with the construct systems people employ, and to use these to engage in a debate about possible action. In this sense, the approach assumes that problems are artefacts of the human imagination. Therefore, individuals who have different perceptions will tend, as discussed in Chapter 3, to frame problems differently. Different construct systems will lead to different framing. To work as an effective group or team, these people need jointly to define the problems on which they will work. This involves negotiation and may include powerplay and argument. SODA aims to support the negotiation and argument and to help people move to a joint commitment to action.

Stress on cognition

As part of its justification comes from cognitive psychology, the approach assumes that humans try to make sense of their environment and of their experiences. In both versions of SODA, the analyst strives to work with the 'sense-making systems' people use rather than with the world as the analyst sees it. Hence, the stress is upon linked constructs, which are psychologically based rather than logically based. The idea, in the cognitive mapping stage, is to develop a graphical scheme of the linked concepts that people seem to employ when thinking about the problem situation. The intention is to help participants see that situation in new ways so that they may act.

Cognitive mapping

A cognitive map is a form of influence diagram, similar to the ones used in system dynamics (see Chapter 7). Eden, Ackermann and Cropper (1992) regard cognitive maps as a subset of cause maps, or 'causal submaps' to use the terminology of Fiol and Huff (1992). The map consists of nodes, known as concepts, linked by arrows. The concepts are ideas and issues that have some meaning for the people involved and, as far as possible, are expressed in the words they use. The arrows represent causal links between concepts, as in Figure 6.1, in which concept 2 (Live in town . . . not on campus) leads causally to concept 1 (Want a more normal life . . . not living like a student). The arrows may carry a sign at the arrowhead, although the absence of a sign is usually taken to indicate a positive link, and a negative sign indicates a negative link. Figure 6.1 shows two concepts linked in a positive way. The direction of the arrow is intended to represent the causal direction of the relationship. This means that, as expressed, concept 2 tends to lead to concept 1.

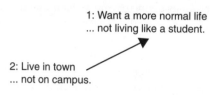

Figure 6.1 Concepts and links.

Concepts (nodes)

A concept is an idea, issue or concern that has been expressed by someone or agreed by a group. A concept should capture the views and outlook of the person who has expressed it. Sometimes, as shown in Figure 6.1, a concept may consist of two poles separated by ellipses, which should be read as 'rather than'. Two poles are needed if a single pole is ambiguous, and should clarify its meaning. Thus, the person may have said that their goal is to live a more normal life, but what does this mean? The second pole, not living like a student, helps to clarify what is being said. Hence, this bipolar concept should be read as 'I wish to lead a normal life, by which I mean that I do not wish to live on campus'. A second pole is often not needed, for example when someone says that they do not wish to pay more than £75 per week in rent. Cause maps built by groups as in SODA II contain few bipolar concepts.

If a concept does have two poles, it is important to realize that these are psychological opposites as expressed by the people or group with whom the map is being developed. The poles need not be logical opposites, as they are intended to capture the views of the people involved. It is important to use labels for concepts that somehow capture the words used by that person. The second pole is not simply the negative of the first pole, because 'psychological opposites are rarely as simple as simple negatives' (Brown, 1992).

Ideally, these bipolar concepts should be expressed in a way that itself is action oriented; thus, 'Want a more normal life' and 'Live in town' express desires to live in particular ways. This does not mean that this action will eventually be taken, because other concepts may interfere with it. For example, the person's thinking might include another concept such as 'Spend less than £75 per week on rent', and this may be impossible unless the student lives on campus. This concept, whatever its opposite pole, might mean that the preference for living in town must be moderated in some way or other. Both concepts are geared towards action, and their interaction is what will, eventually, lead to some action.

The basic rule is simple. If the concept is clear without a second pole, then one is not needed. However, if it is ambiguous, then the mapper needs to ask the person involved to clarify things along the lines of the following: 'OK, you want to live a more normal life, but I'm not clear what you mean by this, can we explore it a bit?'. The discussion will then have one of two effects. Either a second pole will emerge that clarifies the concept, or the concept will be rephrased so that no second pole is needed.

Arrows (arcs)

The arrows are intended to show the relationships, as expressed, between pairs of concepts. The concept at the start (or tail) of the arrow can be thought of as the means to achieving the concept at the end (or head) of the arrow. Thus, higher-order concepts sit at the end of a chain of arcs and concepts. The highest-order concepts are, in effect, goals. The map should ideally be drawn so that it flows upwards towards the higher-level goals. As an example, consider Figure 6.2, which relates to some of the concepts employed by someone in deciding where to go on holiday.

An arrowhead carrying a negative sign is intended to show that there is negative causality between the two concepts. This does not mean that the means–end relationship is reversed. It can mean several things, including the following:

- That an increase in the means (the concept at the tail) will lead to a reduction in the end (the concept at the head of the arrow), if all else remains unchanged.

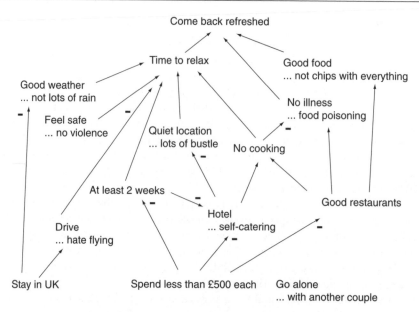

Figure 6.2 Cognitive map – holiday choice.

- That the second pole of the means concept is psychologically linked by the person to the first pole of the end concept. Thus, the wish to spend no more than £500 per person while away for at least 2 weeks will make it very difficult to stay in a hotel.

The negative sign system is employed because concepts with two poles should be expressed with the desirable pole as the first. Thus, this person would prefer to stay in a hotel but would also prefer a cheap holiday. Notice that, at this stage at least, there is no need to force the person to be more specific about what they mean by cheap or expensive. The use of a negative or positive link should be a feature of the concepts expressed by the individual and should not be a reflection of the views of the consultant. For example, Figure 6.2 shows a negative link from 'No cooking . . .' to 'No illness . . .', this being the view expressed by the person whose map this is. Other people, particularly those who cannot cook, might see things differently! In addition, there is nothing to prevent the consultant from developing his or her own map of the situation – indeed, this may be a good idea in some cases.

Drawing the map

Eden, Ackermann and Cropper (1995) suggest 12 guidelines that people should follow when attempting to draw cognitive maps. Rather than repeating them here, I will discuss some of the main points, using Figures 6.2 and 6.3 as examples. Figure 6.3 shows the general map structure that seems to work best. The very top of the map contains the goals; that is, the things towards which the participants are striving. It may also contain things they are trying to avoid, which are labelled as 'not goals' in Figure 6.3. The bottom segment of Figure 6.3 is where actions and options open to participants are located. The aim is to develop a causal trail from these through to the goals (or not goals). The middle segment, labelled as 'strategic directions', contains the important issues that, although not ultimate goals in themselves, must be resolved in order to

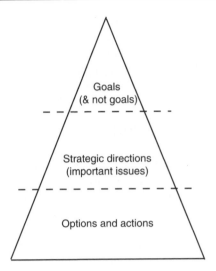

Figure 6.3 A general structure for cognitive and causal maps.

link the options and actions to the goals and not goals. If the map is drawn while interviewing someone or while working with a group, it will probably be very difficult to create one that fits this ideal structure. To do so may require redrawing the map, and this may itself lead to questions and discussion about the goals and strategic directions.

Examination of Figure 6.2 shows that its organization is close to the tripartite form of Figure 6.3, in which goals should be placed at the top of the map. In Figure 6.2 it seems that the main aim of the person involved is to have a relaxing holiday. Thus, using their words, 'Come back refreshed' sits at the top of the map; if at all possible, goals should be identified early in the mapping, as these are the things towards which people are aiming, and they provide the context for the rest of the map.

Below the goals, but leading into them, are the important issues or strategic directions, which have long-term implications, high cost or irreversibility. They may require a portfolio of actions to make them happen, or may even require a change in culture. In essence, these are pivots around which the map is centred. Figure 6.2, not surprisingly, has the concept 'Time to relax' as very important, with many arrows connected to it. Drawn in a different way, a concept to do with food might also be strategic. It may be necessary to prompt the interviewee by asking her what she sees as the key issues.

The bottom layer of the map contains the actions and options, and, as with other concepts, these should be expressed, if at all possible, in an imperative, or action-oriented, way. 'Stay in the UK' is an example of the imperative form, which becomes a statement of intent. If the preferences of the interviewee form the first or only pole of any concept, this directs attention to the preferences, leading to an action orientation. As noted earlier, doing this may lead to some negative links. For example, the concept 'Spend less than £500' leads to several negative links – because it will be hard to achieve, given some of the other preferences in Figure 6.2. With this in mind, it is important to ensure that the arrows have the correct direction of causality. It may be necessary to double-check with participants to be sure how they see this causality, and, in a group, this may cause some argument.

As mentioned earlier, if the map is drawn during the interview, it will need to be tidied up later, and this is advisable for reasons other than just neatness. Working through the map again after the event allows the analyst to think about the links and their structure and to check any aspects that are unclear. This has already been done in Figure 6.2. It reveals that one concept 'Go alone ... with another couple' is totally disconnected from any other concepts. This is an interesting point and is something that might be further explored.

Software support for mapping

Any attempt to understand and interpret people's ideas will produce information that must be organized and analysed. Although this can be done by hand, it gets rather tedious when a map consists of a large number of constructs. Even if it is arguable whether computer software should be used interactively during a client interview to develop a map of the ideas expressed, there are uses for computer support.

First, as a map is developed, its appearance can grow increasingly scrappy and untidy, with lines that cross, writing that becomes nearly illegible, attempts to fit into a space more than was originally intended and so on. Thus, the first use for software support is to make a sketch map rather neater, better organized and easier to read. According to Eden and colleagues, there is little to be gained from a map with only a few concepts that cannot be achieved by a straight verbal account of the ideas and their links. However, they argue that many useful maps may contain over a hundred concepts, and considerable layout skills are needed to draw these legibly. If software is not available or its use seems undesirable, then concepts can be written on Post-it® notes that are stuck to a white board on which the links can be drawn. If the map grows messy and needs to be redrawn, this can be done by moving the Post-it® notes and redrawing the links.

Second, once a map has been developed and is properly drawn, it needs (as will be seen later) to be analysed. This is to link together any concepts that seem to have similar meanings and, possibly, to prepare the maps for aggregation with other maps in the SODA I process.

Finally, if the aim is to develop a group cause map as in SODA II, then this can be done by providing participants with a networked laptop PC, through which they can offer suggestions about which concepts should be displayed and how they should be linked.

Eden and colleagues developed the software system Decision Explorer (Banxia, 2009), which was originally known as Graphics COPE, as a single-user aid in drawing and using these maps. It can be used by an individual to draw and clean up maps or by a facilitator working with a group and displaying the map via a PC projector onto a large screen. The software allows a user to examine and develop a map through a number of views, each of which can display about 40 concepts if they are linked or about 60 if they have been brainstormed and have yet to be linked into a map. Concepts and links are entered directly into the map using a keyboard and mouse and can be freely placed or moved around the view. The user and reference guides (Banxia, 2009) give a complete coverage of the facilities available in Decision Explorer. The Banxia website (www.banxia.com) contains useful tutorial material and examples of the successful use of Decision Explorer.

Group Explorer (Phrontis, 2009) provides mapping support for working with groups of people collaborating on an important issue. Its use requires the presence of a facilitator, who alone has direct access to the map. In essence, a wireless LAN connection allows users to communicate with the facilitator without other participants knowing what they are suggesting. The facilitator must decide when their input is displayed and in what form. As will be clear later, this facilitation using Group Explorer is best done by two people, the second being a 'chauffeur' who manages the communications with the participants. The Phrontis website (www.phrontis.com) contains tutorial material and examples of the use of Group Explorer.

Consulting styles and consulting processes

Schön (1982) argues that many professionals employ what he terms 'technical rationality' in justifying what they do and what they offer to their clients. This embodies a view that professional knowledge sits in a hierarchy in which 'general principles' occupy the highest level and 'concrete problem-solving' the lowest (Schön, 1982, p. 24). In this model, the professional aims to apply the general principles to specific problems. This implies that professionals have a systematic knowledge base that is specialized, firmly bound, scientific and standardized. Hence, most professions require their members to sit exams designed to test their understanding of this knowledge base. Further, the professional is consulted because of this expertise. Schön argues that most professions recognize that the use of this knowledge to give specific help is far from straightforward, but they tend to subsume this under 'craft skills' or something similar. Technical rationality implies that professionals function best as experts who themselves define the problems of clients on which they are working.

However, a different approach is possible, and this is what Eden, Jones and Sims (1983) term the negotiative approach, which they contrast with other approaches as shown in Figure 6.4. This shows three styles of helping or consulting in common use, the first of which is a coercive approach, which has some of the features of Schön's technical rationality. In this coercive approach, consultants use their professional power to persuade and convince clients of how their problems should be framed and how they should be tackled. In this approach, problem definition is the responsibility of the consultant, although this may be cloaked in an approach that is apparently based on consultation. An empathetic approach is the opposite of a coercive one, and this refers to an approach in which consultants set out fully to understand the problem as the clients see it. The consultants work with the clients to help them to frame their own view of the problem. In one sense, the consultant is a passive reflector of the client's concerns.

Rather than these two, Eden, Jones and Sims (1983) recommend a negotiative approach based on a period of negotiation between consultant and client. The idea is to negotiate a problem frame in which both parties are interested and to which both are committed. This approach sits between the other two. It assumes that both parties have something they bring to the venture and both may have something to gain from it. It accepts, as given, that the problem as initially expressed by the client may not be the one on which the consultant eventually cooperates, and vice versa. Thus, problems are seen as negotiated.

A negotiative approach underlies the process advocated by Eden and colleagues with respect to cognitive mapping and to the SODA I and II methodologies. In this, the aspects that technical rationality would relegate to 'craft skills' are taken as fundamental to a successful intervention

	Coercive	Negotiative	Empathetic
Consultant	Frames	Negotiates frame	Passively reflects
Client	Supplies context	Negotiates frame	Frames

Figure 6.4 Consulting approaches.

using cognitive mapping. The cognitive maps should not be the consultant's imperious interpretation of what the interviewee has said, rather they should reflect the meaning of what is said. The consultant's job is to help the individual or group to establish goals, options and key issues, so as to support their decision-making. This partly explains the stress laid upon expressing concepts in the words used by the interviewee. On the other hand, the maps should not result from the consultant acting like a bland sound-recorder who just plays back what the interviewee has said. It is important for the mapper to interpret what the client has said, and it is important that the two of them discuss this interpretation.

Case study: the music merger

To help understand how these methods may be used, consider the following, hypothetical case study.

Background

Hungry Records has recently been taken over by The Continental Corporation, a multinational entertainments company. The Continental Corporation website describes it as 'A family of businesses working in the communications and entertainment industries around the world'. These include Continental Music and Continental Entertainment. The website claims that Continental Entertainment aims 'to bring you the very best in film and television, the very best in music and the very best in TV, video and hi-fi equipment'. Continental Entertainment was formed in the late 1980s by a merger between some of Continental's interests and those of Sezah Electronics.

Continental Music consists of Continental Records, Continental Music Europe and Continental Music America, and the latter is a very successful record label, with its recordings consistently in the top five bestsellers. Continental Records began in the UK and, prior to the takeover of Hungry Records, had merged with the US-based Imagic group to form Continental Music.

The Hungry Records website makes its outlook very clear:

> *Hungry's philosophy is simple: the very finest in music. Everyone at Hungry believes in our artists:*
>
> * *We never sign artists solely on the basis of commercial potential, but on the basis of quality.*
> * *We never tell our artists what to write or how to sound.*
>
> *That philosophy has made us one of the biggest independent labels in the world. It is built on respect for the artists and respect for the fans. You can be sure that, every time you pick up a Hungry record, it will be a record made with love and with care. We will never, ever, try to sell you second best.*

Bob McTag is head of Continental Music and he has asked for your help. He is in the early stages of formulating a strategy for working with Hungry Records. It seems he is having trouble finding any sort of common ground, and has been in touch with you to ask whether cognitive mapping could be used to help them move the situation forward. Paul Mitchell is head of Hungry Records, and it seems that at least he and Bob will need to be involved in this exercise.

An interview with Bob McTag

Interviewer: What do you see as the most important issues facing Hungry at present?

Bob McTag: Well, they have to learn how to live within a new, corporate context. The reason that we have been able to take them over is that, businesswise, their organization left a great deal to be desired. Artistically, they are very strong, and it is not in our interests to interfere with that, but we can help them by introducing some discipline into their business dealings. Also, we hope to develop their strong branding.

Interviewer: What sort of discipline?

Bob McTag: They will have to justify their budgets to the board of the wider company. Projects will not be allowed to run wildly over budget without prior approval. Artists must begin to understand that they, like the rest of us, work within a commercial context. Without that discipline, Hungry will never be turned into a long-term profitable concern. Instead, it would remain on the edge of profitability forever, and any small run of bad luck or unfashionability would see it going under.

Interviewer: So you expect this discipline to impact on the relationship between the company and the artists?

Bob McTag: Not really. We fully intend to keep as many of the Hungry staff as we can. We do not see them as being overstaffed. We see the relationships with the artists being managed by the same people as at present, the Hungry A&R staff. They will be situated as a subdepartment of Continental's A&R department. Paul Mitchell will be involved, but not directly as line manager. This is necessary to gain the sort of financial control we need. So the relationships will be the same, but within a new context of business discipline. That means that the A&R staff will have to manage the relationship on a business level as well as a personal and artistic one. They will have to make sure that the artists know about the budgetary restrictions and requirements, and work to justify budget extensions or to generate ideas for ways around the problem. Each artist is different, so the ideas will be different.

Another important issue is the dance music division, Ravenous Tunes. It has never made money, and I see no prospect of it ever doing so. It remains away from the cutting edge of its own genre, and does nothing for the image of Hungry. I see some of the acts on Ravenous being transferred across to our own dance music label, and others being dropped. That is unfortunate, of course, but it is also necessary.

The purpose of being in this business, as with any business, is to make money. If, along the way, we can put out great records, then so much the better.

Interviewer: What happens when a label doesn't make money?

Bob McTag: A label that does not make money ultimately ceases to exist, no matter how good the music. We have shareholders, and they are interested in the bottom line, ultimately.

Interviewer: What do you see happening with the branding?

Bob McTag: Hungry is a strong brand, but marketing branded merchandise is not our area of competence. We would envisage franchising off control of the brand to a reputable company. They would then exploit the brand in whatever way they see fit. We (and we would expect to take Paul Mitchell's advice heavily in this matter) would retain some right of veto, but, the way that these contracts work, that right is limited: we can only say no to a certain percentage of the ideas, or we become liable for certain payments. However, the royalties from this kind of merchandising can be enormous if you have a strong brand with which people identify, like their favourite football club, or their favourite record label. Merchandising is one of our short-term ideas for making good some of our initial investment.

The long term depends on the music, and how well it sells. The continued credibility of Hungry as a brand depends fundamentally on the quality and success of the music that is issued under that brand. The exploitation of that brand in other ways is nothing more than a lucrative sideline, with no real impact in the long term.

Interviewer: How much independence do you see Hungry having in terms of signing new artists?

Bob McTag: They will be independent. We cannot do what Hungry do in terms of feeling which way the market for their sort of music is going to go, or what fits. They have a good idea of their own subculture. We would expect their staff to listen for suggestions from our A&R staff for artists to sign, and perhaps to move one or two of our suitable artists onto their label, but they can say no. I think it would be unhelpful for them to say no every time, however. It would be likely to cause bad feeling elsewhere around the corporation. I think it is important to stress that I see this partnership as a cooperation, not a series of battles.

Continental can bring significant expertise in the music industry to this partnership, as well as financial strength and business discipline. We expect Hungry staff to cooperate with ours, not simply to fight them. Our Corporation could not allow those kinds of conflict to occur.

Interviewer: What would happen if those kinds of battle were to take place?

Bob McTag: We would have to deal with that as a personnel issue. Those of our staff who work for Hungry would be employees like any others, with the same rights and the same expected standards of behaviour.

An interview with Paul Mitchell

Interviewer: Tell me about the most important issues facing Hungry records at the moment.

Paul Mitchell: Obviously, the most serious issue to face us, given that Hungry has now been sold to Continental, is the negotiation of the power to make the ultimate decisions. We entered the deal with the guarantee that we would retain artistic control, but, understandably, Continental has retained control of the purse strings. If we can make use of the fantastic resources that Continental has, on our own terms, then we can go on to build Hungry as one of the classic names in the history of the music business. At the same time we can make ourselves, our artists and our new parent company a great deal of money.

What we must beware of, however, is losing the brand identity of Hungry in the merger with Continental. It is the identification with Hungry's political and cultural position that makes us strong. If we end up losing control of our own output, the fans will know, and our brand will lose its potency. That is in nobody's interest.

We are fundamentally a healthy business, but we have been forced into this position through cash-flow difficulties. It is my job now to ensure that the company lives on, even if it is ultimately owned by Continental. We have not been making much money over the last few years, that's why we're here, but with Continental's resources we will carry on releasing great music.

Interviewer: What are the most important factors in maintaining Hungry's brand identity?

Paul Mitchell: We must retain ultimate control over the music we put out. Our A&R function (which manages signing new artists and maintaining the relationship with existing artists) must remain independent. We must have a veto over what Continental decides to do with the Hungry brand name. Sometimes, executives in large corporations have no idea whatsoever about the integrity of branding, and we must be able to tell them no. Even if a particular product were to make money in the short term, it is the long-term image of the brand that I have to think about.

Interviewer: What could happen to hurt that?

Paul Mitchell: Well, if we cashed in on the brand with shoddy or inappropriate goods, it might make good money in the short term, but it would damage the credibility of the brand in the long term. We want Hungry fans to feel assured that, every time they buy something with the Hungry logo on, they can rely on it being decent. And, if we produce merchandise that our followers think is rubbish, that reflects back on the brand. Maybe not immediately, but the trust between us and our fans is damaged.

Interviewer: And that applies to whatever product, whether it be records or other Hungry-branded products?

Paul Mitchell: Yes. At the moment, we only produce records and T-shirts, and I can see that there is a market for other products branded as Hungry. Of course, the music is the most important thing, and, if we lose the quality of our musical releases, everything else suffers too.

Interviewer: How will you maintain the quality of the music?

Paul Mitchell: By doing what we've always done, and trusting to the instincts and tastes of our staff, myself included.

Interviewer: And how could you see that going wrong?

Paul Mitchell: With too much interference from Continental. Our artists trust us, and they do not trust large corporations. In a lot of cases, they wanted to be with an independent company, so they signed for us despite having had larger offers from bigger companies. Unless we retain the characteristics that made us what we are, we might as well close down now. Which means we conduct business in our own way, and appoint the staff we want to. Without the right staff, we cannot get the right atmosphere. And we must maintain our own lines of management. Without that, the decisions will be corporate in nature, not Hungry. Which will lead to disaffected artists, who will either leave us or not produce their best work. That way, everyone loses.

Interviewer: What is your ultimate aim for Hungry?

Paul Mitchell: To be regarded as a great label, ultimately. Also, to make money and to enjoy myself. I look for those priorities in the staff I appoint, too.

Maps from the two interviews

It seems clear from the interview transcripts that Bob and Paul have some things in common, but also that they have major differences in their outlook. Drawing maps based on the two interviews can help clarify these differences and may also help to identify common ground on which the two of them can build.

Figure 6.5 shows a map based on the interview with Bob McTag, the Head of Continental Music, the company taking over Hungry Records. It seems that Bob's ultimate goal is to satisfy the shareholders of the Continental Corporation, which means ensuring that the business is consistently profitable. To this end, he needs to have records that sell and would like to supplement this income with cash raised from selling merchandise (T-shirts, etc.) relating to Hungry's artists. He feels that, to do this, he will have to improve the Hungry organization, adding some of the business discipline that has made Continental Music so successful. In an ideal world, he would allow Hungry to keep the artistic freedom represented by its own A&R staff, but that may not be possible. Figure 6.5 shows the flow of concepts, each one stated with an action orientation where possible – that is, with Bob's preferred action or option uppermost.

With his background in Hungry Records, Paul Mitchell's view looks very different and is captured in the map shown in Figure 6.6. His ultimate goal seems to be very different from

Figure 6.5 Cognitive map – Bob McTag.

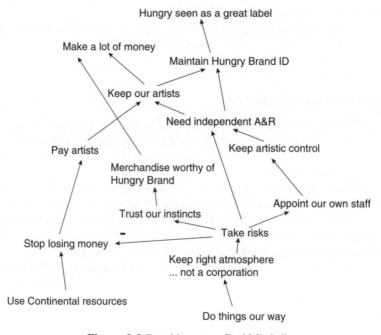

Figure 6.6 Cognitive map – Paul Mitchell.

Bob's, for Paul's aim is for his audience to regard Hungry Records as a great label – whatever that may mean. The rest of the map explores what this means by linking concepts together in a hierarchy with Paul's preferences uppermost in the different concepts shown. Paul, too, wants to make money, but it is not clear whether he will do this if it means degrading what he sees as the integrity of Hungry's name. He is willing to develop the merchandise side of the business if he thinks that the goods are worthy of the Hungry brand. Indeed, it seems that most things are subservient to the development of the Hungry label and its brand, including the type of staff appointed. For Paul, decision-making comes down to following hunches that seem promising for the further development of the Hungry ethos.

Can the two maps be used to help the Hungry business be incorporated within Continental? This is a hard question to answer, but certainly they help to clarify the important differences between the two men. They both wish to see their businesses make money, and both see the need for Hungry to keep a distinctive approach to its A&R, if this is possible. Beyond that, there is much negotiating to be done.

Working with cognitive maps

Cognitive maps are intended to help people to think through the actions they might take, so it is clearly of some importance to consider how these maps might be used. A later section of this chapter discusses the SODA I and II methodologies, which are the processes by which Eden *et al.* suggest that the maps might be used to negotiate problem definitions leading to agreed action within teams of people. In this sense, the methodologies provide a form of group decision support and, with the software systems, form a group decision support system (Eden and Ackermann, 1992). Note that the software is only one part of this system; human beings and their interactions are also important. Before discussing the methodologies, however, it is important to consider how these maps might be understood and analysed. The first part of this section will consider how the mapper might work through the map with the interviewee, clarifying and working towards some agreement about possible actions. The second part will discuss ways in which more complex maps can be handled.

Working through a map

Eden (1989) suggests that there are two ways of working through a map with someone, and a similar approach applies when working with groups of people. The two approaches are top-down or bottom-up. Both aim to check whether the map is complete enough to be used, and to move the discussion from expressing ideas (the mapping phase) to considering actions that might be taken. Doing this requires some skill, for it is not just a simple-minded move from the top to the bottom of the map, or vice versa. While working through a map, the consultant must keep returning to the key issues to organize the discussion and description.

It is important to note that working with and through a map is part of the negotiative approach advocated above. The map serves as a vehicle by which the two people can move towards aspects on which they can agree and on which they might cooperate. It thus serves as a vehicle for negotiation by separating, for a time at least, the interviewee from his or her thoughts and ideas. This must be done with some care, for people's ideas can seem a bit trivial and rather banal when sketched out. The idea is not to show how foolish the client is; the idea is to find some way to move towards sensible action that can be defended in rational terms. This relates to the view that the outcome of the work is a product of the content and the process by which the people work with that content.

In a top-down approach, the idea is to start with the concepts at the top of the map and to work back down through the others. If the map has been drawn as suggested earlier, then the concepts at the top will be an attempt to capture the goals of the interviewee. Hence, Paul Mitchell might be asked why he is so concerned about having music lovers see Hungry as a great record label. Note that this can seem dangerously close to an 'idiot question' (see Chapter 3) and needs to be approached carefully, but it cannot be ignored. Presumably, Paul does not really want to achieve this end at all costs, for he also recognizes the need to make money and to run Hungry Records as a business. Perhaps the mapper needs to elaborate on this concept so as to discover what Paul means by a 'great label'? Again, though, this should only be done with great care, for this may be a very sensitive issue if he has invested years of his life in the company. The idea is that each refinement of the concept moves the map further up its hierarchy until some point is reached at which the new top concept is 'self-evidently a good thing' (Eden, 1989, p. 31). At this point, the idea is to work back down the hierarchical network by asking what actions might be taken to change and improve things other than the ones already placed on the map. The idea is to identify actions that might be taken. The discussion can then, if desired, shift to considering how these actions might be taken.

A bottom-up approach starts by examining the tail of the map; that is, with those concepts at the bottom of the hierarchy with no predecessors. As with the top-down approach, the idea is to search for options that might provide ways of taking action. For example, the map of the interview with Bob contains 'Improve Hungry's marketing' as one of the driving forces. What action might be taken to achieve this? As in contact sports, there are two ways to deal with pressure: roll with it and find some opportunity to turn it to your advantage, or stand your ground and accept the hit. There may be some way in which the pressure being applied could be used to improve other things at Hungry as part of a deal that could be struck. Working up the map by examining each concept should lead to similar discussions, for there may be other ways of improving Hungry's marketing than by using third-party franchisees. The idea, in each case, is to examine the concepts to see if there are other options that could be considered. In this way, the cooperative thinking of the client and consultant can be expanded.

Analysing a map: loop analysis

As mentioned earlier, cognitive maps look very like the influence diagrams used by system dynamics modellers (see Chapter 7). As with the system dynamics diagrams, it is possible to examine cognitive maps for loops, the idea being to see if there are any which may be self-reinforcing (positive feedback) or self-maintaining (negative feedback). A loop occurs when arrows leading out from a concept end up back where they started, if followed forwards through intervening concepts. An abstract example of this is given in Figure 6.7. This hypothetical map contains two loops, both of which start from concept 2. The larger of the two loops starts at concept 2 and returns there via concepts 9, 10 and 11. The smaller of the two loops goes to concept 9, then concept 11 and back to concept 2 again. Checking a large map for these loops is rather time consuming; however, this task is simple to automate and can be managed by tools such as Decision Explorer if the map data are in a computer-readable form.

Having found loops on a map, what do they signify? The first possibility is that they may simply indicate a mistake – either by the person being interviewed (they were muddled) or by the mapper. Thus, the first check is that the loops are intended to be there; if not, reversing

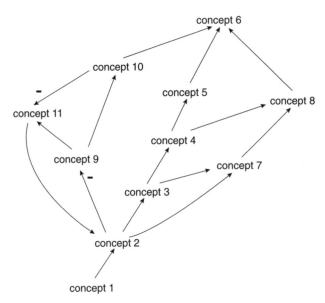

Figure 6.7 Abstract map segment showing loops.

one arrow's causality will remove the loop. If so, then the next stage is to check their signs so as to consider what this might imply in dynamic terms. Checking the sign of the loop allows the mapper to see in what direction the causality lies. As with normal multiplication, an odd number of negative signs indicates that the loop has negative feedback. In terms of control theory, this means that a system will be self-controlling in the sense that it will tend to dampen down fluctuations. The small loop that links concepts 2, 9 and 11 is an example of such negative feedback. An even number of negative signs implies positive feedback, which will therefore be amplifying – precisely what would be expected from a set of concepts linked by positive relationships. The larger loop linking concepts 2, 9, 10 and 11 has two negative signs, making it a positive feedback loop.

The aim of the loop analysis is to check for mistakes and then to check the sign of any remaining 'correct' loops. The mapper and the client can discuss these to try to understand their implications. The loop analysis is best conducted before any attempt to cluster the concepts.

Analysing a map: clusters

As practical cognitive maps may contain a hundred or more concepts, even when produced for a single person, some way is needed to support their use. Decision Explorer provides some support in this, but the basic principles need to be understood so as to avoid the risk of inappropriate use of such a tool. One important feature of such analyses is the idea of a cluster of concepts. These are sets of concepts that are similar in some way and could, in some sense, be more or less separated from the rest of the map. Clearly, if a map contains concepts that are all strongly interlinked, it may not be fruitful to attempt this sort of analysis. This might be the case if the ratio of links to nodes is high.

A cluster indicates that there is an issue of some importance that may have an effect rather greater than just on a single input and output link. Underlying the cluster identification is the notion that 'language is the common currency of organizational life'. That is, people's words have meanings, and a good starting point is to assume that, although the meanings will change over time, the same words may have more or less the same meaning. Clusters can be formed around the names and words that are used, which explains the importance of capturing the words used by the interviewee. Note that this question of meaning is crucial and will be revisited when considering SODA, journey-making and the question of how to merge the maps of different people. This is less of an issue when working with a single person.

Eden, Ackermann and Cropper (1992) suggest two approaches to cluster formation:

1. *Linkage clustering.* In this approach, the labels given to the nodes (that is, the words employed in the concepts) are examined for their similarity. Nodes with similar labels are aggregated into clusters which, once developed, should identify issues of sufficient importance to warrant further discussion. As mentioned above, this relies on the mapper capturing the words used by the interviewee and then coding them in a consistent way. If the map, its nodes and its links are captured in a computer data file, it should be possible to parse the text into separate words and to subject it to a semantic analysis. Then, some scoring system could be used to establish the similarity of different labels. This could then be used as a stopping rule to indicate when a concept should or should not be added to a cluster. The resulting clusters should provide a summary of the overall map. Although it is impossible to do this in Decision Explorer, it can be done manually, or by using software such as Nud*ist (QSR, 2002).
2. *Hierarchical clustering around core constructs.* This approach relates back to the ideas of Kelly (1955) that constructs are organized in a hierarchical way. If this is so, and if the mapping concepts relate to these constructs, it may sometimes be useful to examine the map for hierarchies. In one sense, each node will have a supporting hierarchy, apart from those at the very bottom of the map. However, the purpose of the analysis is usually to show the linkages from certain 'core constructs' (Eden, Ackermann and Cropper, 1992). These can be identified by a count of the in and out arrows at each node, as it might reasonably be supposed that important nodes will have more such links. A single node may well appear in more than one hierarchical cluster; indeed, if it does so, then this may well indicate that the concept is of considerable importance in the map. In Eden's terms, such concepts are regarded as 'potent'. This process of hierarchical clustering can also be automated if the map data are held in some suitable form.

Working with groups and teams: SODA I and II

Cognitive mapping also provides the basis for helping teams of people to decide on an action plan. One criticism of much Management Science is that, although valuable at a tactical level, many of the methods and techniques turn out to be of limited value at the strategic level in most organizations. As argued in earlier chapters, this is probably because strategic decision-making and planning are characterized by great uncertainty, not just about how to do something, but often also about what should be done and why. That is, there is debate about ends as well as about means. In the terms used in the introduction to Part II, this suggests that 'soft' methods might be able to make a useful contribution. The SODA acronym (Strategic Options Development and Analysis) covers two distinct approaches developed by Eden and colleagues to enable groups of people to commit themselves to action by careful and rational consideration of the possibilities they can envisage. As with SSM, these are methodologies in two senses. They provide an approach that should be followed, but also embody a set of assumptions based on cognitive mapping – stressing action and working with people's expressed ideas. The main differences

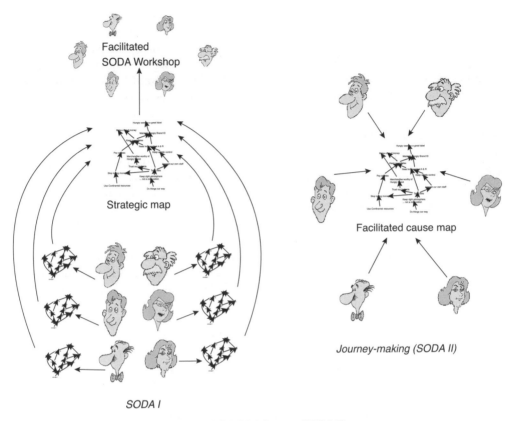

Figure 6.8 SODA I versus SODA II.

between the two approaches are shown in Figure 6.8. Whether to use SODA I or SODA II normally depends on the circumstances. When working with a group in a situation where time is short, SODA II will be preferable to SODA I.

SODA I is useful for situations in which a group of individuals have their own views and outlooks but need to be blended into an effective strategic decision-making team. It starts with separate interviews with each individual member of the team, the idea being to develop a cognitive map for each one. The map will show how they express their thinking about the issue that the team has been formed to address. These individual maps are then merged into a single strategic map that forms the basis for group discussion and negotiation. The strategic map is displayed, usually by PC projection, and is used by a skilled facilitator who works with the group, helping them to reach agreement on what to do.

SODA II, and its sister, journey-making, is an approach described in Eden and Ackermann (1998) and intended for use directly with a team rather than starting with individuals. It usually relies on the use of software such as Group Explorer (Phrontis, 2009) and the use of laptops linked via a wireless LAN. Helped by a facilitator, the team builds a cause map that reflects their concerns and the options open to them in the issues they face. This, like the strategic map of SODA I, is used by the facilitator to help the group to reach agreement on what to do.

Both approaches involve divergent and convergent stages. Chapter 2 discussed Hudson's (1967) early work on convergers and divergers, convergers being very good at analysis, divergers being excellent synthesizers and developers of new ideas. Chapter 2 also argued that both abilities are needed when tackling complex problems, and that they should not be seen as in opposition to one another. The first stage of both approaches is divergent, gaining the views and opinions of individual members of the group. The second stage is convergent, as the group starts to identify the crucial concepts and issues that must be dealt with. A skilled facilitator will help the group to move from one mode to another when that is necessary.

Merging maps in SODA I

The first stage of the SODA I approach is to interview the individual participants in order to develop their individual cognitive maps of the situation. The next stage is to look for links, differences and similarities between the maps of the participants to enable these to be merged into the strategic map. A slightly subtle point underpins this merging process: to whom does the strategic map belong and whose views does it express? When we have described how the merging process works, we will return to this point.

The idea of this merging is to produce a strategic map with which the participants can all identify. The aim is to move the group towards a position where its members are committed to some appropriate action. It is therefore vital that this is done in such a way that they do not feel compromised. Agreement may not be complete, it may be slightly grudging, but each member is willing to work at the actions that emerge from the process. Hence, as has been said several times before, this means that the processes involved in SODA I must be carefully managed.

Eden also stresses that it is important to ensure that some of the words used by each individual and appearing on their own maps are preserved on the strategic map. There are two reasons for this. The first is that words may have several meanings, and the substitution of apparent synonyms may obscure the original meaning. The second is that it may help the individuals involved to be committed to the outcome if they see their own words on the strategic map. The consultant must strive to preserve the meanings of concepts; that is, the intentions behind the words. Of course, if a large number of people are involved, the consultant may need to decide who are the key people, whose views must be shown. In this sense, both SODA approaches recognize the reality of power in organizational life.

There are four processes in merging the individual maps into a strategic map:

1. By examining the individual maps, it should become clear that at least some of the participants are using similar concepts. If there are no such similar concepts, then this indicates that the participants are framing the issues in radically different ways, and this may be the most important observation that can be made. The fact that the concepts are presented as pairs of opposing poles helps the recognition of the similarity. So does the fact that the analyst has worked with the individuals in drawing their maps. The similar concepts can be overlaid on one another in the strategic map, much as transparent sheets may be overlaid, one on top of another.

2. Once overlaid in this way, it may be possible for the consultant to add extra links between the concepts used by individuals. This is a way for the consultant to suggest to the team that their ideas can fit in a synergistic way. The strategic map is to be used as a device to enable the team to negotiate with one another and with the consultant. Any extra links are created with this in mind because the consultant is not just a disinterested observer or referee.

3. While overlaying and linking, the analyst needs to ensure that the strategic map preserves any hierarchies of links that were present in the individual maps. This may be difficult to achieve, but the dependencies are important.

4. The strategic map needs to be analysed for loops, clusters, potent concepts, etc., as described in the previous section. This is a crucial part of the process, for it helps to identify the issues in people's minds to which attention must be paid.

To whom does the strategic map belong? After the merging, the answer is presumably that it belongs to the consultant but is intended to reflect the views of the participants. The approach is, as mentioned earlier, negotiative and does not assume that the consultant acts only in a bland role as a benign sound recorder. The strategic map is the result of a deliberate attempt by the consultant to pick out what seem to be crucial issues from the mess or issue stream (see Chapter 3) with which people are working. If the individual maps are subjective statements about these issues, the strategic map is an intersubjective statement. That is, it shows where people's subjective views are close or distant. Whether the group will accept this is another matter, and this, too, requires careful process management via SODA workshops.

Workshops: general aspects

In SODA I, the strategic map is developed beforehand as the basis for a workshop that is directed by a facilitator but involves the whole group. In SODA II, the action takes place entirely within such a workshop, as the group constructs a cause map, which then supports discussion and debate. Chapter 3 developed the idea that, rather than working on self-contained and well-understood problems, it is more common for people to find themselves working with messes or issue streams in strategic decision-making. These are systems of interconnected problems and issues that are hard to pull apart without losing some of the meaning. The strategic map or cause map is the first stage in helping the group to develop their own views of that mess. The core of the approaches is one or more deliberately planned workshops that employ the strategic or cause map.

The idea of a workshop is to gain commitment to agreed and negotiated action. As would be expected in this negotiative approach, the consultant is not just a neutral facilitator, but also has interests and may have other expertise. One outcome of the workshop may be that there is scope for traditional Management Science of the type discussed in Part III. In this sense, SODA I and II can be regarded as approaches to problem-structuring. However, it is not uncommon for people to find that, once they have negotiated an acceptably common perspective on the issue stream, the action needed is fairly clear. Discussions of the conduct of the SODA I and II workshops are to be found in Eden and Ackermann (1992), Eden and Simpson (1989) and Eden and Ackermann (2001).

The consultant needs to be aware that he or she is taking on a difficult, though manageable, task in attempting either type of SODA workshop. Most teams of managers have a shared life or culture of some kind if they are at all cohesive, and they may not be overwelcoming of attempts to question their ideas. It is thus vital that the consultant starts these workshops in a carefully planned and facilitative mode. The strategic or cause map is to be used as a vehicle for discussion and negotiation, led by the consultant, who needs to remain in control of the proceedings. Given that many senior managers are extremely powerful personalities, this may be easier said than done! Perhaps the best approach is for the consultant to be explicit with the group about his or her role as chair. Even having done this, however, the consultant must try to retain control without losing credibility. It has been found useful for the consultant to be assisted by a second person, often known as the chauffeur, who can keep control of the hardware and software used to develop and display the map to the group.

When planning for a workshop, the facilitator must establish a clear set of workshop objectives and should anticipate the potential workshop stages that might be useful. This process design should be negotiated with the client, during which the facilitator and client both learn their way into the problem situation and the issues that need to be tackled. It should hardly need saying, but the room, lighting, seating and other comfort factors are important. The group will be spending a day or two in intense discussion and debate, and it is important to create an atmosphere that is workmanlike and yet enables people to relax a little. If they are unable to see the map clearly as it develops and changes, they are hardly likely to contribute to a positive debate.

The choice of activity at any particular point during a workshop depends on what the facilitator considers most appropriate to the task. The facilitator must select and shape each step of the workshop, as there is no rigorous, step-by-step procedure. In their presentation of strategic choice, another soft OR approach, Friend and Hickling (1987) point out that a group will shift its focus as it works, and that it is wrong to assume that these shifts follow a particular sequence. In cognitive mapping, these shifts emerge as the map is developed and discussed. During the course of a typical workshop, a group might be involved in several different brainstorming activities, structuring the brainstorm material through clustering and linking, coding concepts according to their type, identifying key concepts to be further developed, voting on the priority of the key concepts, elaborating these concepts through discussion, establishing goals and options, generating actions and finally agreeing a way forward. The facilitator is not limited to using the cognitive mapping to achieve all of this. He or she may choose to incorporate any appropriate activity, which may or may not exploit the software. Managing this contingent approach is important and relies on key craft skills.

SODA I workshops

The consultant has a definite role to play and must come to the workshop with an agenda to be addressed. This must focus on the concepts, issues, problems and relationships that must be addressed if progress is to be made. These should emerge from the strategic map and from the client and should be identifiable on the map. Thus, the strategic map serves as the basis of an agenda for the SODA I workshop.

Eden (1989) suggests that a SODA I workshop should consist of a two-pass approach:

1. *The introductory pass.* This should be led by the consultant with little or no opportunity for the group to comment or to discuss. The consultant should take the group through the strategic map so as to identify the key goals that have emerged, the different problems that have been identified and their relationships, the options for action that people seem to have identified and the assumptions that seem to have been made. As when working with individuals, this could be done in a top-down or bottom-up mode. Discussion needs to be limited to points of clarification. The idea of this first pass is to start a process in which the participants see their views as part of a larger picture, and also start to understand the concerns of other people. The map is a neutral device that separates concepts and concerns from the people themselves. They may recognize their own concepts on the strategic map, but other people may not. People can think about the concepts rather than judging the person who has proposed them.

2. *The second pass.* This may take a considerable time, depending on the group and the complexity of the map. The idea is to take the individual clusters and issues in priority order, and work on them in more detail by encouraging discussion. This second pass fits the notion of cyclic learning mentioned in the chapter on soft systems methodology (Chapter 5). The approach

assumes that most people learn new ideas gradually and at different rates and may need to return to them as their understanding gradually changes. In this second pass the consultant may need to extend or elaborate the map as new issues or linkages emerge in the discussion. It is important that these are visible to the participants so that their commitment may be obtained.

SODA II workshops

As there is no map in existence before the workshop, the group must first develop a cause map, guided by the facilitator and chauffeur. Most often this stage takes the form of a brainstorming session in which the participants type their concerns and concepts into their computers. In effect, the participants form a nominal group during this divergent stage. The concepts and concerns are accessible to the facilitator and the chauffeur via their own computers, but are not projected onto the large screen. The facilitator ends this blind gather (Shaw, Ackermann and Eden, 2001) whenever he or she feels that there are enough rich concepts available. Typically, this requires around 50 contributions. The facilitator and chauffeur must then roughly organize and cluster these concepts so that they can be displayed on the screen. Much of this clustering and organization can be done during the blind gather. The facilitator will know who has contributed which concepts, although this information will not be displayed on the screen. At the end of the blind gather, the consultant will project the organized concepts on the screen for the group to see.

The second stage of brainstorming is to elaborate the map as participants view the emerging cause map and add further ideas and links and suggest how things might be clustered. The blind gather is desirable so as to avoid groupthink (Janis, 1972), and the second stage enables people to build on one another's ideas, which is very important if some form of agreement is to be reached. In essence, the brainstorming and the organization of these ideas into a map help the group to surface what they see as the important ideas and issues. However, it must be recognized that the consultant has a role and responsibility that go beyond acting as recorder of the group's views. The consultant must help the group to develop an action plan, and this may involve posing questions and issues.

The consultant must help the group to develop clusters that they regard as sensible and useful. This can be done in a number of ways. For example:

- links may be added between concepts;
- key concepts might be identified using a round robin of contributions;
- concepts might be colour coded according to their type;
- clusters might be isolated and developed through in-depth discussion.

The facilitator may decide to add the concepts and links suggested by the group, or may ask the participants to do so themselves through their computers. Typically, once the brainstorm material has been structured, the group identifies a set of key concepts and then ranks them by voting. The ranking might be used to prioritize the issues on which to spend workshop time, or used as a tool to note and share divergent opinions. Voting is also used to establish whether the participants' opinions are aligned and may identify outliers – people who may be aware of information of which the rest of the group is ignorant (Westcombe and Pidd, 2002). In discussing the voting patterns, the group can share meaning and understanding and establish agreement. A second vote on the same issues generally involves a shift towards group consensus.

Why display the maps?

What is the role of the maps and why is it important to display and update them during the workshop? First, the maps are non-linear representations that can display complex interactions that are almost impossible to reproduce in the text that forms the agenda and the minutes of a conventional meeting. Most conventional meetings have an agenda that is worked through, point by point. There may be some passing reference to the fact that the issues being discussed are interconnected, but the format discourages thinking and debate that is holistic. The maps, though, make the links clear, and any participant can see this and can refer to it in what they have to say. It should be noted, however, that this non-linear representation does make it hard to write up conventional textual minutes of a cognitive mapping workshop, should that be necessary. However, recording the actions and responsibilities agreed as a result of using SODA is not so difficult.

Second, the map is a public display space that is owned by the group, and in which each member has some investment, and that acts as a reminder. It shows the issues that the group regards as important or that the facilitator has introduced. Quite literally, it enables the group all to face the same direction and to see whether they have developed enough shared understanding to enable agreement. Thus, it serves a similar purpose to the use of hexagons in scenario planning as developed by Shell (Hodgson, 1992). Developing this may take some time and may not be a calm and measured process, as it may involve heated debate, and votes may be needed to find some way forward. No approach can guarantee that people will honour their commitments, but the public display of the map during the workshop makes it more likely that everyone will understand the interconnectedness of the decision space.

Third, as discussed earlier, the approaches advocated here have phases during which they encourage divergence and stages during which they encourage convergence. The use of the map enables the facilitator and the group to operate in whichever mode is most appropriate.

Some reflections on cognitive mapping, SODA and journey-making

Part I introduced the general idea of modelling as used in Management Science and discussed its advantages and disadvantages as a way of anticipating the consequences of events. It also discussed views of rationality, given that these models are part of an attempt to use rational methods in managing organizations. Finally, it covered the idea of problems and decisions to try to relate what are often abstract ideas to the world of organizational life. Part II, of which this is the second chapter, addresses the question of soft or interpretive modelling. How do cognitive mapping, SODA and journey-making sit within all this?

First, there is great stress laid on the need for facilitation skills. Thus, the analyst, or consultant, is not seen as exercising the form of 'technical rationality' identified by Schön (1982), in which these skills are reduced to the notion of 'craft'. Instead, they are seen as central to the success of the approach. Hence, unlike SSM, the SODA methodologies make concrete suggestions about how to generate commitment from individuals who, initially at least, take up different positions from one another. Thus, to distort the views of Simon (1976) slightly, SODA provides a way of implementing procedural rationality in social or organizational terms. That is, SODA is a form of social heuristic that can give no guarantee of success but that has been found to be very useful.

SODA I and II are also, like SSM, pluralistic in their outlook and assumptions. They recognize that in some situations there may be conflict and disagreement, and, in helping to generate a debate, they also implicitly recognize that conflict is not always dysfunctional. Sometimes, change can only occur through conflict, but, when conflict gets out of hand, the results are very uncertain. With this in mind, there is no assumption that organizations are systems designed to achieve some goal. Instead, there is the idea that they are composed of people with all sorts of mixed agenda who choose to cooperate for some reason. One common workshop goal is to uncover the areas of common interest so as to enable progress to be made.

The approaches are also explicitly cyclic and multilevel. In working with both individuals and groups, the approaches recognize that people operate in this way and that this must be acknowledged. This is important because people often bring mixed agendas to their work, and these must be teased out, which takes time. The cyclic nature of the approach may be less clear, as, unlike SSM, there is no argument that one study leads into another, nor that the approach could be started at any point. Instead, Eden and colleagues are firm in their view that, in either form of SODA, mapping must precede discussion and decision. Nevertheless, the approach of SODA I is cyclic, as individuals get at least three chances to develop their understanding. They are interviewed for their own map, they hear the consultant's synthesis in the first part of the SODA workshop and they take part in the debate that forms the second part of the workshop. They therefore have the chance to reflect on the different issues as they are returned to.

Finally, SODA is organizationally sophisticated. It makes no assumption that an organization is a machine, or even that it is an organism. Instead, as pointed out in Pidd (1995), it is closest to the view of organization that Morgan (1986) characterized as 'flux and transformation'. This is a view of organizations that stresses verbs rather than nouns. There is thus an interest in how they develop and change rather than in the positions and roles that people fill within them. Thus, the focus is on the development of methods that will help organizations to manage that change rather better than they might do if they were firefighting the whole time. This view of organizations takes for granted that things are constantly changing within and without them, and that people will employ all sorts of strategies to achieve their ends.

Summary

Cognitive mapping is an approach that can be used as an interview technique or within one of the SODA methodologies. It is used to try to help people to think through the options that face them. Its basic technique involves drawing a graph of ideas or concepts that are linked together in means–end relationships. Fundamentally, the approach is individualistic and makes no claims to rest on explicit systems ideas, unlike soft systems methodology (Chapter 5). The originators of the ideas stress the need to ensure that it is used as part of a negotiative approach that neither acts in a coercive mode nor as a passive tape recorder of people's views. Instead, the idea is to use the map as part of the process of helping the client or group to commit to some action that will help achieve whatever their goals are found to be.

References

Axelrod R. (ed.) (1976) *Structure of Decision: the Cognitive Maps of Political Elites.* Princeton University Press, Princeton, NJ.

Bannister D. and Fransella F. (1986) *Inquiring Man: the Psychology of Personal Constructs*, 3rd edition. Croom Helm, London, UK.

Banxia (2009) *Decision Explorer*. Banxia Software, Glasgow, UK: www.banxia.com

Brown S.M. (1992) Cognitive mapping and repertory grids for qualitative survey research: some comparative observations. *Journal of Management Studies*, **29**(3), 287–308.

Bryson J.M., Ackermann F., Eden C.L. and Finn C.B. (2004) *Visible Thinking: Unlocking Causal Mapping for Practical Business Results*. John Wiley & Sons, Ltd, Chichester, UK.

Buckingham Shum S. (1996) Design argumentation as design rationale, in *The Encyclopaedia of Computer Science and Technology*, Vol. 35, Suppl. 20. Marcel Dekker, Inc., New York, NY, pp. 95–128.

Checkland P.B. (2001) Soft systems methodology, in *Rational Analysis for a Problematic World Revisited*, ed. by Rosenhead J. and Mingers J. John Wiley & Sons, Chichester, UK.

Downs R.M. and Stea D. (1977) *Maps in Mind. Reflections on Cognitive Mapping*. Harper & Row, New York, NY.

Eden C.L. (1989) Using cognitive mapping for strategic options development and analysis (SODA), *Rational Analysis for a Problematic World*, ed. by Rosenhead J. John Wiley & Sons, Ltd, Chichester, UK.

Eden C.L. and Ackermann F. (1992) Strategy development and implementation – the role of a group decision support system, in *Computer Augmented Teamwork: a Guided Tour*, ed. by Bostrom R.P., Watson R.T. and Kinney S.T. Van Nostrand Reinhold, New York, NY.

Eden C.L. and Ackermann F. (1998) *Strategy Making: the Journey of Strategic Management*. Sage, London, UK.

Eden C.L. and Ackermann F. (2001) SODA – the principles, in *Rational Analysis for a Problematic World Revisited*, ed. by Rosenhead J. and Mingers J. John Wiley & Sons, Ltd, Chichester, UK.

Eden C.L., Ackermann F. and Cropper S. (1992) The analysis of cause maps. *Journal of Management Studies*, **29**(3), 309–324.

Eden C.L., Ackermann F. and Cropper S. (1995) Getting started with cognitive mapping. Supplied with *Decision Explorer*. Banxia Software, Glasgow, UK.

Eden C.L., Jones S. and Sims D. (1979) *Thinking in Organisations*. Macmillan, London, UK.

Eden C.L., Jones S. and Sims D. (1983) *Messing about in Problems*. Pergamon Press, Oxford, UK.

Eden C.L. and Simpson P. (1989) SODA and cognitive mapping in practice, in *Rational Analysis for a Problematic World*, ed. by Rosenhead J. John Wiley & Sons, Ltd, Chichester, UK.

Fiol C.M. and Huff A.S. (1992) Maps for managers. Where are we? Where do we go from here? *Journal of Management Studies*, **29**(3), 267–286.

Friend J. and Hickling A. (1987) *Planning under Pressure: the Strategic Choice Approach*. Pergamon, Oxford, UK.

Hodgson A. (1992). Hexagons for systems thinking. *European Journal of Operational Research*, **59**(1), 220–230.

Hudson L. (1967) *Contrary Imaginations. A Study of the English Schoolboy*. Penguin, London, UK.

Huff A.S. (ed.) (1990) *Mapping Strategic Thought*. John Wiley & Sons, Inc., New York, NY.

Janis I.L. (1972) *Victims of Groupthink: a Psychological Study of Foreign-policy Decisions and Fiascos*. Houghton Mifflin, Boston, MA.

Kelly G.A. (1955) *The Psychology of Personal Constructs, Vols 1 and 2*. Norton, New York, NY.

McNamara T.P. (1994) Knowledge representation, in *Thinking and Problem Solving*, ed. by Steinberg R.J. Academic Press, San Diego, CA.

Morgan G. (1986) *Images of Organisation*. Sage, London, UK.

Phrontis (2009) *Group Explorer*. Phrontis Ltd, Banbury, Oxon, UK: www.phrontis.com

Pidd M. (1995) Pictures from an exhibition: images of operational research. *European Journal of Operational Research*, **81**, 479–488.

QSR (2002) Nud*ist software: www.qsr.com.au

Rowe D. (1983) in *Applications of Personal Construct Theory*, ed. by Adams-Webber J. and Mancuso J.C. Academic Press, Toronto, Canada.

Schön D.A. (1982) *The Reflective Practitioner. How Professionals Think in Action*. Basic Books, New York, NY.

Shaw D., Ackermann F. and Eden E. (2001). Sharing ideas in groups – a research report on electronic group brainstorming for real-world workshops. Working paper RP01113, Aston Business School, Birmingham, UK. Available at http://research.abs.aston.ac.uk/wpaper/0113.pdf

Simon H.A. (1976) From substantive to procedural rationality, in *Models of Bounded Rationality: Behavioural Economics and Business Organisation*, ed. by Simon H.A. (1982). MIT Press, Cambridge, MA.

Tolman EC (1948) Cognitive maps in rats and men. *The Psychological Review*, **55**(4), 189–208.

Westcombe M. and Pidd M. (2002) Problem structuring: the process of SODA modelling. Working paper MS 02/02, Lancaster University Management School, Lancaster, UK.

7   System dynamics

Introduction

The first two chapters of Part II discuss two approaches intended to help managers and decision-makers to see the consequences of their actions by developing qualitative models. This chapter focuses on system dynamics, an approach that can be used qualitatively or quantitatively. It thus serves as the first stage of a bridge between Part II and Part III, which deals with quantitative modelling.

Jay Forrester is the prime developer of the ideas now known as system dynamics, and these were first published in his book *Industrial Dynamics* (Forrester, 1961). In this he showed how models of the structure of a human system and the policies used to control it could help to develop understanding of its operation and behaviour. That is, he showed the value of explicit models that combine business process and organizational structure. Forrester developed a set of tools and an approach to simulation that have become known as system dynamics. Others, for example Sterman (2000) and Morecroft (2007), have taken these ideas and shown how they can be applied to help manage organizations, and Senge (1992) used the ideas to develop insights into organization learning. The tools of system dynamics were based on those used by control engineers to analyse the stability of mechanical and electrical control systems – an idea first suggested by Tustin (1953). Although originally intended for use in the industrial sector, the method has also been applied in other areas such as epidemiology (Roberts and Dangerfield, 1990), the management of health care (Lane, 2000), project management (Howick and Eden, 2004), policing (Newsome, 2007) and global modelling (Meadows, 1972).

System dynamics may be used in several ways. The underlying approach provides a way of viewing human systems by stressing the importance of certain structural features, such as feedback control. If human systems are analysed in this way, then Wolstenholme (1990) argues that it is possible to provide useful insights into their operation even without recourse to computer software. The second mode of operation, however, is to use these structural features to develop a simulation model of the systems. This computer-based model can also be used to understand why they behave as they do. Finally, the simulation models can be used to help find better ways of operating the systems by demonstrating their consequences. In all these cases, the idea is to use system dynamics models as tools for thinking, but, whereas our mental models are hidden, the system dynamics models are explicit.

Some writers on system dynamics seem to regard its use as fundamental to any systems thinking, the best-known example being Senge (1992). The manuals accompanying the Stella II software (Richmond and Petersen, 1994) are also explicit in making this case. It should be clear from the earlier chapter on soft systems methodology (SSM) (see Chapter 5) that this book is less sweeping in its claims. The case being made here is that system dynamics is one of the tools available to people wishing to think through the consequences of their possible actions. A core assumption of system dynamics is that the world can be regarded as a set of linked systems whose boundaries depend, in part at least, on the viewpoint of the observer or analyst.

Feedback and delays in human systems

Feedback control

One feature of human systems identified in Chapter 5 is that they are self-maintaining by the use of feedback control. Sometimes this control may be highly formalized, as in standard costing, statistical process control or performance-related payment systems. On the other hand, it may be rather informal, such as when a decrease in earnings causes a reduction in family expenditure – although optimists may delay the implementation for some time! The basic idea of feedback control was shown earlier in Figure 1.4. This shows that control is exercised by feeding back the output to be compared with a target value. Corrective action is then taken to bring the process back within desired limits. This implies that the system has some fairly stable target state (possibly expressed as minimum and maximum performance levels). If the control is based on the difference between the target and the actual output, this is known as control by negative feedback.

Some systems display positive feedback; indeed, this is the basis of electronic amplifiers. These devices produce a signal that loops back round to the input side, adding itself to the existing input, thus producing amplification. Properly controlled, this gives us the pleasure of listening to hi-fi systems. Badly controlled, it produces the screeching of audio feedback that occurs in some public address systems when the microphone is placed in front of the loudspeakers. This positive feedback is also found in human systems. As an example, if a company places its spare cash on deposit, then the returns offered may well increase as the amount deposited increases, the idea being to encourage the deposit of larger sums. Indeed, it could be argued that any system of compound interest represents positive feedback, as the interest earned is added on to the original amount deposited.

The presence of feedback loops, whether positive or negative, usually makes the behaviour of human activity systems hard to understand (Dangerfield and Roberts, 1995). In *Industrial Dynamics*, Forrester (1961) called this 'counterintuitive behaviour', which is especially prevalent when several feedback systems are linked in some way or other.

Delays

A further feature, which can make the behaviour of these systems hard to predict, is the delays that occur in transmitting and receiving information. A fundamental principle of control is that, the closer to the action the control is exercised, the more effective it is likely to be. As a simple illustration of this, consider Figure 7.1, which depicts someone standing in a shower, attempting to control the water temperature. The graph alongside shows the tap settings and the resulting temperature fluctuations. Imagine that you are the bather. You enter the shower, turn it on and are hit by a blast of cold water – not what you were hoping for. There is a slight increase in temperature as the water heats up, but not much. So, you grab the control knob and twist it towards the hot side, but nothing happens immediately, you are still awash in cold water. Thus, you wrench the knob yet further to the hot side. And then? A surge of overhot water hits you somewhere painful and you wrench the knob back to the cold side ... and the process begins all over again, although eventually you should get the temperature right.

There are two reasons why a simple task such as controlling water temperature while having a shower can be so hard to control, in spite of the rapid physical feedback. The first is the delay between turning on the shower and the arrival of any hot water. That is, the pipes of the system may be full of cold water, unless someone else used the shower just before you. The second is

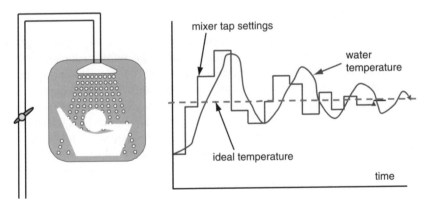

Figure 7.1 Problems with delays in feedback control.

that there is a delay between turning the control valve and the effect reaching the showerhead – the water must run through the intervening pipe. Hence, your action in twisting the mixer valve turns out to have delayed and unexpected consequences. This scenario can develop even further if, as in many British houses, the same cold water system also fills WC cisterns elsewhere in the house – if someone flushes a toilet while you are trying to get the shower temperature correct, an external instability is introduced that makes your task even harder. We have all heard of road rage – perhaps shower rage will be next?

As another example, some years ago a plumber installed a new central heating radiator in our house. The radiator was an unusual design but, nevertheless, should have been available at 24 hours' notice from local merchants. One week after the plumber first came, no radiator had appeared. 'The local merchants are out of stock, they've ordered one.' Another week passed, still no radiator. 'The manufacturers are out of stock, they're making some more.' After a few more days with no radiator, I phoned the manufacturers – a delivery was promised. Meanwhile, the merchant, the plumber and his mate had all also phoned the manufacturer – who now probably believed that there was massive demand for his product. Thus, the combination of delays (the plumber not ordering in advance, the merchant running out of stock, the manufacturer running out of stock) and amplification (four of us phoning the manufacturer independently) might have led to the manufacturer overestimating demand for his product. This would have been bad enough, but suppose that I, and others like me, had grown tired of waiting and had found a substitute product. Then, rather than facing normal demand, let alone an increase, the manufacturer may have faced a slump in demand. Thus, the familiar stop–go cycle of batch manufacturing would have occurred.

Fundamental to system dynamics is the notion that delays and feedback loops are responsible for much of the behaviour of organized human systems. Thus, if any such system is to be understood, let alone improved, these two features need to be thoroughly accounted for. System dynamics provides a way of doing this via diagramming techniques and a computer-based modelling approach.

Basic concepts of system dynamics models

To use system dynamics, it is important to understand the basic concepts, which are very simple. They are based on two pairs of ideas: resources and information, and levels and rates.

Resources and information

This is a fundamental distinction in system dynamics modelling. Resources correspond to the 'stuff' or 'physics' of the system and are the main concerns of the transformation process in which the system engages. Examples of resources might be products in the case of a manufacturing company, patients in the case of a hospital or money in the case of a finance company. These are the people, objects and other things with which the system is concerned, and they flow around the system and will change state. Thus, materials become products which become deliveries, patients become people recovering back at home and cash is collected from customers and lent out to other people. Sometimes the state change marks a complete change in the resource (as when raw materials are transformed into products), and sometimes it denotes a change in location or in concern (as when patients are discharged).

In the view of Richmond and Petersen (1994), it can also be useful to subdivide the resources into two:

- *Consumable resources.* These are depleted as activity in a system proceeds. For example, a manufacturing process will consume materials of some kind as they are transformed into work in progress or finished products. Similarly, a hospital will use up supplies of drugs and blood in its day-to-day operations.
- *Catalytic (non-consumable) resources.* These are rather less obvious but also need to be considered. They are enabling resources, which enable other transformations that involve consumable resources. As an example of this, the rate at which an item is sold may depend on the prices charged by competitors. Price is a catalytic resource in such cases, because the sales rate is dependent on the price, and thus, although the physical stocks are consumed by the sales, the prices simply fluctuate.

By contrast, information is the non-physical means by which control of the resource transformations is exercised. The principle is that information about the current state of the resources is used as a basis for making decisions about the use of those resources. Thus, a manufacturer may decide to increase production if market research reveals that demand is likely to increase; or a doctor may discharge patients when hospital staff provide information that the patients are fit to return home. Note that there is no need, in a system dynamics model, to assume that the information used in decision-making is correct. The information may be delayed in transit, it may be misunderstood and it may be distorted. In the case of the freezing/scalding bather in the shower, one problem was that he thought more hot water was needed, but this was wrong. The amount of hot inflow was fine – he just needed to wait a little longer. In a business system, market research may be wrong or out of date, and in a hospital the diagnosis of the doctor may be wrong or may be based on a misinterpretation of laboratory tests. Nevertheless, distorted or not, this information may well be the basis for real decision-making. Understanding the effects of such distortions and delays may be the reasons for the modelling exercise.

Levels and rates

In Forrester's (1961) original development of system dynamics, such models of human systems were built on two basic concepts: levels and rates. Since the appearance in the late 1980s of the Stella and iThink software (High Performance Systems, 1994, 2009), some people prefer the term 'stock' to level and the term 'flow' to rate. In this chapter, the two terms will be used

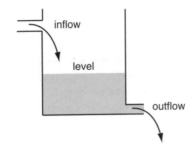

Figure 7.2 Levels and rates as tanks and flows.

interchangeably, although the Stella II concept of stock provides some extensions to the basic system dynamics concept of levels.

Levels are accumulations of resources within the system. Sometimes they may literally be physical stocks, say of materials, finished goods or drugs. The same idea can also be used in a more conceptual way to represent notions such as price levels. Rates are the movements of resources, which cause levels to rise, fall or to remain constant. For instance, an increase in the rate of patients being referred to a specialist physician will lead to an increase in the waiting list of new patients if the physician has no more time to offer and if the rate of discharge for existing patients does not increase.

Perhaps the easiest way to illustrate this is to consider a simple analogy of a tank into which liquid flows and from which it may flow. This is shown in Figure 7.2. When the inflow rate exceeds the outflow rate, the level in the tank rises; when this relation is reversed, the level falls. The transformations of resources and information are modelled, in system dynamics, as a sequence of linked levels and rates. The rates act to increase or decrease the levels that are interconnected by the flows. In a manufacturing company, raw material flows from raw material stocks (thus decreasing their level) and, once transformed, into finished stocks (thus increasing their level), which is the transformation process known as 'making to stock'. Analogous transformations occur in other types of human system.

Levels represent the state of the system at any point in time. They continue to exist even if the flow rates all drop to zero in an instant. The analogy from Figure 7.2 should be obvious: if the inflow and outflow both drop instantaneously to zero, then the level is frozen at some value. The other use for levels is that they represent stocks or buffers within the system, and they thus act to decouple the flow rates. Most systems include stocks of some kind used for this purpose. This is true even in most just-in-time (JIT) manufacturing systems where deliveries may be received, say, twice per day. The stocks act as buffers that soak up variations in the flows. Of course, if an inflow and outflow are persistently different, then the system is unbalanced. This provides two tests for thinking about whether a factor should be considered as a level:

1. Will it continue to have a value even if all activity ceases for a while?
2. Does it act to decouple flows?

Clearly, these both apply to physical stocks of machines and goods, but they also may apply, for example, to the number of people employed in a business or to cash balances. Such factors may therefore be regarded as levels.

The activity within a human system is modelled in system dynamics by the rates of flow that connect the levels within the model. Unlike levels, rates of flow immediately drop to zero if there is no activity in the system. Thus, the purchasing rate for raw materials and the payment rate to creditors may drop to zero if a business goes bankrupt. Similarly, the admission rate to a hospital drops to zero if the hospital is closed. Flows represent rates of change in resources or in information. Information flows are used to link knowledge about the levels to the flow rates. Resource flows deplete and increase the levels through time. If what appears to be a flow rate persists even if activity ceases, then this factor needs to be represented by a level. An example of this might be a calculation of average sales over a period – this persists even if the sales rate ceases, and is therefore to be modelled as a level.

Diagramming methods

Causal loop diagrams

Perhaps the first stage in using system dynamics is to try to understand the feedback loops that are part of the system being studied. One way of doing this is to use causal loop diagrams, which were first suggested by Maruyama (1963) and are sometimes known as influence diagrams (Wolstenholme, 1990). They are intended to be of use in understanding the broad structure of a system rather than its detail, and they are therefore kept deliberately simple. As an example, consider the following:

> Lancaster Decor Company (LDC) makes wall coverings that are supplied to customers throughout the world. Its production method is to buy coated paper and to print it in fashionable patterns. These are held in stock for despatch to customers. Ideally, it keeps 3 weeks' finished stock on hand. Orders received from customers are despatched the week after they are received, and production is also planned on a weekly basis. Thus, when all is running well, LDC should have an order backlog of 1 week, and it should be possible to meet this from stock. Stockholding is planned by forecasting the order rate for the next period; thus, LDC tries to hold 3 times the forecast of the next period's orders.

A causal loop diagram for LDC is shown in Figure 7.3, which reveals a number of the conventions used in these diagrams. The first is that each link is represented by an arrow that carries a sign at its head to indicate the direction of causality of the link. A positive sign indicates that a change in the factor at the tail of the arrow will tend to cause the factor at the head of the arrow to change in the same direction, other factors remaining constant. (That is, an increase

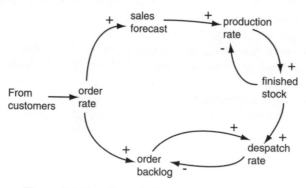

Figure 7.3 Causal loop for Lancaster Decor Company.

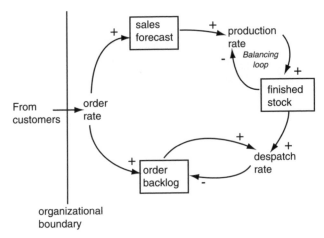

Figure 7.4 Influence diagram for Lancaster Decor Company.

will lead to an increase and a decrease to a decrease.) A negative sign indicates that the change will be in the opposite direction. Figure 7.3 shows that an increase in the orders received per week (the order rate) will tend to lead to an increase in the sales forecast. Conversely, an increase in the despatch rate to customers should lead to a decrease in the order backlog, other factors remaining constant.

The slight variation in these diagrams presented by Wolstenholme (1990), known as system dynamics influence diagrams, distinguishes between levels and rates as shown in Figure 7.4. In these, a level is shown as a rectangle surrounding the name of the level. Rates are shown as only text with no box. Finished stock, order backlog and sales forecast would remain unchanged and frozen if all activity ceased in LDC, and these are therefore levels. Some people refer to levels that result from such smoothing processes as 'implied levels'. Use of the terms 'production rate', 'despatch rate' and 'order rate' indicate that these may be treated as system dynamics flows or rates, as long as they are not averages. Also, brief thought leads to the realization that these flows drop to zero if all activity ceases. This influence diagram also emphasizes one of the points made earlier: information about levels is used to set the rates. This means that levels are not connected directly to one another but only via intervening rates. Hence, if any loop is followed round, it should always pass through alternating levels and rates.

In spite of their simplicity, either of the diagrams shown in Figures 7.3 or 7.4 can be used to make inferences about the system and its operation. As with cognitive maps (see Chapter 6), the sign of a loop is easily calculated by counting the number of negative signs in the loop. An odd number indicates negative feedback (sometimes known as a balancing loop), and an even number or zero indicates positive feedback (sometimes known as a reinforcing loop). In Figure 7.4, the main loop displays negative feedback and is therefore a balancing loop. Effective control relies on negative feedback, and this is, thankfully, evident in LDC. It is also clear from the diagram that, apart from the order rate, the other factors in the large control loop are all within the LDC organization, which means that they have some chance of maintaining control. Whether this control will achieve any desirable end cannot be known just from the diagram. To check this would require the modeller to go further and develop a system dynamics simulation.

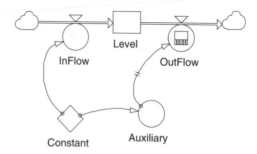

Figure 7.5 Powersim symbols.

System dynamics flow diagrams

Useful though an influence diagram may be, there are times when we wish to go much further. The next stage may therefore be to sketch out a system dynamics flow diagram. The original diagrams are to be found in Forrester (1961). As might be expected, the main point of these diagrams is to represent the relationships between the levels and rates that make up a system dynamics model. The main symbols used by the Powersim system dynamics software (Powersim Corporation, 2009) are shown in Figure 7.5. Flow rates (InFlow and OutFlow) are shown as valves on a double line, terminated with an arrowhead. Information flows are shown by a single arrow, and, if the information may be delayed, this is shown by the two short lines that cross the information flow – as in the case of the flow from the auxiliary to the OutFlow in Figure 7.5. Because this information flow is delayed, Powersim also automatically modifies the OutFlow symbol to indicate the delay. If there were no delay, the InFlow and OutFlow symbols would be identical. An important convention on these diagrams and in system dynamics modelling is that flow rates are not directly controlled by the levels but by information about the levels, whereas flow rates have a direct effect on the levels. This explains why the information flow lines are needed in Figure 7.5.

Forrester (1961) recommended different line styles to represent different types of resource flow – for example, material flow would be shown as a solid line and monetary flows by a solid line interspersed with dollar ($) symbols. This distinction is not applied in contemporary system dynamics software, which only requires that information flows be distinguished from resource flows. Resource flows are usually shown as double-line arrows, and information flows (known as links in Powersim) by single-line arrows. The basic analogy of system dynamics is with fluid flows, and this is emphasized by the diagram symbols that show flows and rates controlled by a tap (spigot in the USA) or valve.

When Forrester first developed the system dynamics approach, the idea was that the modeller would develop the system dynamics diagram and would use this as an aid in writing a set of equations that could be used to simulate the system. This mode of model construction is rarely followed nowadays, as most system dynamics models are constructed with visual interactive modelling systems (VIMSs). Examples of VIMSs for system dynamics modelling include Stella/iThink (High Performance Systems, 2009), Vensim (Ventana Systems, 2009) and Powersim (Powersim Corporation, 2009). The screen dump shown in Figure 7.6 is from a Powersim model simulating the LDC. Different versions of these system dynamics' VIMSs are available for PCs running Microsoft Windows and for the Apple Macintosh.

The circles are known as auxiliaries in Powersim, or as converters in some of the other software. They are used for a number of purposes such as combining several information flows

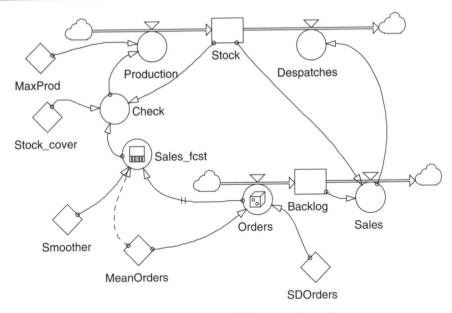

Figure 7.6 Powersim diagram for Lancaster Decor Company.

into one, splitting one flow into several, converting units or just to simplify algebraic expressions. The diamonds represent constants and system parameters – which may be varied by the user when simulating.

Lancaster Decor Company: Powersim diagram

The previous section introduced the LDC. Figures 7.3 and 7.4 provide a simple view of its operations by causal loop or influence diagrams. Figure 7.6 shows a system dynamics diagram of LDC's operations, using the Powersim symbols. The first point to note is that the diagram shows two resource flows. The top resource flow is the physical transformation of the raw material into stock via a production process to finished stock, from whence it is despatched to customers. The stock is clearly a level, as it serves to decouple production and despatch, both of which are flow rates that vary over time. The bottom resource flow is catalytic and is used to control the physical flow. It represents the incoming flow of orders, which are held for a time in an order backlog and are then translated into sales. The order backlog is clearly a level, as it serves to decouple the incoming order rate and the outgoing sales rate.

The diagram also shows the information links between the two flows, which represent the instantaneous flow of information unless otherwise indicated. The despatch rate is linked only from the sales rate, the two being, in effect, the same rate; they must, therefore, be kept in step with one another. The sales rate is computed from the order backlog and the actual stock on hand – presumably the lesser of the two will be sold and therefore despatched. The production rate is controlled by information about the current stock level, the sales forecast (actually the order forecast) and a maximum limit on the production rate. To simplify the representation, an auxiliary, Check, is used to link the sales forecast and current stock level. Smoother is a parameter used to compute the sales forecast.

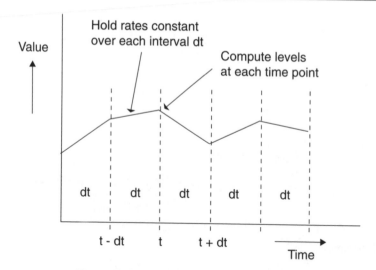

Figure 7.7 Time-handling in system dynamics.

Behind the diagrams – system dynamics simulation

Interesting though it can be to develop the diagrams, they are often just one step on the way to an investigation of the dynamics of the systems being studied – hence the name of the approach. To take this investigation further, the diagrams need to be put into a computable form, as a set of equations, so that a dynamic simulation may be based on them.

Time-handling in system dynamics

The basic system dynamics simulation approach uses simple time-slicing (Pidd, 2004), and a simple way to understand this is to consider an analogy. Suppose that you wish to record what is happening, say in a car park, over a 24 hour period. Suppose, too, that you have been given movie film for this purpose, but not enough to record continually, so you will have to sample what is happening. One way to do this would be to take a shot of the car park at regular intervals. When the film is played back, the effect would be to speed up the movement in the car park – this is what TV nature programmes do when they use time-lapse photography to record the growth of a plant. System dynamics simulation works in a similar way, using the time increment dt. It computes what is happening in the system at regular points of time, each one separated by dt, as shown in Figure 7.7. Imagine that time has just reached a known point t at which a sample (actually a computation) is due. Because a fixed time slice (dt) is being used, we know when the previous computation was done (time $t - $ dt) and when the next one is due (time $t + $ dt). In essence, in a system dynamics simulation, the values taken by continuous variables are sampled at regular intervals, dt, and are held constant over that interval.

A system dynamics model has two main types of equation: level or stock equations and rate or flow equations. As with all such simulation systems, simulated time is moved from point to point, and computations are made at each point before moving to the next one. The basic method of handling time and of the resulting computations is as follows:

1. At time t, compute the new values for the levels or stocks, using the level or stock equations. Use the current values of the rates or flows, computed at time $t - dt$, for this purpose.
2. Now compute the values that the rates or flows will hold over the next time interval dt. These will depend on information about the current values of the levels.
3. Move time forward by one increment (dt) and repeat the process.

Thus, levels are computed for the current point of time, and then the rates are computed over the next known interval. Rates are assumed to be fixed over that interval once they are computed and are only revised after the next computation of the levels.

Equation types

A system dynamics model includes two main types of equation: level equations and rate equations. A level equation has a simple format, which can usually be interpreted directly from the system dynamics diagram, as follows:

$$\text{Level (now)} = \text{Level (previous)} + dt \times (\text{InFlows} - \text{OutFlows})$$

Thus, at the current time point, the value of the level or stock is simply its value at the previous time point plus the net inflow or outflow over the interval (dt) that has passed since the last time point. This is bound to be true if the inflow and outflow rates are held constant over the interval dt. The diagram shows how many such inflows and outflows exist for any level, and therefore the equation usually follows automatically. Hence, VIMSs such as Powersim can generate level equations from the diagram.

Rate equations cannot be inferred from the system diagram, for this shows only which information flows affect the rate computation, not how this influence is exercised. Thus, in Figure 7.6, the sales rate is seen to depend on two factors: stock and backlog. How it is affected cannot be determined from the diagram alone, as this is an expression of the way in which the information is used to control the system. This inability to infer the rate equations from the flow diagrams is a serious weakness, because the same links can represent quite different policies, leading to very different behaviours. If system dynamics is to be used for the dynamic simulation of a system, the nature of the rate equations is crucial, but this cannot be determined only from the level rate diagram.

LDC equations in Powersim

Powersim does not bother to write the full level equations in their proper format, but, if it did so, those for the LDC model would be written as follows:

$$\text{Stock}(t) = \text{Stock}(t - dt) + dt \times (\text{Production} - \text{Despatches})$$
$$\text{Backlog}(t) = \text{Backlog}(t - dt) + dt \times (\text{Orders} - \text{Sales})$$

where $\text{Stock}(t)$ and $\text{Backlog}(t)$ are the values at time t, and $\text{Stock}(t - dt)$ and $\text{Backlog}(t - dt)$ are the values at the previous time point $t - dt$.

The rate equations are as follows:

$$\text{Despatches} = \text{Sales}$$
$$\text{Orders} = \text{NORMAL}(\text{MeanOrders, SDOrders, 999})$$
$$\text{Production} = \text{MIN}(\text{MAX}(0, \text{Check}), \text{MaxProd})$$
$$\text{Sales} = \text{MIN}(\text{Stock, Backlog})$$

Thus, as mentioned above, despatches are equal to sales. The orders are generated from a normal distribution with a mean of MeanOrders, a standard deviation of SDOrders and using a random number seed of 999. The production rate is generated from the Powersim function MIN as the smaller of Check (see below) and MaxProd – the maximum production rate. To ensure that Check cannot be negative, this is enclosed in a Powersim function MAX, which compares its value with zero. The sales rate will be the smaller of the actual stock and the order backlog, and this is computed via the MIN Powersim function.

There are also auxiliary equations as follows:

$$\text{Check} = \text{Stock\_cover} \times \text{Sales\_fcst} - \text{Stock}$$
$$\text{Sales\_fcst} = \text{DELAYINF}(\text{Orders, Smoother, 1, MeanOrders})$$

The equation for Check computes the actual stock needed to provide Stock_cover weeks of the weekly sales as forecast, less the actual stock. The equation for Sales_fcst computes a forecast for orders based on simple exponential smoothing, with the smoothing constant equal to 1/Smoother.

Finally, some constants need to be given values:

$$\text{MaxProd} = 150$$
$$\text{MeanOrders} = 100$$
$$\text{SDOrders} = 20$$
$$\text{Smoother} = 10$$
$$\text{Stock\_cover} = 4$$

These ensure that no more than 150 units can be produced in each month; they specify the parameters of the order distribution, give Smoother a value of 10 (which leads to a smoothing constant of 0.1) and add the requirement that the factory aims at a stock cover of 4 weeks.

Using Powersim to simulate LDC's operations

All that is needed for a Powersim model has now been specified, and so the model may be used to show how LDC might be expected to operate. The result of running the LDC model in Powersim for 20 time units is shown in Table 7.1. Notice that this makes clear the starting conditions for the simulation, which were that the initial stock was set at 300 and the initial backlog was set at 100. The table, as presented by Powersim and as reproduced here, is slightly deceptive. To be properly accurate, it should have twice as many rows, with the alternate rows dedicated to the levels/stocks, that is to stock and to backlog. If the results were to be displayed in this way, the intermediate rows would be dedicated to the flows/rates.

Table 7.1 Results of a Powersim simulation for LDC.

Time	Orders	Despatches	Stock	Backlog	Production	Sales_fcst
0	99.25	100.00	300.00	100.00	100.00	100.00
1	66.00	99.25	300.00	99.25	99.70	99.93
2	63.56	66.00	300.45	66.00	85.69	96.53
3	103.16	63.56	320.13	63.56	52.82	93.24
4	60.46	103.16	309.38	103.16	67.53	94.23
5	93.72	60.46	273.76	60.46	89.65	90.85
6	115.17	93.72	302.95	93.72	61.61	91.14
7	111.76	115.17	270.83	115.17	103.33	93.54
8	110.86	111.76	258.99	111.76	122.46	95.36
9	112.15	110.86	269.70	110.86	117.96	96.91
10	105.11	112.15	276.79	112.15	116.95	98.44
11	109.03	105.11	281.60	105.11	114.82	99.10
12	108.24	109.03	291.30	109.03	109.08	100.10
13	97.71	108.24	291.36	108.24	112.28	100.91
14	102.47	97.71	295.41	97.71	106.95	100.59
15	84.11	102.47	304.65	102.47	98.46	100.78
16	100.86	84.11	300.64	84.11	95.81	99.11
17	100.04	100.86	312.33	100.86	84.81	99.29
18	106.06	100.04	296.28	100.04	101.17	99.36
19	121.90	106.06	297.41	106.06	102.72	100.03
20	76.07	121.90	294.07	121.90	114.81	102.22

For example, the first row should refer to $t = 0$ and should contain just two values: stock should be 300 and backlog should be 100. The next row should refer to the time interval $(0, 1)$, assuming that the time increment dt is set to a value of 1. This row should have the values for the rates over that interval, computed as follows using the flow equations defined earlier:

- Orders $= 99.25$ (sampled from a normal distribution with mean $= 100$, standard deviation $= 20$).
- Despatches $= 100.00$ (this being the value of sales, which is not shown in the table; sales is the minimum of the previous stock and backlog values, and is thus 100.00).
- Forecast $= 100.00$ (this being the starting value given to the function used to compute an exponentially smoothed average of orders).
- Production $= 100.00$ (this being the initial value).

The computations proceed through time in this manner. Time is now moved from 0 to 1 (if d$t = 1$) and the levels/stocks are computed, and the flows/rates are then computed for the interval $(1, 2)$, followed by the auxiliaries. Time is then moved to 2, and so on, until the simulation is complete.

Model building in system dynamics

Two approaches: inside-out or outside-in?

So far, this chapter has described the main features of the system dynamics approach, has illustrated the diagrammatic approaches employed and has shown how computer software builds an equation structure for simulation from the diagrams. However, there has been no discussion of how system dynamics models could or should be built, which is the focus of this section. It will assume that the user of a system dynamics approach has access to contemporary software such as Powersim, iThink or Vensim. There seem to be two ways of building models within system dynamics, depending on the reasons for the modelling. This chapter will call the two approaches 'inside-out' and 'outside-in'.

Inside-out modelling assumes that we know a lot about the structure of the system to be modelled, and that we wish to understand how it behaves. This is how many system dynamics models will be built by management scientists who wish to find better ways to operate some system or other. Hence, a refinement of this approach is that, having satisfactorily modelled how a system is now, we may wish to modify the model to foresee the consequences of operating the system in new ways.

By contrast, outside-in modelling assumes that much is known about the overall behaviour of a system, but that not enough is known about why it happens. Hence, data are available that describe how the system seems to operate ('when we get a short-lived increase in orders, it takes us months to get back to normal again – look at this graph of what happened last time') under certain conditions. The aim is to develop a model that provides systemic structures that produce output mimicking the observed behaviour. This type of modelling aims, primarily, to develop some understanding about why things happen.

It is clearly possible to develop a system dynamics model, or indeed other types of Management Science model, by working simultaneously outside-in and inside-out. However, to clarify the issues in the discussion that follows, it may help to distinguish between the two approaches.

Modelling from the outside in

This approach relies on an assumption that there are a number of characteristic system structures that will lead to certain types of behaviour. As mentioned above, the modeller begins with some idea of the type of behaviour that would be expected from the system and its components. For example, it might display exponential growth under certain conditions. These types of behaviour can be related to standard structures that are easily modelled in system dynamics terms. The modeller selects the appropriate structures by thinking through the observed behaviours. The model becomes an assembly of these standard structures. It must be noted that standard structures and processes will rarely be used in an unmodified form, but they do provide a useful basis from which to begin the modelling. Richmond and Petersen (1994) use this outside-in approach when presenting a set of generic structures that may be employed when modelling in Stella II and iThink. Note, though, that, even when such structures have been selected, they must still be parameterized – values must be given to the variables in the underlying equations.

The first, and simplest, structure is one that occurs when a level and a flow are connected in such a way that there is exponential growth or exponential decay in the level. This form of growth may be evident in financial systems based on compound interest and in some ecological systems in which there are no limits on available food, nor predators to prey on the population. This type of decay happens when a proportion of a level is removed during each time interval. An example of this might be a company reducing its workforce by releasing a proportion in each time period. In the jargon of system dynamics, the proportion applied to the growth or the decay is known as the compounding fraction (shown as CF in Figure 7.8). The compounding fraction itself need not be a constant, but could be the result of other factors elsewhere in the model. Figure 7.8 shows Powersim diagrams and the resulting output for these simple compound growth and decay systems.

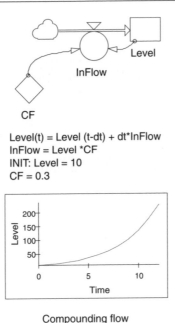

Level(t) = Level (t-dt) + dt*InFlow
InFlow = Level *CF
INIT: Level = 10
CF = 0.3

Compounding flow

Figure 7.8 Structure for exponential growth or decay.

A second type of generic structure occurs in those systems that aim to keep some value at a target level by feedback control. This is sometimes known as a stock adjustment process. Examples of this abound and might include make-to-stock manufacturing, which aims to keep finished stock levels at a certain value. Other examples might be the number of people employed in a business after allowing for recruitment and labour turnover, or the number of patients on a hospital ward. The basic process is just an extension of the compounding/decay structure, except that a target is introduced as a way of modifying the inflow and outflow from the level. In the figure, the target level is set at 30, with an initial value of 10 for the level; thus, the actual level increases quickly at first, and then it asymptotically approaches the target level. If the initial level had been higher than the target, the level would quickly have dropped towards the target, and then would have approached it asymptotically.

The second structure shown in Figure 7.9 is a production process, this term relating to any process in which the output is controlled by reference to another level. Examples might be a manufacturing company in which each machine can produce a specified number of units, or a hospital in which each doctor might be expected to conduct a specified number of outpatient clinics per week. In either case, the capacity of the resource is modelled by the extra level, labelled as 'resource' in Figure 7.9. The unit productivity of the resource is modelled by the CF. Clearly, the value taken by resource could itself be variable and might be the result of other processes elsewhere in the system. It is also clear that the flow could be bidirectional, resulting in a combined stock adjustment and production process.

Modelling from the inside out

The earlier example of LDC was an illustration of this approach, and a second example will be developed here, this time related to the delivery of health care. The example is simplified, but it serves to illustrate how system dynamics models may be developed and used in inside-out mode.

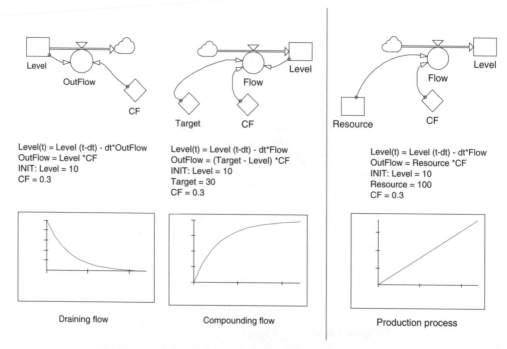

Figure 7.9 Structure for stock adjustment and production processes.

Case study: Lancaster District Hospital

Suppose Lancaster District Hospital (LDH) has a surgical ward into which two types of patient are admitted: emergencies and routine patients — the latter coming from a waiting list that is operated on a first-come-first-served basis. The hospital is required to admit all appropriate emergencies, and any empty beds are taken by routine admissions from the waiting list. To keep the model manageable, it can be assumed that any overflow emergency admissions can be accepted at another hospital, although the board of LDH will have to pay a large financial penalty whenever this happens.

The surgeons who work in the ward have a predictable demand from routine patients, and analysis of their referrals shows that, in total, they add 20 patients per week to the waiting list. The ward is notified of these patients once a week, on a Monday, although they can be admitted to the ward on any day. Demand from emergency patients is much more variable. An analysis of the past 2 years shows that, on any day, the number of emergency cases that need admission can be represented by a normal distribution with a mean value of 4 and a standard deviation of 2.

Although the length of stay (the time that a patient spends on the ward) is slightly variable, it seems reasonable to assume that emergency patients spend 5 days on the ward. At the end of this period they may be transferred to a nursing home if they need further care. Routine patients tend to spend 3 days on the ward. The admissions policy is that all emergencies must be admitted to the ward, and any spare beds are used for routine patients. How many beds will be needed in the ward?

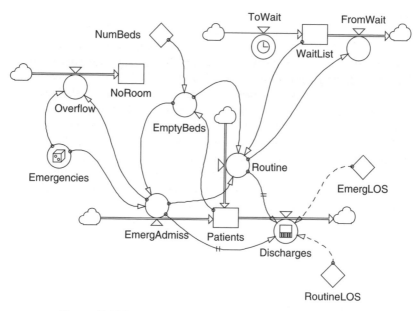

Figure 7.10 Powersim diagram for Lancaster District Hospital.

First stage of modelling LDH using Powersim

In any modelling of systems that involve probabilistic variation it is sensible to begin by working with average values so as to get some idea of the size of the system that is needed. The expected (i.e. average) demand from emergencies is four per day, and they occupy a bed for 5 days, making a total of 20 bed-days per admitting-day. Similarly, each admitting-day for routine patients must cope with about three patients for 3 days, making a total of 9 bed-days. Thus, the use of average values suggests that the ward may need about 29 or 30 beds if it is to cope with the demand.

Note that the term 'cope with the demand' is rather vague at this stage. What does it mean? Perhaps an initial view might be that all emergencies should be admitted on the day that they arise and that no routine patient should wait more than 3 weeks for admission after having been placed on the waiting list. The basic Powersim flow diagram for this system is shown in Figure 7.10. It assumes that the time slice d*t* is equal to 1 day.

The model shown in Figure 7.10 has three levels and associated flows, but it may not be obvious why the system has been modelled in this way. Consider, first, the physical flow of patients into the ward and their subsequent discharge. Patients are admitted to the ward from two sources: as emergencies or as routine. Emergencies will always be admitted unless there is a bed shortage, in which case they are diverted elsewhere. Routine admissions, modelled by the flow rate Routine, are computed by taking up any slack in the ward after emergencies are admitted. These two physical flows are modelled by the Patients level, with two input flows: Routine (which represents the daily admission rate for patients from the waiting list) and EmergAdmiss (which represents the daily rate at which emergencies are admitted). The corresponding outflow is modelled by Discharges, which represents the total number of patients of both types that are discharged each day. Hence, this sector of the diagram handles the 'physics' of the system. The other two stocks/levels and associated flows are used to model the emergency patients who cannot be admitted because no bed is available and the waiting list used for routine patients.

The actual number of emergencies arising on any day is generated by the Emergencies auxiliary, which will take samples from a normal distribution. Ideally, all such emergencies will be admitted immediately, but there may be occasions when this cannot happen because there are not enough beds free. Hence, the actual number of emergency admissions (EmergAdmiss) on any day is modelled by comparing the number of free beds at the start of the day (shown by the EmptyBeds auxiliary) and the number of Emergencies that arise. Should there be a bed shortage, then excess emergencies must be treated elsewhere. The number so treated on each day is modelled by the flow rate Overflow, and the total to date is accumulated in the level labelled as NoRoom. Thus, the number of EmergAdmiss on any day will be the minimum of the EmptyBeds and the actual Emergencies on that day.

The waiting list and the resulting demand from routine patients are modelled by the third level known as WaitList. Patients are added to this by the flow rate labelled as ToWait, and the depletion rate of the list is modelled by the flow rate labelled as FromWait. Note that the latter is a direct reflection of the input rate of routine patients (Routine) to the Patients level. Thus, the diagram shows that the Routine flow rate stems from the size of the waiting list, the number of empty beds and the number of emergencies admitted.

The equations for LDH

As stated earlier when introducing Powersim, the software can generate the level equations from the links that are shown on the flow diagram. The flow equations, however, have to be input by the modeller.

The initial values are

$$\text{Patients} = 0$$
$$\text{NoRoom} = 0$$
$$\text{WaitList} = 0$$

The level equations are

$$\text{Patients}(t) = \text{Patients}(t - dt) + dt \times (\text{Routine} + \text{EmergAdmiss} - \text{Discharges})$$
$$\text{WaitList}(t) = \text{WaitList}(t - dt) + dt \times (\text{ToWait} - \text{FromWait})$$
$$\text{NoRoom}(t) = \text{NoRoom}(t - dt) + dt \times \text{OverFlow}$$

The rate equations are

$$\text{Discharges} = \text{DELAYPPL(EmergAdmiss, EmergLOS, 0)}$$
$$+\text{DELAPPL(Routine, RoutineLOS, 0)}$$
$$\text{EmergAdmiss} = \text{MAX(0, MIN(Emergencies, EmptyBeds))}$$
$$\text{Overflow} = \text{Emergencies} - \text{EmergAdmiss}$$
$$\text{Routine} = \text{MAX(0, MIN(WaitList, (EmptyBeds} - \text{EmergAdmiss})))}$$
$$\text{FromWait} = \text{Routine}$$
$$\text{ToWait} = \text{IF((TIME MOD 7), 0, 20)}$$

The auxiliary equations are

$$\text{Emergencies} = \text{ROUND}(\text{MAX}(0, \text{NORMAL}(4, 2, 999)))$$
$$\text{EmptyBeds} = \text{NumBeds} - \text{Patients}$$

The constants are

$$\text{EmergLOS} = 5$$
$$\text{NumBeds} = 30$$
$$\text{RoutineLOS} = 3$$

The level equations should be self-explanatory, as should their initial values, the constants and the auxiliary equation for EmptyBeds. The others, though, may need some explanation.

As patients spend a known time on the ward and as none dies while there, the Powersim function for a pipeline delay, DELAYPPL( ), can be used to hold the patients in the ward for a time equal to RoutineLOS or EmergLOS, depending on the type of patient.

Emergencies can only be admitted if there are enough empty beds, and hence the number admitted, EmergAdmiss, is computed as the minimum of Emergencies and EmptyBeds, with the quantity forced to take a minimum value of zero. The actual number of emergencies is generated from a normal distribution with a mean of 4, a standard deviation of 2 and a seed value of 999. The number of emergency patients not admitted owing to lack of beds is computed in the Overflow equation.

Routine patients are admitted after Emergencies and are taken from the waiting list, WaitList. The number admitted must be the minimum of WaitList and (EmptyBeds − EmergAdmiss), the latter to allow for emergencies admitted on the current day. FromWait is set to the same value as Routine and will be used to update the waiting list. ToWait, the number added, uses Powersim TIME and MOD functions to generate a value of 20 every 7 days.

Running the LDH Model

Although the focus of this chapter is on qualitative system dynamics, one advantage of using system dynamics software is that a simulation can be performed using the above equations. These can be used to give some indication of the suitability of the policies intended for use in this ward of LDH. Because the initial value given to the various levels was zero, it is important to run such a simulation over a long enough time period for the effect of these zero values to be lost. This period, the run-in period, needs to be excluded from the analysis of the result – unless the aim of the modelling is to understand what might happen in the ward on the first few days after it has opened with all beds empty and no waiting list.

Figure 7.11 shows two graphs. The first shows the number of Patients and Overflows for a 200-day simulation of LDH using the above equations. It is clear that, even when the first few days of this simulation are ignored, there is considerable oscillation in the number of patients occupying beds on the ward. This suggests that a different admissions policy might be considered so as to smooth out the number of routine patients admitted each day. A second obvious feature is that Overflow is often non-zero – that is, LDH is unable to meet the demand for emergency beds on all occasions. The second graph of Figure 7.11 shows that the waiting list climbs throughout the simulation, and this is clearly unacceptable.

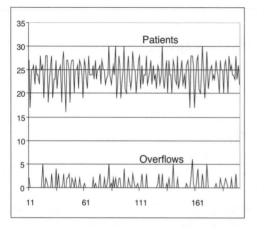 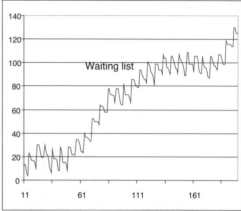

Figure 7.11 Simulation results for Lancaster District Hospital.

If the first 10 days of the simulation are ignored, for the reasons discussed above, a simple analysis of the two flows Patients and Overflow reveals the figures shown in Table 7.2. Thus, this system appears not to make good use of the available beds, the evidence being that the average number of patients on the ward is only 24. In addition, up to six emergencies on any day had to be diverted to other hospitals – not good. It would now be possible to use this Powersim model to conduct experiments with different admissions policies so as to find some better way to operate this ward of the hospital. However, that is beyond the scope of this chapter.

One thing that should be noted, however, is that the LDH model contains several exogenous factors (i.e. things determined outside the system). These can be regarded in one of two ways in any further modelling of LDH. The first is that they are parameters whose values can be varied to see what effects this might have on the performance of the system – what, for example, is the effect of reducing the length of stay? The other view of these factors, shown as diamond-shaped constants in Figure 7.10, is that they are simplifications of what actually happens. There will, for example, be a reason why the length of stay takes the values that it does, and these may be related to other factors in the diagram. Would the length of stay remain the same if the number of beds were increased but staffing levels were unchanged? If this were an important question, then this relationship would need to be properly modelled in Powersim, rather than simplifying it into a constant. This type of thinking about apparently exogenous factors should characterize system dynamics modelling.

Table 7.2 Summary of system dynamics simulation for LDH.

	Patients	OverFlow	WaitList
Mean	24.24	0.73	67.60
Standard deviation	3.56	1.45	5.56
Maximum	30.00	6.00	130.00
Minimum	16.00	0.00	4.00

Summary

This chapter has explained how, in many human systems, control is exercised by feedback processes that use information as the basis for action. This information is often delayed and may be distorted, and this needs to be taken into account when considering how human systems might be managed. System dynamics, as proposed by Forrester, provides a way of modelling such human systems with their feedback, delays and distortions. This relies on a simple analogy between human systems and mechanical or hydraulic systems in which activity is represented by rates or flows and accumulations by levels or stocks. These ideas are embodied in simple-to-use software, including Powersim as used here. Even without using such software, a system dynamics approach may be used via diagramming methods to try to gain some understanding of how a proposed system may operate. Using the software enables a modeller to gain both qualitative and quantitative insight into the proposed system's operations.

It must be recognized that, compared with SSM and cognitive mapping, system dynamics could be a rather mechanistic approach. Certainly, its roots in control theory mean that there is this danger. However, it is very easy, and perhaps best, to use system dynamics in an interpretive mode to try to understand different views of a system and its possible operation.

References

Dangerfield B.C. and Roberts C. (1995) Projecting dynamic behaviour in the absence of a model: an experiment. *System Dynamics Review*, **11**(2), 157–172.

Forrester J.W. (1961) *Industrial Dynamics*. MIT Press, Cambridge, MA.

High Performance Systems (1994) *Stella II Technical Documentation*. High Performance Systems, Hanover, NH.

High Performance Systems (2009) Stella/iThink software: www.hpc-inc.com

Howick S. and Eden C.L. (2004) On the nature of discontinuities in system dynamics modelling of disrupted projects. *Journal of the Operational Research Society*, **55**, 598–605.

Lane D.C. (2000) Looking in the wrong place for healthcare improvements: a systems dynamics study of an accident and emergency department. *Journal of the Operational Research Society*, **51**(5), 518–531.

Maruyama M. (1963) The second cybernetics: deviation amplifying mutual causal processes. *American Scientist*, **51**(2), 164–179.

Meadows D.H. (1972) *The Limits to Growth*. Universe Books, New York, NY.

Morecroft J. (2007) *Strategic Modelling and Business Dynamics: a Feedback Systems Approach*. John Wiley & Sons, Ltd, Chichester, UK.

Newsome I.M. (2007) Using system dynamics to model the impact of policing activity on performance. *Journal of the Operational Research Society*, **59**, 164–170.

Pidd M. (2004) *Computer Simulation in Management Science*, 5th edition. John Wiley & Sons, Ltd, Chichester, UK.

Powersim Corporation (2009) Powersim system dynamics software: www.powersim.com

Richmond B. and Petersen S. (1994) *Stella II. An Introduction to Systems Thinking*. High Performance Systems, Hanover, NH.

Roberts C. and Dangerfield B.C. (1990) Modelling the epidemiologic consequences of HIV infection and AIDS – a contribution from operational research. *Journal of the Operational Research Society*, **41**(4), 273–289.

Senge P.M. (1992) *The Fifth Discipline: the Art and Practice of the Learning Organization.* Century Publications, New York, NY.

Sterman J. (2000) *Business Dynamics: Systems Thinking and Modeling for a Complex World.* Irwin McGraw-Hill, Boston, MA.

Tustin E. (1953) *The Mechanism of Economic Systems.* Harvard University Press, Cambridge, MA.

Ventana Systems (2009) Vensim software: www.vensim.com

Wolstenholme E.F. (1990) *System Enquiry. A System Dynamics Approach.* John Wiley & Sons, Ltd, Chichester, UK.

8 Decision analysis

Basic ideas

Normative versus descriptive decision theory

Chapter 2 introduced the idea of rational choice, which is based on the comparison of known options using an explicit and unambiguous decision criterion. Here, we develop these ideas further under the general banner of decision analysis or decision theory. As with the other approaches covered in this book, there are many texts available that provide detailed accounts of the theory and practice, some of which are listed at the end of this chapter. Here, our aim is to introduce the basic ideas and to set them against the general principles of modelling discussed in Part I.

Decision analysis is an example of normative decision theory – that is, the approach suggests how decisions *should* be made, under certain assumptions. In particular, normative theory insists that decision-makers should be consistent and base their decisions on properly defined choice criteria, as discussed in Chapter 2, around Figure 2.1. In Chapter 8 it will become clear that it is rare to find these assumptions fully satisfied; however, this does not mean that the approach is useless. Used appropriately, normative decision analysis can provide a way to consider options in a systematic way, and doing so can be valuable, as long as its limitations are recognized. Normative decision theory has been around for many years, and early, comprehensive accounts can be found in Raiffa and Schlaifer (1961) and Thomas (1972).

Descriptive, or behavioural, decision theory is, by contrast, concerned with how people *actually* make decisions. Hence, it accepts that people often seem to be inconsistent and that factors other than a narrow view of rationality affect us when we make decisions. As discussed in Chapter 2, Schwartz (2004) provides a readable summary of some research findings in descriptive decision theory, much of it based on Kahneman, Slovic and Tversky (1982) and Kahneman and Tversky (1974). Descriptive decision theory discusses, for example, the paradox that when people have more options available they often make worse choices. Thankfully, there are times when normative and descriptive theories lead to the same conclusions, but this not always the case.

Multi-criteria decisions

When making many, if not all, real-life decisions, we often do this against more than a single criterion. Consider, for example, choosing a flight from the UK to the USA. This may be an easy decision for the very rich, but most of us weigh up factors such as ticket price, flight times, the convenience of particular airports and previous experience with different airlines. As a second example, I wrote most of this chapter during the winter of 2008/9; a time when many major banks were close to failure and had to be rescued by governments. Chapter 2 included a simple investment decision (summarized in Table 2.2), and the current real financial climate suggests that we might evaluate our potential investment on three criteria: the guaranteed annual return, the ethical stance of the bank and the likelihood of the bank failing. It is highly likely that no bank on the list is best in all three areas – a very common situation in multi-criteria decision-making. Both normative and descriptive decision analysis can be extended to cope with multi-criteria decision problems. Hence, there are methods, which will be briefly introduced in this chapter, for helping people come to terms with multiple decision criteria. Some writers prefer the term multi-attribute decision-making, although, strictly speaking, multi-attribute theory relates to the development of a single performance measure by the combination of different attributes of a decision.

Independent or linked decisions

Some decisions can be treated as one-off and independent of others within a particular environ-ment. For example, one Saturday I was in a supermarket deciding what to buy for dinner that night. My wife was away and I was staying in. We already had several wines at home, so I had a fairly free choice from what was available (if you're interested, I chose mackerel, cooked it from a recipe found on the Internet and it was delicious). However, many decisions are linked, and making one decision will often constrain the later options. Hence, when making a decision, we may reflect on the degree of flexibility available for subsequent decisions.

A moment's reflection will suggest that virtually all decisions, even mine about what to eat, are linked to others. The main question to ask is whether a choice can be treated *as if* independent of others. Many, if not all, decisions are part of a sequence of choices. For example, if I hadn't had wine at home, I'd have bought some to go with the fish or bought something other than fish, thus creating a sequence of decisions. Later in this chapter we shall see how normative decision analysis is often used to help people think through a sequence of decisions using decision trees. For example, a business may be considering the launch of a new product or service, and may be wondering whether to test-market it in one area of the country before moving to a national launch. Based on the outcome of the test market, it may decide to modify the product, to reprice it, to increase or decrease marketing support or not to proceed to national launch at all. Thus, there is a sequence of decisions in which later ones depend on what happens as a result of earlier choices.

As well as requiring a sequence of decisions and outcomes, planning a new product launch may also require simultaneous decisions on interdependent aspects. For example, deciding to charge a premium price for a new product will require a different approach to its marketing from that needed for a commodity item. Changing the usual pricing policy and marketing approach may require negotiations with other stakeholders (e.g. retailers), and so a set of simultaneous and sequential decisions may be needed when planning this new product launch. Thus, what seems like a single choice may actually involve several decisions, some of which are taken at the same time and some of which occur in a sequence.

Stakeholders

It is usually true that several stakeholders must be considered when making decisions. I only had a free choice of what to eat because my wife was away (she also likes mackerel, though, so may have agreed with my choice). Working with and managing stakeholders is a key concern of Chapters 5 and 6, so the discussion here will be brief. As anyone planning a family holiday will know, it is rare for all stakeholders in a decision to be in complete agreement about preferences or even on the criteria to be applied when making a choice. Having several stakeholders makes it highly likely that a decision will be based on multiple criteria; for example, when buying a family car, one person may be concerned with cost and another with image. Because decisions that are treated as multi-criteria often involve several stakeholders with rather different views, methods such as soft systems methodology (Chapter 5) and cognitive mapping (Chapter 6) were devised to cope with these. Sometimes it is possible to reach a compromise or, as argued by Checkland (1999), to reach an accommodation so that the stakeholders agree to proceed in a particular way. At other times, the reality of power intervenes as particular stakeholders either exert their power explicitly (e.g. it's my budget, I decide), or more subtly, by clever use of political processes.

Multi-criteria decision analysis

As mentioned earlier, many decisions involve multiple criteria in which no single criterion dominates the rest. There are several different formal approaches to multi-criteria decision analysis (MCDA), each reflecting slightly different assumptions. Some of the ideas have been around for many years, and early discussions can be found in Edwards (1971, 1977) and Keeney and Raiffa (1976). For recent, thorough coverage, including good introductions, see Belton and Stewart (2002), Goodwin and Wright (2004) and the e-learning site of Helsinki University of Technology (2009). Many approaches involve the development of explicit value functions to assess the available options, and this will be the focus of this section. Perhaps the most widely used approach that does not use value functions is the analytical hierarchy process (AHP) (Saaty, 1980). AHP is based on the pairwise comparison of available options, and a mathematical manipulation of these pairwise comparisons with the intention of arriving at a consistent set of preferences. A web search will reveal many reported applications of AHP. Expert Choice (2009) offers software to support different aspects of AHP, particularly the mathematical manipulations.

In this chapter we will consider approaches to MCDA based on value functions and explicit weights, illustrating this with SMART (Simple Multi-Attribute Rating Technique) as suggested in Edwards (1971) and expanded in Edwards (1977). This is not because AHP is necessarily inferior, but because the use of value functions and explicit weights enables open debate about the importance of different criteria when making a complex decision, which may be especially important when there are multiple stakeholders. Belton (1986) takes a critical look at both value function methods and AHP, building on earlier work by Belton and Gear (1983). In general, MCDA approaches are not based on probabilistic reasoning, unlike decision trees covered later in this chapter.

Common-sense MCDA

To illustrate the issues to be faced in MCDA, consider an interview panel of four people, plus a chair, that has seen four people for an academic post. In these circumstances it is not unusual for the candidates each to offer different skills and to have different deficiencies. Suppose that, after a long inconclusive discussion, the chair of the interview panel suggests that panel members each score the candidates against several attributes on a 1 to 10 scale, with 10 implying perfection. In the academic world, these attributes might include research track record, teaching skills, collegiality, promise for the future and so on. This might result in something like the performance matrix in Table 8.1, which shows the scores given by each member (1 to 4) for

Table 8.1 Interview panel matrix of performance scores.

PANEL	Member 1				Member 2				Member 3				Member 4			
CANDIDATE	A	B	C	D	A	B	C	D	A	B	C	D	A	B	C	D
Research	7	7	6	7	6	2	6	7	9	8	7	9	6	7	8	8
Teaching	7	8	7	7	3	2	5	5	8	7	7	8	5	4	6	4
Collegiality	6	6	6	6	5	2	6	4	0	5	1	2	4	7	3	3
Promise	8	8	8	10	4	8	2	6	4	8	5	8	6	5	2	3

each candidate (A to D). This shows that only candidate D is regarded as perfect by any panel member on any attribute: she is given a 10 by member 1 on her promise for future.

Suppose the chair now suggests that the panel members add up the scores for each candidate and use this sum to show which candidate should be offered the post. The totals are shown in Table 8.2, in which the highest summary score of 97 is awarded to candidate D. Is it therefore safe to assume that candidate D should be offered the job because she is clearly the best? Also, if she turns down the job, is it clear that the post should be offered to candidate B? The answer is no; that may be unwise. Why should this be? There are several reasons for this, of which the two most obvious are that the summary score assumes that the four attributes are equally important and also that each panel member has used the same internal scale when scoring each candidate. Consider, first, the importance of each attribute. After some discussion, suppose that the chair insists that he will assign a weight to each score, giving a weight of 5 to the research track record, of 2 to teaching ability, of 2 to collegiality and of 1 to promise for the future. If these are used as weights to compute a weighted sum for each candidate, the weighted scores for A, B, C and D are 238, 231, 234 and 260 respectively. Interestingly, this still gives the highest score to candidate D, but puts candidate A in second place, should D decide she does not want the job – which may matter. Using weighted scores is sometimes known as simple additive weighting (SAW) and can be a surprisingly useful way to tease out people's preferences by showing them the effects of different weightings.

Is there, however, a risk that the panel members will vary in their willingness to use the full range of scores and that this may affect the result? Table 8.3 shows the unweighted scores given by each panel member against each attribute. In general, it seems that panel member 1 is the most generous and panel member 2 is the harshest. To check whether this matters, we could use the average values to normalize the scores by using the column averages, the row averages or a combination of the two. It is also interesting to note that only panel member 1 gives relatively high scores for collegiality to all candidates, which may be because the other three members do not regard this as important – that is, they may be using implied weights when giving their

Table 8.2 Total unweighted performance scores.

Candidate	A	B	C	D
Research	28	24	27	31
Teaching	23	21	25	24
Collegiality	15	20	16	15
Promise	22	29	17	27
Total	**88**	**94**	**85**	**97**

Table 8.3 Unweighted scores by panel members.

Member	1	2	3	4	Av.
Research	27	21	33	29	27.50
Teaching	29	15	30	19	23.25
Collegiality	24	17	8	17	16.50
Promise	34	20	25	16	23.75
Average	**28.50**	**18.25**	**24.00**	**20.25**	

apparently unweighted scores. Alternatively, it may be because panel member 1 does not regard this attribute as important, so has given the same cores to all candidates. We would need to investigate further so as to be clear what the numbers imply.

This example illustrates that using a common-sense approach to multi-attribute scoring can be useful, but can also be misleading. For example, if the chair insists that each attribute score be weighted as suggested earlier, then it would be reasonable for panel members to say that they might have given different scores if they had known the weights at the time. Rather than operating in this common-sense way, a more structured approach is needed to avoid providing a pseudoscientific rationale for arbitrary decisions.

Formal MCDA

It is best to regard MCDA as a process in which decision problems are structured and modelled to help participants explore the options that are available or could be available. MCDA inevitably includes some subjectivity because people are asked to make value judgements, but formal methods temper this with an objective and explicit process. Most MCDA approaches assume that a set of decision criteria can be made explicit and agreed upon by those involved, even though the participants may not agree, initially at least, about the relative importance of the different criteria. The MCDA process aims to allow the evaluation of the options against each criterion and then moves to a comparison of those options. The common-sense approach with simple additive weights illustrates a few important features of the way that MCDA problems are typically structured into:

- a stated set of objectives (select the best candidate);
- a set of options that can achieve some or all of the objectives (the candidates);
- a set of performance attributes that relate to the objectives (research, teaching, collegiality and promise);
- a set of weights that are applied to the attribute values to provide scores for each option (arbitrarily set by the panel chair).

Note that none of these features may be obvious when MCDA methods are used in practice, and considerable effort and careful process management may be needed to explicate any or all of them from participants.

Belton and Stewart (2002) review the various approaches to MCDA, providing enough detail for their practical use. Here, we will focus on value function methods, in which the aim is directly to evaluate the options against defined criteria. The common-sense approach described earlier was based on a well-intentioned attempt to develop and use a value function that consisted of the weighted scores of the candidates. However, as we observed, there was no attempt to ensure that the weights were consistent or that consistent and coherent scores were developed. In general, the formal value function methods strive to provide this consistency and coherence. To illustrate this, the next section provides a brief overview of SMART (Simple Multi-Attribute Rating Technique).

SMART

SMART is an approach in which decision-makers are helped, with appropriate support, to evaluate the options open to them using a consistent rating and scoring process. Like all formal methods, it does not guarantee that the 'correct' decision will be made, as the outcome may depend on factors beyond the decision-maker's control. It introduces a relatively objective process to enable consistency in subjective evaluation. It is thus an example of procedural rationality (Simon, 1976), as introduced in Chapter 2. SMART is usually presented as a 10-step approach (based on Edwards, 1977):

1. Identify the person or organization that wishes or needs to make a decision.
2. Identify the issues; that is, the decision or decisions that need to be made.
3. Identify the available options or courses of action. Note that this may not be trivial, as new options may be discovered during the SMART process and participants may need support in developing these options.
4. Identify the relevant performance attributes (dimensions of performance), often by creating a value tree (see below). This may also be non-trivial, particularly if several stakeholders are involved. Edwards (1977) stresses the importance of keeping the number of performance attributes to the bare minimum so as to ensure that only important weights are used.
5. Rank the dimensions in order of importance.
6. Rate the dimensions; that is, determine the importance weights to be applied to each attribute. This is also not straightforward, and the different versions of SMART suggest different approaches that can be used to ensure consistency.
7. Normalize the importance weights by summing them, dividing each weight by the sum and multiplying by 100.
8. Score each option on each attribute using a value function (see below). As noted in the common-sense example, care must be taken to ensure that these scores are consistent, which is why value functions are used.
9. Use the scores on each attribute to compute the value of the option. In the simplest cases, this is the weighted sum of the attribute scores.
10. Use the weighted sum to decide which option is best.

One attraction of SMART is that it is close to the type of common-sense MCDA approach discussed earlier, yet adds rigour to the process. We should also note that, as in most quantitative modelling approaches, step 10 is not really the endpoint. In most situations we wish to know how sensitive or how robust a decision is to changes in the data used. In the case of SMART and similar approaches, much of the data are subjective, making it even more important to investigate sensitivity. That is, decisions are provisional until participants are agreed that sensitivity analysis or robustness analysis is complete.

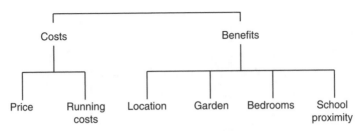

Figure 8.1 A simple value tree.

Value trees

It is important to ensure that the performance attributes used in this form of MCDA are consistent and represent the decision-makers' concerns. One way of developing the attributes is to develop a value tree, which is a hierarchical representation of the relationship between them. The aim is to ensure that the attribute set is complete. As an example, suppose a couple wish to buy a house in which to live with their two children. To keep things simple, assume that the couple agree with one another about everything (unlikely) and can be treated as a single decision-maker, but still need to consider a set of houses that offer different costs and benefits. Suppose they have visited estate agents, studied websites and looked for suitable houses, and are happy to consider eight options in locations around Lancaster in Bare, Caton, Freehold, Galgate, Haverbreaks, Hest Bank, Morecambe and Scotforth.

Houses, sadly, have to be paid for and maintained, so house ownership has a cost. Ownership also has benefits, too, such as living space, garden space, number of bedrooms and location. Hence, as the first stage in developing a value tree, the couple could divide the attributes of the different properties into those they regard as costs and those they regard as benefits. These, in turn, could be decomposed further to give the value tree shown in Figure 8.1. It is important that the attributes should be capable of evaluation by the decision-maker, possibly with help from a skilled analyst. Drawing a value tree enables decision-makers to consider whether the attributes are comprehensive, contain no redundancies (two or more attributes do not duplicate each other) and can be judged independently of one another. Once the couple are satisfied that the tree meets these criteria, the various houses available can be scored on the lowest-level attributes of the tree using value functions.

Value functions

As became clear in the common-sense approach to MCDA, it is important to ensure that attributes are scored on consistent scales, and value functions are used to do this in step 8 of SMART. The idea is to score all attributes on the same range (0 to 100 is typical), although with differently shaped functions (Figure 8.2). Some attributes can be easily quantified – for example, the price of a house, the amount of space and the number of bedrooms. In the simplest case there is a linear relationship between the numeric value and the score, as in Figure 8.2(a) for the house price. This represents a situation in which a house costing, say, £200 000, is half as desirable as one costing £100 000 – which is very unlikely to be true. It is much more likely that there is a non-linear relationship between the score and the house price. As an example of another non-linear relationship, garden size may be important below a certain level, but may grow relatively less important beyond a certain size, as in Figure 8.2(b). There may also be cases,

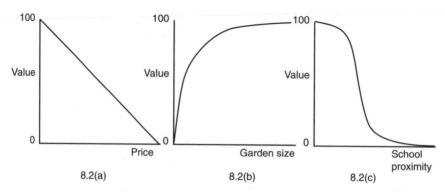

Figure 8.2 Three different value functions.

such as distance from local schools, in which the value function has an S-shape, as in Figure 8.2(c). There are various procedures recommended for eliciting the shape of the value functions, and Belton and Stewart (2002), Goodwin and Wright (2004) and Watson and Buede (1987) cover the main methods in use.

Some attributes are not numeric but can be rank ordered according to the preference of the decision-maker. In the case of housing, this might be the general location of the property – some locations are much more desirable than others for reasons unrelated to other factors such as proximity to schools. A straightforward approach to creating value functions for such attributes is direct rating, in which decision-makers are asked to rank the options in preference order. Suppose the couple do this and their ranking is as follows, from most to least desirable: Hest Bank, Haverbreaks, Freehold, Scotforth, Caton and Galgate, Bare and Morecambe. The most desirable (Hest Bank) is assigned a value of 100, and the least desirable location (Morecambe) is assigned a value of 0. They must now assign values on the scale of 0 to 100 for each of the other locations, and the intervals between their positions on the scale show their relative desirability. Goodwin and Wright (2004) point out that this is an interval scale, rather like those used to measure temperature. In the latter we cannot say that 80 °C is twice as hot as 40 °C; however, we can say that an increase from 40 °C to 80 °C is twice that of an increase from 20 °C to 40 °C. Hence, we might end up with the value scale for location shown in Figure 8.3.

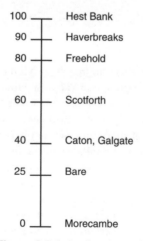

Figure 8.3 A simple value scale.

Using a range of methods, it is possible to develop value functions for attributes of different types, including those that are already quantified and those that are not. All that remains is to apply the normalized weights to the scores derived from the value functions, so as to develop an overall weighted value function. It should be clear why a subsequent sensitivity analysis is needed. Although the processes used to develop the weights and values are explicit, they are still subjective, and it is very important to consider how sensitive the outcome is to those weights and values.

Later versions of SMART include SMARTS (SMART using Swings) and SMARTER (SMART Exploiting Ranks) and are discussed in Edwards and Barron (1994). SMARTS is based on swing weights rather than on weights agreed, possibly arbitrarily, by those involved. Swing weights are derived by focusing the attention of the decision-maker(s) on the trade-offs available in the decision. This is usually done by inviting them to anchor their views on the worst and best decision alternatives. SMARTER is a simplification of SMARTS and is said to reduce the number of difficult decisions and comparisons required of participants.

Normative decision analysis under uncertainty

Normative decision analysis is based on a set of assumptions that relate to the decision-makers and their beliefs and preferences. The first is that a rational decision-maker should have consistent beliefs (for a specific information set) and consistent preferences. In essence, the decision-maker should not be capricious or arbitrary. Another key assumption is that beliefs and preferences can and should be separated. That is, there should be a clear distinction between what a decision-maker would like to happen and what is believed to happen. Just wishing for something will not make it happen.

The term 'beliefs' refers to an individual's assessment of how likely particular outcomes are to occur. For example, a marketing manager may believe that, if a product is launched at a particular price, then some sales levels are more likely than others. She may believe there is a 30% chance of sales being below 100 000 units, a 50% chance they will be between 100 000 and 300 000 and a 20% chance they will exceed 300 000. The calculations used in normative decision theory assume that these beliefs are consistent with probability theory.

Preferences reflect the decision-maker's attitude to the options available, and, in normative decision theory, consistent preferences depend on three factors:

- transitivity;
- the way information is presented;
- invariance.

Transitivity is best understood by considering a situation in which a decision-maker has three options A, B and C available. Suppose that she prefers option A to option B and also prefers option B to option C. Her preferences are transitive if she also prefers option A to option C. Expressed more formally, if $A \geq B$ and $B \geq C$, then $A \geq C$, where the $\geq$ indicates that A is, in the decision-maker's view, never worse than B and B is never worse than C. Hence, in her view, A is never worse than C if her preferences are transitive. As mentioned earlier, Schwarz (2004) has much to say about people's lack of transitivity when making personal decisions. However, this does not mean that normative decision-making is a waste of time, but indicates that it should be used with caution.

Second, preference should remain consistent when faced with the same information presented in the same way. When faced with different information, or if the same information is presented in different ways, most show some inconsistency. A moment's reflection on marketing practices leads to a realization that, in general, marketing expenditure would be wasted were this not so. More generally, as with transitivity, Schwartz (2004) shows that this assumption does not hold for many personal decisions. For example, the sequence in which options are presented or explored can affect someone's preferences – which may be a reason why different wine experts may give rather different ratings to the same wine when presented in different sequences with other wines. As with transitivity, this evidence of inconsistency does not mean that normative decision analysis should be avoided, rather it can be used to explore what might happen were people to be consistent – which can be a very valuable thing to do.

Third, consistent preferences should be *invariant*. This means that the addition of an extra option to an already known set should not affect the existing preferences. Thus, if we already know that, if A ≥ B and B ≥ C, then adding a fourth option D should not alter this, nor should it alter the view that A≥C. That is, adding D to the list of options should not result in B or C becoming more attractive than A, or C becoming more attractive than B. Again, Schwartz (2004) describes situations in which preference are not invariant in personal decision-making.

Decision trees

Decision trees are a way of capturing the essence of linked and sequential decisions made under uncertainty. They display the sequence of options and make a clear distinction between options and the consequences of those options. This book is about modelling rather than algorithms, and hence we stress that the process of developing a decision tree is often as valuable as the end-product, the tree itself. As with MCDA, a carefully planned process is often what makes the decision tree useful. This is because an attempt to develop a decision tree forces the people involved to think carefully about their options and their interactions. Developing the tree can be far from straightforward, but initially we will assume a well-structured decision in which developing the tree is not too difficult. This is a decision about the possible launch of a new industrial product: the Mighty MegaMixer (MMM), a piece of equipment used in food processing. The board of Mighty Manufacturing has agreed that its senior designer should consider two different technologies, which are labelled as micro and nano within the business. The two technologies lead to rather different designs, neither of which is guaranteed to be a success in the market.

A simple decision tree is shown in Figure 8.4 so as to illustrate some of the main features. The tree should be read from left to right and represents a dilemma faced by a camper who is uncertain whether to take a flysheet along with his main tent. The flysheet makes it much more likely that he will stay dry if it rains, but means that he will need to carry more. Decisions are shown as rectangles; hence, his decision is whether or not to take a flysheet. Each of these options has at least one outcome, and, as he cannot control the weather, he uses his previous experience to estimate the probability of rain as 70% (0.7). Because he is only bothered whether it is wet or dry, each option is followed by a chance node, shown by a circle, and these, in turn, have two outcomes – wet and dry. As this tree is only to illustrate the general layout of decision trees, it need not consider further decisions or consequences, and thus the tree ends with end nodes (or terminal nodes) at the branches representing the outcomes.

A simple example

The senior designer has already completed some preliminary calculations based on his view that it is sensible to regard the MMM as either a success or failure in the market. For the

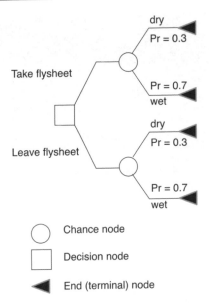

Figure 8.4 Main features of a decision tree.

micro design, he estimates that developing the micro-MMM will produce sales revenue of £15 million if it is successful in the market, but £1 million if it fails. The costs of developing and manufacturing micro-MMM are estimated at £4 million. He is very unsure whether either design will be successful and, initially, considers that the micro design is equally likely to succeed or fail. For the nano-MMM, he estimates that sales revenue will amount to £24 million if the product is successful, and £1 million if it fails. He estimates the development and manufacturing costs of the nano-MMM to be £7.5 million and thinks there is a slightly lower chance that it will succeed, and estimates this as 40%.

It is not essential to use special software to develop and analyse a decision tree, but using such a tool can make life easier. This chapter uses PrecisionTree (Palisade, 2009), an add-in to Microsoft Excel™ that can be used to draw a decision tree and to analyse it. The examples in this chapter were developed in Excel 2007, using PrecisionTree 5.0, but other versions are very similar in their approach. Before use, PrecisionTree must be installed as an Excel add-in and then selected. This leads to a blank worksheet. A new decision tree is created by selecting the Decision Tree option of PrecisionTree, which opens a dialogue box in which the user selects the spreadsheet cell in which the tree will start. In this example, the tree starts in cell A6, which leads to the initial, though useless, decision tree of Figure 8.5. The Decision Tree dialogue box also allows the user to give the tree a name, which, in this case, is *MMM Decision*. Whenever PrecisionTree creates a new node, it assumes that this is an end node of the tree, shown as a solid triangle. It also assumes that this point will be reached with 100% probability and that the end node has no value. Hence, the values 100% and zero are shown by the end node. All of these values can be changed using the dialogue box for Decision Tree Node Settings.

To represent the decision, we need to add options, and do this by clicking on the end node, which opens the Decision Tree Nodes Setting dialogue box shown in Figure 8.6. This has two tabs, which relate to the Node and to its Branches. Figure 8.6 shows the result of selecting the Nodes tab, which confirms that this first node is currently located in cell B7. While on the Nodes sheet, the user may redefine a node as one of four other types. For present purposes, we need

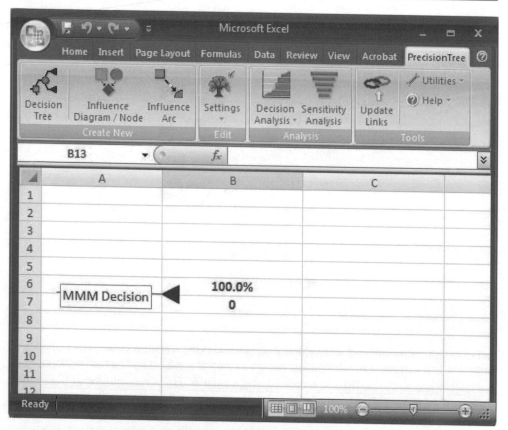

Figure 8.5 Creating a decision tree in PrecisionTree.

only be concerned with decision nodes and chance nodes. PrecisionTree follows the normal convention of decision trees in showing decision nodes as squares, and these, unsurprisingly, occur when a decision must be made. Chance nodes are shown as circles, and these occur as the consequence of a decision. As the designer must decide whether to recommend a micro or nano design, this is a decision node. Hence, we select the Decision option as shown in Figure 8.6 and label the node as *micro or nano*.

Selecting the Branches tab leads to the table shown in Figure 8.7, which allows the user to give names to the branches and values, which here will represent the costs of developing and producing the micro and nano designs. As a default, PrecisionTree assumes that a chance node has two outcomes, to which extra branches can obviously be added if appropriate. In Figure 8.7, the first branch has been relabelled as micro and the second as nano. The corresponding costs have been added in the appropriate cells in the Value column of the table. As the costs of the micro and nano options are £4 million and £7.5 million, the table contains the values −4 and −7.5. The table also contains tick boxes under the Force column, and these should be ticked if the user wishes to explore the effect of insisting on a particular choice or outcome – which is not the case here.

Although not shown here, the completion of the dialogue in Figure 8.7 results in a very simple tree with just two branches: micro and nano. As we have not considered the possible outcomes for the two branches, the tree would simply show that the micro option is cheaper. It would, of

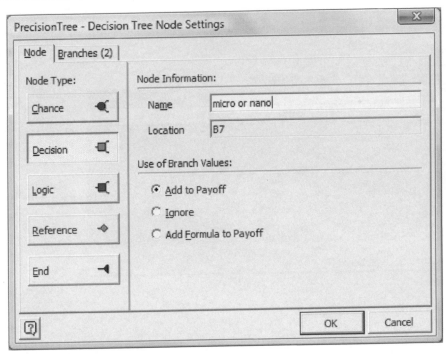

Figure 8.6 PrecisionTree's Decision Tree Nodes Setting dialogue box.

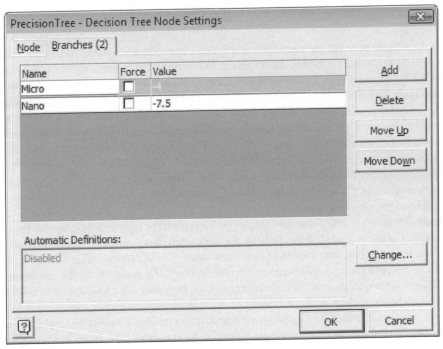

Figure 8.7 PrecisionTree: adding branches to a node.

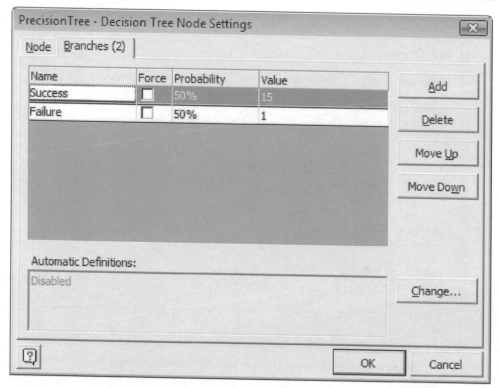

Figure 8.8 Setting probabilities and values in PrecisionTree.

course, be strange to make the decision solely on cost grounds, so we need to add the revenues that result from success or failure. To do this in PrecisionTree, we select the terminal nodes at the end of the decision branches and redefine them as chance nodes, much as the micro or nano decision node was redefined in Figure 8.6. To illustrate this, Figure 8.8 shows the branch table for the outcome resulting from the choice of the micro option. Note that, for chance nodes, this table includes an extra column, labelled as Probability, which will be used to capture the likelihood of the two outcomes, *success* and *failure*. Figure 8.8 shows a completed table using the probabilities and revenues discussed earlier for the micro option. As we are now dealing with revenues, the value of success is shown as 15, representing an income of £15 million. Failure produces revenue of £1 million, so a value of 1 is entered in the table. A similar table needs to be completed for the nano option.

Figure 8.9 shows the decision tree drawn by PrecisionTree after entering the revenues and probabilities of success and failure for both the micro and nano options. As its default decision criterion, PrecisionTree uses expected monetary value (EMV) to determine which of the two options seems preferable. As discussed in Chapter 2, the EMV results from the combination of probability values with the costs and the revenues in an expected value calculation that is basic to probability theory – which is why it is usual, in normative decision theory, to require that beliefs are expressed in ways that are consistent with probability theory. Thus, for example, the sum of the probabilities across all outcomes from an option must sum to 1 (or 100% in PrecisionTree).

It is now possible to compute the EMV of the two options, which is the expected revenue minus the expected costs. To do this, we start from the terminal nodes and work back towards

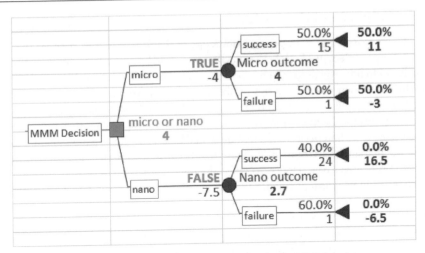

Figure 8.9 Complete decision tree for the simple MMM decision.

the starting node. Consider, first, the nano option and its two outcomes. The revenue from a successful launch of a micro-MMM is £15 million (shown as 15 in Figure 8.9), and from an unsuccessful launch £1 million. Each of these outcomes has a probability of 0.5 (shown as 50% in Figure 8.9). Thus, the expected revenue from the micro option is $(0.5 \times 15) + (0.5 \times 1)$, which is 8, or £8 million – which is not shown in Figure 8.9. Similarly, the expected revenue from launching a nano-MMM is $(0.4 \times 24) + (0.6 \times 1) = £10.2$ million.

Having completed the extreme right-hand nodes in Figure 8.8, the usual computation method for decision trees is to move left, towards the initial node. In this simple example, the next node to the left is the decision node itself. This is a decision node, not a chance node, so rolling the tree back only involves subtracting the costs from the expected revenues. Hence, the EMV of the micro-MMM is £4 million (£8 million expected revenue, less £4 million costs), and for the nano-MMM it is £2.7 million (£10.2 million expected revenue, less £7.5 million costs). Therefore, if EMV is the appropriate decision criterion, the micro-MMM is the best option, as it produces an EMV of £4 million, compared with £2.7 million from the nano-MMM. Hence, a value of £4 million is shown in Figure 8.9 against the initial decision – note, too, that PrecisionTree shows the values of the two decision options as £4 million for micro and £2.7 million for nano, as computed above.

Against the terminal nodes of Figure 8.9, PrecisionTree shows the actual values of each of the four outcomes. These can be rearranged as the payoff matrix in Table 8.4. This shows that, if we ignore probabilities and apply the maximax decision criterion (see Chapter 2), the most preferable option is the nano-MMM, with a payoff of £16.5 million. On the other hand, the same option has the lowest payoff, a loss of £6.5 million if it results in failure. The EMV is a way of steering a course between the two extremes.

Table 8.4 Payoff matrix, simple MMM decision.

	Success	Failure
Micro-MMM	£11 million	−£3 million
Nano-MMM	£16.5 million	−£6.5 million

The value of perfect information

Suppose it were possible to have perfect knowledge of the future; that is, suppose the designer could, somehow or other, predict whether the designs would be a success or failure in the market. How much would it be worth to gain this perfect information? To answer this question, we must imagine the consequence of having this perfect information. We know that a successful launch of the micro model will produce a return of £11 million. We also believe that the probability of a market success for the micro model is 0.5, and hence the expected return from introducing the micro model if we had perfect information would be £11 × 0.5 = £5.5 million. Notice that we ignore the market failure branch of Figure 8.9, because with perfect information we would know which branch was true. Hence, as far as the micro design is concerned, we can calculate how much it would be worth paying for this information: £5.5 million, less the expected return without this information (£4 million); that is, it would be worth paying up to £1.5 million for perfect information about the success of the micro design.

Applying the same logic to the nano design, we see that the expected return from its introduction if we had perfect knowledge would be £16.5 × 0.4 = £6.6 million. Thus, perfect information about the nano design is worth up to £2.6 million (£6.6 million, less £4 million).

Sadly, perfect information is rarely available, and its use, e.g. on the stock market, is often illegal. However, it may be worth gaining extra information that allows us to revise our estimates of market success. This is best done using Bayes' theorem, which is an important tool when using subjective probabilities.

Subjective probabilities

Chapter 2 includes a brief discussion of risk and uncertainty and suggests that the probability of an event occurring is often viewed from the perspective of relative frequency. Thus, if an unbiased six-sided die, as used in gambling and board games, were rolled enough times, most of us would expect an approximately equal number of 1s, 2s, 3s, 4s, 5s and 6s. From this, most of us are content with the idea that each of these outcomes has a probability of 1/6. This relative frequency view of probability is fine when dealing with repeated events. For example, analysis of data from a biscuit factory over a long period may reveal that 0.001% of biscuits are misshaped when produced by a particular machine. We might therefore conclude that this machine has a 1 in 10 000 probability of producing a misshaped biscuit. Although consumers may resent misshaped biscuits, we may be content to allow the machine to operate, as these biscuits will only be found in a small number of packets.

Instead of assuming that probabilities are directly related only to the known frequency of events, other views are possible. One approach is to assume that a statement about probability relates to our belief and knowledge about the events. In fact, many of us may make use of this subjective notion even when assigning a probability of 0.5 to an event such as the toss of a coin producing a head or a tail. We may believe that 20 000 repeated tosses are very unlikely to result in exactly 10 000 heads and 10 000 tails, but this may not affect our view that the probability 'really is' 0.5. We could support this belief, although not challenge it, by asserting, 'Well, we would get the same proportions if we went on almost forever'. This sounds like the earlier relative frequency argument; however, it is not quite the same, and is based on a belief about the process that leads to the event or outcome.

That is, when handed a coin to toss, we might reflect our prior beliefs by saying, 'I think the coin is unbiased and that the system for tossing it is also fair, therefore we should expect equal probability'. This is a subjective approach to probability. Note that 'subjective' does not mean 'wild', 'ludicrous' or 'outrageous'. It simply relates the probability to our beliefs and to our information. It also allows us to change our estimates as more information becomes available. If a coin is repeatedly tossed and we seem to get twice as many heads as tails, we ought to be suspicious of the coin or the tossing system and should examine these. We might also wish to revise our estimates of the probability.

Note that this argument implies that such probabilities are statements of knowledge or belief and may thus change if our knowledge improves or if our previous ideas are shown to be false. Thus, a probability may be a statement about our relative ignorance of some process or other. For example, it could be argued that the process of tossing a coin is wholly deterministic – it's just that we do not understand the process. It might, for example, be possible to design a machine that always tosses a coin in a wholly controlled manner within a static environment, such that it would always come down with heads uppermost. In the absence of such a machine, and with our belief that the coin is unbiased, we may attach a subjective probability of 0.5 to that outcome.

This same approach may be extended to events about which we have too little information to estimate probabilities in any objective sense and for events that are actually unrepeatable. If we are really unable to make any prior estimates of probabilities, then it would be more honest to make all events equally probable – but we rarely do this. Consider gamblers who bet on horse races, who start from form (the recent track record of the horse) and use this, with other information (e.g. how heavy is the going), to consider the odds offered by bookmakers. On this basis, they decide whether or not to bet on the race. Odds reflect people's views of the likelihood of an event occurring and are, in effect, subjective estimates of probability for an unrepeatable event. These odds, or probabilities, change as more information becomes available, particularly as the start time for the race approaches.

Bayesian statistics

Bayesian statistics is the name given to an approach that assumes that all estimates of probability are based on belief and information. The approach is named after the Reverend Thomas Bayes, an eighteenth-century non-conformist minister, best known for Bayes' theorem. Bayesian approaches provide ways in which probability estimates can be updated as beliefs change or as more information becomes available. Most Bayesians distinguish between two types of uncertainty:

- *Aleatory uncertainties.* These are taken to be inherent to a system being analysed if that system is unpredictable, except in a statistical sense. The term 'statistical' carries with it the idea of counting. Thus, in the example of the biscuit machine introduced in the previous section, we can collect data about the behaviour of the machine as seen in the number of misshaped biscuits produced over an extended time period.
- *Epistemic uncertainties.* These are taken to be subjective, arising mainly from limited knowledge; that is, they are due to the person estimating the uncertainty of events. For example, although we can determine the probability of producing a misshaped biscuit by using a relative frequency argument, we cannot use the same argument to assess whether a particular individual, Jane, will complain if she buys a pack of biscuits containing a misshape. We can estimate how likely she is to buy such a pack, but not how likely she is to complain – which may depend on when she finds the biscuits, whether her children like misshapes, and so on. Also, if misshaped biscuits are rare, it may be the first time that Jane has found one in a pack.

Is this distinction between aleatory and epistemic uncertainty a genuine one? Consider again the misshaped biscuits that are observed to occur at a rate of about 1 in 10 000. These occurrences may have deterministic causes; for example, were we to make the extensive effort to investigate further, we might discover that a misshape is due to the coincidence of a speck of dirt on a cam, a slight maldistribution of ingredients or vibration on the machine. As such an investigation may be expensive, we may prefer to use the observed 1 in 10 000 as a probability. That is, many apparently aleatory probability estimates rest on an epistemic base. Seeking further information is not always worthwhile, and understanding and representing uncertainties using probabilities based on relative frequencies is often a wholly acceptable approximation.

The Bayesian world-view has produced a huge literature with many practical applications. However, not all statisticians are convinced Bayesians, many prefer more classical approaches that assume greater objectivity about probability estimates. Here, we are not concerned with the continuing debate between the competing camps, but with the use of Bayes' theorem to improve the estimation of subjective probabilities based on epistemic uncertainty.

Bayes' theorem

As probabilities may be based on beliefs and limited knowledge, it clearly makes sense to have some way of updating these probabilities as new circumstances arise. Suppose we wish to know the probability of an event A occurring, given that another event B has already occurred. Bayes' theorem allows us to compute this as follows:

$$\Pr(A\,|B) = \frac{\Pr(B \cap A)}{\Pr(B)} \tag{1}$$

where $\Pr(A)$ is the probability that event A will occur; $\Pr(B)$ is the probability that event B will occur; $\Pr(A\,|B)$ is the probability that A will occur, given that B has occurred, that is, the conditional probability of A given B; and $\Pr(B \cap A)$ is the probability that both event A and event B will occur.

Thus, the conditional probability of A given B is the ratio of the joint probability of A and B and the probability of B occurring, which, intuitively, makes sense.

As, in this simple case, there are just two events A and B, it follows that

$$\Pr(B) = \Pr(B \cap A) + \Pr(B \cap \bar{A})$$

where $\bar{A}$ indicates that event A does not occur.

Hence, we can restate equation (1) as

$$\Pr(A\,|B) = \Pr\frac{\Pr(B \cap A)}{\Pr(B \cap A) + \Pr(B \cap \bar{A})} \tag{2}$$

Moreover, from equation (1) we can also see that

$$\Pr(B \cap A) = \Pr(A\,|B) \cdot \Pr(B)$$

which leads to

$$Pr(A|B) = \frac{Pr(B|A) \cdot Pr(A)}{Pr(B|A) \cdot Pr(A) + Pr(B|\bar{A}) \cdot Pr(\bar{A})} \tag{3}$$

In Bayesian statistics, $Pr(A)$ is usually known as the *prior* probability of event A, which represents beliefs in the absence of other information. By contrast, the conditional probability $Pr(A|B)$ is known as the posterior probability, as it represents the probability of event A updated in the light of further information.

Using Bayes' theorem

We have already seen how to calculate the value of perfect information, but have also noted that this is rarely available and usually cannot be used. Sometimes, however, we can obtain extra information that allows us to improve the probability of a favourable outcome, and this is a common application of Bayes' rule.

Suppose that the same MMM designer, considering whether to recommend the micro or nano design, now hears of a market research company (MktRC) that will, for a fee, conduct a survey of possible purchasers to provide a better estimate of the probability of success for either design. Will it be worth paying for such a survey, and how much will it be worth? To help him think about this, the designer asks the market researchers about the reliability of their surveys and is told that, with the benefit of hindsight, products for which market surveys are positive are successful in the market 90% of the time. On the other hand, when there is actually an unfavourable market for products, MktRC surveys correctly predict this on 80% of occasions. We can express these probabilities more formally as follows:

Pr(positive survey|success) = 0.9, where success indicates a favourable market
Pr(negative survey|failure) = 0.8, where failure indicates an unfavourable market

If we use Figure 8.8 as the basis for Bayesian updating, we can produce Tables 8.5 and 8.6, which show the posterior probabilities of success and failure after updating the prior probabilities with the historical reliability figures for MktRC surveys.

The term *state of nature* used in Tables 8.5 and 8.6 refers to the true state of the system, were that to be known (of course, it is not known, which is why we face a decision with uncertain outcomes). In this example, the unknown states of nature are whether a product has a successful

Table 8.5 Bayesian analysis of initial MMM options if the survey is positive.

Design	State of nature	Pr(positive survey|state of nature)	Prior probability	Joint probability	Posterior probability
Micro	Success	0.9	0.5	$0.9 \times 0.5 = 0.45$	$0.45/0.55 = 0.82$
	Failure	0.2	0.5	$0.2 \times 0.5 = 0.10$	$0.10/0.55 = 0.18$
		Sum of probabilities	*1.00*	*0.55*	*1.00*
Nano	Success	0.9	0.4	$0.9 \times 0.4 = 0.36$	$0.36/0.48 = 0.75$
	Failure	0.2	0.6	$0.2 \times 0.6 = 0.12$	$0.12/0.48 = 0.25$
		Sum of probabilities	*1.00*	*0.48*	*1.00*

Table 8.6 Bayesian analysis of initial MMM options if the survey is negative.

Design	State of nature	Pr(negative survey|state of nature)	Prior probability	Joint probability	Posterior probability
Micro	Success	0.10	0.5	0.1×0.5 = 0.05	0.05/0.45 = 0.11
	Failure	0.80	0.5	0.8×0.5 = 0.40	0.40/0.45 = 0.89
	Sum of probabilities	*1.00*		*0.45*	*1.00*
Nano	Success	0.10	0.4	0.1×0.4 = 0.04	0.04/0.52 = 0.08
	Failure	0.80	0.6	0.8×0.6 = 0.48	0.48/0.52 = 0.92
	Sum of probabilities	*1.00*		*0.52*	*1.00*

or unsuccessful launch, and these are labelled as *success* and *failure*. In both tables, as in Figure 8.9, the prior probability of a successful launch for the micro design is 0.5, and for the nano design it is 0.4.

Table 8.5 uses information about a positive survey to compute these posterior probabilities by applying Bayes' rule. Thus, if the MktRC survey has a 90% chance of correctly detecting a favourable market, the joint probability of this and a successful launch of a micro-MMM is $0.9 \times 0.5 = 0.45$. Likewise, the joint probability of the survey suggesting a favourable market and a failed launch of a micro-MMM is $0.2 \times 0.5 = 0.10$. The joint probabilities are shown in the fifth column of Table 8.5. The equivalent values for a positive survey for the nano-MMM are also shown in Table 8.5. The final column of Table 8.5 shows the posterior probabilities calculated using Bayes' rule. The values in Table 8.6 are calculated in exactly the same way, but using negative survey results. Thus, we see that the posterior probabilities are as follows:

Micro : Pr(success|positive survey) = 0.82 and Pr(failure|positive survey) = 0.18

Nano : Pr(success|positive survey) = 0.75 and Pr(failure|positive survey) = 0.25

Micro : Pr(success|negative survey) = 0.11 and Pr(failure|negative survey) = 0.89

Nano : Pr(success|negative survey) = 0.08 and Pr(failure|negative survey) = 0.92

The value of extra information

We can now use the posterior probabilities to calculate the return that would result from using the survey. As with perfect information, we are only interested in surveys that produce positive results (that is, they predict that a product will succeed), because, if the survey is negative, they will not develop the product. Consider, first, the micro design and the posterior probabilities if a survey is positive (Table 8.5). If the true state of the market is a successful launch, the expected return is £11 × 0.82 = £9 million. If the true state of the market is an unsuccessful launch of a micro design, the expected return is $-£3$ million × 0.18 = $-£0.55$ million. Thus, using this survey would produce an expected return of £(9.0 − 0.55) × 0.55 = £4.65 million, where 0.55 is the sum of the two relevant joint probabilities. As the expected return in Figure 8.8 for the micro option is £4 million, this suggests it might be worth paying up to £0.65 million for the survey.

If we now consider the nano option and complete the same calculations, we see that the expected return from using this survey is £(16.5 × 0.75 − 6.5 × 0.25) × 0.48 = £5.16 million. Thus, as with perfect information, if the designer has slightly better information as a result of this survey, then he would recommend the nano option, with an expected return of £5.16 million.

This compares with the expected return of £2.7 million for the nano option with no su~~~, £4 million, which means that it could be worth paying up to £1.16 million for the survey. Recall that the added value of perfect information was £2.6 million.

In general, Bayes' rule allows us to estimate the value of gaining extra information before taking a decision. To do so, we calculate the expected value of the decision with no extra information, then use Bayes' rule to compute posterior probabilities from which the expected return from the extra information can be calculated. We should, of course, be very sceptical about the accuracy of any of these expected values, as subjective probability estimation is very much an art rather than a science. This is one reason why the probabilities in Tables 8.5 and 8.6 are rounded to two decimal places; showing more would create a wholly spurious impression of accuracy.

Sequential decisions

Suppose the designer is actually unaware that he could pay for more information but, instead, realizes that either design could be modified, if initially unsuccessful, to make it more acceptable to the market, although at a further cost of £4 million for the micro design and a further £5 million for the nano design. The product would still be sold at the same price, so the revenues from success or failure would remain unchanged. However, the designer reckons that the chance of success with a modified design is now 80% for the micro design and 50% for the nano option. This presents a sequence of decisions that can also be analysed using a decision tree: in effect, this is a multi-stage decision.

Figure 8.10 shows the resulting decision tree drawn and analysed using PrecisionTree. Extra branches and nodes have been added to what were previously the end nodes for failure outcomes from the micro and nano options. As in Figure 8.9, the values beside the new end nodes show the actual returns from options at these points, and these are summarized in Table 8.7. If the EMV criterion is applied, selecting the micro design is the best option, leading to an expected return of £7.6 million, whereas selecting the nano option leads to an expected return of £6.6 million.

Several different decision criteria were introduced earlier in this chapter, and Table 8.7 allows us to consider criteria other than the EMV used in the decision tree. Once again, the maximum return of £16.5 million is gained by selecting the nano option, and, in the modified tree, the second highest actual return of £11.5 million occurs by the successful modification of the nano design. Hence, if the designer and the board of Mighty Manufacturing are all optimists and happy to take risks, the best initial option is to implement the nano design, which should then be modified if initially unsuccessful. It is, though, also true that the worst outcomes result from the initial selection of the nano option, and, if the board is risk averse, it may instead prefer the micro option.

Sensitivity and other analyses

It should be clear that the calculations required on a decision tree are not complicated, apart from the Bayesian analysis, which requires a clear head. Hence, it is reasonable to ask why it is worth bothering with tools such as PrecisionTree. The answer is that, once the decision tree is correctly entered in such software, it is very easy to construct sensitivity analyses. For example, in the sequential decision, we may wish to know how sensitive the expected return and option selected are to the return generated by an unmodified nano design. Currently, this is £24 million,

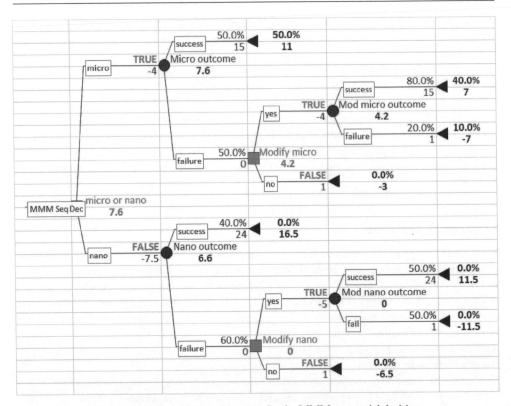

Figure 8.10 Complete decision tree for the MMM sequential decision.

and we may wish to know how big it needs to be to change the preferred option of a micro design, on an expected value basis.

To do this, we select the Sensitivity Analysis button of PrecisionTree (visible in Figure 8.5), which presents us with the dialogue box shown in Figure 8.11. When this appears for the first time, the table in the centre, with three columns marked Cell, Current and Variation, is initially empty. To select a cell for sensitivity, we press the Add button and are then invited to select a cell

Table 8.7 Actual returns from MMM options in the sequential decision tree.

Initial option	Initial outcome	Modify?	Second outcome	Return (£million)
Micro	Success	n/a	n/a	11.00
	Failure	Yes	Success	7.00
			Failure	−7.00
		No	n/a	−3.00
Nano	Success	n/a	n/a	16.50
	Failure	Yes	Success	11.50
			Failure	−11.50
		No	n/a	−6.50

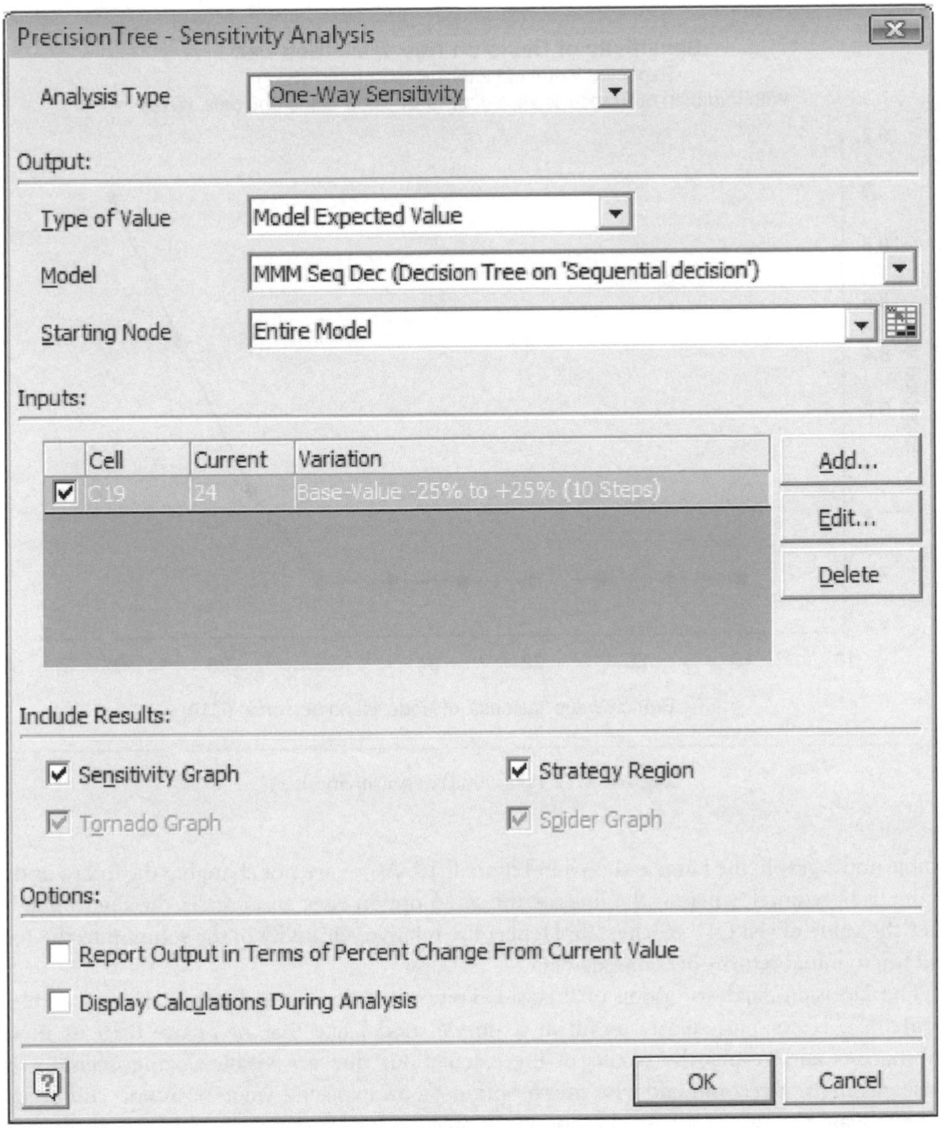

Figure 8.11 PrecisionTree sensitivity dialogue.

on the decision tree and to specify the range over which sensitivity will be checked. I specified that PrecisionTree examine the sensitivity of cell C19 (which contains the value in which we are interested) and that it should, in 10 steps, range this value from 24 less 25% and 24 plus 25%.

Running the sensitivity ranging produces two Excel worksheets, of which the first is the sensitivity sheet, which contains a graph and a table of values that make up the graph. The graph is shown in Figure 8.12, and it is clear that ranging the value from 18 to 26 makes no difference; however, when the value is above 26, the expected value starts to climb, indicating that this makes the nano option preferable to the micro option. The strategy sheet also contains

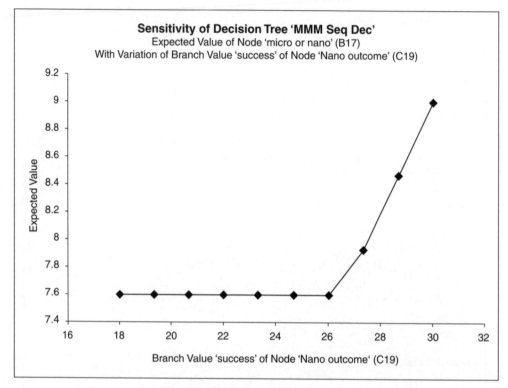

Figure 8.12 PrecisionTree sensitivity sheet.

a table and a graph; the latter is shown in Figure 8.13. As we are not changing the micro option, its line is horizontal, whereas the line for the nano option rises and crosses the micro line just after the value of cell C19 reaches 26. Hence, the relative sensitivity of the solution to the nano and micro initial returns becomes evident.

The Decision Analysis option of PrecisionTree, which is accessed via the button visible in Figure 8.5, is not particularly useful in a simple model like that of Figure 8.10. It merely summarizes and graphs the results of the calculations that are visible on the decision tree. Unsurprisingly, it recommends the micro option on an expected value basis and can be used to investigate the risk profile of the options. Consider, for example, the riskiness of the micro option. The decision tree shows that there is a 50% chance of gaining a return of £11 million, a 40% chance of a return of £7 million and a 10% chance of losing £7 million if this option is chosen. The Decision Analysis option provides graphs that illustrate the risks of these outcomes and comes into its own with larger and more complex decision trees.

Using decision trees

Decision trees provide a simple graphical approach to describing the options available to a decision-maker and the outcomes that result from those choices. The calculations involved are not particularly difficult to master, although they become more complicated if Bayesian methods

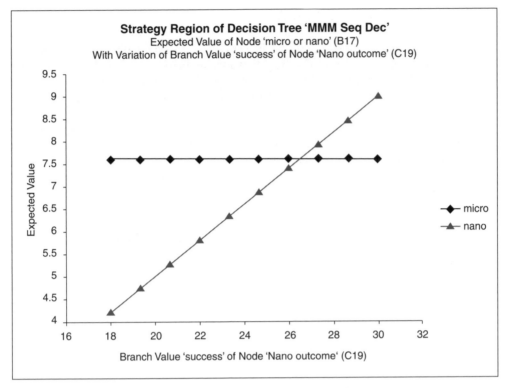

Figure 8.13 PrecisionTree strategy graph.

are employed. Software, as exemplified by PrecisionTree, provides a quick way to draw the trees and to do the calculations, and it has the important benefit of allowing sensitivity analyses to be conducted. This can be really important in real-life decision-making, as there are often things that could be done to reduce risk, and a sensitivity analysis can show the effect of reducing those risks. Thus, it is a mistake to assume that a decision tree provides an answer such as: implement the Micro Mighty MegaMixer and you will make a profit of £7.6 million. No estimate of probability will be 100% accurate, and cost estimates are often also wrong; the tree can be used to see what would happen if these probabilities and costs were to change. They can show how sensitive the decision is to such changes and can indicate the level of risk in making a particular choice.

The description of the Mighty MegaMixer example was chosen because it seems obvious how to lay out the decision tree; however, it is rarely that simple in real life. First, it is often only through questioning and debate that the sequence of interconnected decisions and outcomes becomes clear. Indeed, if the decision is being made by a group, this may be contested by different parties. However, this does not mean that decision trees are a waste of time, but does lead to a realization that one of their values may be in requiring stakeholders to be explicit about the sequence of decisions and outcomes as they see them. That is, as in other modelling approaches taught in this book, the decision tree can serve as the basis for a debate about the structure of the problem being tackled.

Decision analysis – a review

This chapter has extended the discussion in Chapter 2 about decision-making and described how decisions may be approached from a normative standpoint. In the case of MCDA, the approach rests on a procedurally rational approach that aims to increase the consistency and coherence of subjective estimates of the importance of different performance attributes and the values assigned to these attributes for the available options. This does not guarantee that a correct decision will be made, no approach can do that, but it does at least ensure that comparisons between options are based on consistent assessments. Decision trees are also subjective, being based on subjective assessments of the probabilities of events that are usually non-repeatable. Bayesian approaches can be used to enable the updating of those probabilities as more information becomes available. Although this has not been covered in this chapter, it is possible to extend decision trees to situations in which monetary value is not the appropriate decision criterion and approaches exist to develop utility functions that better reflect the value of an outcome to a decision-maker. The methods used to develop these utility functions have some similarity with those used to develop value functions in MCDA.

Does it matter that these approaches assume normative behaviour by decision-makers? The answer, clearly, is yes it does. However, the fact that people actually make decisions somewhat differently does not mean that the approaches are useless. It does mean that treating them like a 'black box' that produces an answer, a choice that must be followed, is a serious mistake. Instead, MCDA approaches and decision trees are best regarded as ways of exploring options and of reducing the subjectivity involved. They can also help to avoid some of the mistakes so easily made when selecting options, as discussed in Schwartz (2004).

References

Belton V. (1986) A comparison of the analytic hierarchy process and a simple multi-attribute value function. *European Journal of Operational Research*, **26**(1), 7–21.

Belton V. and Gear A.E. (1983) On a shortcoming of Saaty's method of analytical hierarchies. *Omega*, **11**(3), 228–230.

Belton V. and Stewart T.J. (2002) *Multiple Criteria Decision Analysis: an Integrated Approach*. Kluwer, Dordrecht, The Netherlands.

Checkland P.B. (1999) *Systems Thinking, Systems Practice: Includes a 30-year Retrospective*. John Wiley & Sons, Ltd, Chichester, UK.

Edwards W. (1971) Social utilities. *Engineering Economist, Summer Symposium Series*, **6**, 119–129.

Edwards W. (1977) How to use multiattribute utility measurement for social decisionmaking. *IEEE Transactions on Systems, Man and Cybernetics*, **7**(5), 326–340.

Edwards W. and Barron H.F. (1994) SMARTS and SMARTER: improved simple methods for multiattribute utility measurement. *Organizational Behaviour and Human Decision Processes*, **60**, 306–325.

Expert Choice (2009) Expert Choice software: http://www.expertchoice.com/

Goodwin P. and Wright G. (2004) *Decision Analysis for Management Judgement*, 3rd edition. John Wiley & Sons, Ltd, Chichester, UK.

Helsinki University of Technology (2009) e-Learning materials on MCDA: http://www.mcda.hut.fi/

Kahneman D., Slovic P. and Tversky A. (eds) (1982) *Judgement under Uncertainty: Heuristics and Biases*, Cambridge University Press, Cambridge, UK.

Kahneman D. and Tversky A. (eds) (1974) Judgement under uncertainty: heuristics and biases. *Science*, **185**, 1124–1111.

Keeney R. and Raiffa H. (1976) *Decisions with Multiple Objectives: Preferences and Value Tradeoffs*. John Wiley & Sons, Inc., New York, NY.

Palisade Corporation (2009) The DecisionTools Suite: www.palisade.com/decisiontools_suite

Raiffa H and Schlaifer R. (1961) *Applied Statistical Decision Theory*. Harvard University, Boston, MA.

Saaaty T.L. (1980) *The Analytical Hierarchy Process: Planning, Priority Setting, Resource Allocation*. McGraw-Hill International, New York, NY.

Schwartz B. (2004) *The Paradox of Choice: Why More is Less*. HarperCollins Publishers, New York, NY.

Simon H.A. (1976) From substantive to procedural rationality, in *Models of Bounded Rationality: Behavioural Economics and Business Organization*, ed. by Simon H.A. (1982). MIT Press, Cambridge, MA.

Thomas H. (1972) *Decision Theory and the Manager*. Pitman, London, UK.

Watson S.R. and Buede D.M. (1987) *Decision Synthesis: the Principles and Practice of Decision Analysis*. Cambridge University Press, Cambridge, UK.

PART III
MATHEMATICAL AND LOGICAL MODELLING

Introduction

Part II introduced four approaches that can be classified as 'soft', starting with Checkland's soft systems methodology and then the cognitive mapping approaches developed by Eden and colleagues. Chapter 7 introduced the system dynamics approach developed by Forrester in the 1960s and since refined by many others. Many management scientists argue that system dynamics is not really a soft approach, but is a form of simulation modelling. However, Chapter 7 argued that it can be used as a way of exploring system behaviour that comes from system structure, as well as for simulation. System dynamics thus serves as the first part of a bridge between Part II and Part III. The final chapter of Part II introduced formal approaches to decision analysis that start from the classical view of rationality but move from that to be much more concerned about how decisions can be supported in practice. Chapter 8 was thus the final part of the bridge to Part III.

By contrast, Part III looks at three approaches that typify what has come to be known as 'hard' Management Science. Each chapter describes an approach to developing mathematical, statistical and logical models, and relies on quantification. The approaches are covered here for two reasons. The first is to provide the reader with enough working knowledge of these approaches and techniques so as to be able to make a start on their use in real situations. Clearly, there is a limit to what can be covered about each in a single chapter, but it should be possible to do something useful with the ideas presented here, and interested readers should follow up the references if they wish to deepen their knowledge.

The second reason is to contrast these approaches with the interpretive methods discussed in Part II. Although it is possible to use 'hard' methods in a partially interpretive mode, this does not come as naturally as the case with the 'soft' approaches. Indeed, as was argued in the introduction to Part II, there are some major differences between the hard and soft approaches.

The three chapters introduce the following:

- *Mathematical programming methods.* These are often strongly associated with Management Science in people's minds, and they are part of the routine toolkit of 'hard' models. They exemplify the way in which models may be used in an optimizing mode, and that is why they are included here. Some people cannot envisage Operational Research or Management Science without optimization methods of this type.
- *Computer simulation approaches.* These are used for situations in which changes through time loom large, and in which entities interact with one another in complicated ways. Computer simulation methods have led to an approach now known as visual interactive modelling, which is why they are included here.

- *Heuristic approaches.* These are methods that aim to find ways of tackling problems that are very close to the ideas of satisficing as developed by Simon (see Chapter 2). Although there are some general principles that may be employed in the development of these heuristics, each application is to a great degree unique. They are included here because they illustrate the creative way in which some of the limitations of optimization approaches are overcome, and because the methods take Management Science to the edge of Artificial Intelligence approaches.

9 Optimization modelling – linear programming

Background

For many people, Management Science is synonymous with the use of optimization techniques. One view of Management Science, common some years ago, was that it was about 'how to get a quart out of a pint pot'. We live in a world of increasingly scarce resources, and it therefore makes sense to use these resources as efficiently and as effectively as possible, and this is the reason for using optimization methods in Management Science. There are many different optimization approaches available to management scientists, but this chapter will concentrate on just one of them, linear programming. It is intended to illustrate how such modelling approaches can be of great value when used properly. There are many excellent books on linear and mathematical programming, and I recommend in particular two books by Paul Williams (1993, 1999). The use of the word 'programming' can lead to some misunderstanding, as it may give the impression that computer programming is required. This is not so; the word 'programming' refers to its old use in planning, as early applications were often focused on planning what resources were needed to achieve some desired plan.

Basic ideas

Linear programming is a subset of mathematical programming, which is itself a subset of constrained optimization. The idea of the latter is that some measure of performance should be optimized (which usually means minimized or maximized) subject to some known constraints. It is very common for this measure of performance to be expressed in monetary terms, but this need not be the case. A simple example that can be expressed in monetary terms is the common need to blend a set of ingredients so as to achieve some required quality of mix while minimizing the total cost of this blend. This might, for instance, be a way of planning the diet of livestock, the constraints being the vitamins and other requirements needed to keep the animals in a healthy condition. These requirements might be available in a wide range of foodstuffs, which could be blended to form some minimum cost diet that satisfies the dietary constraints. Hence, in constrained optimization, there is a measure of performance, often known as an objective function, that must be optimized subject to a set of constraints. The constraints define the solution space for the optimization – that is, any acceptable solution must satisfy the constraints that act as bounds on the solution space.

As an approach, mathematical programming has enjoyed many successful applications since its development in the 1950s. As well as its use in blending and mixing problems, other applications include the following:

- balancing workloads in large organizations (Grandzol and Traaen, 1995);
- credit scoring (Thomas, Banasik and Crook, 2001);
- global supply chain management (Arntzen *et al.*, 1995);
- mail order advertising (Campbell *et al.*, 2001);
- planning telecommunications networks (Cox *et al.*, 1993);
- production scheduling (Hendry, Fok and Shek, 1996);
- understanding the market for wood fibre (Gautier *et al.*, 2000).

The journal *Interfaces* is a good source for keeping up to date with applications.

The ideas that underpin linear programming first appeared in Economics, and its pioneer is generally agreed to be George Dantzig (discussed in Dantzig, 1963). He was the first to suggest the use of an approach, now known as the simplex method, to tackle this type of constrained optimization. Earlier, Kantorovich (1942) had suggested methods for a special type of linear programme, the transportation problem. Since then there have been many developments in solution methods for linear programming, most of which have been dependent on the increasing power of computers for their successful implementation.

Computer software

The benefits of linear programming are greatest in large and medium-scale problems with many variables and many constraints to be considered. Therefore, the development of efficient and accurate computer algorithms has been a major preoccupation among researchers. Suitable programs exist for virtually every commercial computer system that has been developed in the last 20 years, and a very full list can be found at http://wiki.mcs.anl.gov/NEOS/index.php/NEOS_Wiki. Very large-scale problems require large-scale and powerful computer systems, and thus parallel and hypercube systems have been used in recent years (for a discussion of these issues, see Zenios, 1994). However, useful work can be done on single-user personal computers, and packaged software is widely available for these – for example, XPress-MP (FICO, 2009), LINDO (LINDO Systems, 2009) and CPLEX (ILOG, 2009).

The Institute for Operations Research and the Management Sciences (INFORMS) publishes an occasional survey of mathematical programming software in its *OR/MS Today* magazine. Details of the latest survey (2007) can be found on the *OR/MS Today* website (Lionheart Publishing, 2009). For problems of medium scale, the use of add-ons for common spreadsheets has much to commend it. Examples of these include What's Best? (LINDO Systems, 2009) and The Solver (Frontline Systems, 2009), both of which can be run as Microsoft Excel add-ins. The basic version of The Solver comes with the standard versions of Excel, although it needs to be installed as instructed in the Help system of the software. The basic Excel Solver will be used in some examples later in this chapter. Both What's Best and The Solver are well written and are powerful, in spite of their simple appearance, and both come with extended versions to cope with very large problems. Frontline Systems offer an extended version of the Excel Solver, The Premium Solver, and other spreadsheet add-ins for some of the heuristic optimization methods discussed in Chapter 11 (Frontline Systems, 2009). There are also extended versions of The Premium Solver that will cope with very large problems.

Linear programming and rational choice

As will become clear later, linear programming is an example of a modelling and solution approach that corresponds very closely to what was termed rational choice in Chapter 2, as shown in Figure 2.1. At the core of linear programming is a set of assumptions that fit those listed in Chapter 2. These are as follows:

1. A set of alternative courses of action.
2. Knowledge and information that permit the prediction of the consequences of choosing any alternative.
3. A criterion for determining which set of consequences is preferred.

As will become clear later, the number of alternative courses of action may be very large, possibly infinite, but known. The knowledge and necessary information are captured in the constraints and in the objective function. The criterion of choice is usually one of minimization or maximization.

However, it should not be imagined that linear programming must be used in a simple-minded manner in which the only goal is to find some optimum solution. In many cases there are much broader aims than this. Although the search for the optimum is important, it may be even more important to know how sensitive this optimum is to changes in the assumptions that underpin a model. It may sometimes be better to base action on a position that is slightly less than the theoretical optimum if that position is less vulnerable to changes in the environment. Thus, linear programming, like all the other modelling approaches in this book, may be used in an exploratory mode to investigate preferred courses of action.

A simple example

As mentioned earlier, the real power of linear programming becomes apparent when it is applied to problems with many variables and constraints. However, large-scale problems tend to be somewhat confusing to people who are reading about the method for the first time. Hence, it seems sensible to start with a simple example, one that is far too simple to be of any practical value, but that will illustrate the basic ideas of the approach.

Case study: the Lancaster Decor Company

The Lancaster Decor Company (LDC) makes wallpaper that is sold throughout Europe. One of its factories makes two types of wallpaper, pasted and unpasted. Both types of wallpaper are printed by a high-quality gravure process, and both are packed at the same packing plant. The difference is that the pasted wallpaper must pass through a pasting process before it is packed. Although LDC makes many different patterns within these two wallpaper types, for its medium-term plans it need only think in terms of the two categories. The production planner wishes to know how many of each to produce next week so as to maximize the expected gross profit. In the case of pasted, this is £0.090 per metre, and it is £0.075 per metre for unpasted.

There are constraints on the production facilities that will affect the planner's freedom of action. The factory has the gravure print capacity to produce 50 metres per minute of either type of wallpaper, and the gravure printer is available for 40 hours during the week. The capacity of the packing plant is measured in 'packing units', of which there are 300 000 available. A packing unit is the length in metres of so-called standard wallpaper (which is no longer made by LDC). Pasted wallpaper is 3 times as thick as standard, and unpasted is twice as thick as standard, the adhesive accounting for the difference. Thus, it takes 3 times as long to pack a roll of pasted wallpaper compared with a roll of standard wallpaper. The pasting plant has a capacity of 100 000 metres per week.

The LDC Marketing Department insists that the factory must produce at least 30 000 metres of each type of wallpaper. How many metres of each type of wallpaper should be planned so as to maximize the expected gross profit?

Although this example is very simple, it will provide a useful basis for illustrating some of the important concepts within linear programming.

Problem formulation

The first stage in developing a linear programming model is to try to formulate the problem in appropriate terms. This means that a set of equations needs to be constructed so as to capture the objective function and the constraints. The first stage in doing this is to decide on some suitable variables. It seems clear that the planner's aim is to decide how many metres of each type of paper to produce, and there are two types of paper – pasted and unpasted – so it will be convenient to label the decision variables as P and U, where

$$P = \text{metres of pasted wallpaper to be produced next week}$$
$$U = \text{metres of unpasted wallpaper to be produced next week}$$

Hence, it is possible to write a simple algebraic expression that represents the planner's objective, and this is known as the objective function. This is

$$0.09P + 0.075U$$

and the planner wishes to maximize this function.

In a similar manner, it is possible to use simple algebra to capture the constraints that inhibit the planner from simply making infinite amounts of each type of wallpaper. Consider, first, the constrained gravure printing capacity, of which 40 hours is available and which produces 50 metres per minute of either type of wallpaper. There are 40×60 minutes in 40 hours, and, if the print rate is 50 metres per minute, then the gravure print capacity is $(40 \times 60 \times 50)$ metres/week. That is, the maximum total gravure print output is 120 000 metres per week. It seems reasonable to assume that any combination of pasted and unpasted can be accommodated within this limit, and thus this first constraint can be captured in the following inequality:

$$P + U \leq 120\ 000 \text{ metres}$$

This is an inequality, because $(P + U)$ must be less than or equal to the 120 000 metres of capacity that is available. In this inequality, the symbol $\leq$ represents less than or equal to.

The second constraint is that of the packing plant. This can cope with 300 000 metres of standard wallpaper. Pasted wallpaper is 3 times as thick as the standard and unpasted wallpaper is twice as thick as the standard. Hence, the packing constraint becomes

$$3P + 2U \leq 300\ 000 \text{ metres}$$

The remaining three constraints are much easier to handle. The constraint on pasting only affects the pasted wallpaper and limits its production to 100 000 metres per week. Expressed algebraically, this becomes

$$P \leq 100\ 000$$

The marketing constraints are also simple, each requiring the minimum production of the wallpapers to be 30 000 metres. Hence, these two constraints are

$$P \geq 30\ 000$$
$$U \geq 30\ 000$$

where the $\geq$ symbol represents greater than or equal to.

The final formulation of the problem can be summarized as follows:

		Constraint number
Objective function	Maximize $(0.09P + 0.075U)$	
Gravure constraint	$P + U \leq 120\ 000$	1
Packing constraint	$3P + 2U \leq 300\ 000$	2
Pasting constraint	$P \leq 100\ 000$	3
Minimum pasted	$P \geq 30\ 000$	4
Minimum unpasted	$U \geq 30\ 000$	5

Thus, the problem as posed has been formulated as a two-variable linear programme, which is the simplest type of formulation possible. As it is so simple, this formulation can be solved using a graphical approach. Drawing graphs with more than two variables is tricky, and so the graphical approach is useful for illustrating the principles of linear programming, but no more. Anything above two variables requires a mathematical approach, preferably using a computer program. The next section will show how this simple problem may be solved graphically, and the section after that will show the application of the Excel Solver, a powerful spreadsheet extension.

Graphical solution

The key to this approach is the representation of the constraints on a simple graph, but it may not be obvious how a set of inequalities can be so represented. As an example, consider the packing constraint, which is

$$3P + 2U \leq 300\ 000$$

Figure 9.1 shows this constraint drawn on a graph, the vertical axis of which represents U, the number of metres of unpasted wallpaper produced, and the horizontal axis of which

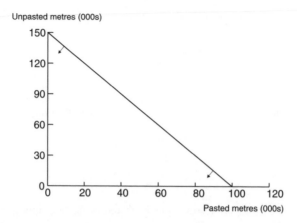

Figure 9.1 Lancaster Decor Company – the packing constraint.

represents P, the metres of pasted wallpaper produced. The sloping line on the graph represents the constraint. This is drawn by considering the maximum values that the variables P and U may take. These values may be found by putting the other variable in the inequality to zero and by treating the inequality as if it were an equation.

Thus, if $U = 0$, then

$$3P \leq 300\ 000 \quad \text{or} \quad P \leq 100\ 000$$

that is, the maximum value of P is 100 000.

If $P = 0$, then

$$2U \leq 300\ 000 \quad \text{or} \quad U \leq 150\ 000$$

that is, the maximum value of U is 150 000.

Hence, the line crosses the P axis at 100 000 and crosses the U axis at 150 000. As this was a less-than-or-equal-to constraint, any acceptable solution must lie to the left of the line, as shown by the arrows on the diagram.

Figure 9.2 shows the effect of drawing all the constraints on the graph in the same way. The first three are all less-than-or-equal-to constraints, but the final two are greater-than-or-equal-to constraints. The combination of these constraints produces a solution space, usually known as the feasible region, which is shown as the shaded area in Figure 9.2. Any combination of P and U must lie in this feasible region if it is to satisfy this set of constraints.

There are two ways to find the combination of P and U that maximizes the objective function and therefore the expected gross profit. The first and preferred way is to use standard algebra on the objective function. In this, the gross profit G is

$$G = 0.090P + 0.075U$$
$$\therefore 0.075U = G - 0.090P$$
$$\therefore U = \frac{-0.090P + G}{0.075}$$
$$\therefore U = -1.2P + \frac{G}{0.075}$$

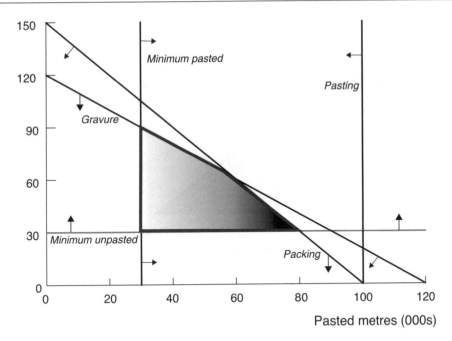

Figure 9.2 Lancaster Decor Company – the feasible region.

which, with U as the vertical axis and P as the horizontal axis, is the equation for a straight line with a slope of -1.2. This value, -1.2 in this case, is known as the isoprofit slope, and it reflects the objective function. Any values of P and U that satisfy the objective function will lie on a line with this slope. That is, the values of P and U can be in any combination that fits this equation. The problem is to find the values of P and U to maximize G.

It can be shown mathematically that the values of P and U that lead to a maximum profit will lie on one of the corners (usually known as the vertices) of the feasible region, which is the hatched area of the graph. The profit will be highest when P and U are as high as possible and when their values lead to an isoprofit slope of -1.2. Thus, to find the solution, imagine a series of parallel lines, each with a slope equal to the isoprofit slope (-1.2 in this case), moving out from the origin of the graph until the lines hit the extreme point of the feasible region. This is shown in Figure 9.3, which demonstrates that this will occur when $P = 60\,000$ and $U = 60\,000$. In this case, the weekly profit will be £9900. This occurs at the intersection of the packing and gravure constraints. These are known as binding constraints.

The way in which the isoprofit slope approaches the optimum vertex can also give some idea of the sensitivity of the solution to changes in the values taken by the coefficients of the constraints and of the objective function. The coefficients of the objective function (0.090 and 0.075 in this example) determine the angle at which the isoprofit slope approaches the edges of the feasible region. The coefficients of the constraints determine the slopes of the sides of the feasible region, and thus determine where the vertices lie. If the slope of one or more of the constraints changes, then so will the angles between two or more of the constraints. Therefore, alterations to the coefficients will change the shape of the feasible region and/or the angle of the isoprofit line. If small changes in the coefficients result in relatively large changes to the isoprofit line or to the binding constraints, then this suggests that the solution may be very sensitive to

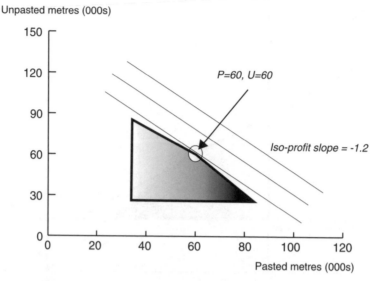

Figure 9.3 Lancaster Decor Company – finding a solution.

the values included in the model. As will be clear later, the sensitivity analysis of an optimum solution is one of the benefits conferred by the use of properly designed computer software for linear programming.

The other way of reaching this solution, which is rather clumsy, is to compute the coordinates of each vertex of the feasible region. As there are two variables (U and P), each vertex consists of two equations. For example, the vertex that we already know contains the solution occurring at the intersection of constraints 1 and 2. Hence, these two equations may be solved as follows:

$$P + U = 120\ 000 \tag{1}$$
$$3P + 2U = 300\ 000 \tag{2}$$

Multiplying constraint 1 by constraint 3 gives

$$3P + 3U = 360\ 000 \tag{3}$$

Subtracting constraint 2 from constraint 3 gives

$$U = 60\ 000$$

and thus

$$P = 60\ 000$$

as well, for which the gross profit = £9900. Similar computations for all the other vertices will show that this is indeed the maximum profit.

Using the Excel Solver

As mentioned earlier, the application of linear programming is no longer restricted by the need for specialist software. Spreadsheet packages often contain add-ins that can be used to tackle problems of non-trivial size. Currently, the most widely used spreadsheet is Microsoft Excel, which comes with an add-in, The Solver. This is very easy to use and, though somewhat slower than specialist software, may be used to tackle problems of a reasonable size. There is, of course, some danger in its ease of use, as there are pitfalls to be avoided in building and running linear programming models that may be glossed over in this friendly software. Nevertheless, the availability of this software is something to be applauded. The discussion here is based on Microsoft Excel 2007. Other versions of the software may have slightly different menu structures, but the basic ideas are the same.

Formulation for The Solver

At the core of any linear programming model is a set of constraints within which some objective function is to be optimized. The simple production planning example of LDC was formulated earlier in this chapter by using conventional algebra as follows:

$$
\begin{aligned}
\text{Maximize} \quad & (0.09P + 0.075U) && \text{Objective function} \\
\text{Subject to:} \quad & P + U \le 120\ 000 && \text{Gravure constraint} \\
& 3P + 2U \le 300\ 000 && \text{Packing constraint} \\
& P \le 100\ 000 && \text{Pasting constraint} \\
& P \ge 30\ 000 && \text{Minimum pasted constraint} \\
& U \ge 30\ 000 && \text{Minimum unpasted constraint}
\end{aligned}
$$

This algebra could be replaced with a different form of expression that relies upon tables (or matrices) for its presentation. This might look as follows:

	P = pasted metres	U = unpasted metres		
Maximize	0.09	0.075		
Subject to:				Limit
	1	1	$\le$	120 000
	3	2	$\le$	300 000
	1	0	$\le$	100 000
	1	0	$\ge$	30 000
	0	1	$\ge$	30 000
				Gross profit
Solution	0	0		0

Apart from the bottom line, this is self-explanatory. The bottom line represents the values assigned to P (metres of pasted) and U (metres of unpasted) before any optimization. In this state, both U and P are set to zero, which results in a gross profit of zero.

The first stage of using The Solver is to set up these matrices on the spreadsheet, and this is shown in Figure 9.4. As in all spreadsheet usage, it is crucial to understand that some cells contain values (constants that do not change), but others contain formulae that lead to values

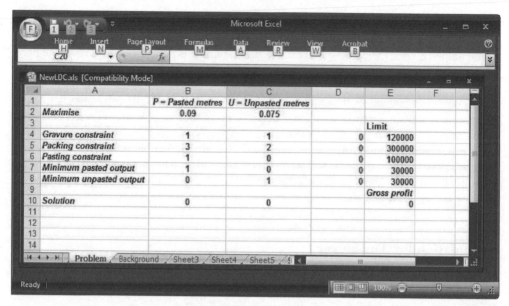

Figure 9.4 MS Excel™ – basic problem formulation.

being displayed in those cells. In this example, Cells D4, D5, D6, D7, D8 and E10 contain formulae. The rest are used for text, to make the example clearer, or for values.

In Figure 9.4, columns B and C are used to set up the values contained in the expressions used in the algebraic formulation and in the above tables:

- Row 2 contains the values of the coefficients of the objective function (0.09 and 0.075).
- Rows 4 to 8 contain the values that represent the coefficients of the constraints.
- Row 10 contains the initial values given to P and U before any optimization.
- Column D contains zeros, but these are computed values that represent the usage of the five constraints.
- Column E shows the limits on the constraints, often known as right-hand sides (abbreviated to RHS by many people).

Examining column D in more detail shows that cell D4 contains the formula

$$= \$B\$10^*\$B4 + \$C\$10$$

which is the sum of two products. The first product represents the gravure usage from P metres of pasted wallpaper, and the second product represents the gravure usage from U metres of unpasted wallpaper. Note that the references to cells B10 and C10 are both absolute. Thus, the formulae underlying cells D4 to D8 are as follows:

$$D4 = \$B\$10^*\$B4 + \$C\$10^*\$C4$$
$$D5 = \$B\$10^*\$B5 + \$C\$10^*\$C5$$
$$D6 = \$B\$10^*\$B6 + \$C\$10^*\$C6$$
$$D7 = \$B\$10^*\$B7 + \$C\$10^*\$C7$$
$$D8 = \$B\$10^*\$B8 + \$C\$10^*\$C8$$

Examining column E shows that there is a limit of 120 000 on gravure usage, of 300 000 on packing and so on. Column D, as mentioned above, is used to store the actual usage of these resources. Thus, cell D4 represents the amount of gravure actually used, and this is zero, as cells B10 and C10 contain zero values before any optimization.

Finally, a spreadsheet cell needs to be used to show the result of the optimization (the gross profit in this case), and this will be placed in cell E10.

The Solver Parameters window

Using normal mouse clicks or keystrokes, The Solver may be selected from the Analysis section of the Data tab in Microsoft Excel 2007. This leads to the Solver Parameters window (see Figure 9.5), which is used to provide the information needed by The Solver to carry out the required optimization. To optimize the above LDC problem, The Solver needs to know the following:

1. Where will the objective function value be placed? This is the result of the optimization and is the effect of computing the function using whatever values of P and U are found by the optimization. In this case, the result will be placed in cell E10. This means that cell E10 must contain the appropriate formula, which in this case will be $= \$B\$2*\$B\$10 + \$C\$2*\$C\$10$. Note that the cell references are absolute – this is advisable, although not absolutely necessary.
2. What are the constraints and what form do they take? To set these up, click on the Add button of the Constraint subwindow of The Solver Parameters window, which produces a dialogue box that is used to enter the details of each constraint. These are entered in the usual way for Excel, by either selecting cells using the mouse or typing in their values. The Add Constraint dialogue is also used to enter the type of constraints and provides a drop-down list for that purpose. Each of the constraints is added using the Add Constraints dialogue, noting that two of them are greater-than-or-equal-to constraints and that therefore the correct symbol must be selected in the Constraint dialogue box.
3. The Solver also needs to know where the decision variables are located on the spreadsheet, and these are defined in the By Changing Cells of the Solver Parameters dialogue, as shown in Figure 9.5. These are the B10 and C10 cells which contain the values of P and U that

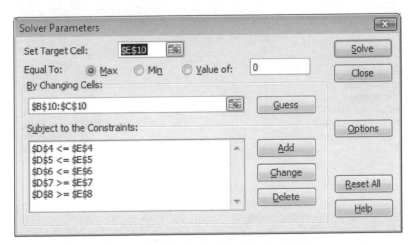

Figure 9.5 The Solver Parameters window.

are to be varied so as to optimize the objective function. As can also be seen in Figure 9.5, the same dialogue box allows the user to specify the type of optimization to be conducted – maximization (Max) in this example. The user provides this information via The Solver Parameters window by entering absolute cell references in the By Changing Cells box. This is a maximization, and thus the Max option is selected.

This is a linear programming problem, and, before performing the optimization, it is a good idea to inform The Solver that all constraints are linear expressions, as is the objective function. This is done by clicking the Options button of The Solver Parameters window. This opens a subsidiary window within which the Assume linear model option should be selected. This will increase the speed of the optimization computation and lead to reports (see below) tailored to linear programming problems.

To perform the optimization, return to The Solver Parameters window and press the Solve button of this window. This results in the output shown in Figure 9.6, which indicates that producing 60 000 metres of unpasted wallpaper and 60 000 metres of pasted wallpaper will result in a gross profit of £9900 and that this is the maximum, given the problem as it was formulated.

It is important to realize that much more information can be gained from the solution to a linear programming problem than just the optimum values of the decision variables. A good computer package such as The Solver provides reports that help the user to understand much more about the solution than this. The Solver provides three standard reports, and it is also possible to export the solution to other computer packages should further analysis be needed.

The Solver Answer Report

This summarizes the results from the worksheet screen and provides a little more information. This extra information could be calculated by the user, but it is useful to have this in

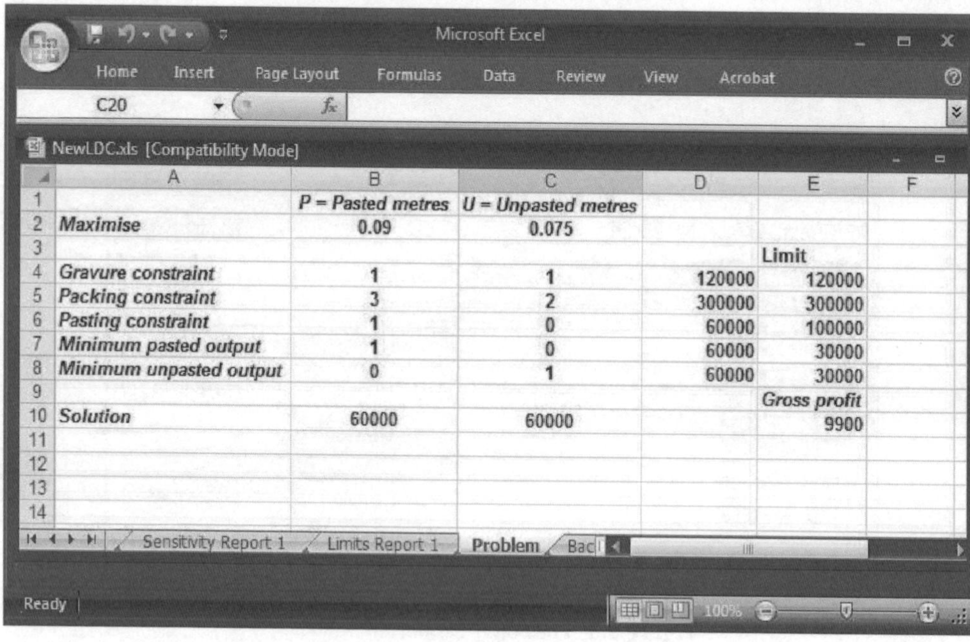

	A	B	C	D	E	F
1		P = Pasted metres	U = Unpasted metres			
2	Maximise	0.09	0.075			
3					Limit	
4	Gravure constraint	1	1	120000	120000	
5	Packing constraint	3	2	300000	300000	
6	Pasting constraint	1	0	60000	100000	
7	Minimum pasted output	1	0	60000	30000	
8	Minimum unpasted output	0	1	60000	30000	
9					Gross profit	
10	Solution	60000	60000		9900	
11						
12						
13						
14						

Figure 9.6 The Solver – solution to the LDC problem.

Microsoft Excel 12.0 Answer Report
Worksheet: [NewLDC.xls]Problem
Report Created: 27/04/2009 11:44:23

Target Cell (Max)

Cell	Name	Original Value	Final Value
$E$10	Solution Gross profit	9900	9900

Adjustable Cells

Cell	Name	Original Value	Final Value
$B$10	Solution P = Pasted metres	60000	60000
$C$10	Solution U = Unpasted metres	60000	60000

Constraints

Cell	Name	Cell Value	Formula	Status	Slack
$D$5	Packing constraint	300000	$D$5<=$E$5	Binding	0
$D$6	Pasting constraint	60000	$D$6<=$E$6	Not Binding	40000
$D$7	Minimum pasted output	60000	$D$7>=$E$7	Not Binding	30000
$D$8	Minimum unpasted output	60000	$D$8>=$E$8	Not Binding	30000
$D$4	Gravure constraint	120000	$D$4<=$E$4	Binding	0

Figure 9.7 The Solver Answer Report for the LDC problem.

one place. The Answer Report for the LDC problem is shown in Figure 9.7 and has three parts:

1. *Target Cell (Max)*. This part shows the maximum profit obtained by The Solver. If this were a minimization problem, this section would contain the minimum value.
2. *Adjustable Cells*. This part shows each of the input variables, the values that they take in the optimum solution and their initial values (zero in this case).
3. *Constraints*. This part indicates the usage of each of the constraints in the problem. The Status column labels each constraint as Binding or Not Binding, the latter being ones that have some unused resource – indicated by a non-zero value in the Slack column. As with the graphical solution presented earlier, only two constraints are binding, those for gravure and packing.

The other two reports provide more information about the sensitivity of the optimum solution, and this can be very important for a number of reasons. First, it is rarely the case that all the coefficients or values in any type of Management Science model are known with complete certainty. Some will be certain, but many will be approximations, estimates or even best guesses. What if these values turn out to be wrong? What would be the effect of such errors in the solution? An optimum solution that turns out to be highly sensitive to the values assigned to the coefficients may, in practice, be worse than another solution that is a little less than optimum. The second reason for the importance of sensitivity analysis is that the world is dynamic, and therefore things are constantly changing. For example, it may be true this week that a raw material has a certain cost per tonne, but, in a month's time, this may have changed. Thus, it is important to know what effect changes in the coefficients may have on the optimum solution.

Microsoft Excel 12.0 Sensitivity Report
Worksheet: [NewLDC.xlsx]Problem
Report Created: 27/04/2009 11:48:19

Adjustable Cells

Cell	Name	Final Value	Reduced Cost	Objective Coefficient	Allowable Increase	Allowable Decrease
$B$10	Solution P = Pasted metres	60000	0	0.09	0.0225	0.015
$C$10	Solution U = Unpasted metres	60000	0	0.075	0.015	0.015

Constraints

Cell	Name	Final Value	Shadow Price	Constraint R.H. Side	Allowable Increase	Allowable Decrease
$D$5	Packing constraint	300000	0.015	300000	30000	30000
$D$6	Pasting constraint	60000	0	100000	1E+30	40000
$D$7	Minimum pasted output	60000	0	30000	30000	1E+30
$D$8	Minimum unpasted output	60000	0	30000	30000	1E+30
$D$4	Gravure constraint	120000	0.045	120000	15000	10000

Figure 9.8 The Solver Sensitivity report.

The Solver Sensitivity Report

The first report that provides information about sensitivity is known as the Sensitivity Report – shown in Figure 9.8 for the LDC problem. The report comes in two parts, shown in the figure, and these are to be understood as follows.

1. *Adjustable Cells.* This part refers to an analysis usually known as objective ranging in the linear programming literature. It gets this name because it shows the range across which each coefficient in the objective function may individually change without altering the values taken by the variables in the optimum solution. Consider, for example, the variable P, which represents the number of metres of pasted wallpaper to be made. In the optimum solution, this takes a value of 60 000 metres. Its coefficient in the objective function is 0.09, and the Allowable Increase and Allowable Decrease columns show by how much this coefficient may change without altering the recommendation that 60 000 metres should be made. The values for the objective function coefficient of U cover the range $0.09 + 0.0225$ to $0.09 - 0.015$; that is, from 0.1125 to 0.075. If the coefficient of P stays within these values, then its optimum value remains unchanged. Similarly, the optimum value for U is 60 000 if its objective function coefficient stays within the range of $0.075 + 0.015$ to $0.075 - 0.015$; that is, from 0.09 to 0.06. Note that this objective ranging only applies to each of the variables independently – if more than one variable changes, then the situation is much more complicated.

   In terms of the graphical solution, objective ranging is equivalent to tilting the isoprofit slope at different angles to see what difference this will make. If the isoprofit slope of the objective function were to vary, eventually it would cease to cross the feasible region at the current optimum solution and would cross at another vertex. Thus, the limits on the ranges relate to the value of the isoprofit slope, which could cause it to cross the feasible region at a point other than the optimum vertex. In the case of LDC, if the gross profit for pasted wallpaper were to rise above £0.1175 per metre, then presumably it would be better to devote more capacity to making unpasted wallpaper than to making pasted wallpaper. The reverse would apply if its gross profit were to fall below £0.075 per metre.

2. *Constraints.* This part reports on what are often termed 'shadow prices' and 'RHS ranging', referring to the limits on the constraints. This is presented as a table with a row devoted to each constraint within the constraint set. The columns should be interpreted as follows:

- *Final Value.* This is the total usage of the constraint in question. In the case of gravure printing, this is shown as 120 000, this being the actual amount of time available as specified by the limit of the constraint. Time for packing is also used up, and thus its final value is 300 000. None of the other constrained resources is fully utilized.
- *Shadow Price.* This is the value of providing a single extra unit of a fully constrained resource. In this solution there are two such fully constrained resources, the time available for gravure printing and for packing. In the case of LDC, this indicates that an extra unit of gravure time is worth £0.045 and an extra unit of packing time is worth £0.015, both expressed in terms of gross profit. Thus, it might be worth LDC paying up to these amounts in order to gain an extra unit of the resource. Note that this is a marginal analysis that only applies within a certain range, and therefore subsequent units outside these ranges will have different shadow prices. The ranges are shown by the values in the last two columns of the table. Note also that, as with objective ranging, these shadow prices only apply to each constraint taken individually. Combined changes require a more complicated analysis.
- *Constraint RHS.* The limits placed on the constraints in the problem formulation.
- *Allowable Increase and Allowable Decrease.* These show the range across which the shadow prices are applicable, and, clearly, these have no meaning unless the resource is fully utilized. Thus, the shadow price of £0.045 for extra gravure capacity applies within a range of values from 120 000 + 15 000 to 120 000 − 10 000; that is, from 110 000 to 135 000. When the RHS values are changed within the allowable limits, the optimum values of *P* and *U* may change, unlike in objective ranging. In graphical terms, this is equivalent to moving a constraint line without altering its slope.

The Solver Limits Report

The second sensitivity report provided by Excel is known as the Limits Report, and the one produced for LDC is shown in Figure 9.9. As this is a maximization problem, the column labelled Upper Limit shows the optimum values for *P* and for *U*, with the corresponding profits in the

Microsoft Excel 12.0 Limits Report
Worksheet: [NewLDC.xlsx]Limits Report 1
Report Created: 27/04/2009 11:48:19

Cell	Target Name	Value
$E$10	Solution Gross profit	9900

Cell	Adjustable Name	Value	Lower Limit	Target Result	Upper Limit	Target Result
$B$10	Solution P = Pasted metres	60000	30000	7200	60000	9900
$C$10	Solution U = Unpasted metres	60000	30000	7650	60000	9900

Figure 9.9 The Solver Limits Report for LDC.

Target Result column. The Lower Limit column shows the minimum value that each variable could take without breaking the constraints. In the LDC problem, both variables have lower bounds of 30 000 metres (the marketing constraints). The Target Result alongside the Lower Limit shows the gross profit that would result if each variable were reduced to its lower bound.

Some useful mathematical concepts

In order to make progress with linear programming, it is important to define and develop a few mathematical concepts, of which the first is the concept of linearity. Linear programming applies to systems in which the objective function and the constraint are all linear expressions. What this means is that each of the variables that appears in the formulation does so in the form

$$\langle \text{constant} \rangle \text{ multiplied by } \langle \text{variable} \rangle$$

Thus, there are no terms such as x^2, e^x, $1/x$ or x/y, where x and y are variables.

This idea is known as linearity because, when there are only two variables in a linear equation, this equation is a straight line when plotted on a graph. For example, the equation

$$x_2 = Ax_1 + B$$

represents a straight line in which x_2 is plotted on the vertical axis and x_1 is plotted on the horizontal axis, and in which the slope of the line is A and the line crosses the x_2 axis at B.

If the objective function were non-linear, then it could not be represented by a straight line, and therefore it might cross the feasible region at more than one point. For example, it might form a tight curve that crosses the feasible region at one point, leaves it and then crosses it again elsewhere. If the constraints were non-linear, the edges of the feasible region would not be straight and there could be no assurance that the objective function would touch it at a vertex. For example, if they were concave, the extreme point at which the isoprofit line touches might not be a vertex, as it might, instead, form a tangent to the curve.

A second mathematical idea useful in linear programming is the summation notation. This uses the Greek capital letter Σ (sigma), chosen because it is equivalent to the letter S, an abbreviation for 'sum of'. It can be very tedious to write down an expression such as

$$a_1x_1 + a_2x_2 + a_3x_3 + a_4x_4 + a_5x_5$$

Instead, we can abbreviate this to the following form:

$$\sum_{i=1}^{5} a_i x_i$$

This enables us to write down general forms of constraints or of objective functions in a much more economical way. In general, this notation may be used to formulate a maximization linear programme with m input or decision variables and n constraints as follows:

$$\text{Maximize } \sum_{j=1}^{m} c_j x_j$$

$$\text{Subject to } \sum_{j=1}^{m} a_{1,j} x_j = b_1$$

$$\sum_{j=1}^{m} a_{2,j} x_j \leq b_2$$

$$\sum_{j=1}^{m} a_{3,j} x_j \leq b_3$$

$$\cdots$$

$$\sum_{j=1}^{m} a_{i,j} x_j \leq b_j$$

$$\cdots$$

$$\sum_{j=1}^{m} a_{n,j} x_i \leq b_m$$

The a values are the coefficients of the constraints, and each of them has a subscript pair i, j. Thus, a_{ij} refers to the coefficient of the ith variable in the jth constraint. The RHS values are represented by the bs, the subscripts of which indicate their constraint.

In the case of minimization problems, the objective function becomes

$$\text{Minimize } \sum_{j=1}^{m} c_j x_j$$

and the constraint set is represented by a set of greater-than-or-equal-to expressions of the following general form:

$$\sum_{j=1}^{m} a_{i,j} x_j \geq b_j$$

where $i = 1, \ldots, n$ and $j = 1, \ldots, m$. There is, of course, no particular reason why minimization and maximization problems cannot contain constraints that are less than or equal to, greater than or equal to or equalities.

The use of matrix algebra provides an even more economical way to write down the formulation of a linear programming model, but that is beyond the scope of this book.

Other types of mathematical programming models

In some circumstances, simplified approaches to linear programming are possible. Two examples of this are transportation and assignment problems. A transportation problem occurs when material must be distributed to several destinations from a number of sources. As an example of this, consider the problem faced by LDC in distributing its pasted wallpaper from its two factories to five customers. This could be represented as in Table 9.1.

Table 9.1 LDC distribution.

	Customer 1	Customer 2	Customer 3	Customer 4	Customer 5	Total supply
Factory 1	1.0	1.1	2.1	1.7	1.5	6 000
Factory 2	1.5	0.9	1.5	2.1	1.2	6 000
Total	1500	3500	2000	2500	2500	12 000

The table shows that the requirements of customers 1 to 5 are for 1500, 3500, 2000, 2500 and 2500 metres respectively, and there are 6000 metres of pasted wallpaper available from each factory. The other numbers in the matrix represent the costs of delivering the wallpaper to the different customers. Thus, it costs 1.0p per metre to deliver pasted wallpaper from factory 1 to customer 1, 1.1p to deliver it to customer 2 and so on. Although this could be formulated as a linear programme in the normal way, it is simpler and usually faster to solve it by using a method known as the transportation algorithm. Most books on the techniques of OR/MS give full details of how to tackle such problems – see, for example, Hillier and Lieberman (2005).

The assignment problem is a simplified version of the transportation problem. It occurs, for example, when there are a number of tasks to be performed by the same number of people, and each person may only perform any one task. Thus, the tasks must be assigned to people, one person per task. As with the transportation problem, this could be formulated as a standard linear programme, but instead it is normal to use a more efficient method, known as the linear assignment algorithm. See any standard text on OR/MS techniques, such as Hillier and Lieberman (2005), for details of this.

Although linear programming is limited to systems in which the objective function and constraints are all linear expressions, extensions to the approach have been devised to cope with other types of equation. Sometimes the expressions are linear, but, in addition, the variables must take integer values – this might be true, for example, in applications for manpower planning where people cannot be subdivided. In these cases, integer linear programming (ILP) methods can be used. The extended versions of The Solver and What's Best? provide algorithms to cope with these types of problem. However, it is important to realize that the formulation and solution of integer linear programs is a complicated matter. Friendly software is a great help, but it would be best for novices to seek expert help before tackling such problems.

Further complications occur when the expressions are non-linear, which might happen when the objective function displays increasing or decreasing returns to scale. Figure 9.10 shows a graph of a function in which there are increasing returns to scale. In these non-linear cases, other algorithms must be employed – although, sometimes, linear approximations may be good enough.

Common types of constraint

In his detailed discussion of model-building in mathematical programming, Williams (1999) examines a number of common types of constraint that are encountered when building mathematical programming models. Some of these will be discussed here in an attempt to shed light on some issues that have to be faced when developing such models.

Figure 9.10 Non-linear function.

Productive capacity constraints

This type of constraint was encountered in the LDC problem discussed earlier in this chapter. They occur when some necessary resource is available in a limited supply, of which the best use must be made. LDC was short of capacity for gravure printing and for packing. Thus, these constraints were as follows for LDC:

$$P + U \leq 120\ 000$$
$$3P + 2U \leq 300\ 000$$

Hence, any optimization had to be conducted within those constraints. Other common examples of these constraints include available labour or time for a particular set of operations.

Raw material availabilities

These are very similar to productive capacity constraints, and they occur when limited raw material supplies are available for use across a range of finished products. A similar situation would occur when facing investment decisions for which a limited amount of cash might be available for investment across a range of possible projects.

Marketing demands and other limitations – simple bounds

There are sometimes rather simple bounds on the values that may be taken by the decision variables, and these occur in two ways. First, when the demand for a particular item requires that at least a minimum amount must be produced. For instance, two such constraints occurred in the LDC example, when at least 30 000 metres of pasted and unpasted output was required. In this case, the constraints were

$$P \geq 30\ 000$$
$$U \geq 30\ 000$$

Thus, 30 000 metres is a lower bound on the amounts of pasted and unpasted wallpaper to be produced. It might occur because of contracts with customers that specify the minimum amounts.

The second, and opposite, case occurs when there is a direct maximum limitation on the amount that is to be produced. This might occur, for example, when a business reckons that there is a limit to the amount that can be sold to its customers. These upper bounds resemble the lower bounds, except they are less-than-or-equal-to constraints.

It is useful to identify this type of constraint for two reasons. The first, connected with the solution algorithms used in most computer software, is that the solution may be reached much more quickly when some constraints are identified as simple bounds. In essence they reduce the amount of searching that the algorithm must do. Some software identifies them automatically, other packages may need a little help. The second reason is more to do with the sensitivity analysis that follows the solution. Marketing constraints are, for example, of a different order to productive capacity constraints. Although the productive capacity may be within the control of the business, the same may not be true of the market for the product.

Material balance constraints

These are less obvious than the previous types of constraint. They represent the simple fact that all the items that go into some process must be present in the outputs from the process – whether as losses or as planned output. This is a typical feature of blending problems in which a number of ingredients are mixed together to form some finished product.

As an example, suppose that feedstuff for animals must be blended from a number of ingredients, and that the feedstuff blender wishes to maximize his profit, subject to a number of constraints such as the nutritional quality of the blend. Suppose that four raw materials make up the blend. Then the objective function might be

$$\text{Maximize } (-c_1x_1 - c_2x_2 - c_3x_3 - c_4x_4 - py)$$

where c_i represents the cost of one tonne of raw material i, p is the gross income received from selling one tonne of the blended feedstuff, x_i is the number of tonnes of raw material i in the final blend and y is the number of tonnes of the blend produced.

Thus, the objective is to maximize the profit, this being the gross income from sales, less the cost of the raw materials that have been blended.

Given this objective function, the constraints must include the following – plus, of course, all the others as required by the circumstances:

$$x_1 + x_2 + x_3 + x_4 - y = 0$$

This ensures that the material will balance. In problems of this type, the objective function will include something like the following:

$$\text{Maximize } \sum_{i=1}^{n} -c_ix_i - py$$

and the constraints will include the following:

$$\sum_{i=1}^{n} x_i - y = 0$$

Case study: gardening department

The problem posed

Suppose that the gardening department of a local authority uses large quantities of compost to grow the plants that it displays at official functions during the year. An external consultant has recommended that they mix their own compost from the four normal materials, known as RS1, RS2, SA1 and SA2. These materials are available at costs of £10, £9, £8 and £5 per tonne. No other material is part of the compost. They would like to produce 20 tonnes of the compost and would like to do so at minimum cost. The compost itself must contain certain quantities of two important organic nutrients, as shown in Table 9.2.

The four materials come from two different sources. RS1 and RS2 come from Robin Smith Quarries, and this company is prepared to deliver up to 10 tonnes in total of these two materials in any proportion. SA1 and SA2 come from Southern Aggregates who are willing to deliver up to 15 tonnes, again in any proportions. The 'feel' of the compost is also important, and for that reason they wish to ensure that the 20-tonne batch contains at least 3 tonnes of RS2 and 3 tonnes of SA2.

A linear programming formulation

As before, the first stage is to define some suitable variables. Suppose that:

$$r_1 = \text{the tonnes of RS1 to be used}$$
$$r_2 = \text{the tonnes of RS2 to be used}$$
$$r_3 = \text{the tonnes of SA1 to be used}$$
$$r_4 = \text{the tonnes of SA2 to be used}$$

Hence, the objective function is

$$\text{Minimize } 10r_1 + 9r_2 + 8r_3 + 5r_4$$

Table 9.2 Compost production

	Amount in each tonne of each of the four materials				Minimum amount needed in total
	RS1	RS2	SA1	SA2	
Nutrient 1	0.10	0.11	0.12	0.12	2
Nutrient 2	0.50	0.40	0.40	0.20	8

Table 9.3 The solution

Material	RS1	RS2	SA1	SA2
Tonnage	6	3	8	3

The constraints are as follows:

1. Minimum quantities of nutrient 1

$$0.10r_1 + 0.11r_2 + 0.12r_3 + 0.12r_4 \geq 2$$

2. Minimum quantities of nutrient 2

$$0.50r_1 + 0.40r_2 + 0.40r_3 + 0.20r_4 \geq 8$$

3. Quantity of compost needed

$$r_1 + r_2 + r_3 + r_4 = 20$$

4. Maximum delivery from Robin Smith

$$r_1 + r_2 \leq 10$$

5. Maximum delivery from Southern Aggregates

$$r_3 + r_4 \leq 15$$

6. Lower bounds on all four materials

$$r_1 \geq 0$$
$$r_2 \geq 3$$
$$r_3 \geq 0$$
$$r_4 \geq 3$$

The formulation is now complete.

Table 9.4 Slack or surpluses available.

Constraint	Usage	Slack or surplus
Minimum quantity of nutrient 1	2.25	2.25
Maximum delivery from Robin Smith	9	1
Maximum delivery from Southern Aggregates	11	4
Lower bound on RS1	6	6
Lower bound on SA1	8	8

Table 9.5 Shadow prices of binding constraints.

Constraint	Shadow price	Range
Minimum quantity of nutrient 2	20	7.9–8.4
Lower bound on RS2	1	0–2
Lower bound on SA2	1	0–2

The solution from the Excel Solver

The solution that emerges from the Excel Solver is shown in Table 9.3. This is achieved at a cost of £166. This means that constraints are non-binding and have slack or surpluses available, as shown in Table 9.4.

The Sensitivity Report reveals that the shadow prices of binding constraints are as shown in Table 9.5. Thus, each unit of nutrient 1 requires costs of £20, and the requirement to use at least 1 tonne each of RS2 and SA2 adds an extra £1 per tonne to the final compost.

Summary

This chapter has provided an introduction to the ideas of linear programming as an example of optimization modelling. It has illustrated this with two simple examples, one of which was solved by graphical means and both of which were used to illustrate the use of computer software by anyone familiar with spreadsheets. The purpose of the chapter was to show how situations might be modelled in which there is a need to make the best use of some limited resources. It also shows that, in many cases, the model is used as a vehicle to explore the solution space in such a way as to understand how sensitive it is to changes in the parameters of the model.

In this way, even mathematical programming models may be used in an investigative mode. It would perhaps be stretching the meaning of the word 'interpretive' too far to regard mathematical programming as an interpretive approach. Nevertheless, there seems no particular reason why the techniques cannot be employed in a complementary way with some of the softer modelling approaches discussed in Part II.

References

Arntzen B.C., Brown G.B., Harrison T.P. and Trafton L.L. (1995) Global supply chain management at Digital Equipment Corporation. *Interfaces*, **25**(1), 69–93.

Campbell D., Erdahl R., Johnson D., Bibelnieks E., Haydock M., Bullock M. and Crowder H. (2001) Optimizing mail streams at Fingerhut. *Interfaces*, **31**(1), 77–90.

Cox L.A., Jr, Kuehner W.E., Parrish S.H. and Qiu Y. (1993) Optimal expansion of fiber-optic telecommunications networks in metropolitan areas. *Interfaces*, **23**(2), 35–48.

Dantzig G. (1963) *Linear Programming and Extensions*. Princeton University Press, Princeton, NJ.

FICO (2009) www.dashoptimization.com

Frontline Systems (2009) The Premium Solver for Excel: http://www.solver.com

Gautier A., Lamond B.F., Paré D and Rouleau F. (2000) The Québec Ministry of Natural Resources uses linear programming to understand the wood-fiber market. *Interfaces*, **30**(6), 32–48.

Grandzol J.R. and Traaen T. (1995) Using mathematical programming to help supervisors balance workloads. *Interfaces*, **25**(4), 92–103.

Hendry L.C., Fok K.K. and Shek K.W. (1996) A cutting stock and scheduling problem in the copper industry. *Journal of the Operational Research Society*, **47**(1), 38–47.

Hillier F.S. and Lieberman G.J. (2005) *Introduction to Operations Research*, 8th edition. McGraw-Hill, Boston, MA.

ILOG (2009) ILOG CPLEX: www.ilog.com

Kantorovich L.V. (1942) O peremeshchenii mass. *Doklady Akademii Nauk SSSR*, **37**(7–8), 227–230; On the translocation of masses. *Comptes Rendus (Doklady) de l'Académie des Sciences de l'U.R.S.S.*, **37**, 199–201; reprinted (1958): *Management Science*, **5**, 1–4.

LINDO Systems (2009) www.lindo.com

Lionheart Publishing (2009) Software surveys: http://lionhrtpub.com/orms/

Thomas L.C., Banasik J. and Crook J.N. (2001) Recalibrating scorecards. *Journal of the Operational Research Society*, **52**, 981–988.

Williams H.P. (1993) *Model Solving in Mathematical Programming.* John Wiley & Sons, Ltd, Chichester, UK.

Williams H.P. (1999) *Model Building in Mathematical Programming*, 4th edition. John Wiley & Sons, Ltd, Chichester, UK.

Zenios S.A. (1994) Parallel and supercomputing in the practice of management science. *Interfaces*, **24**(5), 122–140.

10 Computer simulation – visual interactive modelling and Monte Carlo simulation

Computer simulation defined

The basic idea of computer simulation is shown in Figure 10.1. Strictly speaking, computer simulation is the use of a model as a basis for exploration and experimentation. Like all modelling approaches, simulation is used because it may be cheaper, safer, quicker and more secure than using the real system itself. The idea is that the model becomes a vehicle for asking 'what if . . .?' questions. That is, the simulation model is subject to known inputs so as to see the effects of these inputs on the outputs.

Modelling when things are uncertain

In many situations there is considerable uncertainty about what might happen. In such cases, we need to pay due regard to the likelihood (or probability) of events occurring. One approach to this is to use decision theory based on expected values, as introduced in Chapter 2. Another approach is to use some form of simulation, of which this chapter deals with two types:

1. *Static simulations.* These are sometimes referred to as risk analysis or as the Monte Carlo approach. The latter term stems from the methods used in the Monte Carlo Project, which was part of the US attempt to develop atomic weapons in World War II. In these simulations, dynamic interactions through time are not a major concern, and many such simulations can be executed on a spreadsheet, as in the next section, 'Beyond averages'.
2. *Dynamic simulations.* These are concerned with systems whose behaviour varies through time. In Management Science, these simulations are usually tackled via discrete event simulation if the system behaviour is stochastic, or via system dynamics.

Beyond averages: static simulations

One of the biggest mistakes that we can make is to think that, because something is OK 'on average', then it will be OK. As a simple example, suppose that we need to borrow £100 000, repayable over 25 years, to buy a house. Suppose, too, that current interest rates are 7%, paid annually, on the reducing balance of the mortgage. Is it better to take out a fixed-rate loan or one that can vary? In both cases, the annual payment would be fixed at the same amount. It seems obvious that the result should be the same, but this is not the case.

Spreadsheets such as Excel can be used for most static simulations, and the fixed and variable mortgage loan will be used to illustrate this. The annual payment can be computed using the

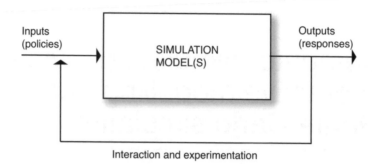

Figure 10.1 Simulation as computer-based experimentation.

PMT() function of Excel, which computes the payment for a loan based on constant payments and a constant interest rate. This gives a fixed annual payment of £8581.05, which reduces the balance to approximately zero after 25 years if the interest rate is constant at 7% p.a.

Figure 10.2 shows part of an Excel spreadsheet for the mortgage, with an annually variable rate that has a mean value of 7% but can vary by ±3%, such that any value between 4 and 10%

	Variable 7% +/- 3%				
	VARIABLE INTEREST RATE				
YEAR	**DEBT (Variable)**	**ACTUAL INTEREST RATE**	**INTEREST PAID**	**7% PAYMENT**	**CAPITAL REPAID**
1	£100,000.00	8.3%	£8,300.00	-£8,581.05	-£281.05
2	£99,718.95	7.5%	£7,478.92	-£8,581.05	-£1,102.13
3	£98,616.82	7.2%	£7,100.41	-£8,581.05	-£1,480.64
4	£97,136.18	4.1%	£3,982.58	-£8,581.05	-£4,598.47
5	£92,537.71	5.4%	£4,997.04	-£8,581.05	-£3,584.02
6	£88,953.69	5.2%	£4,625.59	-£8,581.05	-£3,955.46
7	£84,998.23	6.6%	£5,609.88	-£8,581.05	-£2,971.17
8	£82,027.06	4.7%	£3,855.27	-£8,581.05	-£4,725.78
22	£9,562.33	7.3%	£698.05	-£8,581.05	-£7,883.00
23	£1,679.33	8.9%	£149.46	-£8,581.05	-£8,431.59
24	-£6,752.26	9.3%	£0.00	-£8,581.05	-£8,581.05
25	-£15,333.31	4.1%	£0.00	-£8,581.05	-£8,581.05
26	-£23,914.36	6.6%			
					£123,914.36
				Under/over	£23,914.36

Figure 10.2 Mortgage payments spreadsheet.

Table 10.1 Results of a multiple @Risk
simulation, variable-rate mortgage.

Largest underpayment	£66 798
Largest overpayment	£37 866
Mean overpayment	−£1 968
Standard deviation	22 660
Sample size	100

is equally likely. (Note that years 9 to 21 have been hidden to reduce the size of the figure.) The annual payment, though, is constant at £8851.05, as in the fixed-interest case; therefore, if the sampled interest rate (in column C) is less than 7%, more capital will be repaid that year, and less will be repaid if it is higher. In this spreadsheet, random numbers have been used to generate an interest rate each year. The result shown is pleasing, for it shows that the variable-rate mortgage will lead to total repayments of almost £24 000 less than the fixed-rate mortgage over 25 years – because the average interest rate turned out to be only 6.6%.

However, it is important to realize that, if different random numbers were used, a different result would be obtained. If we repeated the simulation many times, each time with different random numbers, what difference would this make? Later in the chapter we discuss the use of @Risk (Palisade Corporation, 2009), which works with Microsoft Excel to allow repeated simulations. Table 10.1 summarizes the results from 100 replications, using @Risk, each replication using different random numbers. This shows the mean end-of-term underpayment to be about £1968; that is, if we simulate the mortgage repayments 100 times, the variable-rate mortgage is £1968 cheaper, on average, than a fixed-rate mortgage at 7%.

However, that is not the end of the story. In one of the simulations, the end-of-term position was disastrous – a debt of over £37 000. In another, the end-of-term position was very cheering, with a positive end result of almost £67 000. If we do not wish to run the risk of a final debt of over £67 000, then we should stick with the fixed-rate mortgage. If we are happy with this risk, we can expect the variable-rate option to be cheaper, on average. However, the average outcome probably never occurs, and the risk remains of significant overpayment. On the other hand, if we work for the mortgage company that lends the money and does so on many mortgages, it is very clear that lending on these variable-rate terms is worse than offering fixed-rate mortgages. As the mortgage company makes many similar loans, the statistics from the sample distribution produced by the simulation are directly useful.

In summary, common sense tells us that, on average, the out-turn from the variable interest rate should be the same as the fixed rate. But common sense can be wrong, and it is here. Most situations in which it is sensible to use computer simulation include one or more elements about which there is uncertainty. It might, as in the example above, be due to interest rates; or, in another type of simulation, it might be due to observed variation in the arrival time of customers, the demand for a product, the time taken to complete a surgical procedure or to any number of other factors. This variation is simulated by taking samples from a probability distribution believed to be a good representation of the variation.

The basics of random sampling in simulation – top-hat sampling

Suppose that a simulation model needs to include some element that is governed by a probability distribution. How will samples be taken from the distribution as the simulation proceeds? In

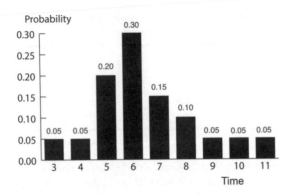

Figure 10.3 A histogram.

most cases, this random sampling is achieved via a two-stage process. Sometimes the sampling process may seem rather complicated, but the underlying principles are very simple, as follows:

1. Generate one or more pseudorandom numbers.
2. Transform this/these into a sample from the required distribution.

To illustrate this, it is best to consider the simplest possible approach to such sampling, known as top-hat sampling.

Top-hat sampling is used to take samples from empirical probability distributions represented by histograms. Figure 10.3 shows such a histogram, which represents the observed times, rounded to the nearest minute, taken by a doctor to see a patient. This tells us that no patients require less than 3 minutes or more than 11 minutes. The most frequent consultation time is 6 minutes, which is taken by 30% of the patients. To understand why this method is called top-hat sampling, imagine a large, cylindrical top hat of the type once worn by English gentlemen and still popular for wedding garb. Suppose that we place 100 plastic counters in the top hat, and on each counter we mark a number according to the probabilities shown on the histogram of Figure 10.3. Thus, no counters have values below 3 or above 11. Five counters will be marked with a 3, five more with a 4, 20 with a 5, 30 with a 6, 15 with a 7, 10 with an 8 and five each with 9, 10 and 11. Thus, the numbers on the counters will be distributed in the same way as the histogram. To take each sample, we shake the hat to ensure that the counters are uniformly distributed within it, and then take a counter from the hat, selecting at random. We note the number on the counter, replace it in the hat and repeat the process. In this way we should end up with samples whose proportions mirror those of the histogram.

As no one would seriously contemplate connecting a mechanical arm and top hat to a computer, an analogous approach is used. This is based on the use of random numbers, or pseudorandom numbers to be precise. These are numbers distributed across some interval (usually from 0 to 1) and presented in a wholly random sequence in which all values are equally likely to occur. These pseudorandom numbers are generated by methods discussed in most books on computer simulation (e.g. Law, 2007; Pidd, 2004). To use such a sequence of pseudorandom numbers in top-hat sampling, we construct a table of the type shown in Table 10.2. This shows that the range of possible random numbers (0.000 to 0.999 inclusive) has been allocated in subranges to each possible value of the consultation time. Thus, 5% of the values (0.000–0.049) have been allocated to a time of 3 minutes, a further 5% (0.050–0.099) to a time of 4 minutes and so on. In this way, the random numbers are mapped on to the time histogram. To carry out

Table 10.2 Sampling scheme for consultation times.

Time (min)	Probability	Random number subrange
3	0.05	0.000–0.049
4	0.05	0.050–0.099
5	0.20	0.100–0.299
6	0.30	0.300–0.599
7	0.15	0.600–0.749
8	0.10	0.750–0.849
9	0.05	0.850–0.899
10	0.05	0.900–0.949
11	0.05	0.950–0.999

top-hat sampling in this way, all we need to do is find some suitable source of random numbers, and then transform them into the required sample – the two-stage process described above.

Table 10.3 shows a sequence of 10 samples taken from this histogram by top-hat sampling, so as to represent the consultation times for 10 patients. The second column shows the random numbers taken from a suitable random number table. The third column shows the resulting sample from the consultation time distribution, using the sampling scheme of Table 10.2. The fourth column shows the running mean after n samples. Thus, after five samples the mean is 5.6, and after 10 samples it is 6.3. The actual mean value of the distribution is 6.5, and, in general, if more samples are taken, the sample mean will be closer to the true mean of the distribution. Of course, in many simulations, unlike this example, the mean of the output distribution is unknown – which is why a simulation is needed. However, the same general comment still applies – if the simulation includes elements that are probabilistic, repeated runs are needed for satisfactory estimates. More is said about this later in the chapter.

Running static simulations on spreadsheets: Monte Carlo simulation

Many financial problems can be tackled by static simulation on a spreadsheet, and the basic ideas will be illustrated using the example of the variable-rate mortgage introduced earlier. Producing

Table 10.3 Ten consultation time samples.

	Random number	Sample	Running mean
1	0.218	5	5.000
2	0.572	6	5.500
3	0.025	3	4.667
4	0.779	8	5.500
5	0.576	6	5.600
6	0.798	8	6.000
7	0.269	5	5.857
8	0.750	7	6.000
9	0.888	9	6.333
10	0.376	6	6.300

an accurate estimate, say of the debt at the end of 25 years, requires repeated sets of random numbers. This could be achieved using the built-in statistical functions of the spreadsheet and writing down 50 or more results, each time with a different set of functions. This is not especially difficult using the recalculate key (F9 in Excel), but it is tedious and there are better ways of using add-ins. The add-ins, unlike The Solver used in Chapter 9, are not provided with current versions of common spreadsheets, but must be bought and installed. Examples of these add-ins include Oracle Crystal Ball (Oracle Crystal Ball, 2009) and @Risk (Palisade Corporation, 2009). To show their potential, this section uses @Risk, which is part of the Palisade DecisionTools Suite.

The Palisade DecisionTools Suite includes elements that all run within Microsoft Excel. These include PrecisionTree, which is used in Chapter 8 to compute expected monetary values on a decision tree, and @Risk, which provides Monte Carlo sampling support. Once installed, @Risk appears as an extra tab on the main ribbon bar of Excel 2007 and in equivalent places on other versions of Excel. Its main benefit is that it allows the controlled multiple replication of a simulation, provides sampling routines for many probability distributions and provides tools for analysing the results. It can thus be used to run the mortgage simulation many times, as described here. Selecting the @Risk tab on the Excel ribbon bar leads to a set of buttons used by @Risk in Excel.

In this variable interest rate mortgage example, the rate paid varies between 4 and 10%, with all values equally likely within that range. Thus, the interest rate payable follows a continuous uniform probability distribution. To simulate this mortgage over its 25-year period, we select the Define Distribution button of @Risk, which leads to an initial window (Figure 10.4) in which the required distribution can be selected by name or shape. Selecting a Uniform distribution and then clicking on the Select Distribution button leads to the dialogue box of Figure 10.5. By

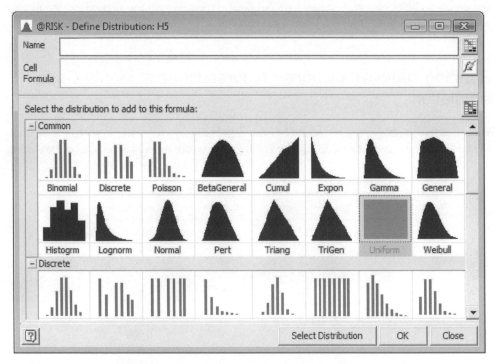

Figure 10.4 Choosing a distribution in @Risk.

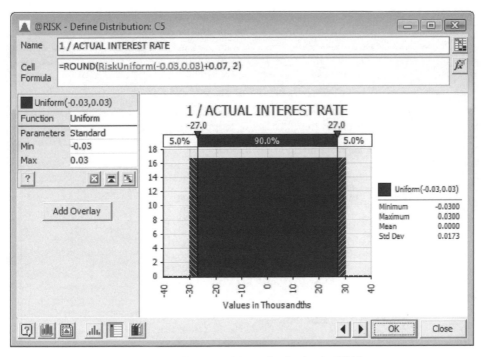

Figure 10.5 Parameterizing a distribution in @Risk.

default, this built-in Uniform distribution assumes a mean value of zero, and hence the user must specify the minimum (Min) and Maximum (Max) values. These are entered as −0.03 (−3%) and 0.03 (+3%), which provides the required range but with the wrong mean. Selecting these values causes an appropriate formula to appear in the Cell Formula section near the top of the dialogue box.

The range needs to have a mean of 7% (0.07), and hence the formula is edited by adding +0.07 in the Cell Formula bar of Excel. Finally, the formula is further edited to round the resulting sample to two decimal places, also in the Cell Formula bar of Excel. This then ensures that, in year 1, the actual interest rate will be sampled from a uniform distribution that produces samples in the range 4–10%. The same formula is copied, in the usual Excel way, into the Interest Rate cells for years 2 to 25. The application is now ready to be simulated.

Before starting the simulation, it is sensible to consider which output variables are of interest. In this case, the most likely candidates are the under/overpayment at the end of 25 years and the average interest rate across the simulations. Figure 10.6 shows the spreadsheet; the rows for years 7 to 23 have been hidden to take up less space. The two output cells (C30 and F32) are marked with borders to make them clearer. To set these cells as outputs, we select the cells one at a time and then the Add Output option from the @Risk ribbon bar. This leads to straightforward dialogue boxes that are not shown here.

We can now run the simulation by entering the number of replications (1000 in this case) in the ribbon bar and pressing the Start Simulation button of the ribbon bar. @Risk will now run 1000 independent replications of a 25-year simulation of the variable mortgage question. Doing so enables us to understand the likely outcome from making this choice by establishing the probability distribution of the results. These distributions are shown in the output histograms for the two variables, and that for the under/overpayment is shown in Figure 10.7, which is the

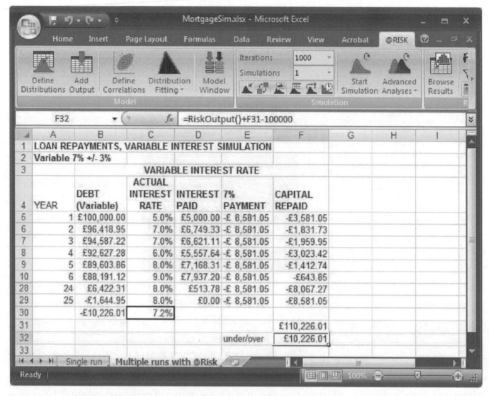

Figure 10.6 Results of a single @Risk simulation of the mortgage problem.

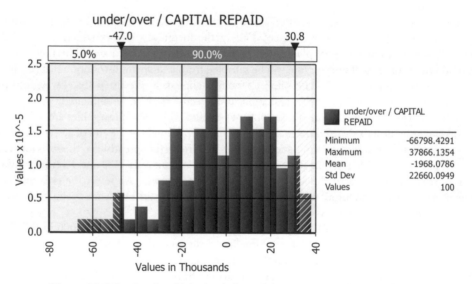

Figure 10.7 Results of multiple simulations of the mortgage problem in @Risk.

source of the data in Table 10.2. In addition, @Risk provides detailed reports on simulation. Examples include:

- detailed data and summary statistics for each cell included in the simulation (for example, for each year of each of the replications);
- regressions linking input and output variables.

The outputs, Figure 10.7 and Table 10.2, show that, across 100 independent 25-year simulations, the variable-rate mortgage is about £2000 cheaper than the fixed-rate option. However, the standard deviation of the results is large (over £22 000). As discussed earlier, if, instead of being the person receiving the mortgage, we were the mortgage company, this graph and table would provide very useful information. From them we can infer that the variable-rate mortgage is likely to be expensive for the mortgage company if it makes many such similar loans. For the person taking out the mortgage, the decision is, in effect, a one-off gamble, and the gamble is likely to lead to a lower overall cost than the fixed-rate option – but it might cost us a lot more.

It should be clear, then, that static simulations are useful ways to gain understanding of the effects of uncertainty and variability. The example given here is very simple, but similar methods underlie much more sophisticated simulations of stock prices and other investments. The next section introduces the ideas of dynamic simulations, which use similar sampling procedures to those of static simulations, but which combine them in complex ways in full-blown models.

Dynamic computer simulation

Given enough time, money, expertise and computer power, almost any system can be simulated on a computer, but this may not be sensible. Hence, the first question to face is, to what type of systems are modern computer simulation methods best suited? The following features tend to characterize the systems best suited to dynamic simulation:

- They are dynamic – that is, they display distinctive behaviour that is known to vary through time. This variation might be due to factors that are not well understood but that may still be amenable to statistical analysis – for example, the apparently random failures of equipment. Or they might be due to well-understood relationships that can be captured in equations – for example, the flight of a missile through a non-turbulent atmosphere.
- They are interactive – that is, the system consists of a number of components that interact with one another, and this interaction produces the distinctive behaviour of the system. For example, the observed behaviour of aircraft under air traffic control will be due to factors such as the performance characteristics of the individual aircraft, the intervention of the air traffic controllers, the weather and any local problems due to political action on the ground. This mix of factors will be varying all the time, and their interaction will produce the observed behaviour of the air traffic.
- They are complicated – that is, there are many objects interacting in the system of interest, and their individual dynamics need careful consideration and analysis.

In short, computer simulation modelling is best suited to systems that are dynamic and interactive as well as complicated. As a technique, it has been in use in Management Science since the early 1950s, and its methods have gradually evolved alongside general developments in computing since then.

Some dynamic simulation applications

In surveys of management scientists, computer simulation usually figures in the top three techniques that they employ in their work. There are thousands of applications across many areas of work in Management Science. This section of the chapter will briefly discuss some of those applications.

- *Manufacturing.* As markets for manufactured goods have become globalized, manufacturers have increasingly attempted to mass-customize their products. That is, they have sought economies of scale by developing products that will have global appeal and should sell in many countries. At the same time they have had to ensure that the products themselves are suited to local preferences, which means they have had to produce local variants of the global designs. This mass-customization, sometimes known as 'glocalization', has placed great pressure on manufacturers to develop and install manufacturing systems that can deliver high-volume, high-quality goods at low cost to meet local needs. This has led to huge investments in manufacturing plant and associated control systems. It is important to ensure that such systems operate as intended, and therefore computer simulation methods have found an important place in the process of designing and implementing these manufacturing plants and systems.

  Examples of this use of computer simulation occur across most manufacturing sectors and include the food industry (Pidd, 1987), semiconductor wafer fabrication (Miller, 1994), beverages (Harrell, 1993), pharmaceuticals (Park and Getz, 1992), automobile manufacture (Beadle, 1986), aerospace (Bier and Tjelle, 1994), shipbuilding (Williams *et al.*, 2001) and materials handling (Burnett and LeBaron, 2001). Simulation is employed because it allows alternative designs and control policies to be tried out on the model before starting to build the physical plant. It helps to reduce the cost and risk of large-scale errors. Simulation approaches are also used on existing plant to find better ways to operate, and these studies might be one-off exercises or may be part of a periodic check on the running of the system.

- *Health care.* As with manufacturing, there is also a need to make effective use of limited resources when providing and delivering health care. Thus, simulation approaches have found widespread application in health care systems around the world. Wears and Winton (1993) report on its use to examine options, particularly those of triage, in prehospital trauma care. Ceric (1990) describes how the methods were used to plan a system to move goods and equipment around a large new hospital in an effective and efficient manner. Günal and Pidd (2008) describe a simulation suite (DGHPSim) that can be used to model whole hospitals and show the effect of performance targets.

  Emergency departments have been a popular application area – see, for example, Fletcher *et al.* (2007), and Günal and Pidd (2006) report on the use of simulation for the planning of effective emergency departments. In all these simulations, and in others, the idea was to test different policies without putting patients to inconvenience or placing them at risk. In a different context, Brailsford *et al.* (1992) describe how the approach has been used to investigate different policies for handling the AIDS epidemic, and Davies *et al.* (2002) use it to assess the value of screening programmes for diabetic complications.

- *Business process re-engineering.* Businesses continually strive to ensure that their core processes are operated effectively and efficiently, and this has been the aim of business process re-engineering (BPR). In BPR the idea is to take a fundamental look at the basic processes without which the business could not function and which contribute in a major way to both profit and cost. In some ways, the stress on BPR mirrors the shift in manufacturing from batch production towards flowline manufacturing. An example of a BPR exercise might be an investigation of the various operations and activities involved in delivering goods to a customer, and in invoicing that customer and in receiving payment. In a traditional system, the paperwork and computer-based documentation might need to pass through several different departments. Taking a radical look at such processes might lead to great simplification and thus to reduced costs and to better service. The aim of BPR is to take an integrated view of such activities and to find ways to provide a better service at lower cost by more effective organization.

Bhaskar *et al.* (1994) identify computer simulation as one of the key approaches to understanding how business processes might be re-engineered to improve performance. Davies (1994) describes how simulation has been used in BPR in the UK financial services industry. Companies providing these financial services in the UK must meet legal time limits for their responses to customers and must also carry out a series of checks required by law – in addition to their own internal monitoring. Laguna and Marklund's (2005) textbook is devoted to the use of Management Science methods, particularly discrete event simulation, in designing and improving business processes.

- *Transport systems.* Computer simulation is also used in a wide range of transportation systems. As with other applications, the idea is to ensure that the system operates as efficiently and as effectively as possible. In the aviation sector, simulation methods have, for example, been used to help plan large passenger terminals. Airport terminals include systems for moving baggage and for ensuring that passengers can get to the departure gates in time for their planes, and a number of simulations have been used to assess their performance (for example, Joustra and Van Dijk, 2001). Also in the aviation sector, air traffic control systems are used to ensure that air space is used efficiently and safely. As part of this, the air traffic controllers must ensure that the movement of aircraft is planned in advance and then managed in real time. Simulation approaches have made a great contribution to safer and more cost-effective air traffic control (for example, Lee, Pritchett and Goldsman, 2001).

  The shipping sector has also been a long-term user of computer methods. Indeed, one of the computer simulation programming languages (CSL) (Buxton and Laski, 1962) was first developed by Esso (predecessor of Exxon) to support simulations of the movement of crude and refined oil around the world. Shipping applications continue to this day, and an example is given in Heath (1993).

  Salt (1991) reports how simulation methods were used to help plan the movement of traffic in the Channel Tunnel that links the UK and France. Although the introduction of this service was controversial, it is clear that one key to its future success is the reliability of the service that it offers. Unlike the ferries, which also ply the route, bad weather should not prevent the operation of the tunnel service. It was therefore crucial that its operations were properly planned and managed. Salt (1991) gives interesting examples of how this was supported by computer simulation approaches.

  The road transport sector is also a major user of computer simulation methods, both to plan individual companies' operations and to investigate road traffic systems in general. Traffic simulators are now a standard part of the armoury of road traffic planners (Pidd, 1995; Rathi and Santiago, 1990; Young, Taylor and Gipps, 1989), as they permit possible road configurations and traffic management schemes to be refined before their physical implementation.

- *Defence.* The defence sector is also a major user of simulation methods, and the Proceedings of the Winter Simulation Conference usually include a range of papers discussing work in this area (see Robinson, 2001, for example). Applications range from studies of logistics operations through to battle simulations, which investigate possible strategies and tactics to be used in defence or attack. Their appeal here is obvious: no battle commander wishes to be defeated, and the chance to develop tactics beforehand and to prepare countermeasures is of some importance. Not surprisingly, the majority of defence simulations are not reported in the open literature.

Discrete event simulation

Whatever the simulation modelling approach adopted, a simulation model must be able to mimic the changes that occur, through time, in the real system. In Management Science it is usual to distinguish between three different approaches to dynamic simulation modelling. These are known as discrete event simulation, continuous simulation and mixed discrete/continuous simulation. The majority of applications of dynamic simulation methods in Management Science seem to use discrete event models, and thus this chapter will concentrate on them. System dynamics (see Chapter 7) supports a simulation approach that is a simple version of continuous simulation. Some system dynamics software, notably Stella/iThink (High Performance Systems, 2009), extends this to allow for the limited inclusion of some discrete elements.

Discrete event simulation is so named because of its main features. Systems to be simulated in this way are considered to consist of discrete entities that occupy discrete states that will change over time. Thus, a hospital will include individual patients whose states may include 'being admitted', 'on Emergency Ward 10', 'in surgery' and so on. Similarly, the staff who treat the patients may themselves be regarded as entities that change state. For example, doctors may be 'examining a patient', 'writing case notes', 'operating on a patient' and so on. Many of these states require the cooperation of two or more classes of entity – for example, 'examining a patient' (the doctor's perspective) is the same as 'being examined by a doctor' from a patient's perspective. Thus, the essence of discrete event modelling is an effort to capture the important features of the system in terms of entities and states.

The bulk of a discrete event simulation model consists of a set of logical statements, expressed in some computable form, which describe how the entities change state. Thus, there might be statements of the following type:

```
If (ThisDoctor=Free) and (PatientsWaiting>0) then {
    Take ThisPatient from PatientsWaiting;
    Engage ThisDoctor to ThisPatient:
    Compute ConsultationTime;
    Release ThisDoctor and ThisPatient after ConsultationTime.
}
```

These statements, which are not written in any particular programming language, describe what must happen for a consultation to begin. The conditions governing this are that ThisDoctor must be Free and there must be PatientsWaiting. If those conditions hold, then a waiting patient and ThisDoctor are placed in an engaged state in which they will remain until the ConsultationTime is over. This example also illustrates another feature of a discrete simulation model: it is concerned with the conditions that govern a state change of the entities. Unless those above are satisfied, the event will not occur. The times at which the entities change state are known as events – hence the term discrete event simulation.

At some stage or other, the logic of a discrete event simulation model needs to be put in a computable form. For large-scale and complex systems this will need a computer program of some size and complexity. In the first 30 years of discrete event simulations, these were usually written in a general-purpose programming language such as, nowadays, Java, C++ or Visual Basic, or in a special-purpose simulation programming language such as SIMSCRIPT or MODSIM (both from CACI). Since the 1990s, software developers have produced easy-to-use, discrete event simulation tools that greatly ease the process of developing and running a simulation. These tools are known as visual interactive modelling systems (VIMS, a plural or singular acronym), and they will be discussed later in this chapter. VIMS have been developed for other types of simulation too, and Powersim (Powersim Corporation, 2009) and Stella/iThink (High Performance Systems, 2009) are examples of VIMS developed for system dynamics. Although there is no formal survey data to support this, it seems that, nowadays, most discrete event simulations are developed using VIMS.

Entities and classes

In order to provide a useful description of discrete event simulation modelling, it is important to define, more precisely, the terminology introduced above. The tangible components of the system are usually known as entities. An entity is an object whose behaviour within the model will be explicitly tracked as the simulation proceeds. As with all modelling, a simulation model is a simplification, and there will be many candidates for inclusion within a model as an entity, but only some need be included. Those included should be those that are relevant to the reason that simulation is being conducted. In a hospital, entities might be patients, doctors, nurses, items of equipment and so on. In an airport terminal they might be passengers, staff, items of baggage, aircraft and other equipment. For each such entity, the simulation system will track their behaviour by maintaining detailed information about their current and possible future states.

In some simulation software, entities may be conveniently grouped into classes. These are permanent groupings of similar objects that, therefore, share similar features or attributes. Thus, we may refer to classes such as patients, doctors, nurses and aircraft, or, in a factory, orders. The individual members of a class need not be identical, but they do have common features. Thus, an attribute of an order in a factory might be the machines (or route) that will be needed in order to meet the order. As mentioned above, many simulations nowadays are carried out using a VIMS. These may be designed for special use in certain application areas. For example, Witness (Lanner Systems, 2009) was originally designed for use in discrete parts manufacturing, and so users are encouraged to think about their system as a set of parts that flow through work centres. Such VIMS provide built-in classes to simulate the behaviour of common entities; in manufacturing systems, examples might be conveyor systems and automatic guided vehicles.

States, events, activities and processes

As introduced above, entities occupy states for a period of time. It is best to assume that these states are disjoint – that is, there is no overlap and no entity can simultaneously be in more than one state. This is obviously a simplification, but it forces the modeller to think about the states that are relevant to the system and situation being modelled. Any entity included in the model must be in one state or other throughout its time in the simulation. If entities are idle, then they should be regarded as in an idle state; fuzziness is not permitted. The entities persist in a state for a period of time, and the time at which they change state is known as an event, or event time. State changes must also be precise, and thus no entity will have states that overlap.

What goes on while an entity is in a known state? From one perspective, what is happening is that the entity is changing state, and this takes time to happen. This is often known as an activity, and an activity may well be cooperative; that is, it may require the cooperation of more than a single class of entity. Thus, in the example above, unless a doctor is free and a patient is waiting, a consultation cannot begin. Once it begins, this activity persists for some time, during which the doctor may be in the 'with a patient' state and the patient may be in a 'seeing the doctor' state. At the end of the consultation activity, the paths of the two entities may well diverge – but

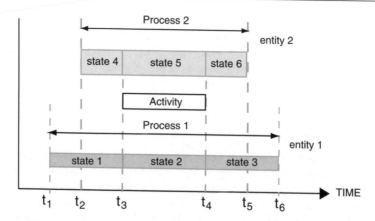

Figure 10.8 States, events and processes in discrete event simulation.

this may depend on what happens during the activity. Any activity begins with an event and ends with an event. Both events cause the entities involved to change state in some way or other.

For convenience it is often useful to think in terms of a process. A process is the chronological sequence of activities (and therefore of events) through which an entity must or may pass. Each class of entity will have one or more processes associated with it. When an entity that is a member of that class appears in the simulation, this process becomes a route through which the entity will pass. The entity's progress through the process will be delayed at times – either because of an activity in which it engages with other entities, or because the entity is in some idle state waiting for something to happen. Figure 10.8 shows the relationship between events, activities and processes.

The dynamics of time

Although it may be true that, in the real world, time is 'like an ever-rolling stream' (Watts, ca 1719), this is not how a discrete event simulation works. Instead, time is controlled via what is usually known as the simulation clock, and this moves forward irregularly from event to event. Thus, in Figure 10.8 the simulation clock moves as follows:

t_1 This event marks the start of state 1, which coincides with the start of process 1, because state 1 is the first state occupied by entity 1 in its process.

t_2 This event marks the start of state 4 which coincides with the start of process 2, because state 4 is the first state occupied by entity 2 in its process.

t_3 This event marks the start of state 2 (entity 1) and state 5 (entity 2) and is the start of the activity in which the two entities jointly engage. This coincides with the end of state 1 for entity 1 and state 4 for entity 2.

t_4 This event marks the end of state 2 (entity 1) and state 5 (entity 2) and is the end of the activity in which the two entities jointly engage. This coincides with the start of state 3 for entity 1 and state 6 for entity 2.

t_5 This event marks the end of state 6 for entity 2 and also the end of process 2.

t_6 This event marks the end of state 3 for entity 1 and also the end of process 1.

That is, time within such a simulation moves forward in unequal amounts depending on when the events fall due. The time between events is ignored in a discrete event simulation, as changes only occur at events. Therefore, if the simulation is driving an animated display of, for example, a factory, then the display will seem jerky unless steps are taken to give it a smooth appearance.

The executive or control program

In the early days of computer simulation, during the late 1950s, it was realized that it was possible to separate out a feature common to all discrete event simulations. This is the need to ensure that events happen as and when they should, and that the entities change state accordingly. The control program, or executive, carries out these tasks of sequencing and scheduling in the simulation. There are several ways in which these executives can be organized (for a thorough description, see Pidd, 2004), but the various approaches are based around similar ideas. As an analogy, imagine a puppet theatre in which a puppeteer must pull strings to ensure that the puppets move around on the stage. Each puppet's possible actions are determined by the ways in which the strings are attached, and their actual actions are determined by the ways in which the puppeteer pulls the strings. In a discrete event simulation, the entities are the puppets, the events, activities and processes are the strings and the executive or control program is the puppeteer.

In controlling the running of a discrete event simulation model, the control program needs access to all relevant information about all entities. In particular, the executive needs to know the current state of all entities and for how much longer they will remain in those states. In simple terms, the executive maintains a diary (usually known as an event list or event calendar) containing information about the simulation entities. As an entity changes state, this information is updated, and these state changes may depend on one of two things. First, the entity will change state only when other resources (typically other entities) with which it will cooperate are available. This activity is cooperative, and the precise time of its occurrence cannot be predicted because it depends on the availability of those resources. Thus, although patients are waiting at 2 p.m., an outpatient clinic will not start until the doctor appears. This, in turn, may depend on when the doctor has been able to deal with an emergency that cropped up in the late morning. Hence, until the doctor appears, the start time of the clinic is uncertain. For such activity, the event time for its start is unknown in advance and the simulation executive can take no direct action, as some other event may intervene before the expected one occurs.

The other type of event is one that will certainly occur at some known time. Hence, an outpatient consultation, once begun, will come to an end. Of course, the time of that event will depend on the duration of the consultation, and, it might be argued, this cannot be known in advance. In a discrete event simulation, this variation in activity durations is handled by taking samples from probability distributions that are known to represent the durations. Thus, it might be believed that the duration of the consultation is normally distributed but truncated, so that no consultation takes less than 5 minutes and no consultation takes more than 30 minutes. When the event that starts the activity occurs in the simulation, a sample is taken from the distribution and may be used to calculate the time that the activity will end. This 'end time' can then be placed on the event calendar.

In general, the first type of event will engage or consume resources that are available, and must therefore await their availability. The second type, in general, will release resources at the end of the activity, and these events can thus be directly scheduled. Events occur under the control of the simulation executive. As they occur, they trigger activity, and this may result in future events being scheduled on the event calendar. Hence, the simulation control program maintains an event calendar on which are entered the times at which these known events of the second type are due to occur. Most of them will be scheduled, or entered on the calendar, when an event of the first type occurs. How this calendar is implemented will vary, depending on the computer software that is in use, as will the terminology used to describe the two types of event. What is important is that the modeller should be able to decide which are the relevant entity classes, what are the events in which they engage and what activity will occur as a result of these events.

Using diagrams to build simulation models

When building a discrete event simulation model, it is important to understand the logic of the system to be simulated and to represent this in terms of entities and their interactions. This is often known as conceptual modelling. This logic can be expressed verbally, but many people find it simpler to use diagrams as an aid to their thinking. Activity cycle diagrams are one way of developing conceptual models, which, though they cannot represent the full complexity of any system, are useful for thinking about the ways in which the simulation entities interact. Their simplicity fits well with the principle of parsimony discussed in Chapter 4.

Activity cycle diagrams

An activity cycle diagram (ACD) is a network that shows how the processes of different entity classes interact, at least in a skeletal form. An ACD has just two symbols, as shown in Figure 10.9:

- An active state is one whose time duration can be directly determined at the event that marks its start. This might be because the time duration is deterministic (the bus will definitely leave in 5 minutes), or because its duration can be sampled from some probability distribution.
- A dead state is one whose duration cannot be so determined, but can only be inferred by knowing how long the active states may last. In most cases, a dead state is one in which an entity is waiting for something to happen, and, thus, some people refer to the dead states as queues.

Each entity class has an activity cycle that shows the sequence of activities and events through which an entity will pass, and is more or less equivalent to a simulation process. To draw an ACD, the first stage is to consider the entity classes that will be needed; then, an activity cycle is drawn for each entity class. Combining the different cycles leads to the completed diagram which shows how the different classes of entity will interact within the simulation model. At this stage there is no need to be concerned with any statistical aspects of the model, those are considered later. As an example, consider the simple system outlined in the case study for Joe's Exhaust Parlour.

Figure 10.9 Activity cycle diagram symbols.

Case study: Joe's Exhaust Parlour

Background

Joe owns and runs an exhaust replacement business on an industrial estate. This exhaust parlour provides a service to private motorists who are concerned about the state of their car exhaust systems. Joe has run the business successfully for a number of years, but is concerned at the competition from a national franchise that has opened up nearby. He knows that most potential customers will visit his parlour as well as that of the national competitor, and he also ensures that his prices are competitive. Given this, he believes that the keys to winning an order are not only surroundings that are clean and business like, though not too plush, but also keeping a customer waiting for the shortest possible time.

Joe's Exhaust Parlour is open from 9 a.m. to 7 p.m., and he and his fitters work throughout that period if there is work to be done. Meals and rest breaks are taken whenever the activity is slack. The mode of operation is as follows. Motorists arrive unannounced and wait for Joe himself to inspect their car's exhaust system. To do this, the car is driven by Joe on to any free hydraulic ramp so that the car's exhaust system may be checked from below. Joe then advises the customer on the necessary work, and 70% of customers elect to stay at Joe's parlour to have the work done. The other 30% go elsewhere.

Those drivers who choose to have the work done at Joe's sit in the lounge from which they can watch one of Joe's fitters work on their car on the ramp. When the fitter is finished, Joe inspects the work, and, if it is satisfactory, he prints the bill for the driver who then pays and leaves. If Joe decides that the work is not satisfactory (which seems to happen to 10% of the jobs), then the fitter must rework the job – and this may take as long as the original work. Rework is inspected in the same way as the original job.

Joe would like some advice from you. He needs to know how many fitters and ramps he should employ in the Parlour. He is very secretive about his finances and will not give you this information, preferring to carry out a financial analysis himself after you have advised him about fitters and ramps. Ideally, he would like to keep his customers waiting for rather less than 10 minutes before he inspects their vehicle after their arrival; he would also like to ensure that customers spend less than 60 minutes in total at the Parlour.

Activity cycle diagram – Joe's Exhaust Parlour

Figure 10.10 shows the activity cycle of the driver/car combination – note that this is the first simplification. We will assume that the driver always stays with the car and never goes off elsewhere to do some shopping while the work is being done. We will also simplify things by assuming that lunch breaks are ignored and the correct parts are always available. Figure 10.10 is not a complete ACD, it just shows an annotated activity cycle for the driver/car, but it serves to illustrate some of the basic ideas. First, note that the diagram consists of closed loops – this is an artificiality that actually can be useful as it forces the modeller to think about what happens to the entity at all times. The loops are closed by the creation of an imaginary dead state *Outside* from which the drivers/cars enter Joe's premises and to which they return.

Second, note that each loop consists of alternate active and dead states. This, too, is artificial, but once again this simplification serves an important purpose. If this alternation is observed, then this means that the states fit neatly together. The duration of an active state can be determined in advance, but that of a dead state cannot. Thus, if a dead state sits between two active states,

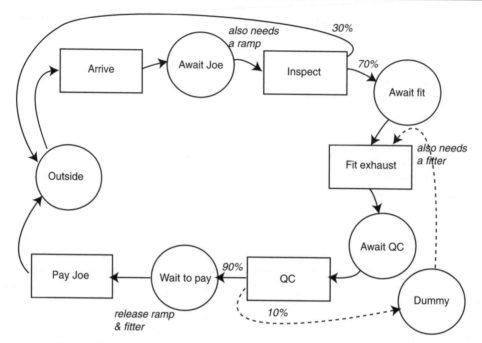

Figure 10.10 Activity cycle diagram – drivers and cars in Joe's Exhaust Parlour.

its behaviour can be inferred from the combined operation of its neighbours. Thus, the time that a driver/car will wait for the final quality control check (dead state *Await QC*) will depend on when the *Fit* active state ends and when the final quality control (active state *QC*) begins.

Finally, it may not be obvious why *Arrive* should be regarded as an active state. It actually represents another artificiality: the interarrival state. To understand this, imagine a machine that takes drivers/cars from *Outside*, and, then, a short time later, delivers them into the dead state *Await Joe*. Once a driver/car enters the dead state, another starts its journey from *Outside*. The time taken to travel from *Outside* to *Await Joe* will be variable unless people arrive according to a timetable. Also marked on the diagram are a few reminders – that 70% of drivers/cars choose to stay with Joe for the replacement work and that 10% of jobs need to be redone. Note that the annotations indicate that extra resources are needed at certain points – namely, ramps and fitters.

Figure 10.11 shows Joe's activity cycles; these are simpler than those of the drivers/cars and also have a rather different appearance. Whereas drivers/cars follow a fairly predictable sequence, Joe has three tasks and may move from one of them to any other. For completeness sake, he is shown as passing through an *Idle* state as he does so.

The activity cycles of drivers/cars and Joe may be linked via their common active states *Inspect*, *QC* and *Pay*. These linkages make it very clear which activities are dependent upon cooperation, and this is one of the points of drawing the diagram. Figure 10.12 shows the final diagram, from which we could, if we wished, write down some of the conditions that govern the activities in the simulation model. For example, for the active state *QC* (the activity of inspecting the new exhaust on a car after it is fitted) to begin, these conditions could be written down as something like the following:

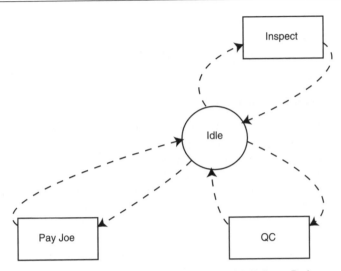

Figure 10.11 Activity cycle diagram – Joe in his Exhaust Parlour.

```
If (at least one driver/car is in state Await QC) AND (Joe is in
state Idle) THEN {
    Change Joe state from Idle to Exhaust QC;
    Take first driver/car, change state from Await QC to Being
    QC'd;
    Decide how long this QC will take;
    Tell the executive to end this QC at this time in the future.
}
```

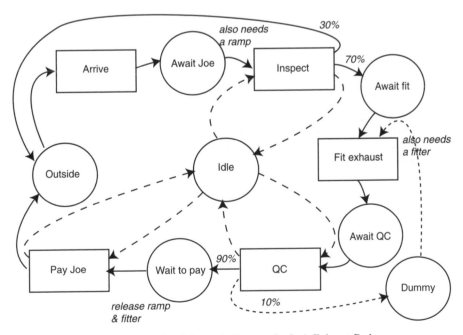

Figure 10.12 Full activity cycle diagram for Joe's Exhaust Parlour.

Note that the active state *QC* needs to be more detailed than the diagram might suggest if we are to enforce the desirable rule that entity classes must have unique states. Thus, we may refer to the state *Exhaust QC* for Joe and to the state *Being QC'd* for the driver/car.

Entities and system resources

What about the ramps and fitters? This has been skated over in the discussion so far. After all, Joe wishes to know how many of them are needed to run his business properly. Why are they not treated as entities in the simulation model? Figures 10.10 and 10.12 show them as annotations, and these imply that they are being treated as system resources rather than as entities. A system resource is something that is used to represent things that can be measured or counted and that are, in effect, identical. This does not mean that fitters are the same as ramps, but does imply that all ramps are the same and all fitters are the same – that is, they are interchangeable. Thus, instead of maintaining state and calendar data about each ramp or fitter, all the program needs to do is keep track of how many are *Free*, *In Use* or whatever other designation we choose. This can be done by the use of simple counters such as *FreeRamps*. If no work is in progress at the start of the simulation, then, if there are five ramps, *FreeRamps* = 5. If *FreeRamps* > 0, this is one of the conditions to be satisfied for the activity *Inspect* to start.

Thus, the logic that governs the inspection of an exhaust on a car that has arrived at Joe's might be expressed in words as follows:

```
If (at least one driver/car is in state Await Joe) AND (Joe is in
state Idle) AND (FreeRamps > 0) THEN {
    Change Joe state from Idle to Inspect Exhaust;
    Take first driver/car, change state from Await Joe to
    Being Inspected;
    Reduce FreeRamps by 1;
    Decide how long this Inspect will take;
    Tell the executive to end this Inspect at this time in the
    future.
}
```

As with the ACD active state *QC*, the active state *Inspect* has been split into two for the two entities involved. At the end of this activity, 30% of the drivers/cars leave the Parlour immediately, in which case the *FreeRamps* would be increased by 1. For the 70% that remain, the ramp is still occupied, and thus *FreeRamps* need not be increased.

Hence, the idea of system resources provides us with a simple way of keeping track of countable, identical items. However, if the items are not identical, or if we needed to keep a detailed track of which ones are in use at any time, then the ramps and/or fitters would need to be modelled as simulation entities. For example, this would be necessary if we wished to monitor the meal-breaks taken by the fitters.

Micro Saint Sharp – a simple VIMS

Many simulations are carried out using VIMS, and this is one of the reasons why computer simulation is discussed in this book. Chapter 7 gives an overview of one such VIMS, Powersim, which is used to develop system dynamics models and which may be used to simulate systems that are modelled in that way. One major technical domain for visual interactive modelling is discrete event simulation. This section of the chapter introduces Micro Saint Sharp or Windows (Micro Analysis and Design, 2009), a simple discrete event simulation VIMS, and shows how it may be used to simulate Joe's Exhaust Parlour. Quite a variety of discrete event simulation VIMS are on the market, and examples include AnyLogic (XJ Technologies, 2009), AutoMod (Applied Materials Inc., 2009), Flexsim (Flexsim Software Products Inc., 2009), ProModel (Promodel Corporation, 2009), Simul8 (Simul8 Corporation, 2009) and Witness (Lanner Systems, 2009). Micro Saint is one of the simpler VIMS, but it is still surprisingly powerful, and this section will provide a general insight into the use of a VIMS.

A VIMS runs within a graphical user interface (GUI), such as Microsoft Windows, or the Apple Macintosh interface. The keyboard, pointing device (e.g. a mouse) and high-resolution, colour graphics screen are used to develop and to run a simulation model. Although using a VIMS does not require fully fledged skills in computer programming, it is usually necessary to define some of the task logic of the simulation using a simplified programming language within a VIMS.

Joe's Exhaust Parlour in Micro Saint Sharp

Micro Saint Sharp is based around the concept of a task network, which is rather like a process map, as shown in Figure 10.13. Thus, to develop the model, the user must decide what tasks must be included in the overall process and must place these in a sequence, which need not be as simple as in Figure 10.13 and could include complex decision points. Each task is shown on the network as a named icon, for which Micro Saint uses a rounded rectangle shape by default, although this can be changed. The tasks are linked by arrows representing the flow of the tasks for the main simulation objects – drivers/cars in this case. Thus, to use a task network of this type, it is necessary to think in terms of the main objects that flow through the system. In essence, everything else is treated as a resource. Figure 10.13 shows a task network for Joe's Exhaust Parlour that contains six tasks: *Arrival, Inspect, Replace, Check, PayJoe* and *Leave*. The links

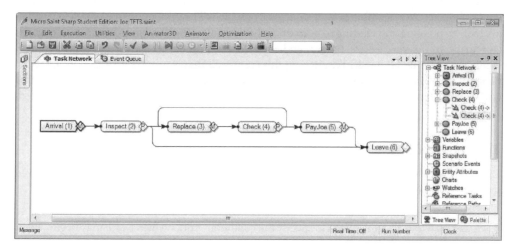

Figure 10.13 Micro Saint task network for Joe's Exhaust Parlour.

between the tasks represent the flow of the main entity class of the system – drivers (or cars) in this example. Thus, for example, Joe checks an exhaust (the *Check* task) only after one has been fitted (in the *Replace* task), and sometimes a car is routed back for a (re)replacement after it has been checked.

Note that the appearance of the arrival task in Figure 10.13 differs from the rest. This is an entity generator, which generates new entities (drivers with cars in this case) into the system at the requisite intervals. Note also that a diamond shape is at the end of each task, relating to the routing decision at the end of the task. The letter contained in the diamond indicates the type of routing decision, and Micro Saint Sharp includes three such types:

1. *Probabilistic.* These contain the letter P and are used when proportions of entities follow the routes after the task. For example, 70% of cars/drivers continue through to the *Replace* task after the *Inspect* task, and 30% move to the *Leave* task.
2. *Multiple.* These contain the letter M and are the default routing applied by Micro Saint Sharp when a task is added to a network. They allow a task to spawn multiple versions of the 'same' entity; for example, to separate cars and drivers at some point in the process were that to be needed. M routings are shown on the *Arrival*, *Replace* and *PayJoe* tasks in Figure 10.13, although none has multiple outputs. This is because, strange though it may same, 'multiple' means any number greater than or equal to 1, and this is why tasks are given an M routing by default.
3. *Tactical.* These contain the letter T, but there are none in Figure 10.13. Tactical routers are used when an entity could move to more than one task after completing its current task and the choice depends on defined factors. For example, Joe might use stronger ramps for vehicles above a certain weight, and this could be represented by a special subnetwork for those vehicles. The T router would check the weight of a vehicle (which would be an attribute of the entity) and route it accordingly.

As with all VIMS, there are forms and dialogue boxes in which the user may provide data to parameterize the elements of the system. Clicking on a task icon in Micro Saint Sharp opens the appropriate dialogue box or window. These cover aspects such as task durations (which may be samples from probability distributions or might be constants), details of decision nodes and limits on queue sizes. Sensible default values are provided. The simulation model is developed in a VIMS by pointing and clicking so as to draw the network using the appropriate icons, linkages and forms. In this way, a basic model can be developed without any computer programming – familiarity with the GUI (MS Windows in this case) is all that is needed. However, to be really useful, a simulation VIMS must allow the user some way to express the logic of the events that govern the behaviour of the entities and their state changes. This logic may be very complicated.

Task logic in Micro Saint

Each VIMS allows the user to express this logic in different ways. Micro Saint is task-based, and it thus allows the user to define the following logic of those tasks:

- *Release conditions.* These are used to specify the conditions under which a task may begin. Thus, in Joe's Exhaust Parlour, Joe must be free and at least one ramp must be available for the *Inspect* task to begin; that is, before a driver/car is released into this task. Micro Saint Sharp will automatically check that there is a driver/car in the queue, as the queue is linked by the system itself to the correct task.

- *Beginning effect*. This defines what happens immediately as the task starts. In the case of *Inspect*, this would be that Joe is no longer free and that there is one less ramp available.
- *Ending effect*. This defines what happens immediately after the end of the task. In the case of *Inspect*, this would be that Joe is now free again. As with incoming queue logic, Micro Saint Sharp links the probabilistic node after *Inspect* to this task and automatically deposits the driver/car into this node. From there they will proceed either to the *Check* queue or to *Leave*.
- *Launch effect*. This is a bit more subtle and permits the user to carry out tasks after the task duration has been computed, which is done automatically by the Micro Saint Sharp control program. This might, for example, allow action to be taken if the task duration would take the task completion time beyond the end of the working day.

Thus, Micro Saint and other simulation VIMS allow the user to specify the detailed event logic of the system. One problem with these VIMS is that each one seems to use its own programming language for this purpose. Micro Saint Sharp is so named because it uses the C# language for this purpose and also relies on the Microsoft.NET framework to link it to other Windows applications. This is convenient, but does require programming expertise. For example, the C# code for the beginning effect of the *Inspect* task might look as follows:

```
JoeFree = false;
FreeRamps--;
InspectQ--;
Entity.WaitInspectTime = Clock - Entity.ArrivalTime;
if (Entity.WaitInspectTime > MaxWaitTime) {MaxWaitTime =
Entity.WaitInspectTime;}
```

The first line sets Joe as not free (he is required to inspect the exhaust) by using a Boolean variable, *JoeFree*. The second line reduces the number of free ramps by 1, using an integer variable *FreeRamps*. The third line reduces the count of those waiting for an inspection by decrementing an integer variable *InspectQ*. The fourth line computes the time that an entity (a car/driver) has waited by calculating the difference between the current time in the simulation (*Clock*) and the time at which the entity arrived (the integer variable *Entity.ArrivalTime*, in which the dot indicates that *ArrivalTime* is an attribute of the *Entity*). The final line uses an integer variable *Max* to keep track of the maximum time for which any entity has waited so far and enables Joe to see if his 10-minute target is being met. The Tree View at the right-hand side of Figure 10.13 is used to define and keep track of the variables used by Micro Saint Sharp.

As well as providing an easy way to develop a model on screen, a VIMS such as Micro Saint Sharp supports parsimonious modelling. When using a VIMS there is no need to develop a complete model before running it to see how it behaves. In the case of Joe's Exhaust Parlour, it would be possible to place just two tasks on screen (*Arrive* and *Inspect*, for example) to provide some parameters for these tasks and then to run the model. Once this all-too-simple model runs OK, then other tasks can be added. Similarly, the existence of default logic in the VIMS means that almost 'empty' tasks can be added, and the simulation may be run with them in place. The 'proper' logic may then be added, a step at a time, until the model reaches the required level of detail. This stepwise development is crucial and is an entirely normal part of simulation model development. It is unlikely that the precise specification of the model can be known in advance for most simulations.

Running a Micro Saint model

A VIMS should also provide an interactive environment within which the model may be run. This means that the simulation can be carried out like a video game with interactive experimentation. As the simulation is run, the screen can be arranged to provide a display that shows the main features of the system being simulated. In some systems, these features can appear in multiple on-screen windows. Thus, the user can watch the model run and might observe, for example, that queues build up very quickly and are not dissipated. This suggests a shortage of system resources of some kind, and the display may make it clear where this bottleneck is occurring. Thus, the user may interrupt the running simulation, may add extra resources and may then restart the simulation or may continue the run, but with extra resources. In this way, the user will use the visual interactive features of the VIMS to navigate towards an acceptable system design. As part of this run-time support, Micro Saint allows the user to watch a number of different windows as the simulation proceeds. Examples include the following:

- *The network diagram.* This is the task network drawn on screen to develop the model. As the simulation runs, this can be animated to show the build-up and movement of entities through the system. This gives some idea of the level of activity and of the build-up of queues.
- *The variable catalogue.* All variables defined by the user are accessible, and a selection can be displayed in a window as the simulation runs. Thus, the actual values of queue sizes can be watched as the simulation proceeds.
- *Animator.* This is a different iconic representation of the model, in which objects may be drawn to resemble the physical system. Thus, icons may be developed for Joe, the fitters, ramps and cars. Cars may be shown arriving, waiting for service, and moving on to and from ramps, and the fitters and Joe may be seen attending to them. This can be useful for demonstrating the simulation to a client and convincing them of its acceptability.
- *The event queue.* This is the technical heart of the Micro Saint control program, and it shows the calendar on to which events are entered and from which they are executed at the correct simulation time. This can be very useful for debugging a model.
- *Watches.* This window is used to keep track of particular variables as the simulation runs – for example, the maximum waiting time for initial inspection.

Thus, like other VIMS, Micro Saint Sharp provides visual tools for model development, for debugging, for client presentations and for model refinement. In addition there are analysis tools for the analysis of the results of simulation runs, and the simulation output can also be exported in common formats to be read by spreadsheets and statistical analysis packages.

Simul8 – a powerful, low-cost VIMS

Simul8 (Simul8 Corporation, 2009) is another VIMS that runs under Microsoft Windows and has the significant advantage over many other simulation VIMS of a price structure closer to that of standard PC software. As simulation VIMS are specialist software packages with limited markets, their prices tend to be high, often well over £10 000 per copy, whereas that of Simul8 is much more sensible. Simul8 has many similar features to Micro Saint and is just as easy to use. The main difference is that a Micro Saint simulation is based on a task network, whereas the

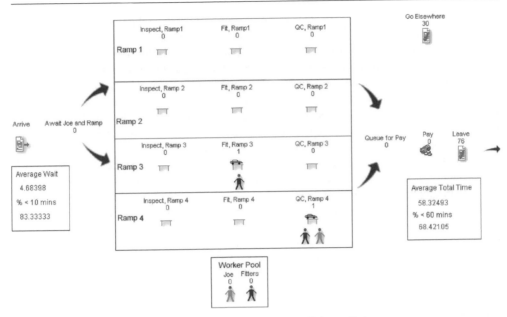

Figure 10.14 Simul8 model for Joe's Exhaust Parlour.

Simul8 model is based around a machine network. A Simul8 diagram for Joe's Exhaust Parlour is shown in Figure 10.14. and its objects are as follows.

The central part of the diagram shows four rectangles, each representing one ramp, and each ramp has three associated tasks: *Inspect*, *Fit* and *QC*. The left-hand side of the diagram is used to represent the arrival of cars/drivers and the queue in which they must wait until a ramp is free and one of the four ramps is unoccupied. Below the ramps is a worker pool that represents the fitters and Joe, these being needed for the tasks in the model. On the right-hand side of the diagram, the objects represent the cars/drivers as the ramp work is completed. Thus, they queue to pay, they pay and then they leave. At the top right-hand corner of the diagram there is a further object that is used to represent those cars/drivers that decide not to have their exhaust replaced at Joe's Parlour after he has inspected them. Some simple output statistics that can be used to understand how well the system is running are shown in the two rectangles labelled as *Average Wait* and *Average Total Time*.

As with Micro Saint Sharp and other VIMS, each Simul8 object has properties that can be given values. For example, the properties for *Arrive* include the probability distribution used to generate the new customers and the out-routing from this that leads to *Await Joe* and *Ramp*. Similarly, the properties of *Inspect, Ramp 1* include the probability distribution for the time taken for an inspection, the in-routing (from *Await Joe* and *Ramp*), the out-routing (to *Fit, Ramp 1*) and the resources needed – Joe in this case. The properties are set using standard Windows forms. Also, like Micro Saint, it is possible to open other windows as the simulation runs so as to check on the detailed internal workings of the simulation using a simulation monitor. Finally, like Micro Saint, Simul8 includes its own programming language, known as Visual Logic in this case.

There is, though, at least one important difference between the Micro Saint Sharp and Simul8 models. The task metaphor used by Micro Saint Sharp means that there is no need to show a separate set of tasks for each ramp. Instead, Micro Saint Sharp just shows the overall task logic, and the ramps are treated as resources that are needed to start a task and are released when a task sequence is complete. This makes it simpler to change the number of ramps, but has the disadvantage that an animation will not show the state of each separate ramp. On the other hand, in the Simul8 model, icons that represent cars/drivers, Joe and the fitters can show the state of each repair that is in progress. Users may find this a great help in understanding the simulation as it runs. A similar animated display can be produced in Micro Saint Sharp, using the Animator window, but this needs to be developed after the task network is complete. In this way, it is possible to make Micro Saint Sharp show each ramp separately, and it is possible to reduce the clarity of the Simul8 representation. However, in either case, this means that the underlying metaphor of the VIMS is violated.

As mentioned earlier, the underlying metaphor of Micro Saint Sharp is that a model consists of a sequence of tasks for which resources are needed. This leads to a task network that hides the state of individual resources that are used and released as the simulation proceeds. Simul8, though, is best regarded as based on a machine network in which the machines may undertake several tasks. It is impossible to say which approach is better, as it depends on the system to be simulated and the form of visual output that is required. If, however, the underlying metaphor starts to become a problem, it may be time to use a VIMS based on the opposite approach.

The effects of stochastic variation

As was mentioned earlier, the time that an entity spends in a state (e.g. being served) may not be deterministic but may be variable. That is, if we were able to observe how long a particular activity took on a number of occasions, we may find that the time taken varies and that this variation may be represented by a probability distribution. This variation through time is known as stochastic variation and is a feature of many systems simulated by discrete event methods. The inclusion of stochastic elements within a simulation model means that great care must be taken when analysing its results. This book is not the place to go into a detailed discussion of the statistical analysis of such models; excellent coverage of this is given by Law (2007) and Kleijnen and van Groenendal (1992). Instead, some of the basic principles will be spelled out here.

Figure 10.3 showed a histogram of patient consultation times with a doctor, and this was used in Table 10.2 to develop a sampling plan so as to take random samples from the histogram using top-hat sampling. Table 10.4 is an extended version of Table 10.3 and shows the result of 10 top-hat samples from the histogram. The second column shows the random numbers, and the

Table 10.4 First 10 consultation time samples.

	Random number	Sample	Running mean	Running SE	Lower CL	Upper CL
1	0.218	5	5.000	0.000		
2	0.572	6	5.500	0.707	−3.485	14.485
3	0.025	3	4.667	1.080	0.019	9.314
4	0.779	8	5.500	1.202	1.675	9.325
5	0.576	6	5.600	0.908	3.078	8.122
6	0.798	8	6.000	0.849	3.819	8.181
7	0.269	5	5.857	0.724	4.086	7.628
8	0.750	7	6.000	0.639	4.489	7.511
9	0.888	9	6.333	0.661	4.808	7.859
10	0.376	6	6.300	0.589	4.968	7.632

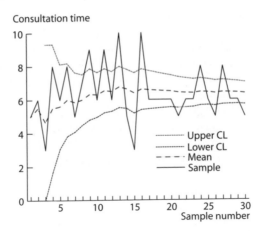

Figure 10.15 Confidence limits in stochastic simulation.

third column is the sample produced by using Table 10.2 to transform them into the required distribution. The fourth column shows the running mean, this being the mean of all the samples produced at this stage. The true mean of this histogram is 6.5, and the running mean is an estimate of the true mean. In order to show the likely accuracy of this estimate, we can compute 95% confidence limits, and these are shown in the last two columns. The confidence limits (CL) are computed in the standard way as follows:

$$\text{Lower 95\% CL} = x - t_{0.05,n-1} \times \text{SE}$$
$$\text{Upper 95\% CL} = x - t_{0.05,n-1} \times \text{SE}$$

where $t_{0.05,n-1}$ is the t value for a two-tailed Student's t-distribution with a probability of 0.05 at $(n-1)$ degrees of freedom (n is the sample size), and SE is the standard error of the samples (being the sample standard deviation divided by the square root of the sample size).

Student's t-distribution is needed because the sample size is small. An extended set of 20 more such samples, giving 30 in all, is shown in Figure 10.15. This shows four lines: the sampled times, the running mean and the lower and upper confidence limits. We can be 95% sure that the true value of the mean (which we actually know is 6.5) is within the two confidence limits (4.97–7.63). Note how the limits converge as the sample size increases. Initially the convergence is rapid, but then it becomes rather slow. Repeated stochastic simulation results display similar behaviour to the simple example.

This simple example illustrates a number of important aspects of any stochastic simulation, no matter how complicated. The first is that such simulations need to be regarded as sampling experiments. The results of each experiment will depend on the random number streams that are used to produce the required samples. Different random numbers will transform into different samples, and thus simulations that use different random numbers will produce different results. For confidence in the results, it is important to ensure that a set of results is produced and analysed using appropriate statistical methods. The greater the number of runs, the greater the degree of confidence that the results are representative. As is clear from Figure 10.15, the confidence limits converge quickly at first and then rather slowly. The smaller the gap between the limits, the greater will be the precision of the results. The simulation literature includes variance reduction techniques to be employed to help speed up this convergence.

The second point is that, if a stochastic simulation is being used to compare two or more policy options (e.g. do we need 10 or 16 emergency beds?), then, as far as is possible, each option should be run with the same random numbers. This is to ensure that the comparison is a fair one, given that the random numbers used will affect the results. This technique, known as streaming or common random numbers, seeks to ensure that the effects of randomness are properly contained across policy comparisons.

The third point is that, if a stochastic simulation is being used, any experimentation needs to be properly and carefully designed. The analysis of experiments is a statistical minefield for the unwary and a source of some amusement among professional statisticians. Simulation modellers whose knowledge of experimental design and analysis is slight should seek statistical help in some form or other.

These points remain valid whether the simulation model is a static one developed in a spreadsheet or is a discrete event simulation implemented in a specially written computer program or via a VIMS such as Micro Saint Sharp, Simul8 or one of the expensive packages. If a VIMS is used, then interactive experimentation should be used to reduce the size of the set of sensible experimental options. For example, a hospital may be considering how many emergency beds are needed, and it may become clear from a VIMS simulation that with fewer than 10 beds the system cannot cope, and that providing more than 20 beds is unnecessary. If this is so, then the options between 10 and 20 should be carefully investigated with properly designed experiments.

Summary

Computer simulation offers a way to investigate systems that are uncertain or variable. A computer model is built and is then used to carry our experiments to understand how the system will operate. The uncertainty and variability can be represented by probability distributions from which random samples are taken, and this sampling forms a major part of most simulation models. If the system of interest is dynamic, complicated and highly interactive, then a discrete event simulation may be required.

Progress within computer simulation has depended on general developments in computing. Thus, it seems that most discrete event simulations are now built into VIMS, which make it possible for people who are not expert computer programmers to develop discrete simulation models and permit dynamic displays to be used to show the results of the simulation experiments as well. Further, these VIMS fit well with the principles of modelling discussed in Chapter 4. In particular, they enable the modeller to 'model simple and think complicated', and they support the principle of parsimony.

Simulation methods can also be useful in situations that are less dynamic and interactive, such as in financial modelling and risk analysis. Using spreadsheet add-ins, powerful simulations can be constructed of such systems.

References

Applied Materials Inc. (2009) Promodel software: www.appliedmaterials.com/products/automod_2.html
Beadle R. (1986) Designing the control of automated factories, in *Simulation Applications in Manufacturing*, ed. by Hurrion R.D. IFS, Kempston, UK.

Bhaskar R., Lee H.S., Levas A., Pétrakian R., Tsai F. and Tulskie W. (1994) Analyzing re-engineering business processes using simulation, in *Proceedings of the 1994 Winter Simulation Conference, Lake Buena Vista, FL*, ed. by Tew J.D., Manivannan S., Sadowski D.A. and Seila A. IEEE, Piscataway, NY.

Bier I.J. and Tjelle J.P. (1994) The importance of interoperability in a simulation prototype for spares inventory planning, in *Proceedings of the 1994 Winter Simulation Conference, Lake Buena Vista, FL*, ed. by Tew J.D., Manivannan S., Sadowski D.A. and Seila A. IEEE, Piscataway, NY.

Brailsford S.C., Shahani A.X., Roy R.B. and Sivapalan S. (1992) Simulation modeling for HIV-infection and AIDS. *International Journal of Bio-Medical Computing*, **31**(2), 73–88.

Burnett D. and LeBaron T. (2001) Efficiently modeling warehouse systems, in *Proceedings of the 2001 Winter Simulation Conference, Arlington, VA*, ed. by Peters B.A., Smith J.S., Medeiros D.J. and Rohrer M.W. IEEE, Piscataway, NY.

Buxton J.N. and Laski J.G. (1962) Control and simulation language. *The Computer Journal*, **5**(3).

Ceric V. (1990) Simulation study of an automated guided-vehicle system in a Yugoslav hospital. *Journal of the Operational Research Society*, **41**(4), 299–310.

Davies M.N. (1994) Back-office process management in the financial services – a simulation approach using a model generator. *Journal of the Operational Research Society*, **45**(12), 1363–1373.

Davies R., Roderick P., Canning C. and Brailsford S. (2002) The evaluation of screening policies for diabetic retinopathy using simulation. *Diabetic Medicine*, **19**(9), 762–770.

Fletcher A., Halsall D., Huxham D. and Worthington D. (2007) The DH Accident and Emergency Department model: a national generic model used locally. *Journal of the Operational Research Society*, **58**(12), 1554–1562.

Flexsim Software Products Inc. (2009) Flexsim simulation software: www.flexsim.com

Günal M.M. and Pidd M. (2006) Understanding accident and emergency department performance using simulation, in *Proceedings of the 2006 Winter Simulation Conference, Monterey, CA*, ed. by Perrone L.F., Wieland F.P., Liu J., Lawson B.G., Nicol D.M. and Fujimoto R.M. IEEE, Piscataway, NY.

Günal M.M. and Pidd M. (2008) DGHPSim: supporting smart thinking to improve hospital performance, in *Proceedings of the 2008 Winter Simulation Conference, Miami, FL*, ed. by Mason S.J., Hill R., Mönch L., Rose O., Jefferson T. and Fowler J.W. IEEE, Piscataway, NY, pp. 1484–1489.

Harrell C.R. (1993) Modeling beverage processing using discrete event simulation, in *Proceedings of the 1993 Winter Simulation Conference, Los Angeles, CA*, ed. by Evans G.W., Mollaghasemi M., Russell E.C. and Biles W.E. IEEE, Piscataway, NY.

Heath W. (1993) Waterfront capacity-planning simulations, in *Proceedings of the 1993 Winter Simulation Conference, Los Angeles, CA*, ed. by Evans G.W., Mollaghasemi M., Russell E.C. and Biles W.E. IEEE, Piscataway, NY.

High Performance Systems (2009) Stella/iThink software: http://www.hpc-inc.com

Jacobson S.H., Sewell E.C. and Weniger W.G. (2001) Using Monte Carlo simulation to assess the value of combination vaccines for pediatric immunization, in *Proceedings of the 2001 Winter Simulation Conference, Arlington, VA*, ed. by Peters B.A., Smith J.S., Medeiros D.J. and Rohrer M.W. IEEE, Piscataway, NY.

Joustra P.E. and Van Dijk N.M. (2001) Simulation of check-in at airports, in *Proceedings of the 2001 Winter Simulation Conference, Arlington, VA*, ed. by Peters B.A., Smith J.S., Medeiros D.J. and Rohrer M.W. IEEE, Piscataway, NY.

Kleijnen J. and van Groenendal W. (1992) *Simulation: A Statistical Perspective*. John Wiley & Sons, Ltd, Chichester, UK.

Laguna M. and Marklund J. (2005) *Business Process Modeling, Design and Simulation*. Pearson/Prentice Hall, Upper Saddle River, NJ.

Lanner Systems (2009) Witness software: http://www.lanner.com

Law A.M. (2007) *Simulation Modeling and Analysis*, 4th edition. McGraw-Hill, New York, NY.

Lee S., Pritchett A. and Goldsman D. (2001) Hybrid agent-based simulation for analyzing the national airspace system, in *Proceedings of the 2001 Winter Simulation Conference, Arlington, VA*, ed. by Peters B.A., Smith J.S., Medeiros D.J. and Rohrer M.W. IEEE, Piscataway, NY.

Micro Analysis and Design (2009) Micro Saint for Windows software: www.maad.com

Miller D.J. (1994) The role of simulation in semi-conductor logistics, in *Proceedings of the 1994 Winter Simulation Conference, Lake Buena Vista, FL*, ed. by Tew J.D., Manivannan S., Sadowski D.A. and Seila A. IEEE, Piscataway, NY.

Oracle Crystal Ball (2009) Oracle and Crystal Ball: www.oracle.com/crystallball

Palisade Corporation (2009) The DecisionTools Suite: www.palisade.com/decisiontools_suite

Park C.A. and Getz T. (1992) The approach to developing a future pharmaceuticals manufacturing facility (using SIMAN and AutoMod), in *Proceedings of the 1992 Winter Simulation Conference, Arlington, VA*, ed. by Swain J.J., Goldsman D., Crain R.C. and Wilson J.R. IEEE, Piscataway, NY.

Pidd M. (1987) Simulating automated food plants. *Journal of the Operational Research Society*, **38**(8), 683–692.

Pidd M. (1995) The construction of an object-oriented traffic simulator, in *Proceedings of the 3rd EURO Working Group on Transportation, Barcelona, Spain, September 1995*, ed. by Barcelo J. Institut Català d'Estudis del Transport, Barcelona, Spain.

Pidd M. (2004) *Computer Simulation in Management Science*, 5th edition. John Wiley & Sons, Ltd, Chichester, UK.

Powersim Corporation (2009) Powersim software: http://www.powersim.com

Promodel Corporation (2009) Promodel software: www.promodel.com

Rathi A.K. and Santiago A.J. (1990) The new NETSIM simulation model. *Traffic Engineering and Control*, **31**(5), 317.

Robinson T. (2001) ODIN – an underwater warfare simulation environment, in *Proceedings of the 2001 Winter Simulation Conference, Arlington, VA*, ed. by Peters B.A., Smith J.S., Medeiros D.J. and Rohrer M.W. IEEE, Piscataway, NY.

Salt J. (1991) Tunnel vision. *OR/MS Today*, **18**(1), 42–48.

Simul8 Corporation (2009) Simul8 software: http://www.simul8.com

Watts I. (c. 1719) O God Our Help in Ages Past, hymn based on Psalm 90.

Wears R.L. and Winton C.N. (1993) Simulation modeling of pre-hospital trauma care, in *Proceedings of the 1993 Winter Simulation Conference, Los Angeles, CA*, ed. by Evans G.W., Mollaghasemi M., Russell E.C. and Biles W.E. IEEE, Piscataway, NY.

Williams D.L., Finke D.A., Medeiros D.J. and Traband M.T. (2001) Discrete simulation development for a proposed shipyard steel processing facility, in *Proceedings of the 2001 Winter Simulation Conference, Arlington, VA*, ed. by Peters B.A., Smith J.S., Medeiros D.J. and Rohrer M.W. IEEE, Piscataway, NY.

XJ Technologies (2009) AnyLogic simulation software: www.xjtek.com

Young W., Taylor M.A.P. and Gipps P.G. (1989) *Microcomputers in Traffic Engineering*. John Wiley & Sons Research Studies Press, Chichester, UK.

11 Heuristic search

Background

This final chapter of Part III considers a third approach to modelling in Management Science – heuristic search. The term 'heuristic' has a number of meanings, but here it refers to approaches that give no guarantee that they will reach the best solution. This contrasts with the optimization methods such as linear programming, discussed in Chapter 9. In linear programming, the method guarantees that an optimum solution to a correctly formulated model will be found, if it exists. As has been consistently argued in this book, this does not guarantee that the optimum solution to the model will be the best solution in practice. This can only be the case if the model is a perfect fit to the system being modelled, which is unlikely.

Heuristic search, like computer simulation, gives no guarantee that any proposed solution will be optimum – even in the context of the model, let alone in the context of the system being modelled. Although these search methods share this limitation with simulation approaches, there is also an important difference – a simulation approach is usually based on experiments guided by humans (see Figure 11.1). The idea is that the experimenter thinks up possible options and uses the simulation model to see what would happen if these were followed. In common parlance, this is known as a 'what if' approach. By contrast, heuristic search methods provide ways of automatically generating solutions to problems that have been formulated in certain ways. They are approximate approaches (Foulds, 1983) in that they aim to come as close as possible to some optimum – but they may fail to do so. For example, some people believe that always taking the second turn to the right is a rapid way to escape from a maze such as the one at Hampton Court. It would seem that their confidence is misplaced.

Heuristic search methods are included here for two reasons. First, their use in Management Science is increasing because they offer ways to tackle certain types of problem that are computationally rather complex and yet have a practical payoff. Examples of this might be the scheduling of transport systems, the control of emergency services or the timetabling of large events. The second reason for their inclusion is that they take Management Science to the edge of Artificial Intelligence methods as seen in Evolutionary Computation. Although the honeymoon period of Artificial Intelligence is long over, there are great benefits in being able to design human–machine systems that are able to cope with complicated circumstances. Management Science practitioners can help play a part in the design and appraisal of such systems, which means that they and their customers may need to be aware of these methods.

This chapter covers three metaheuristics: tabu search, simulated annealing and genetic algorithms. The term metaheuristic implies a generic approach that needs to be made more specific in order to apply it to a particular problem. Thus, within each of the three metaheuristics covered here, there are multiple variations on the same theme. Extensive coverage of widely used metaheuristics, including the three covered here, can be found in Reeves (1995a) and Glover and Kochenberger (2003).

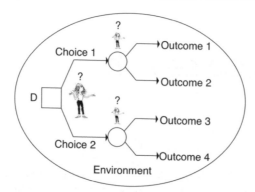

Figure 11.1 Decision-making as sequential search.

The basic idea – two analogies

Most metaheuristics are based on the idea of search. The principle is that some feasible starting solution is found and that an iterative procedure is used to search, sequentially, for better solutions. Two analogies may help to clarify this. The first is the idea of sequential searches through a decision space, which is close to the ideas proposed by Simon and Newell (1958). As discussed in Chapter 2, Simon was concerned to understand how humans made decisions, and he proposed a view that is sometimes described as linear, or sequential, search. The basic idea of this is shown in Figure 2.1 and is shown here, in a slightly revised form, in Figure 11.1. In essence it imagines that the task of a decision-maker is to start from the left-hand side of the figure and move towards the right-hand side, hoping to end up at a destination that is either optimal or satisfactory. To do so, the decision-maker is faced with a series of choices that constitutes the solution space of the problem. Simon points out that decision-makers do not have perfect information and that, for this and for other reasons, they do not actually optimize. Instead, they satisfice – they find solutions that are satisfactory in some sense or other, and they employ heuristics to do so. This implies that the search starts from the left and proceeds towards the right but could go on for a very long time. The search stops when a good enough point is reached.

This idea of a heuristic, as proposed by Simon and Newell (1958), was that it should provide a rule of thumb by which choices could be made as the decision-maker moved through the network of options. Simon (1978) was specifically interested, at one stage, in decision-making in the game of chess. He suggested that experienced chess-players develop heuristics that enable them to rapidly scan through possible options when faced with recognizable positions on the board. Thus, he argued, experienced (and successful) chess-players learn to recognize clumps of similar situations and develop heuristics for dealing with them. As has been made clear elsewhere in this book, especially in Part II, there are many situations in which this sequential search view of decision-making breaks down. Nevertheless, it does have its uses, especially when its limitations are understood.

As a second analogy, imagine an explorer searching, in the dark and without a map, for the deepest valley in a mountain region. Suppose she has been dropped off by a helicopter and told to find her way down – how can she do this? An obvious strategy is to head downward whenever possible, feeling her way slowly in the dark. This will work if the explorer is fortunate enough to find herself in terrain containing only a single valley. However, in most such explorations, there will be more than one valley and some of them may sit above one another. In Figure 11.2

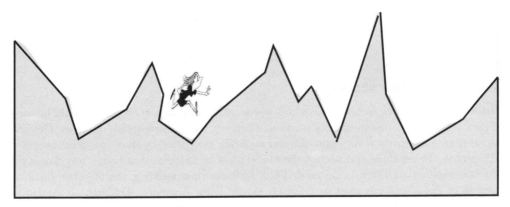

Figure 11.2 Exploring in the dark.

our explorer has found the bottom of one valley, but this is not the lowest point in the terrain. The problem facing her is to find some way of climbing over the intervening hills so as to find her way to the lowest point. In Figure 11.2 we have a great advantage over her, we can see where she needs to get to; that is, we have perfect knowledge. However, if we were the explorer, then neither we nor anyone else would have perfect knowledge, and we would be, figuratively, floundering in the dark.

The metaheuristics discussed here attempt to provide strategies that enable the search to proceed until we have a reasonable assurance that we are at, or near, the minimum point. Note that there can be no certainty about this unless we know the shape of the terrain – and, if we knew that, we would not need to search in this way. If the problem is one of maximization, then the analogy is with searching for the highest point in the dark. Simple though this analogy is to understand, it perhaps does not convey the scale of problems for which modem heuristic methods are suited. It is easy to imagine the search problem in three dimensions, which certainly complicates things. Problems to which these methods are applied have the mathematical equivalent of huge numbers of dimensions. Thus, efficient search procedures are vital.

To use these heuristic search methods, a number of things are needed. The first is that there must be some objective function. As discussed in Chapter 9, when referring to linear programming, this is a consistent way of working out the cost or return from any choice that is made. In terms of the search for the lowest point in Figure 11.2, the objective function might measure the depth at which the search is currently located. Thus, it must relate directly to the choices and actions that are available. That is, the notion of 'cost' need not imply cash or monetary value. As in optimization, this objective function must be minimized or maximized. In a minimization problem, for example, it may refer to distance (in a situation where vehicles need to be routed), deaths (in a situation where a limited budget needs to be spread over a range of treatments) or time (when best use needs to be made of available time). In a maximization problem, the measure might be something like the number of customers served (in a situation in which goods need to be distributed) or the number of patients within 30 minutes' travelling time of a clinic (in a situation where clinics need to be located). In either case, the 'cost' could be a combination of factors rather than a single value.

The second requirement for their use is that, to use the analogy of the terrain again, it is desirable to be able to get from any point to any other point. This does not mean that the journey must be straightforward; it may be very tortuous indeed. But the search procedures require the different options to be interconnected in some way or other if they are to work properly.

The third requirement is a search procedure that will enable the heuristic to find its way, step by step, to a desirable solution.

Why use heuristic search?

Before looking at three metaheuristics, it is worth asking why such approaches should be used if they cannot guarantee an optimal solution. There are two answers to this question. The first stems from a comparison with optimization methods, as typified by linear programming (see Chapter 9). To use these approaches, the model must be formulated in such a way that it fits the optimization approach being used. Thus, in linear programming, the objective function and all of the constraints must be relatively simple linear functions. Although, as argued in Chapters 3 and 4, all models are simplifications and approximations, for many applications such simplification may be an approximation too far. The model may have to be so distorted that its solutions are far, far removed from the real world in which they need to be implemented. In such cases, it may make much more sense to use a heuristic approach even though there is no guarantee of optimality. A near-optimal solution to a good model may be much better than an optimum solution to a bad one.

The second reason relates to the computational demands made by many optimization algorithms. This book is not the place to discuss this in detail (for a readable and thorough account, see Reeves and Beasley, 1995), but the issue is simple enough. Consider the problem of designing a laminated material with 10 distinct inner layers sandwiched between some outer coating. If all the layers must be present once, but their order is irrelevant, then there are $3\,628\,800\,(10 \times 9 \times 8 \times \cdots \times 2 \times 1)$ permutations. If the number of layers increases to 12, then the number of permutations rises to over 479 million. The problem is that the number of options available may increase exponentially as the size of the problem increases. Many optimization algorithms, although guaranteeing an optimum solution, have a solution time that increases exponentially as the size of the problem increases. Thus, for many very large problems, even if the model is a good representation of the real system and even if very powerful computers are brought to bear, the solution times are simply too long to be of use. This is particularly true of situations in which frequent changes are made to the number and type of options being compared. In such situations, the only practicable way forward may be to use an approximate, that is, heuristic, approach.

Metaheuristics and heuristic strategies

Strictly speaking, an individual heuristic is devised for a particular situation or problem. However, within Management Science, a number of general approaches have developed that are sometimes known as metaheuristics. These approaches provide general guidelines that are valuable across a range of mathematically formulated problems. Useful reviews of these metaheuristics are to be found in Eglese (1986) and Reeves (1995a). This chapter will discuss the basic ideas of three common metaheuristics: simulated annealing, tabu search and genetic algorithms. The premium versions of The Solver (Frontline Systems, 2009) and What's Best (LINDO Systems, 2009) software allow problems to be set up in such a way that some of these metaheuristic approaches can be used. There is not enough space here to give the detail needed for immediate implementation; instead, the aim is to demonstrate their value so that you may decide whether to make the effort to find out more.

Foulds (1983) provided a four-way classification of strategies for heuristic search:

1. *Construction strategies.* These typically begin with the data and information that comprise the problem situation. This is examined for elements that might seem to make a valuable contribution towards some very good final solution. Successive other elements are added if they seem likely to contribute towards improvement. Thus, the starting point is an incomplete solution that is gradually completed. Many of us would do this intuitively when trying to construct a timetable. We might build a conference timetable by, initially, placing all the most popular sessions in non-overlapping time slots. Other sessions are then added around these.
2. *Improvement strategies.* In these approaches, the heuristics begin with some complete and feasible solution to the problem, and this initial solution is gradually modified in a progressive mode so as to improve on it. An example might be a conference timetable that fits within the time allotted to the conference but that could be improved by swapping some sessions.
3. *Component analysis strategies.* These heuristics are based on a 'divide and conquer' approach and are useful when the situation is so complicated that it has to be broken into smaller pieces. The idea is to tackle the components and then put everything together again in some acceptable way. An example of this might be to ensure that two full streams of a conference are scheduled for different days. The individual days are then assembled to form a composite timetable.
4. *Learning strategies.* These heuristics are closest to the idea of sequential search as introduced in Chapter 2 and discussed above. The different options are envisaged as mapped out like the branches of a tree, and some method is devised to move through the tree while seeking to find the best solution. These are close to the ideas of improvement as discussed above.

In many practical situations, two or more of these four strategies may be combined. For example, the overall approach might be based on component analysis, but an improvement strategy might be employed within each component.

Applications of heuristic approaches in Management Science

The field of modern heuristics is changing rapidly, and so any survey of applications is quickly out of date. An interesting review is provided by Rayward-Smith (1995) who reports on a number of successful applications from several countries. In addition, the Management Science journals frequently contain papers that discuss developments, both of theory and practice. For example, work by Dullaert *et al.* (2007) comprises a special cluster within the *European Journal of Operational Research* that is devoted to applications and manufacturing and supply chains. There are also web pages that keep up-to-date lists, including a useful Wikipedia entry, and some of these are in later sections of this chapter. Among the applications reported in Rayward-Smith (1995) are the following:

- *The control of continuous chemical processes.* Cartwright and Cattell (1995) report on the use of genetic algorithms to improve the control of continuous chemical processes. In such processes, feedstock is continually imported into a reactor vessel and the products and other materials are continuously pumped from the vessel at a rate equal to the input of feedstock. Such continuous plants are often much cheaper than comparable batch plants in which the vessel is filled, the reaction takes place and the vessel is then emptied. One important problem in continuous processes is the control of the reaction so that variations in the output product stream are minimized and the process is safe. Heuristics, based on genetic algorithms, were developed so as to control the reactions in a way that was superior to more conventional control systems. This is an application in which the heuristics form part of a control system.

- *The design of telecommunications networks.* Chardaire (1995) reports on the use of simulated annealing to design computer networks that include concentrators employed to link groups of computers into the network. In one form of 'ideal' network, the computers would be organized in a star formation in which each is directly connected to a central server. The problem with this formation is that it is expensive to connect up and therefore local concentrators are employed. In one simple form of this approach, each concentrator becomes the centre of a small cluster of machines and the concentrators are then linked to the central server. Thus, the network becomes hierarchical. Chardaire (1995) reports on how simulated annealing methods can help to design efficient networks that employ such hierarchical concentration. This is an application in which the heuristics are used in design.

- *Timetabling county cricket fixtures.* Wright (1994) describes how he has successfully used a form of tabu search as the basis of a computer system that organizes the fixture list for first-class cricket matches in England. The fixture list needed to be one that reduced unnecessary travel for players and that met a whole series of other constraints. The situation has many complications, such as the long tradition of many first-class teams to play their home games on more than one ground in their home county. Other issues included the need to take account of international fixtures that occur in the season. Wright's efforts were successful, and his system is the basis of the English County Cricket fixture list.

- *Timetabling sessions at a large multistream conference.* Eglese and Rand (1987) discuss the use of simulated annealing heuristics to develop working timetables for multistream conferences so as to minimize undesirable clashes of events. In this case, their aim was to minimize the disappointment suffered by the delegates at the conference if events they wished to attend were scheduled at the same time.

- *Vehicle routing.* Christofides (1985) discusses different approaches to problems connected with vehicle routing, the idea being to meet service criteria while not incurring excessive cost. Eglese (1990) discusses the general ideas of applying simulated annealing methods for this type of application.

Some fundamental ideas

Iterative improvement

The three heuristic strategies to be discussed here – tabu search, simulated annealing and genetic algorithms – have a number of features in common. The first is that they adopt an iterative approach in a quest for improvement. By iterative, we mean that the algorithms proceed step by step, each one building on the previous one – much as our explorer creeps over the terrain in pitch darkness. At each place, she checks her height above sea level to see if she is lower than she last checked or higher. The idea being to proceed in directions that will lead to the best point – whether it be the lowest in the case of minimization or the highest in the case of maximization. It should therefore be clear that, in the terms used by Foulds (1983), these three metaheuristics are primarily to be viewed as improvement strategies. They assume that it is possible to generate some initial, feasible solution from which the improvement may proceed. How long they will take to converge at a point that is near or at the optimum may depend on the starting point as well as on their search strategy.

Neighbourhoods

A second feature of these approaches can also be understood from the analogy of our explorer. Given that the approach is iterative, it also makes sense to limit the number of options considered at each step to those close to the current position. This is the idea of neighbourhood search, in which opportunities for improvement are sought within the immediate locale. Thus, the algorithms need some way of defining the neighbourhood and of knowing the cost of moving from the current position to others within the same neighbourhood.

The strict definition of a neighbourhood is that it comprises the set of solutions that can be reached from the current solution by a simple operation. This is equivalent, in our analogy, to those points that our explorer can reach in her next move. Any point beyond that is not in the neighbourhood. What is meant by a simple operation will depend on the metaheuristic itself. The solution that is better than all others within the current neighbourhood is said to be optimum with respect to this neighbourhood. Within each iteration, the search processes operate by examining the options within the current neighbourhood and then selecting one of them as the next point to move to.

Simple neighbourhood search

Glover and Laguna (1995) suggest that the approaches taken by some of the heuristic strategies discussed here can be generalized within a framework. This consists of the general, iterative algorithm summarized in Figure 11.3. More formally, Glover and Laguna assume that there is a set of feasible solutions, known as X, in which an individual feasible solution is represented

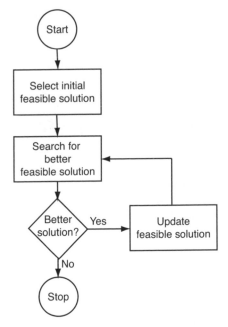

Figure 11.3 A general, iterative, heuristic algorithm.

by the variable x, which is a member of that set. The idea is to start from a feasible solution, possibly selected at random, and then to examine the neighbourhood to find a better feasible solution. The neighbourhood N is defined as the subset of X that can be reached in a simple move. Having found a better solution in the neighbourhood, we now look in its neighbourhood for a better solution until there is no improvement. Thus, each move may redefine the area within which the search is made.

More formally, the general iterative approach, which represents the current solution as x^{now} and its cost as $c(x^{now})$, is as follows:

Step	Activity	Detail
1	Initialization	Select a starting solution x^{now} from X.
		Define $best\_cost = c(x^{now})$.
2	Choice and termination	Choose a solution x^{next} from $N(x^{now})$ such that $c(x^{next}) < c(x^{now})$.
		If no solution qualifies to be x^{now}, then STOP, else proceed to step 3.
3	Update	Put $x^{now} = x^{next}$.
		Put $best\_cost = c(x^{now})$.
		Go to step 2.

Thus, the method searches around the neighbourhood in a tentative way. It accepts moves to any new point that leads to a lower value for the cost function. Once no other point in the neighbourhood leads to an improvement, then the algorithm terminates.

Neighbourhood search with steepest descent

A common variation of simple neighbourhood search is to use the principle of steepest descent when choosing the next solution x_{next} from $N(x_{now})$. This is equivalent to our lost explorer attempting to search around in the neighbourhood of her current location. If she were able to visit all the locations in her neighbourhood, then an intuitively appealing strategy would be to move to the point that takes her deepest. Hence, she does more than just find any point in the neighbourhood that is lower. Instead she finds the lowest point in the current neighbourhood, which, intuitively, should lead to faster convergence on the lowest point.

If the basic algorithm is modified to allow for steepest descent, then it can be expressed as follows:

Step	Activity	Detail
1	Initialization	Select a starting solution x^{now} from X.
		Define $best\_cost = c(x^{now})$.
2	Choice and termination	Choose a solution x^{next} from $N(x^{now})$ such that $c(x^{next}) < c(x^{now})$ and $c(x^{next})$ is $Min(N(x^{now}))$.
		If no solution qualifies to be x^{now}, then STOP, else proceed to step 3.
3	Update	Put $x^{now} = x^{next}$.
		Put $best\_cost = c(x^{now})$.
		Go to step 2.

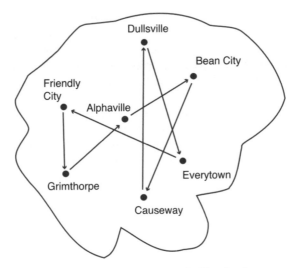

Figure 11.4 A chaotic route in Transitania.

Illustrative example: the travelling salesman problem

Consider Figure 11.4, which shows seven cities in the imaginary country of Transitania. Suppose someone wishes to know the shortest route to follow, starting at Alphaville, visiting each city only once and ending up back at Alphaville. This is a simple example of a general 'problem' called the travelling salesman problem (TSP), which is often used to illustrate heuristic methods. 'Problem' is in quotes because, to use the terminology of Chapter 3, this is really a puzzle to which there is, in fact, a correct solution. The example of Figure 11.4 is very small and could easily be solved by complete enumeration – simply try all the possibilities, compare them and select the one with the lowest total distance. However, although this is possible with just seven cities to visit, the number of options to compare rises exponentially with the number of cities. Nowadays, heuristic methods are used to tackle TSPs with the equivalent of several million cities.

Suppose that this problem has arisen because the one salesman employed in Transitania by Lancaster Products Ltd has just left that company and has been replaced by Jane Wiley. She has to visit the seven cities in Transitania every Friday and would like to minimize the distance that she drives. She starts next week and would like to organize a route that starts from the base at Alphaville and returns there on Friday evening. The Transitanian Automobile Association has given her the data in Table 11.1, which shows the distance (in kilometres) between each pair of

Table 11.1 Distances between Transitanian cities.

	A	B	C	D	E	F	G
A		30	25	32	23	25	32
B			55	33	30	60	70
C				52	37	33	18
D					45	43	57
E						52	50
F							21

cities. Her predecessor was a likeable man, popular with his customers, but a bit disorganized. Piecing together the scraps of paper that he left her, Jane concludes that his usual route was to begin at Alphaville (A), proceed to Bean City (B), then to Causeway (C) and then on to Dullsville (D), arriving back at Alphaville via Everytown (E), Friendly City (F) and Grimthorpe (G). This route is shown in Figure 11.4, which gives the clear impression that it could be improved upon.

It can be convenient to represent such a route by listing the cities in the order in which they are visited, remembering that she needs to return to the base after visiting the last city on her route. The strange route inherited by Jane can be represented by a list, or vector, of the initial letters of the cities that she will visit, presented in the sequence of her itinerary. Hence, if she were to accept her predecessor's rather odd route, then this could be represented as [A, B, C, D, E, F, G]. From Table 11.1, this route incurs a distance 'cost' of $(30 + 55 + 52 + 45 + 52 + 21 + 32)$ km; that is, 287 km.

Neighbourhoods in the TSP

For heuristic methods based on neighbourhood search, it is important to define the neighbourhood, as it constrains the search region for each iteration. In a simple TSP it can be useful to define a two-swap neighbourhood; that is, one that would permit the replacement of any two links with another two. For example, if those between A and B were replaced with those between D and E, this might be written down as remove (A, B) and (B, E) and replace them with two other links. If the current route is [A, B, C, D, E, F, G], then this leads to a new tour of [A, D, C, B, E, F, G]. An alternative expression of the same move would be that the positions of cities B and D are swapped. Both expressions of this move have only one feasible result.

The larger the neighbourhood, the larger the set of options that must be searched within it, which means that the algorithm is slow. However, a small neighbourhood may lead to a search converging quickly on a value that is a long way from the global optimum. The neighbourhood structure restricts the search, and, in simple neighbourhood search, there is an implicit trade-off between neighbourhood size and the likelihood of convergence nearer to the global optimum. Small neighbourhoods result in rapid and efficient searches but may not lead to good solutions. Large neighbourhoods are slow to search, but the search should get closer to a global optimum.

If a TSP includes n locations, the number of possible different tours is

$$\frac{(n-1)!}{n}$$

where $(n-1)!$ means multiply out $(n-1) \times (n-2) \times (n-3) \times \cdots \times 2 \times 1$. In our example there are seven towns, which means that 360 possible tours could be devised. As mentioned earlier, in such a small problem it is feasible to use complete enumeration; that is, to check all the possibilities in order to find the one that involves the shortest overall distance. But combinatorial explosion makes this impossible with larger numbers; if $n = 10$, there are over 180 000 possible tours; if $n = 12$, there are almost 20 000 000.

As mentioned earlier, we need to define the neighbourhood over which the search will take place. Suppose we decide that we will take two cities and swap their positions in the list. With this two-city neighbourhood, the number of possible swaps is

$$\frac{n(n-1)}{2}$$

This is because each of the seven cities has six partners with which they could be swapped, hence the top line of $n(n-1)$. Also, the distance from one city to another is the same as a move in the reverse direction – which is why we divide the top line by 2. Therefore, at any time, there will be 21 possible swaps in each neighbourhood for this example.

Devising shorter tours with a steepest descent strategy

This is straightforward with the algorithm presented earlier. It works as follows if $k = 2$ (i.e. if pairs of cities are swapped in our attempt to find a better route):

Initialization	1	$x^{now} = [A, B, C, D, E, F, G]$; *best_cost* $= 287$ km.
Iteration 1	2	Swap cities C and E; $x^{now} = [A, B, E, D, C, F, G]$; $C^{next} = 243$ km.
	3	$x^{now} = [A, B, E, D, C, F, G]$; *best_cost* $= 243$ km.
Iteration 2	2	Swap cities F and G; $x^{now} = [A, B, E, D, C, G, F]$; $C^{next} = 221$ km.
	3	$x^{now} = [A, B, E, D, C, G, F]$; *best_cost* $= 221$ km.
Iteration 3	2	Swap cities A and D; $x^{now} = [D, B, E, A, C, G, F]$; $C^{next} = 193$ km.
	3	$x^{now} = [D, B, E, A, C, G, F]$; *best_cost* $= 193$ km.
Iteration 4		STOP, no improvement is possible.

This suggests that Jane's route should be [A, C, G, F, D, B, E], and the distance she can expect to drive is 193 km, a reduction of 94 km on the distance driven by her disorganized predecessor. Given that we have used a heuristic procedure, there is no guarantee that it is the one route of the 360 with the lowest total distance. However, it has only taken us four iterations to find this route, which is rather less than the 360 that would be needed to check all possibilities. It also looks a sensible route when drawn on the map (see Figure 11.5).

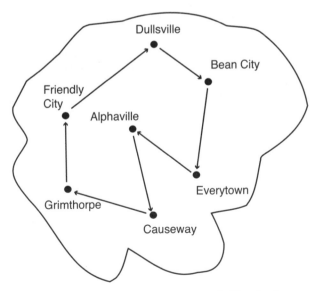

Figure 11.5 A better (the best?) route in Transitania.

Why the interest in travelling salesmen?

Why should general 'problems' such as the TSP be of such interest to the developers of heuristic approaches? It is not because many of them have ever been travelling salesmen or women. The reason is that it is representative of a whole class of more specific 'problems' of which instances are found in the real world of organizational life. One way to appreciate this is to consider again the representation of a TSP tour by a vector that shows the places to be visited and their sequence. In the case of the problem facing Jane, her predecessor seemed to follow a tour that could be represented by the vector [A, B, C, D, E, F, G]. This form of representation can be used in a whole host of generic problems.

For example, a company may need to deliver its products to customers who are spread all over a region. It might be necessary to divide the deliveries by day of the week – for which a component analysis strategy might be used, as discussed in Chapter 4. There then remains the question of the sequence in which the sites are to be visited. This could clearly be modelled in the same way as in the TSP tour. Similarly, a health care organization may need to offer an ambulance service to non-emergency patients, and some form of TSP-based analysis might help in the daily scheduling of pick-ups. In a manufacturing company, a set of jobs may need to be in the warehouse by a certain date, and it can be expensive to make those jobs in the wrong sequence. The sequence of jobs could be represented in a similar manner to the tour faced by the travelling salesman. The distance function might be related to the cost of the jobs, it might be the overall lateness for some deadline or it might be some function of the expected profitability of the work. A rather different type of application might be the design of microelectronic circuits in which components can occupy different places on a three-dimensional grid.

Avoiding premature convergence

The problem with basic neighbourhood search is that it may settle on a local optimum and be unable to move to the global optimum. Figure 11.2 shows that our explorer is currently at a local optimum, the bottom of a valley. The problem she faces is to find some way to move towards the global optimum, the lowest point overall. The following three metaheuristics described in this chapter adopt different approaches to this problem. One approach would be to vary the size of the neighbourhood. Another might be to permit, in the short term at least, a move that actually makes the current situation worse, in the hope that this may lead to her climbing over the next peak en route to the lowest point. None of these ideas fully captures how the following three metaheuristics improve on basic neighbourhood search. But they give some idea of the thinking behind the development of improved methods.

Tabu search

The basic idea behind the modern tabu search seems to have been suggested by Glover (1986), who systematized and developed some common-sense notions that had been around for many years. As with the other two approaches that are discussed here, it is only possible to scratch the surface of the subject; for a thorough introduction, see Glover (1989, 1990a, 1990b) or

Glover and Laguna (1995, 1997). There are many excellent websites that contain up-to-date information on tabu search, including tutorials, software, conferences and applications. The basic idea is to develop procedures to guide a search process past difficult regions, attempting to avoid local optimum solutions. As with many metaheuristics, the strategy consists of a number of principles intended to make the search process more intelligent. This is achieved by the use of flexible memory in which information about past solutions, as well as current ones, is stored.

Tabu (or taboo) search is so called because it rests on procedures that declare certain moves to be tabu (meaning forbidden), even though they are part of the current neighbourhood. In a simple neighbourhood search, all members of the neighbourhood are potential solutions from the current point. In tabu search, this neighbourhood set is restricted by declaring some of them to be tabu and placing them on a tabu list. This means that the heuristic will, normally, choose the lowest-cost no-tabu neighbour. Thus, the modeller needs to decide, in advance, on a set of rules that will be used to mark certain moves as tabu according to their current status. Tabu moves are based on the short- and long-term history of the search, guiding the search procedure to avoid clearly bad moves to ensure that they (or their components) are not attempted time after time in a vain attempt at improvement. That is, tabu avoids thrashing around.

Flexible memory allows a tabu search algorithm to monitor some aspects of the history of the search. The precise way in which this memory is organized will depend on the tabu procedure in use, and also upon the way in which the heuristic is programmed for computer use. Glover and Laguna (1995) suggest that this flexible memory may have four aspects: recency, frequency, quality and influence.

Recency – restricting the search

This refers to some way of counting the number of iterations made since a particular element of a solution was last altered in some way or other. There are many ways of representing this, but one way is in a simple matrix as shown in Table 11.2 for Jane Wiley's problem in Transitania. It shows a way of representing recency at the start of the fourth iteration, based on a strategy that requires moves to be tabu for three iterations after they have occurred. Thus, a non-zero value indicates that a move is tabu, and this value is decreased by 1 at every subsequent iteration. Three iterations after its last move, the move becomes non-tabu and may be used in a new solution. Thus, when considering candidates for moves in the neighbourhood search, the basic idea is that only non-tabu moves should be considered. This prevents swaps being continually made and then quickly reversed as the heuristic hunts for a new solution. It helps to prevent the heuristic from thrashing around in vain.

Table 11.2 Recency matrix at the start of iteration 4.

	A	B	C	D	E	F	G
A				3			
B					1		
C							
D							
E							2
F							

Frequency – diversifying the search

A second way of using flexible memory in tabu search is to monitor how many times that particular move has taken place. In most cases the frequency notion is employed when the descent has reached a local optimum. This happens when no move in the neighbourhood offers an immediate improvement. Frequency is employed as a way to diversify the search; in terms of the analogy of our lost explorer, it may permit her to climb uphill in order to find her way over an intervening peak into the next valley. If the basic principle of the recency tabu is to restrict the search, the basic principle of frequency is to diversify the search.

A simple implementation of frequency-based search would deploy a similar memory structure to that used in recency-based memory. Thus, one method might be to employ a matrix similar to the one shown in Table 11.2. However, this time the cells would show how often the particular move or swap had occurred. Thus, if cell (A, B) contained the value 5 and cell (D, E) contained the value 3, this would indicate that the (A, B) move had occurred 5 times and the (D, E) move had happened 3 times since some defined cut-off point. The essence of the approach, then, is to allow a move among non-tabu candidates that have a low-frequency score. The lower the frequency value, the less often that this move has been considered in the past. Thus, this use of frequency serves to diversify the search into regions that have not yet been considered. In essence, both recency and frequency serve to influence the choice of neighbour from a current solution. Their implementation will depend on the application.

Influence and quality – using aspiration criteria to break the tabu

Sometimes progress from a local optimum is only possible by breaking the tabu, and Glover and Laguna (1995) suggest the concept of influence to do this. The tabu is broken if a move meets some defined aspiration criteria that define conditions that allow the tabu status of a move to be overridden. The aim is to encourage moves that may have a great influence in improving the solution. Thus, the search algorithm examines the available moves and selects one that is clearly better than the others, even if it is tabu. The aspiration criteria define what is meant by better.

A move is considered to be influential if it shifts the solution substantially – that is, to a degree beyond that offered by non-tabu moves. In conceptual terms, this may be equivalent to being able to leap over an intervening peak into the next valley. This opens up whole new possibilities for the search to proceed and may avoid it getting stuck at some local optimum. The modeller thus needs to specify these aspiration criteria, which may be static (i.e. wholly determined in advance) or might be dynamically computed as the search proceeds. This relates to the fourth concept of solution quality, which is a measure of the way in which a particular move contributes to a shift towards a global optimum.

A basic tabu search algorithm

An earlier section of this chapter presented a general algorithm for neighbourhood search and for its steepest descent variant. This same general scheme may be employed to capture the essence of tabu search. It employs a history record, H, which is initially empty and to which solutions visited are added at each iteration and may be later removed if the search continues and they have been in H for too long. This enables some solutions to be regarded as tabu for a period so as to avoid their inclusion. Needless to say, the length of time a solution is allowed to remain in H can affect the degree to which the algorithm converges on a global optimum solution. The general algorithm is thus as follows, using the nomenclature defined earlier:

1	Initialization	Select a starting solution x^{now} from X.
		Define $best\_cost = c(x^{now})$.
		Create an empty history record, H.
2	Choice and termination	Choose a solution x^{next} from $N(H, x^{now})$ to minimize $C(H, x^{now})$ over this set.
		After a specified number of iterations, STOP or else proceed to step 3.
3	Update	Put $x^{now} = x^{next}$.
		Revise H.
		If $c(x^{now}) < best\_cost$, then $best\_cost = c(x^{now})$.
		Go to step 2.

Simulated annealing

The physical analogy

Like tabu search, simulated annealing algorithms try to avoid convergence on local optima, and the approach owes its name to an analogy between the physical operation of annealing and a search process. In the physical world, annealing is a process of heat treatment that is commonly applied to metals and to other materials such as glass by careful control over their heating and cooling. When metals are heated and cooled, their physical structure changes, and annealing is used to soften metals that have grown hard and less ductile from attempts to reshape them at low temperatures. The effect of the process is to change the crystalline structure of the metal in such a way that it can be worked without the breaking and cracking that would occur had it not been annealed. The essence of this physical process of annealing is careful temperature control.

A way to understand this annealing analogy is to consider the analogy of the lost explorer who is stuck in a valley higher than the point she is seeking, and is wishing to continue her search. Physical annealing is a carefully designed process that avoids the points at which the metal would normally harden and break, which is analogous to a local optimum. When the metal is approaching the point at which it might start to fail, it is reheated to permit further work to continue. In a simulated annealing algorithm, this 'reheating' permits the search to continue beyond an apparently local optimum. In a physical annealing process, the amount of extra work that is possible will depend on the temperature of the annealing, and this is carefully controlled. In simulated annealing, the same concept is used to control the search that occurs around some local optimum.

The method itself was proposed, in a form relevant to Management Science, by Kirkpatrick, Gellat and Vecchi (1983), and readable accounts can be found in Eglese (1990) and Dowsland (1995). As with all the metaheuristics described here, the approach has been considerably enhanced since its introduction, and there are many variants in use. The basic idea is that a random choice is made between available moves from the current neighbourhood. Strict local search would only permit such moves if they led to immediate improvement, but simulated annealing permits some uphill moves in an attempt to shift the search to new ground.

The underlying analogy of simulated annealing

In its original form, simulated annealing employed an equation from statistical thermodynamics. The use of this equation in this way is commonly attributed to Metropolis *et al.* (1953). It is usually presented as follows:

$$\Pr(\delta E) = \exp\left(\frac{\delta E}{kt}\right) \tag{1}$$

where E represents energy, δE represents a change in energy, t represents temperature and k is known as Boltzmann's constant. Metropolis *et al.* were simulating what happens to metals as they are cooled and heated in a heat bath. In their simulation they generated a small change, and from this they computed the change in energy. In their model of the physical world, if the energy decreased, then the system moved to a new state. However, if the energy increased, whether it moved to a new state depended on a probability computed by equation (1). In simulated annealing, a probability function governs whether a new move is allowed. That is, some randomness is injected into the search process.

Perhaps the part of the analogy that is most important to understand is that, in its original form, simulated annealing employed an exponential probability function. An example of the shape of such a function is shown in Figure 11.6. This shows that the function has a sharp decline when x is small, but that it levels off as x increases. Relating this back to the probability equation, this means that the probability is high when the temperature t is high or the cost increase is low. Thus, applying this to simulated annealing, a high control parameter means that there is a high probability of accepting an uphill move. The usual approach is to allow such an exponential decay in the probability as the number of iterations increases. The idea is that the search should be encouraged to roam widely in the early iterations so as to remove the effect of the starting solution. As it proceeds, the search should get increasingly restricted.

A basic simulated annealing algorithm

As with tabu search, the general scheme presented earlier may be used to show the essential features of a simulated annealing algorithm. There are considerable differences between this

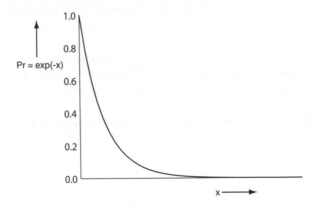

Figure 11.6 An exponential function.

and the algorithm for neighbourhood search with steepest descent:

- The algorithm requires a control parameter (temperature) function to be established, which takes the form

$$T_{next} = f(t_{now})$$

  that is, the control parameter t is recalculated at each iteration, based on a function of its previous value. The control parameter must be given some initial value t_0.
- The value of x^{next} is selected from its neighbourhood $N(x^{now})$ and is accepted as the new value of x^{now} if it produces a lower cost. The selection may be random or the choices may be considered in some defined sequence.
- If x^{next} produces a higher cost, then it may be accepted as a new value of x^{now} if it meets a probability criterion. This usually involves taking a sample from a uniform probability distribution in the range 0 to 1. This random sample is then compared with a function based on equation (1).
- If this comparison results in a rejection of the x^{next} value, then the process is repeated until an acceptable value is found or until some predetermined number of attempts is reached. Without the latter condition, the algorithm could loop forever.

The algorithm works as follows:

1	Initialization	Select a starting solution x^{now} from X.
		Define $best\_cost = c(x^{now})$.
		Set $t_{now} = t_0$, its initial value.
		Specify n_rep, the maximum number of attempts.
		Set $n = 0$, use as number of attempts so far.
2a	Choice	If $n \geq n\_rep$, then STOP.
		Increment n by 1.
		Select x^{next} from $N(x^{now})$.
		Compute $\delta = c(x^{next}) - c(x^{now})$.
		If $\delta < 0$, then go to step 3, else go to step 2b.
2b	Accept	Generate u from Uniform(0,1) distribution.
		If $u < \exp(-\delta/t_{now})$, then go to step 3, else go to step 2a.
3	Update	Put $x^{now} = x^{next}$ and $c(x^{next}) = c(x^{now})$.
		Compute $t_{next} = f(t_{now})$, put $t_{now} = t_{next}$.
		Go to step 2a.

Comparing simulated annealing with tabu search

Comparing the two basic versions of these approaches presented here, one major difference is apparent. Although both strategies have been devised to reduce the risk of getting stuck at some local optimum, they tackle this in completely different ways. In tabu search, the history of the search is used to guide the search in the future. In basic simulated annealing there is no attempt to do this; instead, obviously good moves are accepted automatically without regard to their history. If no obviously good move exists, then a potentially bad one is accepted at random according to a probability based on equation (1). A second difference is that, in the forms presented here, tabu search is more 'conservative' than simulated annealing. Tabu search tries to choose lowest-cost neighbours, whereas simulated annealing uses a random element in the hope that this will eventually lead to improvements.

Which of the two basic strategies is better? The two camps each have their own advocates, and the answer will depend on the precise problem on which they are being used. There is no obvious reason why the two approaches cannot be combined if that makes for a more reliable algorithm.

Genetic algorithms

The genetic analogy

The third heuristic strategy discussed here is also based on an analogy – this time from population genetics. It stems from the belief that random mutations at genetic level can, in the right circumstances, lead to a healthy population that contains those genes. The notion is that the circumstances (the environment) temper the random mutation by selecting some individual mutations as better suited to survival and prosperity than others. Thus, like simulated annealing, genetic algorithms rely on some kind of randomness. A readable but fairly detailed introduction to the basic idea of genetic algorithms as they might be used in Management Science is given by Reeves (1995b). The method was first suggested by Holland (1975), and a detailed account of the ideas is provided by Goldberg (1989). A website (ai-depot, 2009) provides a useful source of up-to-date material.

The basic concept is that of a chromosome, which is usually represented as a binary string, such as the following example:

[1010010]

This example chromosome has seven binary variables that are often known as alleles. Each allele has a position in the string, often known as its locus. Thus, an allele with locus 2 in a chromosome of length 9 is occupying the second position in a string of nine (0, 1) variables. Each solution in the search needs to be represented by such a chromosome if a genetic algorithm is to be used. Strictly speaking, the alleles need not be restricted to (0, 1) variables, but most straightforward algorithms are based on this representation. The coded chromosome structure processed by the algorithm is known as the genotype. The decoded version of the chromosome string is known as the phenotype. Thus, different problems with the same structure may share genotypes while having different phenotypes.

The basic approach

Like simulated annealing, genetic algorithms use randomness to improve upon simple neighbourhood search, but the way that this is done is very different. The first difference is that, whereas simulated annealing methods move from one solution to another, genetic algorithms maintain a population of solutions. In genetic terms, this is a population of potential parents within which breeding will occur. The assumption is that alleles present in the parental chromosomes will find their way into the chromosomes of the offspring. Thus, the intention is to encourage the most suitable offspring to survive each generation to become the next generation of breeding parents. The second difference is that the basic form of algorithm representation shown earlier for neighbourhood search, steepest descent and tabu search is not a suitable way to represent the approach.

Instead, it is more helpful to envisage the basic approach as consisting of a series of generations stemming from reproductive activity. Each phase of reproduction develops as three steps:

1. *Crossover.* Two parents mate to produce a new chromosome.
2. *Mutation.* Random changes with low probability are introduced into the chromosomes.
3. *Selection.* Which chromosomes will survive is decided.

These three stages are repeated as the basis of the algorithm.

Crossover and mutation

Crossover is the normal way of simulating breeding between two parent chromosomes, and its mechanism is best illustrated by an example. Suppose there are two parents, which are represented by the following chromosomes, each of length 7:

$$[1010101] \quad [0000111]$$

These will be mated by the exchange of alleles around some randomly chosen crossover point. Suppose that the crossover point is at 3, which means that it lies between the third and fourth allele in each string. Hence, the two chromosomes swap their alleles in loci 1, 2 and 3 for those of the other at loci 4, 5, 6 and 7. Such a crossover would result in the following pair of offspring:

$$[1010111] \quad [0000101]$$

The crossover point is often selected by sampling from a uniform probability distribution as part of the randomness of the algorithm. Operators other than simple crossover are sometimes employed in these algorithms; an example would be having more than one crossover point in the breeding process.

Mutation occurs when, as a result of the swap, one or more of the alleles take a new value. If binary strings are used as the chromosomes, then this simply means that a 0 becomes a 1, or vice versa. Mutation is intended to introduce new attributes into the genetic make-up of the population, thus reducing its dependence on its starting chromosomes.

Selection

During each cycle, the population completes its mating phase, and some of the candidate offspring are selected to survive as the next generation of breeding parents. Thus, the algorithm must specify a selection mechanism that includes some measure of fitness. This fitness function is equivalent to a cost function or an objective function. That is, offspring that make the greatest contribution to the objective function will be selected for survival. Having set a fitness function, there are several possible intergenerational mechanisms that could be used in selecting survivors from the breeding and mutation. In discussing this issue, Reeves (1995b) lists the following options:

- Replace each generation en bloc after breeding, which was the mechanism originally proposed by Holland for genetic algorithms. Thus, selection is automatic.

- Replace incrementally after breeding. That is, only keep those offspring that do not duplicate chromosomes present in the parent population. This helps avoid recessive breeding.
- Employ elitist selection by forcing the best member of the current population to be a member of the next. This ensures that good chromosomes pass forward.
- Use termination with prejudice. This removes members of the parent population that have below-average fitness, replacing them with a randomly selected member of the offspring.
- Employ parental selection by encouraging breeding between parents with the highest fitness values.
- Finally, some algorithms employ speciation. This is a way of avoiding indiscriminate mating between different 'species'.

Other coding methods

In the basic approach, the chromosome is a binary coding of the solutions. There are many problems in which this is not a convenient form of representation. One example is the TSP, in which it is much more normal to use a string representation of the type shown earlier for the simple, seven-city trip of Jane Wiley. In this case, we might have two parents such as the following:

$$[A, B, C, D, E, F, G] \qquad [C, A, B, F, G, E, D]$$

Simple crossover mechanisms are not suited to this form of representation, and various others have been suggested. However, it may be that genetic algorithms are not well suited to this form of sequence representation, but, instead, are better suited to other types of application in which fitter parents are likely to create fit offspring. Simple crossover will not guarantee this in TSP, as it depends on the labelling system in use for the nodes to be visited.

Summary

The argument in this chapter is that, when some form of mathematical search is a useful way to proceed, optimization approaches of the type exemplified by linear programming in Chapter 9 are often unsatisfactory. This is because, for large-scale problems, the solution methods may take far too long to converge on the optimum. In addition, there are other problems for which search is needed, but for which no optimizing algorithm exists. Hence, for these types of problem, heuristic search is a sensible way to proceed. The discussion employed the TSP as a simple-to-understand, generic application that needs heuristic approaches for problems of a reasonable scale. Many situations to which these methods are applied are much more complicated than the simple TSP and do not lend themselves to simple visual representation.

The heuristic search methods discussed here proceed towards a solution in an iterative manner, each step hoping to find a better solution, although with no guarantee that it will be optimal. They usually employ a form of neighbourhood search at each iteration, rather than examining all possibilities. Strategies such as tabu search and simulated annealing have been devised to avoid early convergence on very suboptimal solutions. A rather different approach is taken in genetic algorithms, the expectation being that aspects of good solutions will be propagated from generation to generation, each time getting better.

References

ai_depot (2009) Genetic algorithms: http://ai-depot.com/knowledge/genetic_algorithm

Cartwright H.M. and Cattell J.R. (1995) Studies of continuous-flow chemical synthesis using genetic algorithms, in *Applications of Modern Heuristic Methods*, ed. by Rayward-Smith V.J. Alfred Waller, Henley-on-Thames, UK.

Chardaire P. (1995) Location of concentrators using simulated annealing, in *Applications of Modern Heuristic Methods*, ed. by Rayward-Smith V.J. Alfred Waller, Henley-on-Thames, UK.

Christofides N. (1985) Vehicle routing, in *The Travelling Salesman Problem. A Guided Tour of Combinatorial Optimisation*, ed. by Lawler E.L., Lenstra J.K., Rinnoy Kan A.H.G. and Shmoys D.B. John Wiley & Sons, Ltd, Chichester, UK.

Dowsland K.A. (1995) Simulated annealing, in *Modern Heuristic Techniques for Combinatorial Problems*, ed. by Reeves C. McGraw-Hill, Maidenhead, UK.

Dullaert W., Sevaux M., Sörensen K. and Springael J. (2007) Feature cluster on the applications of meta heuristics. *European Journal of Operational Research*, **179**(3), 601–735.

Eglese R.W. (1986) Heuristics in operational research, in *Recent Developments in Operational Research*, ed. by Belton V. and O'Keefe R.M. Pergamon Press, Oxford, UK.

Eglese R.W. (1990) Simulated annealing: a tool for operational research. *European Journal of Operational Research*, **46**, 271–281.

Eglese R.W. and Rand G.K. (1987) Conference seminar timetabling. *Journal of Operational Research*, **38**, 591–598.

Foulds L.R. (1983) The heuristic problem solving approach. *Journal of the Operational Research Society*, **34**, 927–934.

Frontline Systems (2009) The Premium Solver for Excel: http://www.solver.com/

Glover F. (1986) Future paths for integer programming and links to artificial intelligence. *Computers and Operations Research*, **5**, 533–549.

Glover F. (1989) Tabu search – part i. *ORSA Journal on Computing*, **1**(3), 190–260.

Glover F. (1990a) Tabu search – part ii. *ORSA Journal on Computing*, **2**(1), 4–32.

Glover F. (1990b) Tabu search: a tutorial. *Interfaces*, **20**(4), 74–94.

Glover F. and Kochenberger G.A. (eds) (2003) *Handbook of Metaheuristics*. International Series in Operations Research and Management Science, Vol. 57. Kluwer, Boston, MA.

Glover F. and Laguna M. (1995) Tabu search, in *Modern Heuristic Techniques for Combinatorial Problems*, ed. by Reeves C. McGraw-Hill, Maidenhead, UK.

Glover F and Laguna M. (1997) *Tabu Search*, Springer, Berlin, Germany.

Goldberg D.E. (1989) *Genetic Algorithms in Search, Optimization and Machine Learning*. Addison-Wesley, Reading, MA.

Holland J. (1975) *Adaptation in Natural and Artificial Systems*. University of Michigan Press, Ann Arbor, MI.

Kirkpatrick S., Gellat C.D. and Vecchi M.P. (1983) Optimization by simulated annealing. *Science*, **220**, 671–680.

LINDO Systems (2009) Optimization modelling tools: http://www.lindo.com/

Metropolis N., Rosenbluth A.W., Rosenbluth M.N., Teller A.H. and Teller E. (1953) Equation of state calculation by fast computing machines. *Journal of Chemical Physics*, **21**, 1087–1091.

Rayward-Smith V.J. (ed.) (1995) *Applications of Modern Heuristic Methods*. Alfred Waller, Henley-on-Thames, UK.

Reeves C. (ed.) (1995a) *Modern Heuristic Techniques for Combinatorial Problems*. McGraw-Hill, Maidenhead, UK.

Reeves C. (1995b) Genetic algorithms, in *Modern Heuristic Techniques for Combinatorial Problems*, ed. by Reeves C. McGraw-Hill, Maidenhead, UK.

Reeves C. and Beasley J.E. (1995) Introduction, in *Modern Heuristic Techniques for Combinatorial Problems*, ed. by Reeves C. McGraw-Hill, Maidenhead, UK.

Simon H.A. (1978) On how to decide what to do. *The Bell Journal of Economics*, **9**(3), 494–507.

Simon H.A. and Newell A. (1958) Heuristic problem solving: the next advance for operations research. *Operations Research*, **7**, 1–10.

Wright M.B. (1994) Timetabling county cricket fixtures using a form of tabu search. *Journal of the Operational Research Society*, **45**(7), 758–771.

PART IV
MODEL ASSESSMENT
AND VALIDATION

Because models are used to think through the consequences of possible actions, it is important that some form of quality assurance is applied to them. This final part of the book, which applies to both 'soft' and 'hard' approaches, aims to introduce ideas relevant to this theme. The apparently simple question of model validity turns out to be rather complicated, and this is true whether we are concerned with the hard approaches of Part II or the soft methods described in Part III. In neither case can we ever be sure that a Management Science model is wholly valid; the best we can say is that it is acceptable and credible for the purpose for which it is intended. This suggests that reusing a model developed for one purpose in a way not anticipated during its construction can be very dangerous.

12 Model assessment and validation

Introduction

The theme running through this book is that modelling is a great help in facing up to complex issues. Part I introduced some general ideas that affect virtually all types of model employed in Management Science. Part II described the basics of some commonly used interpretive approaches to modelling, and Part III covered similar ground for quantitative modelling. Whatever the type of model in use, it seems important to ensure that it is suitable for the purpose for which it was built. This process goes under a range of names, of which model assessment and model validation are probably the most common. This final chapter discusses how Management Science models should be assessed and validated.

First, it introduces some of the general issues that seem to be important when considering the validation of any type of model in Management Science. Following this, there is discussion of some general principles for the validation of quantitative models. Then, the slightly more vexing question of the validation of the soft models used in interpretive approaches is examined. As will be clear, the validation of quantitative and interpretive models rests on rather different assumptions. Finally, the different threads will be drawn together.

Foundations of validation

A naive approach to validation would be something like the following:

A model is a representation of the real world, or of at least part of it. Therefore, the validation of the model is really quite straightforward – in principle. All we have to do is check that the model behaves as the real world does under the same conditions. If it does, then the model is valid. If it doesn't, then it isn't.

Although this view is appealing in its simplicity, there are reasons why it is described as naive. To understand this requires some consideration of epistemology, the subject concerned with human knowledge – how, in the famous words of Donald Rumsfeld, do we know what we know? In two fascinating papers, Déry, Landry and Banville (1993) and Roy (1993) show that validation is more complex than it might seem at first sight.

Epistemology

Déry, Landry and Banville (1993) argue that, if Management Science is to be viewed as a scientific or even a technological activity, the dominant epistemologies of science ought to be seriously considered when thinking about the question of validation. They discuss three different perspectives on the epistemology of science: philosophical, historical and sociological.

Philosophical perspective Philosophers of science and others have long been concerned to understand the relationship between scientists, the objects they observe and the ways that those observations are captured as knowledge or scientific truth. Some go further than this and are concerned with making prescriptive statements about what should characterize those relations. Déry, Landry and Banville point out that three threads are woven into this particular philosophical garment:

- A view, based on logical empiricism, that a statement can be regarded as an addition to scientific knowledge if it is an objectively correct reflection of factual observations that are translated into logicomathematical terms. Thus, objectivity and rigorous quantification are crucial to the development of scientific knowledge.
- A later view, credited to Popper (1959, 1964) that all scientific knowledge is, in one sense, conjectural because no experiment could conclusively prove a theory to be true. This does not mean that all theories or conjectures are equally valuable. In this view, truly scientific experiments are ones that could disprove a theory or part of a theory rather than ones that seek to confirm it.
- Alongside this there is the commonplace notion of utilitarianism: that scientific and technological knowledge is that which is practical. Thus, a theory that does not have any consequences in the real world may be interesting, but it is not scientific. This provides a partial explanation of why theories may continue in use even though they have been refuted. Thus, Newtonian mechanics is widely used in spite of its replacement with relativistic notions.

Combining these three views might suggest that a valid Management Science model should satisfy these three criteria. That is, the model should be based on objective research, expressed mathematically, should be shown to be useful and should pass crucial tests designed to show its inadequacy.

Historical perspective This is mainly concerned to account for the ways in which different theories have actually dominated scientific communities; that is, to theorize about actual behaviour. Thomas Kuhn (1970) is perhaps the best-known historical analyst of scientific epistemology. He argues that a scientific community is bound together by a disciplinary matrix that defines its interests by specifying what its members regard as scientific knowledge. In a period of 'normal science', the members of a scientific community share a stable matrix, and most research is devoted to activity that confirms the validity of the matrix. During periods of 'revolutionary science', the matrix is threatened by alternative paradigms, which may result in periods of fierce conflict and argument.

From such a historical perspective, validity relates to the acceptability of an idea, theory or model in the expert community of scientists who are operating within a dominant paradigm. Thus, in these terms, validation is the concern of the professional community of management scientists who ought to define rules for validation. In 'normal science', validation is therefore partly a test of whether the theory fits the paradigm. Interestingly enough, Gass (1993) makes a plea for a quantitative measure of model acceptability, which seems to imply that management scientists operate within something equivalent to normal science.

Sociological perspective This takes a yet wider view and looks at scientific communities in the same way as any other groups or social system. In these terms, scientific knowledge is defined by social processes, including conflict, power play and other social activity, as well as rational argument – much as are other areas of life. Thus, in these terms, a theory is regarded as knowledge when it is accepted by the community, and much the same range of ploys are used to achieve this acceptance as in any other social group. This accounts for peer-group pressure, for power play and the rest. However, if the community of scientists gets too far out of kilter with the rest of society, then it ceases to be effective because it has no wider franchise. Thus, the social processes operate within the scientific communities and between them and other groups. This is one reason why utilitarian views may be espoused to justify scientific activity.

In these terms, model validation is based on a model's acceptability to those who dominate the Management Science community, as they define the rules of acceptability. Those who wish to develop models deemed by those in power to be unacceptable must either face exclusion or find ways to upset the applecart.

These three viewpoints illustrate the naivety of the naive approach, which seems to stem from views about scientific knowledge that take little account of the history of the development of scientific knowledge and ignore the social processes at work as models are developed and used. From a historical perspective it is clear that the scientific community adopts validation rules that fit the dominant paradigm, and that these may shift over time as new problems are faced. Hence, although the naive approach might be fine for quantitative models, it could be wholly inappropriate for interpretive approaches that are aimed at quite different targets. From a sociological perspective we see that the scientific community is not immune to the same pressures as the rest of society. Social relations affect scientific work and are part of what scientists have to say about the objects that they observe. Irrelevance will be rewarded with indifference.

The declaration of independence

Underlying the naive approach is what might be termed 'the declaration of independence', an implicit view that the problems on which management scientists work are independent of the observer or of other people. They are somewhere 'out there'. But is this true? Is the management scientist clearly separate from the context of the problem? Chapter 3 argued that problems are social and psychological constructs that need to be negotiated between the management scientist and the client or user. For example, Figure 5.1 showed how Checkland's soft systems methodology (SSM) requires the analyst to be aware of his or her own influence on the system being studied. Advocates of soft approaches are, in general, sceptical of such declarations of independence.

The declaration should, however, also be questioned in quantitative modelling in Management Science. For example, Roy (1993) attacks this view of observer independence in his discussion of validation from the perspective of multicriteria decision-making (MCDM), an approach discussed in Chapter 8. Roy accepts that, like social scientists, management scientists form part of the systems with which they are concerned. This applies just as much to quantitative modelling as to interpretive work, and it makes validation a difficult issue. Roy (1993) addresses this by considering three paths, or quests, towards scientific knowledge.

The first he calls the 'realism' path, which, when followed, is intended to lead to a description of what the world is really like. This, he points out, may lead to a belief that the elements of a model represent real objects. But all models are approximations, and even in relatively simple investment decisions it is reasonable to ask what is meant by the 'cost of capital'. As Roy (1993) points out, 'some costs that play critical roles in numerous models refer to virtually unspecifiable realities'. This is not just restricted to investment decision-making; for example, the system dynamics model of Lancaster District Hospital (Chapter 7) included variables concerned with length of stay (LoS). However, even this simple idea hides a multitude of complications that exist in the real hospital.

The 'axiomatic' path is Roy's second route and refers to the view that a science needs a consistent set of axioms (frames of reference) by which to make sense of things. This seems to correspond to 'normal science' with a dominant paradigm, when validity may be assessed against these axioms. For example, there are highly consistent theories of choice based on expected subjective utility (see Chapter 2). These theories may be employed to model how decisions should be taken; that is, they may be used in a normative way – which may be in marked contrast to the ways in which people actually make decisions. This view is related to the idea of logical empiricism discussed above and is open to exactly the same criticism.

Roy's third path is that of 'constructivism', in which models are not used in an attempt to discover truth but in an attempt to discover useful 'keys' that might help to organize a situation. In this sense, models become working hypotheses. This is close to a utilitarian view, but also close to the idea running through this book that models can be interpretive tools that may shed light on difficult and complex situations.

Validation is impossible, but desirable

The preceding argument leads us to a sombre conclusion. This is that validation, if taken to mean a comprehensive demonstration that a model is fully correct, is impossible. What, then, is possible? And is this better than nothing? It would perhaps be best to answer the second question first. Validation is best regarded as an ideal towards which we must strive if we are to be at all faithful to the idea that Management Science aims to support action in the real world. It actually matters whether our models are wrong, as this may cause people to embark on action that has very negative consequences. Hence, management scientists have a responsibility to aim at some form of validation, but should begin by recognizing that this may be limited. Among many scientists it is recognized that theories and knowledge can never be comprehensively demonstrated to be true, and yet these same theories turn out to be very useful. They also have an impact on the world outside the scientific community, especially if they resonate with wider social concerns and needs.

What, then, is possible in the way of validation? That depends on the type of model and the use to which it is put. This is the subject of most of the rest of this chapter, after a short diversion into the world of validation errors.

Validation errors

Statistical inference

In many areas of life it is neither possible nor desirable to test a complete population about which we wish to know something. Statistical inference enables us to draw conclusions from a sample of the population and gives us some idea of the reliability of that inference. For example, the only way to know how long a light bulb will last is to test it to destruction. But if the manufacturer were to test all his production in this way, none would be left for sale. Instead, he will test a sample and will use the results of this to make statements, or inferences, about his entire output.

It is not unusual to need to make inferences about a population by examining a sample of items from that population. This would be simple if all the items were identical; however, there is likely to be at least some slight variation. For example, not all light bulbs will last for exactly the same time. If all members of the population were clones of one another, there would be no problem, for a sample of any size (one, say) would contain all the information about the population. This variation is usually handled by computing a statistic for some attribute of the sample and then using this to make estimates of the same attribute for the whole population. We may thus measure the life of each member of a sample of light bulbs and compute the mean life of the sample and its variance. Thus, the statistic being measured might belong to the items themselves, such as the expected life of a light bulb, or it might be the result of a comparison, such as knowing whether one light bulb type lasts longer than another. Using suitable statistical methods, we may use the sample observations to estimate the likely life of a typical light bulb from the population. To provide support in making these inferences, statisticians have devised a whole armoury of tests and approaches that can be employed.

In all of these tests and approaches, inferences about populations are made from samples taken from those populations. As a sample may not be representative, these inferences may, in the light of full and complete information, turn out to be wrong. For instance, a comparison of samples of two types of light bulb may suggest that, on average, type A lasts longer than type B. However, even though the samples might have been selected at random from the two populations, this inference may be wrong. It could be that the random sampling led us, unwittingly, to a set of type-B bulbs that was unaccountably bad. Thus, the sample comparison was not a fair one. To cope with this possibility, statistical theory suggests confidence levels for the statistic that fixes boundaries on the likely values of the statistic. Thus, a statement that the 95% confidence limits for the expected life of a bulb are 2010 hours and 1850 hours gives an upper and lower bound for this expected life. The 95% figure simply implies that there is a probability of 0.95 that the true average life of the whole population of bulbs lies within those limits.

Type-I and type-II errors

One application of statistical inference is hypothesis testing. We may, for example, wish to know whether two different types of light bulb have different lives. One way to check this would be to take random samples of each type, measure how long each lasted and then compute the average life for each sample. To test whether type A lasts longer than type B, we need to decide whether the difference between the two average values is greater than zero. Thus, we have a null hypothesis that the difference between the two average lives is zero, and an alternative hypothesis that there is a positive difference in favour of A. Hypothesis tests, like confidence intervals, allow a statistically trained person to compare the two hypotheses by estimating how likely it is that the difference between the means is a true difference, which reflects the entire population. Thus, these tests result in statements such as, 'Reject the null hypothesis at a confidence level of 95%', which means that there is a probability of 0.95 that the difference observed in the samples is actually non-zero in the whole population.

This statement of statistical confidence reflects the fact that there is a risk of drawing the wrong conclusion. The difference might be very small in the whole population, effectively zero, in spite of a reasonably large difference in the samples taken. To cope with this risk, statisticians use the terms type-I and type-II errors. A type-I error occurs, in classical hypothesis testing, when a correct hypothesis is wrongly rejected. In the light bulb example, the application of statistical theory may lead us to conclude that there is a significant difference between the average lives of the two types of light bulb. If we had access to the entire population of these bulbs, then we might know that this conclusion from the samples was wrong, because their average lives are effectively the same. This would be a type-I error. The higher the level of significance, then the lower this risk will be – but this may require very large samples. A type-II error occurs, by contrast, when an incorrect hypothesis is wrongly accepted. Thus, we might accept, at some confidence level, that the average lives of the two types of light bulb are effectively the same. If this turns out to be an error, then it would be a type-II error.

It is sometimes naively assumed that the validation of a model involves the straightforward application of these ideas of statistical inference to a sample of results from the model against a sample from the real world. As will be seen later, this is a gross oversimplification for both quantitative and interpretive models. However, the general notion is still a useful one. In general validation terms, a type-I error is the risk of wrongly rejecting a valid model. A type-II error is the risk of wrongly accepting an invalid model.

Type-0 errors

A type-0 error (called a type-III error by Balci, 1994) occurs when the modeller sets out on the wrong track altogether. The result is a model that does completely the wrong thing and is of no value at all. This can happen with the cleverest and most complicated of models and is the most important error to avoid in any modelling. It can also happen when a model that in overall intention is sensible ends up with detail in irrelevant places and with sketchy coverage of aspects that turn out to be important.

The best way to avoid these fundamental type-0 errors is to pay careful attention to problem and model formulation. This is one aspect that comes across very clearly in Willemain's (1995) study of expert modellers and their modelling, referred to in Chapter 4. Although the experts studied might have been expected to focus almost exclusively on the technical aspects of their modelling, they spent about 30% of their time on careful consideration of the problem context and on thinking about model assessment and validation. This time was devoted even in the short space of the 60 minutes they were given to think aloud. Thus, experts recognize the importance of avoiding these type-0 errors.

The assessment and validation of quantitative models

Some basic ideas

Perhaps the discrete computer simulation community has put most effort into the validation of quantitative models, with notable contributions from Balci (1987, 1994), Sargent (1988) and Zeigler (1976, 1984). The US Department of Defense Modeling and Simulation Coordination Office (M&SCO) maintains an extensive website (MSCO, 2009) that offers advice on simulation model assessment for defence-related simulations. A detailed discussion of some general issues related to validation and validity is to be found in Zeigler (1976, 1984).

Zeigler (1984) suggests that the real system can be regarded as a black box that transforms defined inputs into observed outputs. This transformation defines the input–output relation of the real system, and we can only observe it at some point of time t (of which there may be many). What we observe will vary at different time points and will depend on how the system is operated. Zeigler (1984) introduced the concept of an experimental frame, as the precise definition of the circumstances under which this input–output relation is observed and can be obtained. Thus, although we wish to know the 'full' input–output relation of the real system, this can only be known at some time t within some defined experimental frame. If it is true that we may view the input–output relations of the real system within some experimental frame, then the same is true of the model; it, too, has input–output relations to be viewed within an experimental frame.

Zeigler's view embodies two important notions. First, that validation involves the comparison of observations (some from the model, some from the real system). Thus, it may be possible to use statistical tests and investigations of the type discussed earlier if we wish to compare the input–output relations of the real system and the model. Second, Zeigler's concept of experimental frame reminds us that any validity statement must be made within some defined purpose, as validation is a test of fitness for purpose.

What do we mean by model?

Chapter 1 developed a definition of model as used in Management Science, but we need to go further if we wish to discuss the validation of quantitative models. Zeigler (1976) is careful to distinguish between the following (shown in Figure 12.1):

- *The real system.* This is defined as the source of observable data. Even if we do not understand the real system, we can still observe its behaviour. The observable data consist of a set of input–output relations that need not be simple.
- *An experimental frame.* This is defined as the limited set of circumstances under which the real system is to be observed or experimented with.
- *The base model.* This is defined as some hypothetical model that would account for all the input–output behaviour of the real system. This may not exist in any tangible form, although it must do so if there is no real system, such as when a new system is being developed from scratch.
- *A lumped model.* This is defined as an explicit and simplified version of the base model and is the one that will be used in Management Science.
- *A computer program.* In this, the lumped model is implemented and is intended to generate the input–output relations of the lumped model.

Thus, the idea is that, when faced with the need to develop a model of some complex system, we begin with a conceptual or base model, which we keep in mind as we try to build the lumped model that may then be implemented in a computer program. The intention is that the models should be used in relation to the purposes defined by the experimental frame.

Validation and verification in simulation modelling

Each of the four elements in Figure 12.1 has its own input–output relation. Given the earlier definition of the base model, it follows that its input–output relation should be the same as that for the real system at some defined time t, under some defined experimental frame. In the usual sense in which the term is used, validation is a process of assessing the degree to which the input–output relation of the lumped model is the same as that of the real system, within some defined experimental frame.

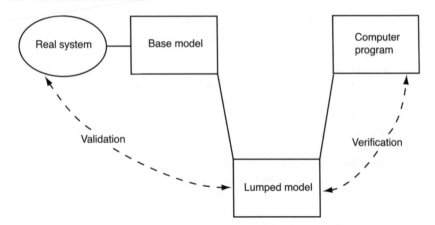

Figure 12.1 Zeigler's view of modelling.

Verification, another term in common use, usually refers to a test of the computer program to check that its input–output relation is the same as those of the lumped model. This is more straightforward than validation, as both the lumped model and the computer program are fully defined.

Simulation model validation

Balci (1994) points out that computer simulation studies are cyclic, because models are refined gradually as time progresses, which accords with the principle of parsimony advocated in Chapter 4. In a proper sense, therefore, assessment and validation are activities that should continue throughout a simulation project. The same should be true of any quantitative modelling in Management Science that follows the principle of parsimony. Therefore, it is wrong to focus all the assessment and validation effort at the end of a modelling project. Instead, it should be a fully fledged part of all stages of the modelling work, part, indeed, of a critical approach. Balci (1994) suggests tests and assessments that can be made at each point of the simulation modelling cycle. He suggests that many of them could be built into simulation support environments.

Robinson (1996) points out that 'Three terms are often used in the context of simulation model and simulation study assessment: validity, credibility and acceptability'. He quotes Schruben (1980) as arguing that 'credibility is reflected in the willingness of persons to base decisions on the information obtained from the model'. This credibility reflects the trust that the model user or client places in the analyst or group building the model, and the credibility of the model is clearly only a part of this. The third term, acceptability, usually refers to the entire study, which includes the model and is also clearly a reflection of the relationship between the modeller(s) and the user or client.

Kleindorfer, O'Neill and Ganeshan (1998) explore ten different positions in the philosophy of science, a rather finer set of distinctions than those of Déry, Landry and Banville (1993), and relate them to the validation of simulation models. The paper includes a discussion of objectivism (at its simplest, model validation can be divorced from the model builder and the context) versus relativism (at its simplest, the model builder and the model are inseparable) in the recent philosophy of science. In conclusion, Kleindorfer, O'Neill and Ganeshan (1998) suggest a metaphor derived from the law courts, that of demonstrating validity beyond reasonable doubt, which stresses the careful consideration of evidence. This is very similar to the way in which the term 'credibility' is used in more general parlance, as a judgement based on evidence.

Validity, credibility and acceptability are all aspects of the trust that the client and model-user feel that they can place in the model and in the modeller(s). This is developed as the model is built and not just by testing a completed model. Although these statements are based on experience in simulation modelling, it seems likely that they apply to other types of quantitative model as well.

Program verification

In computer simulation, validation is the process of assuring that the model is useful for its intended purpose. It needs to be distinguished from verification, a term usually applied to a computer program, given that many Management Science models are implemented in computer programs. Program verification is the process of ensuring that the program embodies the model correctly – that is, it assumes that the model has been correctly specified. Within the computer simulation world, Law and Kelton (1991) suggest the following eight considerations when verifying a computer simulation program. My comments have been added:

1. Write and debug the program in modules. Develop and add submodules as needed until the model is complicated enough. (This advice fits well with the principles of parsimony and divide and conquer described in Chapter 4.)
2. With large models, have other people read through the code or walk it through to avoid the programmer getting stuck in a rut. (Note, though, that reading other people's computer programs is rarely a pleasure.)
3. Run the simulation under a variety of conditions for input parameters and check that the output is reasonable. (Sensitivity testing of this type is always sensible, but not always done.)
4. Make use of variable traces, especially to check the program's behaviour under extreme conditions. Make use of interactive debuggers if they are available. (Many computer programming systems have very good debugging tools, but they take time to master.)
5. Run the model under simplifying assumptions for which true characteristics are known or can easily be computed. (Simple arithmetic can be very useful in checking that a computer program is producing sensible results.)
6. If it seems sensible, watch an animation of the output from the model. (This can apply to heuristic search methods as well as to computer simulation models.)
7. Check the observed sample moments against those specified for the input distributions. (This is specific to computer simulations with stochastic elements.)
8. Where possible, use a simulation language/package to reduce the lines of code. (More generally, if a tried-and-tested package is available, use it. It may seem expensive but it will probably be cheaper in the long run.)

General approaches to validating quantitative models

Black-box validation: predictive power

There are many different approaches to model validation, but they can be divided into two groups: black-box and open-box validation. In black-box validation, the model is treated as if it were an input–output system of unknown internal construction – hence the term 'black box'. A Turing test, the basic idea of which was introduced in Chapter 1 and is shown in Figure 1.2, is the essence of black-box validation. The test is based on a comparison between the output of the model and that produced by the system(s) being modelled. This assumes that both model and system(s) operate under the same circumstances. If the model output is indistinguishable from that of the system, this implies that the model is in some sense a valid representation of that system. This type of black-box validation focuses on the predictive power of the model.

It is important to realize that any black-box validation is based on the comparison of two sets of observations. The first set comes from the model and the second from the system with which it is being compared – its reference system. As with all observations, those used in validation are open to errors due to recording, transcription, analysis and interpretation. It is highly unlikely that the observations of the output from the model will be identical to those observed in the reference system. Indeed, it would very suspicious if they were. Therefore, the aim of black-box validation is not to test whether model and reference system produce the same results. Rather, the aim is to test whether the two sets of observations are close enough to be confident that the model has adequate validity. Thus, the usual armoury of a statistical test may be brought to bear on this comparison in order to make some statement about the degree of confidence that may be placed in the similarity between the performance of the model and its reference system.

There is an obvious problem with black-box validation in studies for which no referent system exists. In such cases, it is impossible to compare the output from the model with that of the real system, for there is no real system. The same problem also occurs in those studies for which a referent system does exist, but in which the model is being used to investigate how that system could be improved or would operate under new conditions.

Open-box (white-box) validation

A black-box validation assumes that the model has unknown internal workings, but this is clearly wrong. Someone built the model and therefore someone understands its internal workings. The model is a deliberate creation of human minds, and it includes relationships that ought to be understood by its creators, if not by its users. Thus, the box can be opened – hence the name of this type of approach, which is sometimes known as white-box validation (Pidd, 1984). As a closed white box is just as hard to peer into as a closed black box, the term 'open box' seems preferable. The idea of this approach is that the detailed internal structure of the model should be compared with that of its reference system. It should be apparent that there is an immediate problem here, because the reason for building the model may be to help understand the structure of the reference system. Nevertheless, there are ways for open-box validation to proceed, depending on the type of model being built. In the case of quantitative models it is possible to check a number of key features.

Open-box validation is based on a critical assessment of the variables and relationships that comprise the model. For example, Chapter 9 introduced linear programming as a form of optimization modelling. It discussed the material balance constraints that are common in optimization problems involving physical processes that observe conservation laws. Without their inclusion, many such models would be invalid, as the model might allow matter to be created or destroyed. An examination of these constraints and their relationship to the objective function is therefore a crucial part of any validation of such optimization models.

Another aspect to be considered in some models is the probability distributions included. If any probability distributions are employed, are they reasonable, given the phenomena being modelled? For example, in queuing-type systems it is often reasonable to assume that a distribution based on the Poisson process may be used to model the arrival pattern of customers. This is true when there is believed to be no relationship, other than a random one, between the arrival of successive customers. As another example, certain probability distributions such as the Weibull distribution are useful in modelling the ways in which items of equipment tend to fail in service. It is much better to think about the process that the probability distribution represents than just to collect some data to try and fit any old distribution to it. The analytical probability distributions are all derived from different assumptions about the process that generates the results. At its most basic, some distributions assume a continuous variable (such as the weight of an item), whereas others assume a discrete variable (such as the number of people arriving during a time interval). Continuing with the same point, some distributions assume that the variable covers an infinite range (i.e. it has no limits); some assume that the value can go negative and others that the range is strictly bounded by a maximum and minimum value.

A related issue might be whether the model employs what is believed to be appropriate theory. For example, a model for air traffic control might need to track aircraft as they move through some three-dimensional airspace. The time taken for an aircraft to get from one point to another may therefore be of great importance and may depend on the aircraft type (e.g. a wide-bodied Boeing 747) and its load. It will also depend on whether the departure and arrival points are at the same altitude, and on any wind patterns. It is important to ensure that any well-understood theory is embodied in the model.

Clearly, open-box validation is not a once-and-for-all exercise conducted by the management scientist after the model is built. It is part of the modelling process itself and needs to be carried out throughout the modelling. It should also be conducted hand-in-hand with the client for the study or user of the model. The modeller may be skilful at modelling, but the other parties are more likely to be well informed about the problem domain. In large-scale modelling, much of this validation may be handed over to a third party whose task is to examine the detail of the model so as to assure the model-user or client that it can be used with some degree of confidence.

Validation difficulties

There are several reasons why validation is less straightforward than might be imagined at first sight. The first, introduced earlier, occurs when a model is being built to help investigate how something works or how something might work. In these circumstances, the model is a theory about the operation of its reference system, but there is no fully understood reference system with which the model may be compared. For example, complex manufacturing systems are often simulated so as to find better ways to operate them. Because these manufacturing plants are very complicated, it is not unusual for them to perform below their specified levels of output and efficiency. Rather than experiment with the plant itself, which might be dangerous, costly or even illegal, it may be better to experiment with a computer simulation model. In these cases it is important to consider whether the reference system, or lumped model, is the manufacturing system as it was intended to be, or its actual, current implementation.

A second difficulty, closely related to the first, occurs when a model is built to see how a system might perform after modifications or under new circumstances. The model can be compared with the existing reference system in both a black-box and open-box sense. However, that is not true of its operation after modification or under new conditions. Although the management scientist and the client may be happy that the model is a valid representation of the system as it now is, there can be no such certainty about its operation in new modes. Partial open-box validation is possible, because use of appropriate theory, etc., can be assessed, but system theory makes it clear that emergent properties are hard to predict. Note that this is not an argument about whether the model is slapdash, simply a statement that its extension into uncharted territory is a process of exploration in which trust may gradually be earned.

A third problem, closely related to the second, occurs when the model is used to predict the future. A golden, if somewhat cynical, rule among forecasters is 'when asked for a forecast, always give a number or a date, but never both'. The future is uncertain and unknown, that is why it is being modelled. Therefore the future is the reference system. As an example, newspapers are fond of competitions to find the best economic forecaster or the best investor. In the former case, distinguished economic commentators are asked to estimate various statistics about economic performance (such as percentage growth in gross domestic product). In the latter case, investors are given a hypothetical amount of cash and are invited to 'invest' this over a year so as to produce the maximum return. The winners are lauded a year later as the best economic forecaster or the canniest investor. A pause for thought reveals that, in a race, someone must win unless all perform identically. Suppose that economic performance or the stock market were entirely random, then someone would still win – but this would not be a reflection of their ability, simply a result of their luck on two more of life's lotteries. In other words, even predictive success is no guarantee of a model that is valid. If, on the other hand, the same person were to win the competition year after year, then it would begin to look as if their model was rather good. But hindsight always helps when dealing with the future.

Assessing and validating the models resulting from interpretive Management Science

Part II of this book is devoted to three 'soft' modelling approaches commonly used in interpretive Management Science. That is, they are used with the deliberate intention of helping to support a debate among people who have differing views and make different interpretations of the way things are, or of the way things might be. As Checkland (1995) points out, one of the fundamental differences between quantitative Management Science models and models that result from interpretive work is their approach to validation. The first section of this chapter pointed out that there are better approaches to validation than simple attempts to see how well the model maps on to a chunk of the real world. The argument presented by Déry, Landry and Banville (1993) suggests that these other approaches are, in fact, necessary for all types of model. Certainly, they are important for interpretive models. Roy (1993) points the way forward by suggesting that validation might be related to axiomatic or constructivist ideas.

Validation in SSM

Checkland (1995) points out that the type of quantitative validation discussed above is based on a view that is close to that espoused in the physical sciences. He describes this as based on the three Rs:

1. *Reductionism.* As discussed in Chapter 5, this is the notion that a complex system may be decomposed into its constituent parts without any loss of information, predictive power or meaning.

2. *Repeatability*. This is the idea, dominant in the scientific literature, that any experiment ought to be, in concept at least, repeatable. Most scientific journals require enough detail in their papers to enable other investigators to replicate any experiment. Thus, they may check the work that led to the claims of the paper.
3. *Refutation*. As mentioned earlier, this notion is mainly due to the philosopher of science Karl Popper (1959, 1964), who argued that no experiment could conclusively prove a theory to be true. Thus, truly scientific experiments were ones that could disprove a theory or part of a theory. In this sense, all scientific theory is conjectural – which does not mean that all theories are equally valuable.

The three Rs themselves rest on logical empiricism, an outlook that is suspicious of any thought (including would-be scientific hypotheses) that is incapable of being reduced to direct observation.

Hence, in these terms, the approaches to model assessment and validation discussed previously are attempts to devise tests that measure how close a fit a model may be to the system being modelled. This is because these models are intended for use in efforts to decide how to improve these real systems. In one sense they are intended as surrogates for those systems. In Checkland's terms, they are 'would-be representations of the world'. By contrast, Checkland (1995) argues that, in SSM (see Chapter 5), the idea of a model is much more subtle. SSM makes use of conceptual models developed from a consideration of root definitions of relevant systems. These conceptual models are attempts to show the relationships between those activities that must, in concept, be present in any system that could realize the root definition. That is, they are not intended to be models of the 'real' world.

As Figure 12.2 shows, models in SSM are devices that are intended to be relevant to a debate about X, rather than being attempts to develop a model of some real system X. They are developed in an attempt to support a debate intended to lead to agreed action. The same claim could certainly be made about cognitive maps and the strategic options development and

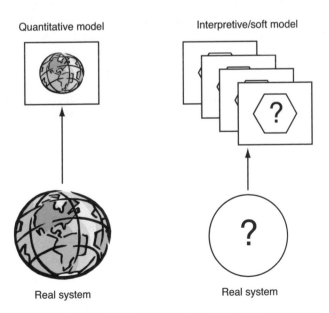

Figure 12.2 The nature of models in SSM.

analysis (SODA) methodology, and could easily be extended to system dynamics when used in an interpretive mode as discussed in Chapter 7.

What are the implications of this claim for validation? Checkland (1995) argues that 'the validity question becomes the question of how we can tell a "good" device from a "bad" one'. According to Checkland, this 'good' or 'bad' notion includes two aspects. First, is the model, as developed, in any sense 'relevant'? Second, is the model competently built?

Before assessing this view, it is necessary to stand slightly further back and recall that SSM is a systems methodology; therefore, it employs systems ideas and is itself systemic, a learning system. The employment of systems ideas might lead one to assume that conceptual models in SSM must be based on systems ideas. Checkland and Scholes (1990) argue that this is not necessary; that is, there is no need to employ any formal systems ideas in assessing whether a conceptual model is acceptable. Instead, they suggest that a conceptual model must be defendable only in the sense that its activities each follow directly from words or concepts in the root definition. The same should be true, argues Checkland (1995), of any measures of performance suggested for a conceptual model. Figure 5.4 showed that the components of a root definition can be viewed as parts of an input–output system contained in an environment. Thus, even when checking the linkage between a conceptual model and a root definition in SSM, there is implicit recourse to formal systems ideas. That is, although Checkland and Scholes state otherwise, it is hard to see how a valid SSM conceptual model will not be related in some way to formal systems ideas. Thus, the validation of a conceptual model in SSM is, in part at least, related to an axiomatic view from systems theory.

Checkland (1995) suggests two questions to ask when assessing the validity of such a model: is the model relevant and is it competently built? Both of these questions can themselves be interpreted in two ways. The first interpretation relates to the previous paragraph. That is, it addresses the degree to which the models are relevant to, and competently built from, the root definitions that have been produced. That is, once again, the validation is related to an axiomatic approach. The second interpretation would be that of its relevance to the outcome of the work and the competence of the analyst in the eyes of the client group. This is captured in Checkland's view that models should have some notion of efficiency, effectiveness and efficacy (three of the five Es), as mentioned in Chapter 5. This relates to a constructivist view, in that the question is whether the models provide any keys, and to an instrumental view about whether the models are of any use.

Thus, we see that model validation can be attempted in SSM, provided we forsake the view that these models are intended as would-be representations of the real world. If, instead, we view them as ways of supporting a debate about systemic issues, then some validation is indeed possible.

Validation in cognitive mapping and SODA

What, then, of the models that characterize cognitive mapping and the SODA methodologies discussed in Chapter 6? How can they be validated, if at all? Eden, Ackermann and Cropper (1992) state that cognitive maps are 'tools for reflective thinking and problem-solving'. When built for individuals, it can be argued that their design stems from personal construct theory and its notions about how people, individually, make sense of their worlds. Hence, as with conceptual models in SSM, some form of validation is possible with cognitive maps, and, as with SSM, this validation is based on axiomatic, constructivist and instrumentalist approaches. If they are built as cause maps for groups, as in SODA II, this is trickier because it would be simply wrong to claim that personal construct theory provides their justification.

Thus, individual cognitive maps can be validated axiomatically by checking the degree to which they conform to the underlying ideas of construct theory. For example, a fundamental assumption of Kelly's personal construct theory (Chapter 6) is that a person's construct system is composed of dichotomous constructs; that is, each construct has or implies two poles. Thus, a construct can be represented as statements, one pole of which denotes agreement and the other the opposite. As an example, a person may believe that a pleasant holiday involves a relaxing time. Its opposite, which may be implied and not stated, is that a holiday that is not relaxing will not be enjoyable. This is based on Kelly's view that we cannot affirm one thing without explicitly denying something else within a particular context. It is important to note that the poles are psychological rather than logical. There is, for example, no particular logical reason why a person should not enjoy a holiday that is strenuous as well as one that is relaxing. Thus, to be valid in axiomatic terms, an individual cognitive map must be expressed as a set of these psychological opposites. If there is ambiguity about the concepts on the map, then it is presumably invalid in axiomatic terms.

The analysis of these individual maps, which was discussed in Chapter 6, can also be assessed in these axiomatic terms. The analysis aims to identify clusters of related concepts according to some ideas about organization. For individuals, this organization is based at least partially on the assumption of construct theory that constructs are hierarchically ordered. If no such organization can be detected in a map, then it seems reasonable to question its validity in axiomatic terms – it appears not to correspond to construct theory. A similar argument could be made about the merging of maps prior to a SODA I workshop. Two more assumptions of personal construct theory are as follows:

1. If two people employ similar constructions of an experience, then we can infer that their psychological processes are similar.
2. People are able to understand one another's construct systems, and this is the basis of social interaction.

If people appear to have no concepts in common, and if the theory itself has any validity, either the maps are invalid or the people at the SODA I workshop truly have nothing in common.

As in SSM, it seems reasonable to invoke the constructivist and instrumentalist approaches to the validation of cognitive maps. They are developed as a means to an end and not as an end in themselves. If they serve to move a group towards commitment to action, then they have, in some instrumental sense, demonstrated their validity. If they provide insights previously hidden or unknown, they are acting as keys that unlock things. They may thus be regarded as valid in a constructivist sense.

As far as the cause maps used in SODA II are concerned, there can be no basis on construct theory and, so, no possibility of axiomatic validation. Instead, we must fall back on constructionist and instrumentalist approaches.

Validation in system dynamics

System dynamics models differ from conceptual models in SSM or cognitive maps because they can be used in much the same way as other quantitative models or as interpretive models. Writing about validation in system dynamics, Lane (1995) points this out and captures it in the

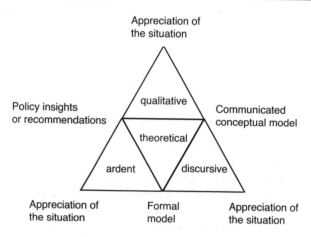

Figure 12.3 Lane's folding star.

idea of a folding star, shown in simplified form in Figure 12.3. The star is an extension of a simpler tetrahedron model proposed by Oral and Kettani (1993), and it can be imagined as a tetrahedron whose sides have been unfolded. Its faces represent four different ways in which system dynamics is put to use.

The vertices represent four different aspects of a system dynamics modelling process:

1. *Appreciation of the situation.* This stems from efforts to collect data from, and to reflect on, the 'world'. It is thus a conceptualization that provides data that will be used later. In some senses it resembles Zeigler's notion of a real system as a source of data. When the star is folded into a tetrahedron, the three identically named vertices coincide.
2. *Communicated conceptual model.* This is the expression of the appreciation of the situation within some ordered framework so that it can be communicated to, and understood by, other people. This is close to Zeigler's idea of a lumped model.
3. *Formal model.* The representation of the communicated conceptual model, probably using a computer package such as Powersim (see Chapter 7). It may be used for experimentation.
4. *Policy insights or recommendations.* These are the results, in qualitative or quantitative terms, of the use of a system dynamics model.

The faces emphasize the fact that system dynamics may be put to a range of different uses, only some of which are properly interpretive.

- *Ardent system dynamics.* This links the left-hand trio of vertices and represents the use of a formal model, captured in computer software to develop a set of recommendations for change in the real world. This is indistinguishable from the type of modelling discussed in Part III of this book, and thus the techniques for validating quantitative models may be applied.
- *Qualitative system dynamics.* This links the top three vertices and represents a mode of use in which system dynamics provides a language that allows people to discuss their views of the systems under consideration. In a limited sense, this is therefore an interpretive mode of use.
- *Discursive system dynamics.* This links the right-hand three vertices and represents the use of a formal model to help understanding and to develop learning. This, too, has some interpretive features.

- *Theoretical system dynamics.* Note that none of the vertices of this face is about appreciation of the situation. This might be thought to imply the worst kind of speculative modelling in which there is no concern whatsoever with a real system, in the terms that are used by Zeigler. Lane uses it to describe work done for the system dynamics community to demonstrate the power of the approach, or models for which there is no obvious client or user. This has some interpretive features.

Reference points for validity

The argument so far might lead a critical reader to one of two false conclusions. The first would be that the models used in interpretive Management Science are so far from notions of rationality that they have no place in Management Science and can be dismissed out of hand. The second would be that validation of these models is irrelevant as long as they seem to be useful. Neither of these conclusions is justified. To understand why, we need to think about the role of frameworks or presuppositions.

Chapter 2 was a brief tour of rationality, as the idea is often used in Management Science. It began in the pleasant foothills of the classical rationality of choice, as espoused by many economists. In this terrain, routes were found through the meadows by a map containing every feature of the terrain, and the only problem was to decide which way to go. The tour climbed into the steeper slopes of procedural rationality as proposed by Simon, in which it becomes clear that there is no complete map of the terrain, but it can be surveyed – at a cost. Individuals or groups may decide that they have only so much resource to expend on the survey and may thus settle for a route that is pleasant but that could be bettered if perfect information were available.

The bus then took us to the steeper slopes of non-rational and intuitive ideas as espoused by Mintzberg and his colleagues. These might seem, at first sight, to support a view that the best way to select the route is to choose one that looks immediately appealing from where we happen to find ourselves. In fact, it is more subtle than this, for it is more concerned to argue that there are more things in life than can be measured or assessed – positivism is a false god or guide. There are times when an inspired leader may choose a route that, with helicopter vision, we might see is a relatively bad one, yet the group may get there owing to the tour-guide's personal qualities. Finally, the tour ended on the high peaks of Damasio's suggestion that emotion and reason are in fact closely linked in the brains and bodies of healthy people. Put together, they allow routes to be chosen that are pretty good and permit emotion and social processes to keep the tour together.

Figure 12.4 shows the interpretive and quantitative approaches as extreme points on a spectrum – which they are, because even a quantitative model can be clearly used in an interpretive

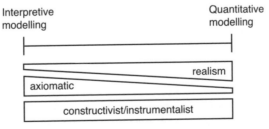

Figure 12.4 A spectrum of approaches.

way. Underneath the spectrum are three wedges, which attempt to show the importance of the three 'paths' suggested by Roy (1993). The thickness of the wedge is intended to show its importance for the two extremes. With quantitative models it may be very important to demonstrate that they are valid 'would-be representations of the real world'. Hence, realism is very important. This is less so for interpretive models, but it would be dangerous to argue that all concepts of reality have no importance.

Axiomatic validation is crucial for interpretive models, for the aim is to provide a language that will enable debate to flourish at a new level. Thus, the models need to be checked against the language. This might also be true of quantitative models when they are being used in an attempt to shed new light on something – and it may also be part of open-box validation. Constructivist validation is also important, especially for interpretive models, as the idea is to provide new keys that might unlock new insights.

Summary

Validation is an important issue in Management Science modelling and should not be ignored, although this often happens owing to the pressure of time. The validation of quantitative models of short-term operational problems is relatively straightforward, although it can be time consuming in practice. The suggestion of Kleindorfer, O'Neill and Ganeshan (1998) that neither extreme objectivism nor extreme relativism is appropriate is sensible. This leads to a view that validation is a judgement based on available evidence and avoids an overprescriptive approach. The validation of the models used in interpretive work is not so simple and may be very specific to the interpretive approach being used. For example, SSM models need to be consistent with root definitions and should also be defendable in terms of systems theory.

Whatever the model used, the modeller must go way beyond the simple Turing-type tests that dominate much thinking about validation in Management Science.

References

Balci O. (1987) Credibility assessment of simulation results: the state of the art, in *Proceedings of the Conference on Methodology and Validation, Orlando, FL*. IEEE, Piscataway, NY, pp. 19–25.

Balci O. (1994) Validation, verification and testing techniques throughout the life cycle of a simulation study. *Annals of Operations Research*, **3**, 53; also in *Simulation and Modelling*, ed. by Balci O. J.C. Baltzer, Basel, Switzerland.

Checkland P.B. (1995) Model validation in soft systems practice. *Systems Research*, **12**(1), 47–54.

Checkland P.B. and Scholes, J. (1990) *Soft Systems Methodology in Action*. John Wiley & Sons, Ltd, Chichester, UK.

Déry R., Landry M. and Banville C. (1993) Revisiting the issue of validation in OR: an epistemological view. *European Journal of Operational Research*, **66**(2), 168–183.

Eden C.L., Ackermann F. and Cropper S. (1992) The analysis of cause maps. *Journal of Management Studies*, **29**(3), 309–324.

Gass S.I. (1993) Model accreditation: a rationale and process for determining a numerical rating. *European Journal of Operational Research*, **66**(2), 250–258.

Kleindorfer G.P., O'Neill L. and Ganeshan R. (1998) Validation in simulation: various positions in the philosophy of science. *Management Science*, **44**(8), 1087–1099.

Kuhn T.S. (1970) *The Structure of Scientific Revolutions*, 2nd edition. University of Chicago Press, Chicago, IL.

Lane D.C. (1995) The folding star: a comparative re-framing and extension of validity concepts in system dynamics, in *Proceedings of the 1995 International System Dynamics Conference, Tokyo, Japan, 30 July–4 August*.

Law A.M. and Kelton W.D. (1991) *Simulation Modelling and Analysis*, 2nd edition. McGraw-Hill International Editions, New York, NY.

MSCO (2009) VV&A recommended practices guide: http://vva.msco.mil/

Oral M. and Kettani O. (1993) The facets of the modelling and validation process in operations research. *European Journal of Operational Research*, **66**(2), 216–234.

Pidd M. (1984) *Computer Simulation in Management Science*, 1st edition. John Wiley & Sons, Ltd, Chichester, UK.

Popper K.R. (1959) *The Logic of Scientific Discoveries*. Hutchinson, London, UK.

Popper K.R. (1964) *Conjectures and Refutations*. Routledge, London, UK.

Robinson S. (1996) Service quality management in the process of delivering a simulation study. Paper presented to the 14th Triennial Conference of the International Federation of OR Societies, 8–12 July 1996, held in Vancouver, BC.

Roy B. (1993) Decision science or decision aid science? *European Journal of Operational Research*, **66**(2), 184–203.

Sargent R.W. (1988) A tutorial on validation and verification of simulation models, in *Proceedings of the 1988 Winter Simulation Conference, San Diego, CA*. IEEE, Piscataway, NY, pp. 33–39.

Schruben L.W. (1980) Establishing the credibility of simulations. *Simulation*, **34**(3), 101–105.

Willemain T.R. (1995) Model formulation: what experts think about and when. *Operations Research*, **43**(6), 916–932.

Zeigler B.P. (1976) *Theory of Modelling and Simulation*. John Wiley & Sons, Inc., New York, NY.

Zeigler B.P. (1984) *Multi-facetted Modelling and Discrete Event Simulation*. Academic Press, New York, NY.

Index